Diplomacy in the Age of Artificial Intelligence

Ahmet Turan
https://orcid.org/0000-0002-0227-6161
Inonu University, Turkey

Hasan Ucuzal
https://orcid.org/0000-0003-4870-3015
Inonu University, Turkey

IGI Global
Scientific Publishing
Publishing Tomorrow's Research Today

Vice President of Editorial	Melissa Wagner
Director of Acquisitions	Mikaela Felty
Director of Book Development	Jocelynn Hessler
Production Manager	Mike Brehm
Cover Design	Jose Rosado

Published in the United States of America by
IGI Global Scientific Publishing
701 East Chocolate Avenue
Hershey, PA, 17033, USA
Tel: 717-533-8845 | Fax: 717-533-7115
Website: https://www.igi-global.com E-mail: cust@igi-global.com

Library of Congress Cataloging-in-Publication Data

LCCN: 2025040084 (CIP Data Pending)
ISBN13: 979-8-3373-4937-4
Isbn13Softcover: 979-8-3373-4938-1
EISBN13: 979-8-3373-4939-8

British Cataloguing in Publication Data
A Cataloguing in Publication record for this book is available from the British Library.

Table of Contents

Detailed Table of Contents

This study explores the evolution of Russian foreign policy from traditional Realpolitik to a hybrid model shaped by digital technologies, termed Digitalpolitik. While maintaining classical power tools like military force, Russia has integrated digital capabilities to expand influence, control information, and reinforce sovereignty. Key developments such as the annexation of Crimea, and the invasion of Ukraine illustrate this shift. The rise of cyber diplomacy, AI-driven strategies, and a focus on digital sovereignty highlight a new paradigm. Framed by ideological narratives and institutionalized hybrid warfare, Russia's approach challenges global norms and demands new multi-layered responses from the international community.

This section examines the profound transformative impact of the strategic synergy between quantum technologies and artificial intelligence on the international system, security paradigms, and global governance. The analysis, conducted through a multidimensional conceptual framework, details the different strategies of global actors such as the United States, China, and the European Union in this new era of technological competition by assessing changes in military strategy, economic competition, and normative orders. It also explores significant risks and geopolitical tensions arising from this synergy, such as cybersecurity vulnerabilities, the emergence of lethal autonomous weapons, and increasing technological dependence. argues that effectively managing these disruptive technologies is critical to ensuring global stability, preventing a potentially deepening "quantum divide," and aligning technological progress with ethical standards and international security, and discusses the need for robust international governance and cooperation mechanisms.

The 21st century has ushered in an era of profound technological transformation, marked most notably by the rapid evolution of artificial intelligence (AI). Once confined to the realm of science fiction, AI has become an integral part of daily life and global industry, revolutionizing sectors from healthcare and finance to transportation and education. As nations grapple with the economic and societal implications of this digital revolution, AI is also increasingly finding its way into the traditionally human-centric domain of international diplomacy. This intersection of cutting-edge technology and global governance represents both an unprecedented opportunity and a complex set of challenges for statecraft, international relations, and the preservation of global norms. Diplomacy, as one of the oldest instruments of statecraft, has historically relied on human intelligence, negotiation, subtlety, and strategic communication. From ancient emissaries sent between kingdoms to modern-day foreign service officers and multilateral institutions.

In this chapter, we discuss how narrative diplomacy has emerged as an International Relations characteristic in a period of artificial intelligence and digital transformation. It positions storytelling and strategic communication as the heart of international relations where governments, international organizations, and non-state actors are increasingly putting algorithm-based platforms as a means to shape world problems, cover policy justification, and sway opinion. With an interdisciplinary approach invoking non-traditional disciplinary themes that incorporate foreign relations and media studies and AI ethics, the chapter deciphers how narratives are developed, challenged, and reformulated in major international diplomatic forums namely the Munich Security Conference, the Raisina Dialogue, and the United Nations General Assembly.

In the rapidly evolving digital age, Artificial Intelligence (AI) has emerged as a transformative force across numerous sectors, profoundly reshaping how information is created, disseminated, and interpreted. Among the most impacted domains are media and diplomacy, two fields historically reliant on human judgment, nuanced communication, and complex decision-making. AI's integration into media and diplomacy is no longer a futuristic concept but an unfolding reality, presenting unprecedented opportunities while simultaneously surfacing significant challenges. The rise of AI technologies—from machine learning algorithms and natural language processing (NLP) systems to advanced data analytics and autonomous agents—has revolutionized traditional processes, enabling new modes of interaction, insight generation, and influence. In the realm of media, AI is redefining the landscape of journalism, content creation, and audience engagement.

Food system has become a tool of global anxiety and collaboration in the context of technical convergence and the urgency of climate. International cooperation is necessary to meet the challenges of food security and climate change. Agri-Tech Diplomacy is defined as the integration of artificial intelligence and international collaboration to meet the challenges of food security globally. This chapter shows how international and regional cooperation, such as the Indo-Africa partnerships, EU-South Asia, and the FAO-ITU AI bridges initiative, is using yield forecasting

and strategies to challenge marginalisation and assert digital sovereignty. Concluding with a call for institutional redesign, the chapter advocates for participatory, rights-based approaches that embed inclusion into the normative core of global governance.

This chapter examines sports diplomacy as part of the twenty-first-century shift from traditional state-centered diplomacy to a multi-actor, multi-level practice spanning culture, economy, communication, and governance. It defines sports diplomacy through its links to soft power and public diplomacy, distinguishing it from broader sport–politics debates and nation branding. Tracing its evolution from the Olympic Truce to Cold War bridge-building and post-Cold War mega-events, the chapter highlights key actors such as states, federations, NGOs, athletes, and corporations. It also addresses issues like sportswashing, governance deficits, and human rights concerns, emphasizing the uneven and often temporary nature of soft power gains. Looking forward, it argues that the credibility of sports diplomacy depends on digital engagement, sustainability, inclusivity, and ethical governance aligned with global development goals.

This chapter explores the "techno-geopolitical turn" in diplomacy, where artificial intelligence, big data, and digital platforms are reshaping the tools and arenas of international relations. It examines how AI enhances intelligence gathering and scenario planning, how big data enables predictive and proactive foreign policy, and how digital platforms transform public diplomacy through narrative contestation. While these technologies expand opportunities for cooperation and strategic foresight, they also introduce risks of bias, disinformation, and widening digital divides. The chapter highlights emerging debates on digital sovereignty, multilateral governance, and cyber diplomacy, arguing for balanced policy frameworks that promote innovation, accountability, and inclusivity while affirming the enduring role of human judgment in global diplomacy.

This research analyzes the concept and role of security diplomacy in the Middle East, tracing its development through the various historical eras the region has experienced. The main research problem lies in whether the mechanisms currently used contribute to strengthening security diplomacy in the Middle East. Based on this problem, the study proposed several hypotheses, including that the lack of collective political will among the member states of the Arab League and the Gulf Cooperation Council (GCC) limits the effectiveness of security diplomacy.And the weak implementation of artificial intelligence applications to develop traditional diplomatic performance and move towards modern digital diplomacy.

This chapter critically interrogates ASEAN's digital turn, arguing that while successive Summits have rhetorically placed digital diplomacy, cybersecurity, and AI governance at the strategic frontier, the gap between ambition and implementation remains stark. Despite headline initiatives such as DEFA, the ASEAN Digital Masterplans, and emerging AI governance frameworks, national fragmentation, weak enforcement, and the gravitational pull of US–China techno-strategic rivalry constrain ASEAN's agency. The chapter contends that achieving the digital dimension of the ASEAN Community Vision 2045 demands not continuity of the "ASEAN Way," but its recalibration toward regulatory convergence, agile governance, and a more networked posture in the contested global digital order.

This chapter examines how Cambodia has changed from a historically passive position in international relations to a proactive and adaptable role in digital diplomacy

Preface

1. OVERVIEW OF THE SUBJECT MATTER

The twenty-first century has witnessed the rapid diffusion of artificial intelligence (AI) across nearly every domain of human activity, including the traditionally human-centric practice of diplomacy. Once defined by in-person negotiation, linguistic precision, and symbolic gestures, diplomacy is now being reshaped by algorithms that process data, generate narratives, and even simulate empathy. The intersection of AI and diplomacy has emerged as a critical field of study that bridges international relations, communication studies, ethics, and computational sciences.

This volume, *Artificial Intelligence in Diplomacy*, responds to this intellectual and practical transformation. It explores the ways in which AI technologies, ranging from large language models and predictive analytics to machine vision and quantum computation, are altering diplomatic behaviour, decision-making, and perception. The book aims to map how these technologies are redefining not only the mechanics of diplomatic engagement but also the philosophical foundations of trust, agency, and sovereignty in global affairs.

By uniting contributions from scholars and practitioners across diverse regions, this collection provides a panoramic view of the emergent "AI-diplomatic complex", a sphere where human judgment and machine intelligence coalesce to produce new forms of influence, cooperation, and conflict.

2. RELEVANCE IN THE CONTEMPORARY WORLD

The integration of AI into diplomacy cannot be viewed in isolation from the broader transformations of international society. The global order is increasingly defined by the twin forces of digitalization and interdependence. Diplomatic communication is now mediated through digital platforms; decision-making relies on data-driven insights; and states deploy AI for cybersecurity, economic forecasting, and strategic communication.

In this context, diplomacy has entered a new epistemic era, one characterized by algorithmic mediation. AI-driven tools now assist in analysing negotiation patterns, translating complex documents, and monitoring international crises in real time. Yet these tools also introduce new vulnerabilities: misinformation, data asymmetry, ethical ambiguity, and the erosion of human interpretive control.

This book positions AI diplomacy as both a transformative opportunity and a site of critical tension. It argues that the future of diplomacy will depend not only on technological capacity but on human adaptability, institutional learning, and ethical governance. As such, the insights contained herein are relevant not merely for diplomats and policymakers, but for all stakeholders engaged in shaping a just and cooperative digital future.

3. TARGET AUDIENCE

This volume is designed for a wide yet academically engaged readership, encompassing scholars and students of international relations, political science, and communication studies who are interested in exploring the theoretical and empirical implications of artificial intelligence for global governance. It also addresses the needs of practicing diplomats, foreign service officers, and policymakers seeking to understand how AI is being operationally integrated into negotiation processes, public diplomacy, and multilateral coordination. Furthermore, the book appeals to technology experts, ethicists, and AI developers working at the intersection of computational design and international policy, as well as to journalists, civil society representatives, and think-tank researchers concerned with the societal and communicative dimensions of AI in diplomacy. By bridging theory and practice, this volume provides analytical frameworks, regional perspectives, and policy-relevant insights, positioning itself as a foundational text for understanding AI's transformative role in shaping the next generation of diplomatic conduct.

4. OVERVIEW AND IMPORTANCE OF EACH CHAPTER

Chapter 1: From Realpolitik to 'Digitalpolitik' – Russia's Diplomatic Shift in the Age of AI

This chapter offers a country-specific perspective on how Russia is incorporating AI into its diplomatic and strategic apparatus. It examines digital propaganda, cyber operations, and data-driven diplomacy, positioning Russia's *Digitalpolitik* as a new mode of geopolitical engagement grounded in technological sovereignty.

Chapter 2: The Impacts of Quantum Technologies and Artificial Intelligence Synergy on International Relations and Security

By examining the convergence of AI and quantum computing, this chapter highlights the technological frontier of security diplomacy. It explores how quantum-AI integration will redefine intelligence gathering, encryption, and strategic deterrence, emphasizing both the potential and perils of a quantum-AI world order.

Chapter 3: Artificial Intelligence in Diplomacy

This foundational chapter defines the scope and conceptual boundaries of *Artificial Intelligence in Diplomacy*. It positions AI not merely as a technical adjunct but as an institutional and epistemic force within international relations. The chapter develops a typology of AI tools, such as machine learning, large language models, computer vision, and autonomous systems, and maps their application across the diplomatic cycle: information analysis, decision support, negotiation, implementation, and evaluation. It also establishes the methodological framework of the volume, integrating comparative case studies, computational text analysis, and policy ethnography. Finally, the chapter introduces the book's central normative themes, accountability, transparency, bias mitigation, and human oversight, laying the theoretical groundwork for the subsequent empirical chapters.

Chapter 4: Narrative Diplomacy and Strategic Communication

This chapter examines the narrative power of AI technologies in shaping global discourse. It argues that AI systems, through social media algorithms and automated messaging, play a crucial role in constructing diplomatic narratives, amplifying certain worldviews while marginalizing others. The discussion bridges narrative theory and AI ethics, demonstrating how digital storytelling has become a strategic instrument of statecraft.

Chapter 5: AI in Media Framing, Public Diplomacy, and Diplomatic Influence

Expanding on the communicative dimension, this chapter analyses AI's impact on the framing of international events. It provides empirical evidence on how machine learning models influence media representation, perception management, and soft power projection. The chapter underscores the growing interdependence between public diplomacy and algorithmic influence.

Chapter 6: Agri-Tech Diplomacy – AI-Driven Agricultural Collaboration Across Borders

This contribution turns to the intersection of AI, sustainability, and development. It explores how AI-enabled agricultural technologies facilitate cross-border collaboration, improve food security, and create new avenues for environmental diplomacy. The chapter presents Agri-Tech as a form of "functional diplomacy" where technology acts as a mediator of cooperation rather than competition.

Chapter 7: AI in Digital Communication Practices – The Reconstruction of Symbolic Capital within Digital Diplomacy

Drawing on Pierre Bourdieu's concept of symbolic capital, this chapter theorizes how digital diplomacy reconstructs legitimacy in online environments. It demonstrates that AI not only shapes information flows but also redefines who holds symbolic authority in the digital public sphere. The study contributes to a sociological understanding of AI's influence on diplomatic prestige and credibility.

Chapter 8: Digital Inclusion and AI Diplomacy – Addressing Inequality Through Multilateral Forums

This chapter examines digital inequality as a central challenge to global governance. It discusses how international organizations employ AI to promote inclusion, capacity-building, and equitable participation in the digital economy. The analysis highlights the diplomatic importance of ensuring that AI development serves global justice rather than deepening existing disparities.

Chapter 9: Bridging Nations through Sports – The Strategic Role of Sports Diplomacy in Global Relations

Although sports diplomacy may seem distant from AI, this chapter innovatively connects the two by exploring how data analytics and machine intelligence enhance sports diplomacy initiatives. It argues that the integration of AI into sports performance, broadcasting, and fan engagement can strengthen people-to-people ties and serve as a subtle yet effective diplomatic tool.

Chapter 10: The Techno-Geopolitical Turn – AI, Big Data, and the New Diplomacy

This chapter situates AI within the broader geopolitics of data. It explores how nations deploy AI to reinforce sovereignty, monitor information ecosystems, and project influence in cyberspace. The "techno-geopolitical turn," as defined here, refers to the transformation of global power from territorial control to data control, a key shift in contemporary diplomacy.

Chapter 11: Security Diplomacy and Artificial Intelligence in the Middle East – The Arab League and the Gulf Cooperation Council

Focusing on the Middle East, this chapter explores how regional organizations integrate AI into security and counterterrorism diplomacy. It assesses the institutional capacities of the Arab League and the GCC to manage AI governance and cybersecurity cooperation, providing an empirical understanding of AI's regional security implications.

Chapter 12: ASEAN Summits at the Digital Frontier – Forging Networked Diplomacy, Cybersecurity Resilience, and AI Cooperation

This chapter analyses ASEAN's efforts to incorporate AI into its diplomatic and economic frameworks. It conceptualizes *networked diplomacy* as a regional innovation model, emphasizing shared digital infrastructure and collaborative governance for cybersecurity resilience and technological integration.

Chapter 13: Digital Diplomacy in Cambodia – Embracing Artificial Intelligence for Strategic Engagement and National Development

This case study illustrates how smaller states, such as Cambodia, are leveraging AI to enhance digital diplomacy and national branding. It presents Cambodia's strategy as a microcosm of how developing nations can utilize AI to strengthen soft power and regional connectivity.

5. CONCLUSION: SCHOLARLY AND PRACTICAL CONTRIBUTIONS

Artificial Intelligence in Diplomacy contributes to the academic and policy discourse by framing AI not as a technical adjunct but as a transformative epistemic actor in international relations. By offering theoretical insights, empirical research, and comparative case studies, this volume broadens the conceptual scope of diplomacy to include digital, algorithmic, and data-driven dimensions.

The book's contribution lies in articulating a framework of *"algorithmic diplomacy"*, a paradigm where human and machine intelligence interact in the creation of meaning, the management of trust, and the pursuit of strategic goals. Through its interdisciplinary engagement, this collection provides scholars, practitioners, and policymakers with both analytical tools and normative guidance for navigating the diplomatic challenges of the digital century.

Ultimately, this work aspires to establish AI diplomacy as a formal field of inquiry, one that recognizes the enduring value of human judgment while acknowledging the inevitability of technological co-agency in shaping the future of global relations.

Chapter 1
From Realpolitik to 'Digitalpolitik': Russia's Diplomatic Shift in the Age of AI

Ahmet Turan
https://orcid.org/0000-0002-0227-6161
Inonu University, Turkey

ABSTRACT

This study explores the evolution of Russian foreign policy from traditional Realpolitik to a hybrid model shaped by digital technologies, termed Digitalpolitik. While maintaining classical power tools like military force, Russia has integrated digital capabilities to expand influence, control information, and reinforce sovereignty. Key developments such as the annexation of Crimea, and the invasion of Ukraine illustrate this shift. The rise of cyber diplomacy, AI-driven strategies, and a focus on digital sovereignty highlight a new paradigm. Framed by ideological narratives and institutionalized hybrid warfare, Russia's approach challenges global norms and demands new multi-layered responses from the international community.

1. INTRODUCTION

In contemporary international relations literature, a prominent trend is frequently described as the "resurgence of Realpolitik." Following the optimistic climate of globalization in the 1990s and the intense counterterrorism campaigns and insurgency operations of the early 2000s, great power rivalry and geopolitical calculations have once again assumed a central role. Walter Russell Mead illustrates this development by pointing to events such as Russia's annexation of Crimea, China's

DOI: 10.4018/979-8-3373-4937-4.ch001

growing maritime assertiveness, Japan's increasingly resolute responses, and Iran's efforts to establish influence in the Middle East through its alliances with Syria and Hezbollah, emphasizing the reemergence of classical power politics on the global stage (Wohlforth, 2015). This shift marks a decisive end to the post-Cold War liberal international order, where economic interdependence and institutional cooperation were once seen as the primary drivers of global politics, and a return to an era where raw national interest and military might be paramount.

However, the transformations in international affairs throughout the 21st century have also reshaped Russia's approach to Realpolitik. Pagen characterizes this new orientation as "Putin's Operationalization of Psychology and Propaganda." According to him, President Putin frames his political actions and strategies not only through the lens of traditional Realpolitik, but also through what he terms the "new Realpolitik" (Pagen, 2020: 61). This modern iteration retains the core Realpolitik focus on securing state interests and expanding spheres of influence but fundamentally updates its methods. It moves beyond the traditional reliance on overt military and economic coercion to incorporate a sophisticated, multi-domain toolkit designed to achieve strategic objectives while maintaining plausible deniability and avoiding costly direct confrontation.

This "new Realpolitik" is distinguished by its heavy reliance on asymmetric and non-kinetic tactics. Central to this approach is the weaponization of information, where disinformation campaigns and cyber operations are deployed to sow discord within rival nations, undermine the credibility of democratic institutions, and manipulate public perception. The Kremlin employs a strategy of "reflexive control," feeding an opponent information designed to make them voluntarily choose actions beneficial to Russian interests. This is complemented by the use of cyber-attacks to disrupt critical infrastructure and the funding of fringe political groups to exacerbate social divisions in target countries, creating internal weaknesses that can be exploited for geopolitical gain.

Furthermore, Russia's strategy leverages economic interdependencies as strategic weapons, a tactic often termed "geoeconomics." While traditional Realpolitik viewed economic power as a blunt instrument of sanction or trade, the new model employs subtler forms of coercion, such as control over energy supplies to Europe to create political leverage and division within NATO. The construction of pipelines like Nord Stream was not merely a commercial project but a calculated geopolitical manoeuvre to bypass Eastern European transit states and increase German dependency on Russian gas, thereby weakening a unified European response to aggression (Wigel & Vihma, 2016). This exemplifies how economic relationships are instrumentalized to achieve political dominance.

The ultimate objective of this modernized Realpolitik remains consistent with its classical forebearer: the revision of the international status quo and the re-establishment of Russia as a preeminent great power with a recognized sphere of influence. Actions such as the 2008 war with Georgia, the 2014 annexation of Crimea, and the ongoing involvement in Syria are all traditional power plays aimed at altering borders and challenging US hegemony. However, the "new" element is found in the accompanying narrative warfare, where these actions are justified through an alternative history and information sphere that portrays Russia as a defender of traditional values against a decadent and aggressive West, seeking to legitimize its actions for both domestic and international audiences (Allison, 2017).

In conclusion, the current international landscape is indeed defined by a return to power politics. Yet, to fully understand the strategies of actors like Russia, it is necessary to recognize that Realpolitik itself has evolved. It is no longer solely about the blunt exercise of military and economic power but has integrated a pervasive psychological dimension. By masterfully blending traditional hard power aggression with 21st-century tools of cyber warfare, information manipulation, and economic coercion, Vladimir Putin has operationalized a hybrid model of statecraft. This "new Realpolitik" presents a more complex and insidious challenge to the international order, one that demands a sophisticated and equally adaptable response from the West.

1.1. Realpolitik: Russia's Geostrategic Foundations

Since the dissolution of the Soviet Union, Russia has faced a decisive crossroads. In recent years in particular, President Vladimir Putin's policies have become firmly rooted in the absolutist tradition, seeking to construct a strong centralized state that grants only limited autonomy domestically. The consolidation of political authoritarianism has led observers to label Putin's system a "managed democracy," marked by an increasingly dominant focus on geopolitical affairs (Eriksen, 2016).

The most recent iteration of Realpolitik in contemporary Russia, however, is increasingly being replaced by what may be termed Digitalpolitik. Some scholars argue that digital transformations do not necessarily imply merely useful reforms or technological shifts; they may also be driven by political motives (Wijermars, 2020, p. 17). A significant turning point in the Russian Federation's digitalpolitik approach dates back to 2012. During Dmitry Medvedev's presidency, a Ministry of Open Government was established, marking an important institutional innovation.

The promotion of open government led to a considerable increase in the accessibility of public data. For instance, government procurement information became available through the Goszakupki (Government Procurement) portal (zakupki.gov.ru), while a variety of datasets were consolidated on the official open data platform (data.gov.ru). Moreover, the transparency of the legislative process was enhanced through the creation of specialized online platforms. For example, video recordings of the Russian State Duma sessions are publicly accessible via video.duma.gov.

ru, and draft laws can be submitted for public consultation on regulation.gov.ru (Wijermars, 2020, p. 18).

Since the late 2000s, Moscow's approach to internet governance has undergone a marked transformation, driven by a growing perception of Western technology as a tool for foreign espionage, regime change, and projection of influence. Sherman (2024) characterizes this transformation as a kind of "internet awakening" within the Kremlin. This awakening was accelerated by a series of critical developments: the role of Georgian bloggers in shaping the narrative during the 2008 Russo-Georgian War; the decisive impact of social media on mass mobilization during the Arab Spring (2010–2013); the digitally organized protests in response to electoral fraud in the 2011 parliamentary elections and Vladimir Putin's return to the presidency in 2012; the 2013 Snowden revelations exposing the scope of U.S. global internet surveillance; and finally, the Euromaidan Revolution in Ukraine in 2014, which was significantly driven through social media platforms (Sherman, 2024).

These events reinforced long-standing digital threat perceptions among conservative, security-oriented circles within the Putin administration. No longer limited to issuing warnings, these actors have increasingly gained institutional capacity and strategic tools to shape the trajectory of Russia's internet policies from within the political system (Sherman, 2024).

The primary proposition is that Russian foreign policy has taken on a unique momentum during Vladimir Putin's leadership. From the outset of his presidency, he has actively sought to lay the groundwork for fulfilling his imperial ambitions. His strategy is premised on a mixture of geopolitical and geoeconomic ideas, sometimes involving military action (as in the case of the war with Georgia and the fighting in Ukraine) but at other times assumes an institutionalized form, as in the case of the establishment of the Eurasian Union earlier this year. Russia's confrontational approach to Realpolitik reflects the increasing regional risks and at times the strategic interest in the states in which Putin aspires to implement control (Eriksen, 2016).

Of these, Ukraine is a particularly important case. Prior to the annexation of Crimea, Ukraine was making blatant moves towards closer integration with the West, involving NATO cooperation and the desire for EU membership. The idea of losing Ukraine from Moscow's area of influence was a serious worry not only for the Kremlin, but a direct threat to Putin's goals for the future. Ukraine's resiliency to Russian pressure and domination is one of the reasons for the ferocity of the measures taken against it during the 2014 crisis (Eriksen, 2016).

A similar trend appears in relation to Moldova. Exploiting a moment of domestic vulnerability born out of the civil conflict between Moldovan and Transnistrian authorities, Putin was able to increase Russian influence at its moment of weakness. Moldova moved even closer to Europe by signing its Association Agreement with the European Union in 2014, much like Ukraine, increasing geopolitical competition within the region (Eriksen, 2016).

1.2. Russia's Transition to Digitalpolitik

Digitalpolitik may be broadly defined as the comprehensive domain of both domestic and foreign policy that operates in constant interaction with the components of the digital world. Digital technologies have become one of the principal forces transforming not only Russia's social and economic structures but also its political order. In the mid-1990s, fewer than one percent of the population had internet access; today, with nearly 110 million users (representing three-quarters of the population) Russia ranks sixth worldwide. The spread of affordable smartphones during the 2010s further accelerated this process, and by 2020 the internet had evolved into a mass-access medium, with more than 60 percent of users going online primarily via mobile devices. These developments have positioned Russia as the largest internet market in Europe (Wijermars, 2020, p. 17).

Following the conclusion of the federal "Electronic Russia" program and reforms in the public administration system, e-government applications gained new momentum within the framework of the "information society" initiative. In this regard, the 'Strategy for the Development of the Information Society in the Russian Federation for 2017–2030' was adopted by Presidential Decree in 2017. The main objective of this strategy is to create conditions conducive to the development of an information society in Russia. The document highlights humanitarian aspects reflecting the government's intentions to implement projects in the field of education, establish interconnected networks of information and ideas accessible to citizens, provide a safe digital environment for children, promote the Russian language globally, and support traditional forms of information transfer outside the internet. However, the vast majority of these goals are not supported by feasible and verifiable mechanisms (Martynova & Shcherbovich, 2024).

The most striking aspect of the strategy is not so much the declarations about building an information society, but rather Russia's policy of ensuring its independence from Western-sourced technology and software. The document lists the development and use of national information and communication technologies, making them internationally competitive, and protecting national interests in the digital economy as priority areas. In this context, ensuring the security and technological independence of the infrastructure used to provide goods and services to Russian citizens and institutions is also a critical element. Therefore, the development of national infrastructure with domestic IT solutions has become a priority in terms of state policy. It is observed that similar emphases on ensuring technological independence have become routine in digitalization documents published in subsequent years (Martynova & Shcherbovich, 2024).

Overall, the defining characteristic of this period is a shift from modernization rhetoric towards national security priorities. The frequent repetition of the concepts of 'technological sovereignty' alongside 'economic sovereignty' in bureaucratic language reflects this transformation. This change can also be seen as a result of the disappointment among Russia's top decision-makers regarding opportunities for cooperation with foreign partners and the growing expectation of open conflict with the West, influenced by the sanctions imposed after the annexation of Crimea in 2014. In this context, reducing technological backwardness and ensuring sustainability without dependence on foreign technologies have become fundamental objectives of the state (Martynova & Shcherbovich, 2024).

The impact of digitalization, however, extends well beyond the economic sphere and directly shapes the Kremlin's strategic vision. According to the Ministry of Digital Development, Communications and Mass Media, the Russian internet industry reached a value of 5 trillion Rubles in 2019, accounting for nearly 5 percent of national GDP (Wijermars, 2020, p. 17). At this scale, the internet functions not merely as a driver of economic growth, but also as a tool for controlling information flows, steering public opinion, and reinforcing national security policies. In this respect, digitalization constitutes both the infrastructure and the legitimacy basis of the Putin administration's Digitalpolitik strategy.

In Russia, unlike in many other authoritarian or semi-authoritarian regimes, the internet has provided fertile ground for the emergence of a distinctive "web culture." The substantial investments made by Russian authorities in the digital sphere, combined with the active encouragement of digital technology use by segments of the elite, have accelerated this process. This approach not only seeks to make the internet more accessible to the public, but also involves prioritizing certain domains of the online space with the broader aim of constructing a "sovereign web." (Nocetti, 2011: 6).

2. RUSSIA'S DIPLOMATIC TOOLKIT IN THE AI AGE

The transformation of Russia's diplomatic methods and tools is not unique to the contemporary international system. In fact, the shift in diplomatic practices that began during the reign of Peter the Great in the 17th century marked Russia's transition toward a Western-style diplomacy (Bohlen, 1966). Most notably, in the era of artificial intelligence, the evolution of Russia's diplomatic methods is particularly evident in the use of diplomatic language. While earlier generations of diplomats employed language that was clearer and more precise, Russian diplomacy in the digital age has diverged from this tradition of clarity (Reinhardt, 2020: 3).

Russian diplomacy is a merger of tradition and innovation with strong influences from its own past. Classic Russian diplomacy consisted of an atmosphere of informality, strict compliance with rules of etiquette, and a highly elaborate language of diplomacy. Since the days of the Tsars, long descriptive letters, choreographed negotiations, and a machinery of remote courtesy were the very core of Russia's own diplomatic tradition. Under Soviet conditions, the language turned ideological with stiff etiquette where interstate relations were upheld through protracted bargains kept patiently waiting by waiting negotiation procedures (Reinhardt, 2020: 4).

Modern-day Russian diplomacy has been more frank, concise, and rapid in its manner of expression. And information as well as social media has been successful in providing rapid and efficient dissemination of messages by the Ministry of Foreign Affairs as well as by official spokespersons. As a result, Russian diplomacy has been caustic now and then to a level of being straightforwardly offensive as well as overtly confrontational. Unlike their predecessors who were charged with gathering intelligence information, deep analysis, as well as conducting complex bargaining, their role these days has largely been merely to arrange for direct contacts between high-level leadership (especially presidential-level leadership) and organize required technical as well as protocol support for meetings of such a level (Reinhardt, 2020: 5-7).

In defending national interests, Russia has remained consistent and non-negotiable with both approaches. But where older diplomacy demanded more emphasis on compromise and accord within multilateral institutions, new Russian diplomacy (with particular emphasis towards the West) upholds national interests more aggressively, frequently unilaterally, with limited leeway for compromise. Sovereignty and national security increasingly have been absolute principles with often higher standing than cooperation more generally among nations (Reinhardt, 2020: 4-10).

In the midst of global and domestic politics, Russia has been a strong advocate for multilateralism and observance of international norms. But for the present era, it has developed a sceptical position regarding international institutions it deems to be "Western." What has ensued is a more protectionist foreign policy, a sensitive rhetoric about sovereignty, and aiming to be a member of various alliances like BRICS and the Shanghai Cooperation Organisation. Modern-day Russian diplomacy is hence being increasingly seen as a challenge to Western control over the international order, imparting to it a more divided, competitive, and divisive appearance (Reinhardt, 2020: 11-13).

2.1. Russian Cyber Diplomacy

Digital sovereignty is a necessary term that defines a country's authority over the digital realm, data handling, and cybersecurity. It involves a country's ability to control its own digital infrastructure, data flows, and activity in cyberspace. Digital sovereignty, an issue of critical importance with respect to a country's security, economic freedom, as well as social order, is central to new state politics. Russia's cyber diplomacy has been conceptualized as an extension and part of such an understanding of digital sovereignty. For Russia, cyberspace is both a realm of war or defence but also a strategic instrument of influence in international politics. It is one such fundamental principle governing activity within cyberspace by the state (Kukkola et al, 2017: 11).

Russia's cyber diplomacy is founded upon several fundamental building blocks. In the first place, a mix of laws and regulations has been developed under its information control policy to influence internal as well as international public sentiment. In the second place, through cyber operations, different types such as cyber-attacks and information manipulation are enforced with an aim to influence decision-making processes among target countries or to support its own policy. In third place, as an additional building block, it is engaged with international cooperation to support its strategies through joint practices implemented through information sharing within the framework of cybersecurity (Hakala & Melnychuk, 2021: 13).

Fourthly, laws related to cybersecurity have been introduced to coordinate digital sovereignty. These laws entail legal measures concerning data protection, combating cybercrime, and safeguarding strategic digital infrastructure. Finally, these aspects converge with a view to exerting global influence. Russia utilizes its cyber diplomacy to promote its interests in the international arena and has a unique influence strategy, primarily concerning its tie with the West. Lastly, digital sovereignty is what lies behind Russia's cyber diplomacy. Russia aims to enhance its position internationally as much as its own national security through cyberspace as a defence shield as well as an active tool for projecting power (Hakala & Melnychuk, 2021: 14).

In recent years, cybersecurity has been a decisive factor for Russia-Ukraine-Europe relations. Due to Russia's annexation of Crimea and beginning of war in Donbas in 2014, Russia significantly escalated it cyberattacks against Ukraine. These cyberattacks afforded Russia an opportunity to take Ukraine as a testing ground to refine its cyber war prowess. Cyberattacks targeting critical infrastructure (power grids, banking systems, and public services) signalled widespread destruction caused in war and peacetime (Barichella, 2022: 4).

In addition to technical attacks, information warfare against Western nations also involved Russia's usage of cyber espionage and disinformation campaigns. Psychological operations and deceitful content were utilized to manipulate public sentiment throughout Europe. As a counteraction, the West placed economic sanctions upon Russia. As much as sanctions were regarded as having slightly diminished Russia's cyber armaments, they did also pose a threat to incite additional cyber-attacks (Barichella, 2022: 4-6).

Ukraine then developed extensive cyber resilience and strengthened its expertise with global support. Technology equipment, software, and expertise were provided to Ukraine by American and European countries to enhance its cybersecurity infrastructure. Concurrently, the European Union refreshed its defence policies against cyber-attacks and created harmonized response protocols. Thus, the ongoing battle within the virtual sphere has tremendously affected Russia-Ukraine-Europe relations and directly contributed to global security trends (Barichella, 2022: 14).

2.2. AI Role in the Russia's Diplomatic Practice

At the beginning of the 2010s, a new chapter came to international development of artificial intelligence (AI) after a decade-long slumber. It came driven by innovation in machine learning and its sub-category deep learning enabled by surging computing power, high-end algorithms, but most importantly by increases in datasets being handled. It is reshaping economies with a mix of digital technology, robots, and AI and is set to have significant mid-term socio-economic effects nationally and internationally with further deepening dominant market presence by a few large high-tech multinationals and a widening array of inequalities. But is there a specific 'Russian view' with regard to such essentially international trends? (Nocetti, 2020).

Russia employs AI technologies to several purposes within the realm of diplomacy in order to achieve its strategic objectives. Towards that end, it is significantly reliant upon AI, particularly where information warfare as well as propaganda is involved. Through such false profiles together with deepfake videos over social media platforms, it attempts to manipulate public opinion amongst its target countries. These policies have a tendency to widen societal division by targeting confidence within credible news sources (Bendett, 2024: 6).

Another major area where AI is applied is cyber operations. AI-fuelled cyber-attacks and data gathering operations are employed by Russia to expand threats to critical infrastructures of adversary countries. With AI being utilized to conduct more advanced and specific attacks, it would seek to inflict extensive harm to energy supply systems, communication systems, and financial systems. At the same time, data analysis and prediction tools aid in facilitating diplomatic decision-making procedures. AI-driven analysis helps Russian authorities to gain a strategic upper hand with respect to predicting trends and prospective crises for international relations (Bendett, 2024: 3).

It is boosting military-strategic cooperation by integration with military as well as civilian abilities. Military planning as well as operational execution is being supported with artificial intelligence. Apart from that, to be a leader with an upper hand technically despite competition globally, it is emphasizing home development initiatives with respect to AI. Even in spite of sanctions from outside, it is investing significantly to take benefit from technological sovereignty so that it becomes less dependent on external technology with respect to AI. Russia's strategy to leverage artificial intelligence to assist its diplomacy and foreign relations spans a remarkably broad spectrum, from information manipulation to military operations, and from data processing to technological sufficiency. As such, it strengthens Russia's position within international power politics (Bendett, 2024: 20).

Overall, AI arguments and perceptions within Russia sound much the same as they would in Western countries, for the most part following the dualistic frame encapsulating international AI discussions. AI is scoped by Russia's elites economically and politically as a collection of revolutionary technologies to be accepted across such industries as transport, education, and health. Authorities cite AI's future positive impacts upon the nation, stimulating economic growth alongside diversification. While somewhat unclear, the objective appears to be a dual-sided one: lessening Russia's dependency upon revenue from the energy sector and framing AI itself as a domestically developed entity, changing its implication from an external import to a piece of national pride and security (Nocetti, 2020).

Following annexation of Crimea, international sanctions induced so-called 'import substitution' strategies in various sectors. As much as Russia remains significantly dependent upon high-tech imports itself, its elites redesign and defend their AI strategy within an international scene including a renewed flare-up of protectionism as well as AI nationalism. Reception of AI has a dual connotation: as a publicity campaign (something non-unique to Russia) and as a harbinger of loyalty to the Kremlin within an old imitation-based tradition deep-rooted in behaviour among Russia's political elite (Nocetti, 2020).

Economic elites and top private companies also share optimism regarding AI's value-creation prospects. Referred to as 'nuclear energy of the future,' AI is also believed to be capable of increasing labour productivity by 20-30%. Since 2018, AI events in Russia have multiplied significantly, encapsulating the subject into basically political and economic agendas with an enormous hype. Regular conferences and forums represent principal soft power tools, generating storytelling about the technology. There has been an ongoing increase in panels for digital and technological subjects even at such high-profile forums as the annual St. Petersburg International Economic Forum. In June 2019, for instance, 21 panels debated AI's impact across different sectors (health, labour market, recruitment) while addressing its issues such as middle-class impacts, transparency of algorithms, and mathematics education.

International conferences such as AI Journey, which has been convened since 2019, have brought together scientists, developers, and business leaders to Moscow and such technological innovation centres as Novosibirsk, Tomsk, and St. Petersburg (Nocetti, 2020).

Public opinion in Russia usually is not threatened or single-mindedly optimistic regarding AI. In a recent poll, 54% were positive about AI and robots, but a prior poll showed only 29% felt they knew AI's essence. Most citizens remain either neutral or optimistic about application but anticipate improved public services such as administrative services, health treatment, and education. Fears of lost jobs due to AI-based applications are rare, compared to more cautious public attitudes in France and Britain. But surveillance digital technology concerns have increased due to COVID-19 everywhere, including Russia. 'Chipping' speculation about being ordered by authorities to allow for geo-location has been widespread but confused public knowledge about real technological stakes. In Russia, AI is being framed increasingly as both problem and instrument of sovereignty. Relative to the U.S. or China, where AI is typically seen as some sort of promethean force with intrinsic power unto itself, Russian commentary is usually more measured and mostly dominant only among conferences debating AI's attributes to the international order. AI strategies developed by China and the U.S. are paid close attention to by Russian international relations professionals, such as the European Commission's ethics-driven strategy through its February 2020 White Paper regarding AI (Nocetti, 2020).

3. CASE STUDY OF DIPLOMATIC SHIFT

The annexation of Crimea in 2014 is widely classified as the most aggressive foreign policy intervention undertaken by the Russian Federation since the collapse of the Soviet Union. In recent years, the Russian Federation has grown increasingly aggressive and, at times, militant regarding relations with former Soviet republics. In 2008, it clashed with Georgia employing military instruments and regularly intervened in the energy supplies of neighbouring states, including Ukraine, Moldova, and Lithuania. Apart from that, it has interfered in the internal political matters of such and other regions and so strengthened military presence in post-Sovetic territory with the building of new military bases in Belarus, Kyrgyzstan, and Tajikistan. Apart from that, it has used economic pressure on neighbouring regions as a tool of forcing them to join institutions administered under Moscow control, such as the Collective Security Treaty Organization and the Eurasian Economic Union, and was also involved in similar projects (Götz, 2017). The action was motivated by Moscow regarding the post-Soviet geography as belonging to its domain of influence as dictated in the "near abroad doctrine." The Putin regime perceived the expansion of NATO and the EU and particularly Ukraine's attempts to become integrated with the West as directly jeopardizing national security (Mearsheimer, 2014).

3.1. Ukraine (2014–2024)

During Putin's early presidencies, the Russian Federation mostly worked along a classic realpolitik model in foreign policy, with balance-of-power calculations based on realistic position assuming primary focus. It was reaffirmed in the war over Georgia in 2008, the annexation of Crimea in 2014, and military support Moscow provided for the Syrian President Bashar al-Assad in 2015. It is observed from the chosen examples that Moscow applied hard power as an instrument of securing its interests and increasing its sphere of influence. However, the large-scale invasion of Ukraine in February 2022 was a significant deviation from that pragmatic course. In this process, territorial gains were justified not solely on the grounds of security concerns but also through the rhetoric of "reuniting Russian lands" and fulfilling a historical mission. As a result, Russia's position within the international system has increasingly been framed as a direct challenge to Western hegemony (Graham, 2024).

Indeed, the afore-identified shift in ideology is also reflected in the Foreign Policy Concept, approved in March 2023. In it, Russia is defined not only as a nation-state but also as an 'independent civilisation-state' in the centuries-old conflict with the 'collective West' led by the US. This conceptualisation reveals that Russian foreign policy is acquiring an increasingly ideology-informed nature, substantiated with references to history and defended normatively. Moscow's foreign policy discourse thus began to transcend calculations of interest and instead based itself on Russian identity, civilisation demands, and a multipolar vision of the international order (Graham, 2024).

3.2. Realpolitik Dynamics

The Crimean annexation testified to the re-emergence of classical realpolitik policies based on the employment of hard power. To attempt to justify its transgression of international law, Russia appealed to the argument about 'the Crimean people's right to self-determination.' Nonetheless, such an argument was not taken on trust by the West, and Russia was subjected to the toughest sanctions in its history. In the field of geopolitics, NATO testified to a conspicuous reinforcement of the eastern flank, while the EU initiated activity with the aim of lessening its dependence upon energy. The Kremlin assessed the orientation of Ukraine in the West as a strategic failure on its own part in the framework of the balance of power theory as constituting a zero-sum game. Moscow, as a response, proceeded with a policy of 'subtraction,' with the aim of reducing Ukraine's geo-economic significance in the perception of the West with the aim of preventing a drastic redistribution of the balance of power. This policy gave preference to preventing the pro-Western administration of Kiev from taking advantage of such opportunities over the appropriation of the energy assets of the Black Sea by Russia.

The fact that Russia also possesses plenty of mineral wealth it doesn't require in Crimea merely serves to emphasise the implication of the scenario. Based on this, it is debatable that Moscow is attempting to prevent an alliance between its opponents in the European gas market and thus ensure it maintains control. The fundamental intent of the exercise was to seize Crimea and create chaos in east Ukraine. In regards to the 'wedge strategy,' one is able to argue that the taking of Crimea was driven amongst other motives by military and geopolitical concerns. Military value of the peninsula, apart from Crimea and eastern Ukraine energy assets, played an integral role in the processes leading to the annexation. Moreover, it is revealed in the conclusions that notwithstanding Russia investment of hundreds of millions of dollars in energy infrastructure in Crimea, the country is still yet to realise substantive economic gains. It reveals Moscow was not looking to acquire Crimea energy assets, but an energy nationalisation was part of the process of annexation.

In the aftermath of the illegal annexation of Crimea in 2014, it is obvious that the Russian Federation's foreign policy is founded upon a school of thought that is realistic. According to the thesis that power and interests are the very preoccupation in international relations, ideological and moral considerations are normally sidelined in favour of national security and national interests (Edinger, 2022). In the current case, Moscow has made the pursuit of regional pre-eminence a first principle of foreign policy. The effort at exerting influence over immediate neighbours with the intention of shaping a new region of influence in the former Soviet topography is an exemplification of the same. Putin's actions are less a response to modern geopolitics on people's minds as a declaration of an effort at redefining the position and role of Russia in the past (Edinger, 2022).

The liberal principles and democratic norms preached by the West are perceived in Moscow as a threat to national sovereignty and cultural identity. It is the belief of Putin that such principles are adopted as instruments of strategy by the West, with the potentiality of disrupting Russia's internal order. The eastward expansion of NATO and Western countries' neighbourhoods policies have been perceived in Moscow as an immediate threat to national security. It is this perception that has driven a change in Russian foreign policy in the direction of a brasher and confrontational policy (Edinger, 2022). What Putin sees is founded on the rationale of protecting Russia's national identity and cultural independence. It is a perception with segments of the governing elite and one that has presaged a shift in foreign policy in the direction of a less accommodative and a confrontational track. Western actors' failure to account for Russia's security anxieties has been a contributing factor in escalating international tensions (Edinger, 2022). It is an engagement directly responsible for determining Russia's stance in the international domain.

3.3. Digitalpolitic Dynamics

Amidst the context of a war in Ukraine, the Russian armed forces have invested significant time and resources into developing and preparing a comprehensive hybrid warfare enterprise. Hybrid warfare is described as wars characterized by a combination of the engagement of kinetic force with non-military variables that are arguably core or central, rather than peripheral, to a military operation. Since the annexation of Crimea in 2014, Russia's weaponization of communication policies has certainly received considerable international attention and analysis, which might suggest a developed and well-considered apparatus to shape the international information space in relation to the crisis. Russia's approach weaponizes information, or uses information-based interventions to re-direct the narratives of media outlets, undermine other entities, and manipulate perceptions domestically and globally (Giles, 2015).

The Russian concept of information warfare relies on two interrelated but distinct pillars. First, there are external offensive efforts such as strategic disinformation and propaganda. Externally, the Russian government has undertaken comprehensive disinformation and propaganda strategies in order to achieve several strategic objectives: for example, creating discord and confusion in Ukrainian society, and among its allies, reducing international condemnation of its actions, and cultivating a positive information space that could engender either future escalation or justify future actions. This is facilitated in part through the intentional and systematic use of a variety of state-based media outlets, including RT, Sputnik, organized networks of fake social media accounts, and conspiracy theories. The goal of the Russian action is not necessarily to persuade people of a particular "truth," but rather to inundate the information sphere with opposite and contradictory stories that will reduce confidence in institutions, objective journalism, and, finally, faith in the idea of truth itself, a tactic referred to at times as "reflexive control."

Secondly are domestic defensive measures, which include information control and censorship. In the domestic context, the strategy becomes one purely of control and isolation. Messaging intended for the Russian people aims to create an information space that is perpetually sanitized and will shield the Russian citizenry from alternative perspectives concerning the operation and global events. This is done through laws prohibiting "fake news" or anti-war rhetoric, blocking access to independent media and foreign social media sites, and establishing a patriotic state narrative. This information isolationist strategy fortifies regime security through the creation of consent, nationalism, and deterring a unified anti-Putin domestic movement (Giles, 2015).

These two approaches are codified in Russia's information security doctrine creates the information space as a national security frontier. The main goal of this doctrine is to establish sovereign control over Russia's national information space while conducting power and influence outside of its borders. Russia achieves this through a robust framework of control mechanisms working on both traditional media and digital platforms, thereby positioning the state as the source of information.

The case of Ukraine offers another demonstration of how Russia operationalizes hybrid warfare, interspersing elements of realpolitik (military action, economic leverage, and diplomatic coercion) with elements of digital politics, which could involve cyberattacks on infrastructure, algorithmic manipulation, and cognitive hacking. This hybrid approach challenges many assumptions of classical theorizing on security, particularly the binary between war and peace, soldier and civilian, or the physical and the virtual. Russia's actions in Ukraine demonstrate that modern forms of conflict may take place in the mind as much as on the battlefield, and presents a disquieting frame of reference for the 21st century and international relations, to become plausible that all future politics will be marked by a continuous information confrontation.

4. CONCLUSION

This study shows that Russian foreign policy has changed over the past three decades by reorganising it using the opportunities provided by the digital age rather than by giving up hard tools based on classical power politics (Realpolitik). The annexation of Crimea in 2014, followed by the intervention in Syria in 2015 and the massive invasion of Ukraine that began in 2022, illustrates that traditional calculations of security, balance and influence still remain at play. The situations that we've just described have also demonstrated that military power is no longer an acceptable way of defining power; we are living in a new age of power where networks, data, and information are now also legitimate forms of political power.

"Digitalpolitik" has become a defining framework for Russia's external influence strategy and internal governance in this regard. In order to regulate the flow of information, shape public opinion, and uphold national security priorities, digitisation has been accelerated since the early 2010s and combined with the institutionalisation of open data, e-government, and transparency tools. The idea of a "sovereign web" has become a strategic objective as a result of the Kremlin's increasing belief that "Western technology" could be used for influence projection, regime change, and espionage.

Diplomatic practice is not exempt from this change. In the digital age, the traditional Tsarist and Soviet-era ceremonial/formal language and negotiation patterns have changed to become more straightforward, quick, and occasionally combative. The foreign affairs apparatus's function has evolved into one that quickly distributes messages via digital platforms and enables direct communication between high-level leaders. A line that favours unilateral actions over multilateral institutional agreements is nourished by the focus on security and sovereignty.

The foundation of this new toolkit is cyber diplomacy. Russia's understanding of digital sovereignty is reinforced by internal initiatives in areas such as content control, data localisation, critical infrastructure protection, and legal-regulatory frameworks; externally, it is reinforced by influence operations, disinformation campaigns, and cyberattacks. The institutionalisation of hybrid warfare (a tactic that combines the military, economic, and information domains to influence the opponent's decision-making) has been tested in Ukraine.

This architecture gains speed and scale from artificial intelligence. AI increases the flexibility and cost-effectiveness of Russian foreign policy applications, ranging from decision support systems and predictive analytics to perception management, fake accounts, and deepfake content creation. Simultaneously, the focus on home-grown development and the rhetoric of technological sovereignty align with the substitution tactics brought about by sanctions, positioning AI as both a tool and one of the practical and symbolic pillars of sovereignty.

The definition of "civilization-state" in the 2023 Foreign Policy Concept provides a conceptual framework for this ideological-technological convergence. By situating itself in a historical conflict with the "collective West," Russia produces a language of legitimacy that is normative and identity-based, going beyond the interest- and security-centred rationality of Realpolitik. As a result, digitalpolitik is developing as a strategic vision fed by narratives of sovereignty, history, and civilisation rather than just as an instrumental innovation.

However, there is still a sense of continuity: Russia's zero-sum approach to power distribution, its ultimate determinism of hard power, and its propensity to use military options in its immediate vicinity. It is the operationalisation of a hybrid model that blurs the lines between internal and external, reality and manipulation, and war and peace. The difference is that this traditional tool is now combined with digital tools that concentrate on the information sphere. Because cyberattacks, information operations, and legal ambiguities obscure the threshold and timing of conventional international responses, this model makes deterrence and response mechanisms more difficult.

Therefore, it is possible to interpret Russia's shift from Realpolitik to Digitalpolitik as an adaptive reaction to the structural unpredictability's of world politics. The goal of expanding state capacity through digital layers is to increase regime resilience internally while diversifying foreign policy tools. This duality not only questions Western primacy, but also contributes to understandings of fragmentation and competition in the international order by allowing people to question the legitimacy of laws, organizations and standards within the global information ecosystem.

It is obvious we need to build strong capabilities in areas such as information integrity, cyber resilience, military deterrence, critical infrastructure security, and A.I. governance in response to this duality. The Russian example serves as a reminder that as narratives, data and algorithms are just as important as tanks and rifles when projecting power in the digital age. Developing a framework that emphasizes the overlapping of Realpolitik and Digitalpolitik, sheds light on the structural realities within international relations and can help inform policy drivers.

5. REFERENCES

Allison, R. (2017). Russia and the post-2014 international legal order: Revisionism and realpolitik. *International Affairs*, *93*(3), 519–543. DOI: 10.1093/ia/iix061

Barichella, A. (2022). *Cyberattacks in Russia's hybrid war against Ukraine and its ramifications for Europe*. Jacques Delors Institute.

Bendett, S. (2024). The Role of AI in Russia's Confrontation with the West. *Center for a New American Security*. Pp. 1-31.

Bohlen, A. (1966). Changes in Russian diplomacy under Peter the Great. *Cahiers du Monde Russe et Sovietique*, *7*(3), 341–358. DOI: 10.3406/cmr.1966.1672

Edinger, H. (2022). Offensive ideas: Structural realism, classical realism and Putin's war on Ukraine. *International Affairs*, *98*(6), 1873–1893. DOI: 10.1093/ia/iiac217

Eriksen, M. (2016). Assessing Russia's Doctrine of Realpolitik as Strategic Re-Contouring of Regional Power-Balance in The Post-Soviet Periphery. *Politeja* 41: 305–328. https://www.jstor.org/stable/24920236

Götz, E. (2017). Putin, the State, and War: The Causes of Russia's Near Abroad Assertion Revisited. *International Studies Review*, *19*(2), 228–253. DOI: 10.1093/isr/viw009

Graham, T. (2024). Realpolitik vs. Messianism in Russian Foreign Policy. *Orbis*, *68*(3), 462–469. DOI: 10.1016/j.orbis.2024.05.007

Hakala, J., & Melnychuk, J. (2021). *Russia's Strategy in Cyberspace*. NATO Strategic Communications Centre of Excellence.

Kukkola, J., Ristolainen, M., & Nikkarila, J.-P. (2017). *Game Changer: Structural transformation of cyberspace*. Finnish Defence Research Agency.

Martynova, E., & Shcherbovich, A. (2024). Digital transformation in Russia: Turning from a service model to ensuring technological sovereignty. *Computer Law & Security Review*, *55*, 106075. Advance online publication. DOI: 10.1016/j.clsr.2024.106075

Mearsheimer, J. J. (2014). Why the Ukraine Crisis Is the West's Fault: The Liberal Delusions That Provoked Putin. *Foreign Affairs*, *93*(5), 77–89.

Nocetti, J. (2011). Digital Kremlin": power and the internet in Russia. Russie. Nei. Visions, 59(5).

Nocetti, J. (2020, December). *The Outsider: Russia in the Race for Artificial Intelligence* (Russie Nei Reports No. 34). Institut Français Des Relations Internationales (IFRI).

Pagen, J. (2020). A New Russian Realpolitik: Putin's Operationalization of Psychology and Propaganda. *Global Security and Intelligence Studies*, *5*(1), 55–79. DOI: 10.18278/gsis.5.1.5

Reinhardt, R. (2020). Tweets vs. the Officialese: How the Language of Russian Diplomacy Is Changing amid the Global Transition. *Valdai Papers* 114. Retrived May 13, 2025, from http://valdaiclub.com/a/valdai-papers/

Sherman, J. (2024, July 29). *Russia's digital tech isolationism: Domestic innovation, digital fragmentation, and the Kremlin's push to replace Western digital technology.* Atlantic Council. Retrieved May 9, 2025, from https://www.atlanticcouncil.org/in-depth-research-reports/issue-brief/russias-digital-tech-isolationism/

Wijermars, M. (2020). The Digitalization of Russian Politics and Political Participation. In *The Palgrave Handbook of Digital Russia Studies* (pp. 15–32). DOI: 10.1007/978-3-030-42855-6_2

Wohlforth, W. C. (2015, April). *The Return of Realpolitik*. Russia in Global Affairs. Retrieved May 4, 2025, from https://eng.globalaffairs.ru/articles/the-return-of-realpolitik/

Chapter 2

The Impacts of Quantum Technologies and Artificial Intelligence Synergy on International Relations and Security

Hasan Ucuzal
https://orcid.org/0000-0003-4870-3015
Inonu University, Turkey

ABSTRACT

This section examines the profound transformative impact of the strategic synergy between quantum technologies and artificial intelligence on the international system, security paradigms, and global governance. The analysis, conducted through a multidimensional conceptual framework, details the different strategies of global actors such as the United States, China, and the European Union in this new era of technological competition by assessing changes in military strategy, economic competition, and normative orders. It also explores significant risks and geopolitical tensions arising from this synergy, such as cybersecurity vulnerabilities, the emergence of lethal autonomous weapons, and increasing technological dependence. argues that effectively managing these disruptive technologies is critical to ensuring global stability, preventing a potentially deepening "quantum divide," and aligning technological progress with ethical standards and international security, and discusses the need for robust international governance and cooperation mechanisms.

DOI: 10.4018/979-8-3373-4937-4.ch002

1. INTRODUCTION

The strategic integration between quantum technologies and artificial intelligence is bringing about a profound transformation in the field of international relations and security. This change is not merely a technological advancement but also a multidimensional transformation that is reshaping the functioning of the international system, power balances, and the understanding of security (Derian & Wendt, 2020). This development, which manifests its influence across a broad spectrum from states' security strategies to economic models, from diplomatic practices to international law norms, has made technological superiority the most crucial element of global competition. When the superior computational power provided by quantum computers is combined with AI's prediction and learning capabilities, it creates new strategic opportunities and risks not only for states but also for multinational corporations and international organizations (Boretti, 2024).

The realist perspective, which examines this transformation from a power struggle standpoint, positions quantum and AI as the new frontier of interstate competition. The strategic rivalry between the US and China, in particular, reveals that technological superiority is not only an economic or military issue but also a matter of diplomatic influence and global leadership (Lippert & Perthes, 2020). China's Micius quantum communication satellite, launched into space in 2016, became one of the first concrete examples of the practical applications of quantum encryption and reflected Beijing's determination in this field (Yin et al., 2017). In response, the US has become one of the strongest actors in this race through DARPA's quantum security projects, Google and IBM's quantum computer prototypes, and the integration of AI and quantum by military research centers (AbuGhanem & Eleuch, 2024). The European Union's "Quantum Flagship" initiative and Japan's national strategies demonstrate that this process is acquiring a multilateral character. All these developments, as realism predicts, are affecting power balances, transforming deterrence calculations, and deepening security dilemmas (Riedel, Kovács, Zoller, Mlynek, & Calarco, 2019).

Assessments from a liberal perspective suggest that these technological advances also bring cooperation opportunities. This approach, which argues that technology by its nature spreads on a global scale, considers it imperative to strengthen international institutions, normative regulations, and transparent oversight mechanisms to manage risks (Roco, 2020). The United Nations' ethical debates on AI and autonomous weapon systems, the European Union's AI Act, and NATO's joint work on quantum communication technologies are concrete examples of these quests for cooperation (Sharikov, 2024). Therefore, the effective management of the risks created by quantum and AI-based technologies on a global scale can only be possible through multi-stakeholder cooperation among states, international organizations, the private sector, and academia.

The constructivist interpretation, which deals with this process in its normative and discursive dimensions, emphasizes that technologies are not merely elements of material power but also shape international politics through identities, norms, and discourses. The difference between China's presentation of quantum communication networks as a "symbol of sovereignty and independence" and the European Union's positioning of the same technologies within the framework of "strengthening common security and ethical standards" is one of the most concrete reflections of this approach (Sharma, 2018). A state's definition of quantum-based encryption as a peaceful security measure can be perceived as a threat by another state; this situation further complicates the normative dimension of the security dilemma.

In the context of Risks and Geopolitical Tensions, the quantum-AI integration is creating new vulnerabilities in the international system. The potential of quantum computers to break current cryptographic systems could leave financial markets, military communication networks, and critical infrastructure vulnerable on a global scale. While strategic dependencies increase for countries lagging in the technological superiority race, this could trigger new geopolitical bloc formations (Cyriac, Eswaran, & Selvarajan, 2024). The technology race, shaped under the leadership of great powers like the US, China, and Russia, is intensifying not only bilateral rivalries but also the pressure on third countries to choose sides. In this context, the possibility of a "technological cold war" is becoming a concept increasingly discussed in international security literature (Tung, Zander, & Fang, 2023; Willoughby & Seskir, 2021).

Governance and Cooperation Strategies that stand out to balance these risks aim to align the technological transformation with international law, ethical norms, and institutional mechanisms (Liu, 2024). Establishing quantum encryption standards, developing transparent algorithmic audit mechanisms for AI use, and creating multinational regulatory frameworks are the main elements of these strategies (Sahu & Mazumdar, 2024). NATO's efforts to develop common standards among allies in quantum communication technologies, the European Union's AI Act, and the OECD's AI principles can be cited as examples within this framework (Hildebrandt, 2020; Kgoale & Odeku, 2023). Furthermore, designing technology transfer and capacity-building programs for developing countries to prevent the deepening of global technological inequalities is of critical importance for international stability.

The effects of quantum-AI integration in the military field are becoming increasingly visible (Krelina, 2021). The potential of quantum computers to break current cryptographic systems could leave military communication networks and critical infrastructure vulnerable (Gitonga, 2025). The US's investments in developing quantum-based secure communication systems, China's quantum radar and communication research, and Russia's emphasis on AI and quantum in its military modernization strategies show that this process is not only a race but also a new breaking point for global security (Evsikov, 2022). While autonomous weapon systems become more effective with quantum algorithms, ethical and legal issues are becoming an increasingly urgent agenda item.

On the economic dimension, the impact of the quantum-AI synergy is transforming the parameters of global competition. Google's quantum supremacy experiments, IBM's commercial quantum systems, China's quantum computer investments for financial modeling, and supply chain optimization projects in Europe demonstrate that the economic reflections of these technologies are not only theoretical but also concrete and applicable (Dunjko & Briegel, 2018). While this process creates strategic advantages for developed countries, it makes the establishment of international support mechanisms necessary for developing countries to integrate into this race. Otherwise, the deepening technological gap will increase global inequalities and create new areas of instability for international peace (Willoughby & Seskir, 2021).

The integration between quantum technologies and artificial intelligence is a strategic transformation beyond technical innovation that can be interpreted from different angles by each of the international relations theories. The realist reading through power competition and security dilemma, the liberal approach emphasizing cooperation and governance, and the constructivist view evaluating the process in the context of norms, identities, and discourses allow us to make sense of the effects of these technologies on the global order in different dimensions. China's Micius satellite, the US's DARPA projects, the EU's Quantum Flagship initiative, and Japan's national strategies show that this transformation is not just a theoretical discussion but a reality concretely experienced today (AbuGhanem & Eleuch, 2024; Parker, 2021; Yin et al., 2017). How the quantum and AI synergy is managed in the international system will continue to be one of the critical elements determining the direction of the global security architecture, economic order, and diplomatic relations in the coming decades.

2. CONCEPTUAL FRAMEWORK

Understanding the capacity of the interaction between quantum technologies and artificial intelligence to transform the international system is not limited to focusing on technical details. These two technological fields are creating deep and comprehensive effects on the fundamental dimensions of the international system, such as security, economy, normative orders, and strategic competitions. Therefore, adopting a multi-layered conceptual framework is necessary to examine this interaction. The quantum and artificial intelligence (AI) synergy not only equips the international system with new technological tools but also redefines power balances, raises ethical and normative questions, deepens global economic inequalities, and radically changes the security paradigm. Hence, when assessing technological impact, it is essential to focus not only on technical capacity but also on strategic, normative, and economic conditions.

In the field of security, the potential of quantum computers to break classical encryption methods seriously calls into question the sustainability of current digital security systems. This potential threat materializes in the scenario defined in the literature as "cryptographic apocalypse." Quantum computers can solve certain algorithms much faster than classical computers, and this poses a serious risk for banking systems, energy infrastructures, and data classified as state secrets. Artificial intelligence can make this process more practical by optimizing the error correction processes of quantum computers and selecting the most suitable algorithms (Bernstein, 2008; Tom, Anebo, Onyekwelu, Wilfred, & Eyo, 2023). This combination not only increases interstate cyber competition but also directly affects private sector and critical infrastructure security. For example, financial institutions could become vulnerable to quantum-powered AI attacks in terms of data security. Similarly, power plants and critical communication networks become fragile in the face of this new threat.

Quantum sensors have revolutionary potential in the military field. These sensors can detect magnetic anomalies created by submarines, perform monitoring with precise measurements in airspace and land areas, and determine location without relying on GPS (Kantsepolsky, Aviv, Weitzfeld, & Bordo, 2023). Artificial intelligence reshapes intelligence and deterrence calculations by analyzing the big data flow from these sensors in real-time. Thus, a new security approach based on data-driven decision processes emerges, moving away from traditional weapon and submarine strategies. On the other hand, in the field of cybersecurity, the tension between the code-breaking capacity of quantum computers and the theoretical security offered by quantum key distribution, when combined with AI-based network analysis, drives states into a new cyber arms race. This situation redefines not only attack and defense strategies but also international intelligence sharing and cyber deterrence policies (Krelina, 2021; Lindsay, 2020; Singh & Kumar, 2024).

In the economic field, the interaction between quantum and AI has the potential to transform international productivity and competition. The simulation capacity offered by quantum computers in sectors such as drug development, financial modeling, logistics optimization, and materials science, when combined with AI algorithms, is significantly increasing global productivity. In the pharmaceutical sector, quantum computers can rapidly perform complex molecular simulations; AI algorithms analyze the data obtained from these simulations, enabling faster and more effective drug discovery. In the financial sector, quantum-based computations greatly improve risk modeling, portfolio optimization, and market predictions. In the logistics and manufacturing sectors, quantum and AI integration reshapes global economic competition by optimizing supply chains and increasing efficiency in production processes (He, Govoni, & Galli, 2020; Pfister, Schubert, & Kröll, 2023; Wang, Chen, Yang, Lee, & Tseng, 2023).

However, these technological advantages also give rise to a new source of inequality called the "quantum divide." The intensive investments of the US and China elevating them to a leading position lead to developing countries facing dependency risks, thus creating a deepening asymmetry in global economic balances. This situation brings not only economic but also political dependency and strategic vulnerability problems. Furthermore, the decrease in routine jobs in the labor market increases demand for highly skilled fields such as quantum software engineering, data science, and AI ethics, making it mandatory to restructure education systems according to these new needs. This situation requires the reshaping of international education and human capital policies (Gercek & Seskir, 2024; Hughes et al., 2021; Jang, Choung, & Kang, 2022).

The normative and ethical dimension of quantum and AI technologies is also very important. Dual-use technologies, meaning tools that can be used for both civilian and military purposes, fall outside the scope of the current international legal order. Quantum-based communication networks and sensor systems can be used both for critical infrastructure security and to provide military superiority. When autonomous AI decision-making systems combine with the processing power of quantum computers, ethical dilemmas such as the uncontrolled development of lethal autonomous weapons or the strengthening of mass surveillance regimes emerge (Boretti, 2024; Possati, 2023). The European Union's claim to normative leadership with its "trustworthy AI" principles creates a global struggle of values between the US's market-oriented approach and China's state-controlled surveillance model. This situation highlights the importance of how the ethical and legal aspects of digital technologies will be shaped at the international level (Ashok, Madan, Joha, & Sivarajah, 2022).

From the perspective of military strategy and hybrid threats, the quantum and AI synergy creates new dynamics on the battlefield. Quantum radars and sensors reduce uncertainty on the battlefield, while AI provides real-time simulations and decision support systems, increasing the speed and effectiveness of military planning. However, the fundamental problem that stands out at the strategic and hybrid level is the pushing aside of human judgment due to the extreme acceleration of decision-making processes (Krelina, 2021). When quantum-assisted code-breaking capacity combines with AI's power to generate deepfake content, the impact of cyber warfare and disinformation campaigns is further strengthened. This situation is forcing states to reconsider not only their military doctrines but also their national security policies and international alliance strategies (Shoaib, Wang, Ahvanooey, & Zhao, 2023).

The quantum and AI synergy presents itself as a force reshaping the international system not only as a technical innovation but in all its dimensions, from security to economy, from normative orders to hybrid threats. Understanding this transformation necessitates the adoption of an interdisciplinary approach and the development of a multidimensional conceptual framework. The effects of quantum and AI technologies are redefining not only the power balances of states but also global ethical, normative, and economic structures. Researchers, policymakers, and international actors must address technical, strategic, and ethical elements together to correctly assess this transformation (Dunjko & Briegel, 2018).

In the future, quantum and AI-focused policies will need to be developed in a harmonious manner at both national and international scales. Countries must consider not only investment and R&D strategies to achieve technological superiority but also ethical guidelines, international standards, and normative frameworks. While the quantum and AI synergy creates a profound transformation in international security, economy, and ethics, the balanced and sustainable management of this transformation requires international cooperation and an interdisciplinary approach.

3. STRATEGIES OF GLOBAL ACTORS

The synergy of quantum and artificial intelligence (AI) technologies varies according to states' economic capacity, scientific infrastructure, political system, and geopolitical goals. These technologies are critical not only for national security or economic competition but also for international power balances, normative orders, and technology geopolitics. Understanding the quantum-AI strategies of global actors is essential for analyzing the future technology-based international order.

The United States (US) is developing its strategy in the quantum and AI fields based on private sector innovation, state-supported R&D programs, and cooperation with international allies (Raymer & Monroe, 2019). The US has maintained its technological superiority since World War II and consolidated this leadership during the Cold War with institutions like DARPA, NASA, and NSA (Elliott et al., 2005; Krelina, 2021). Today, both government institutions, for example, the National Quantum Initiative, and private sector giants like Google, IBM, Microsoft, and Amazon play a pioneering role. These institutions are carrying out strategic investments in quantum computing research, AI algorithms, and critical infrastructure security (Alvarado-Valiente, Romero-Álvarez, Moguel, García-Alonso, & Murillo, 2024).

A concrete indicator of the US technology strategy is the CHIPS and Science Act adopted in 2022. This law aims to bring semiconductor manufacturing back to the US and provide over $200 billion in federal investment for quantum information science and artificial intelligence research. Thus, dependency on China in supply chains is reduced, and self-sufficiency in critical technologies is increased (Dhiman, 2025). One of the US's strongest aspects is the dynamism of the private sector. Google's Sycamore processor, with which it announced "quantum supremacy" in 2019, IBM's quantum computer roadmap with over a thousand qubits, Microsoft's Azure Quantum platform, and Amazon's Braket service, which provides quantum computing access via the cloud, are expanding the ecosystem (AbuGhanem & Eleuch, 2024; Devitt, 2016). The main goal of the US strategy is to maintain technological leadership and balance China's rise. In this context, cooperation has been deepened through alliances with NATO allies and the Quad (US, Japan, Australia, India) and AUKUS (US, UK, Australia), and technology export restrictions and sanctions have been imposed on China (Çokgüçlü, 2022).

China, on the other hand, is pursuing a state-directed, centralized, and fast strategy in the quantum-AI race. The New Generation Artificial Intelligence Development Plan announced in 2017 under the leadership of the Chinese Communist Party aims to make China the world's leading AI center by 2030. Quantum technologies have also been made a national priority, with large resources allocated to state-supported research institutions and universities (Wu et al., 2020). Among China's notable achievements in quantum computing is the photonic-based Jiuzhang processor, and the quantum key distribution experiment conducted with the Micius satellite set a first in space-based quantum communication. These developments show that China is focused not only on theoretical research but also on practical and military applications (Lu, Cao, Peng, & Pan, 2022).

One of China's most decisive strategies is the Military-Civilian Fusion policy, which aims to integrate the military and civilian technology sectors. Advanced technologies developed in universities and private companies are directly offered to the service of the People's Liberation Army. This situation reveals that quantum and AI are being used as a lever to enhance China's military capacity. Although the US-imposed sanctions and export restrictions make it difficult for China to access high-quality semiconductors, China is determined to develop its domestic production capacity. This process creates a scenario of technological decoupling and deepening competition between the two superpowers (Can & Vieira, 2022).

The European Union (EU), while lagging behind the US and China in terms of economic and technological scale, follows a different path with its normative power and ethical leadership approach. The EU's quantum-AI strategy is built on an understanding of technological sovereignty and human-centric innovation. The Quantum Flagship program launched in 2018 with a budget of 1 billion euros aims to coordinate Europe's quantum research and keep it competitive (Riedel et al., 2019). The EU is pursuing an effort to set global standards with its "Trustworthy

AI" guidelines published in 2019 and the agreed AI Act (Chahri, 2021; Smuha, 2019). These regulations, emphasizing principles such as transparency, human oversight, privacy, and justice, offer an alternative to the US's free-market and China's state-control models. On the other hand, the relative weakness of private sector investments, the difficulty of coordination among 27 member states, and the migration of talented researchers to the US increase the risk of the EU falling into a secondary position in technological applications.

Russia, although not in a comprehensive race due to resource constraints, is pursuing a strategy focused on creating asymmetric advantages. Russia's quantum-AI investments are primarily directed toward military applications. Research institutes under the Ministry of Defense are working on quantum radars, quantum gyroscopes, and quantum cryptography systems. Maintaining nuclear deterrence and ensuring the security of communication infrastructure are priorities for Russia. The strong mathematics and physics infrastructure inherited from the Soviet Union gives Russia an advantage in theoretical research, but Western sanctions and a lack of capital prevent this knowledge from being converted into practical and commercial products. Therefore, Russia sees these technologies as tools to strengthen its existing military capacity and use in hybrid threats, rather than aiming to be a primary actor in the quantum-AI race (Fedorov et al., 2019).

India is a significant regional power trying to stand out in the quantum-AI race with its rapidly growing economy and strong software sector. The Indian government launched the National Quantum Mission in 2023 with a budget of 1 billion dollars, aiming to develop intermediate-scale quantum computers and establish quantum communication networks within the next five years. The dynamic technology sector in cities like Bangalore and Hyderabad provides a solid infrastructure for India's rapid progress in AI. Furthermore, the large population and data pool provide an advantage in training AI algorithms. Geopolitically, India pursues a balancing policy; it cooperates with the US within the Quad alliance while maintaining relations with Russia and China. This approach shows that India is open to multilateral collaborations in the quantum-AI field (Chakraborty, Bhattacharya, Pal, & Agoramoorthy, 2023; Menon & Adhikari, 2023).

Global South countries, on the other hand, face the risk of marginalization and external dependency in the quantum-AI race. Many countries in the African continent, lacking basic digital infrastructure and R&D investments, have limited capacity and are largely dependent on international aid and cooperation. In Latin America, countries like Brazil, Argentina, and Chile conduct certain quantum research, but most of the region lags behind the global race due to resource shortages and political instability (Orszag, Retamal, Saavedra, & Wallentowitz, 2007). On the other hand, some Asian countries like Singapore, South Korea, and Taiwan are developing niche expertise in quantum communication and AI fields thanks to strong education systems, technology-oriented economies, and state support; these countries stand out as regional innovation centers (Costa & Rodrigues, 2020).

A comparative analysis shows that the strategies of global actors differ significantly. The US follows a strategy of private sector-led innovation, geopolitical alliances, and balancing against China; China adopts a state-directed central planning, military-civil integration, and self-sufficiency approach. The EU offers an alternative model with normative leadership, ethical regulations, and institutional cooperation; while Russia carries the goal of military-focused, asymmetric strategy and preserving existing power. India pursues a balancing policy, software power, and gradual capacity-building strategy, while the Global South remains in a limited position with the risk of marginalization, dependency on foreign aid, and the quest for technology transfer. This situation clearly reveals the multidimensional, multipolar, and dynamic nature of the quantum-AI competition.

In light of all these assessments, the quantum and AI synergy emerges not only as a technological innovation but as a force reshaping the international system in its economic, security, normative, and strategic dimensions. The moves of global actors in this field directly affect both technology geopolitics and international power balances. The strategies of the US, China, the EU, Russia, India, and Global South countries show that the future technology-oriented international order will develop in a multidimensional and dynamic structure.

4. RISKS AND GEOPOLITICAL TENSIONS

The combination of quantum and artificial intelligence (AI) technologies has the potential to reshape the international system in terms of both opportunities and serious risks. The risks created by these technologies can be examined under five main headings: cybersecurity, autonomous weapons and military risks, technological dependency and vulnerability, surveillance and individual freedoms, and geopolitical competition and global security. These areas reveal the multidimensional effects of the quantum-AI synergy on the international system.

In the field of cybersecurity, the potential of quantum computers to break current encryption algorithms poses a serious threat to digital infrastructure. The possibility that widely used cryptographic methods like RSA and ECC can be broken with quantum power creates vulnerability across a broad spectrum, from financial systems to state secrets. This scenario is defined in the literature as "cryptographic apocalypse," and if it materializes, critical infrastructures, energy grids, and water systems could be paralyzed. Artificial intelligence plays a role that can directly affect the timing of this threat by optimizing quantum algorithms and managing error correction processes (Sahu & Mazumdar, 2024).

The effects of the quantum-AI synergy on critical infrastructures also represent a significant risk area. Quantum systems that break codes and AI-powered cyberattacks could target a country's basic services such as energy, transportation, or communication. Such coordinated attacks not only cause economic loss but can also fundamentally destabilize states by causing social chaos and humanitarian crises. In the face of this threat, post-quantum cryptography (PQC) standards are being developed under the leadership of the National Institute of Standards and Technology (NIST). However, the global adoption and implementation of these new algorithms is a long process, and the transition period creates a "risk window" where digital systems are vulnerable (Yesina, Ostrianska, & Gorbenko, 2022).

In the military field, the quantum-AI synergy is accelerating the development of lethal autonomous weapon systems (LAWS). These systems have the capacity to select and attack targets without human supervision (Horowitz, 2019). Misperception or software errors could lead to unforeseen and uncontrollable conflicts. Furthermore, the extreme sensitivity of quantum sensors increases the risk of producing false positive alarms; for example, a pod of whales being detected as a nuclear submarine could trigger an irreversible counterattack in high-tension environments like a nuclear crisis. This situation brings a new and unpredictable escalation risk to the global security environment. The intensive investments of the US, China, and Russia in quantum-based military technologies are triggering a new arms race reminiscent of the Cold War era, undermining international trust, and deepening the security dilemma among states.

Technological dependency constitutes another risk dimension of the quantum-AI synergy. The superconductors, optical systems, and precise cooling devices required for quantum processors can only be produced by a limited number of countries and companies. This makes other countries strategically fragile, and a disruption in supply chains can directly threaten national security. Software and algorithmic dependency similarly create risk; quantum programming languages and large AI models are largely controlled by US-based technology firms. This limits the technological sovereignty of other countries and carries the risk of a kind of "software colonialism" in the digital age. Furthermore, the US's high-tech sanctions and export restrictions against China risk creating a "technological iron curtain" by fragmenting global supply chains. This scenario could divide the world into poles with non-interconnected, competing technology standards (Schmalz, 2024).

In terms of surveillance and individual freedoms, the quantum-AI synergy is creating an unprecedented mass monitoring capacity. The high sensitivity of quantum sensors and the data processing power of AI can penetrate into the most private areas of individuals through applications such as facial recognition, behavior analysis, and social network monitoring. This capacity offers a powerful tool for social control to authoritarian regimes and poses serious threats to democracy and human rights.

Mass surveillance erodes fundamental rights such as freedom of expression, the right to assembly, and privacy, leading individuals to self-censor and causing the weakening of civil society and democratic participation.

In terms of geopolitical competition, quantum-AI is a central element of a new technology-based cold war between the US and China. As both superpowers compete fiercely to gain technological superiority, the world economy and security architecture are directly affected by this struggle. Sanctions, counter-sanctions, and cyber conflicts are becoming routine elements of this cold war. The US-China rivalry is forcing other countries to choose sides; while the European Union tries to maintain its normative independence, India and Southeast Asian countries are pursuing a balancing policy. This situation increases the risk of the re-blocking of the international system and the weakening of the spirit of multilateral cooperation (Yamin, Ullah, Ullah, & Katt, 2021).

Additionally, quantum-AI technologies could make existing regional tensions more dangerous and unpredictable. A sudden cyber-attack or the accidental triggering of an autonomous weapon in high-risk regions like the South China Sea, the Taiwan Strait, Ukraine, and the Middle East could rapidly turn a regional conflict into a global crisis. Therefore, the risks created by the quantum-AI synergy increase the fragility of the international system in every field; giving rise to new and complex problems in different areas such as cybersecurity, military control, economic dependencies, individual freedoms, and great power competition (Maathuis & Cools, 2025).

In light of all these developments, managing the risks of the quantum-AI synergy will only be possible with effective international cooperation and governance mechanisms. Without the establishment of global standards, normative frameworks, and technological cooperation networks, it will be difficult to prevent the crises that these technologies could cause. Furthermore, states must develop both technological and legal strategies to protect both their internal security and global stability. Quantum-AI, as a force capable of having profound effects on international security, economic balance, individual freedoms, and geopolitical relations, emerges not only as a technological innovation but also as one of the most important strategic agenda items of our time.

5. GOVERNANCE AND COOPERATION STRATEGIES

Mitigating the disruptive risks created by the quantum and artificial intelligence (AI) synergy and fairly distributing the emerging opportunities on a global scale has become an urgent necessity for the international community. This necessity mandates the implementation of multilateral, inclusive, and effective governance mechanisms. Global governance should not be limited to interstate negotiations; it also requires the active participation of international institutions, the private sector, academia, and civil society organizations.

International institutions play a central role in managing the risks that quantum-AI will create. The United Nations (UN), as the most inclusive platform, can lead the formation of global norms. While the UN Conference on Disarmament could organize negotiations for the ban or restriction of lethal autonomous weapons (LAWS), the Human Rights Council could report on the use of quantum-based surveillance technologies in human rights violations and set principles. UNESCO can develop education programs to increase quantum and AI literacy in developing countries. Through these institutions, it becomes possible to both determine global normative standards and achieve capacity development goals (Horowitz, 2019; Kathala & Palakurthi, 2024).

Regional security institutions also have critical importance in this framework. NATO can develop common defense protocols against quantum-based cyber threats and autonomous weapons (Sharikov, 2024). Similarly, ASEAN, the African Union, and other regional organizations should create platforms related to these technologies and develop common positions, considering their own security needs (Nesadurai, 2008). Such initiatives can strengthen regional cooperation while also playing a stabilizing role in the global security architecture.

Economic cooperation organizations can also undertake an important task in quantum-AI governance. The OECD and G20 can play a key role in harmonizing post-quantum cryptography standards, coordinating R&D investments, and negotiating multilateral agreements for technology transfer. The G20, by bringing large economies together, offers an ideal forum for establishing a global technology governance framework (Joseph et al., 2022). In this context, economic and technological cooperation is a critical tool not only for growth goals but also for the dissemination of security and ethical standards.

Existing international arms control regimes are inadequate in covering quantum- and AI-based weapons. Agreements regulating nuclear, biological, and chemical weapons are not suitable for new and revolutionary technologies. This legal gap increases the risk of the uncontrolled proliferation of lethal autonomous systems. Therefore, the development of new treaties at the international level is essential. For example, a binding agreement aiming to prevent the development of systems capable of making lethal decisions without human control could be effective in banning or restricting lethal autonomous weapons. Similarly, agreements addressing aggressive actions in cyberspace could establish international norms prohibiting the use of quantum code-breaking capabilities against critical civilian infrastructure. In this context, recent regional wars and their outcomes have clearly demonstrated how the pursuit of technological superiority and the emergence of next-generation weapon systems affect the balance of international security (Turan, 2024).

However, the implementation of such agreements carries serious challenges. The complexity of verification processes, the lack of trust among states, and the fear of losing military advantage limit the effectiveness of negotiations. Yet these challenges should not stop normative framework-building efforts. The primary goal of the international community should be to establish at least global standards and ethical principles regarding technology use.

Support mechanisms for developing countries are of critical importance in reducing inequalities in the quantum-AI field. In this context, education and capacity-building programs can ensure that the Global South does not fall completely behind in the technology race. The UN, the World Bank, and other international organizations can increase the competitiveness of these countries through scholarship programs, online education platforms, and technical support. Furthermore, technology transfer mechanisms should make it possible for developing countries to be not only technology consumers but also producers. Open-source software (Qiskit, TensorFlow Quantum) and multinational companies' local R&D investments can enhance the effectiveness of this process (Bansal, Khanna, & Rajput, 2024).

Regional research centers can also play an important role in reducing inequality. Quantum and AI centers of excellence established in Africa, Latin America, and Southeast Asia will enable local researchers to participate in international collaborations and develop solutions for regional needs. These centers will not only increase technology production but also contribute to strengthening regional capacities (Orszag et al., 2007).

Establishing an ethical and normative framework is a fundamental requirement in the governance of quantum-AI technologies. Multi-stakeholder governance models, by involving states, companies, civil society organizations, and academia in the process, can guarantee that the technology is used in a fair, transparent, and accountable manner. While companies should comply with ethical principles, civil society should undertake the task of oversight and advocacy; and academia should assume the responsibility of independent research and developing ethical standards.

Among the ethical principles that can be adopted on a global scale, human oversight and control, transparency, fairness, data privacy, and accountability principles stand out. Especially in life-and-death decisions, the final authority must always lie with humans. How algorithms make decisions should be understandable and auditable, designed to be free from biases and respectful of individuals' privacy. The EU's AI Act and "Trustworthy AI" principles can be presented as an international model for this ethical framework and should be developed in cooperation with other countries. This approach offers an alternative that centers human rights against China's surveillance model and the US's less regulatory approach (Sharikov, 2024).

Cooperation models are a decisive factor for the success of quantum-AI governance. Open science and open-source models, by sharing research findings and software, encourage the participation of global scientists in collaboration. Public-private partnerships provide an effective mechanism for the funding and commercialization of basic research; the DARPA model in the US and the EU's Quantum Flagship program are successful examples of this approach. Regional cooperations, through organizations like ASEAN, the African Union, or MERCOSUR, can increase the chances of competition for small and medium-sized countries by pooling their resources (AbuGhanem & Eleuch, 2024; Parker, 2021; Yin et al., 2017).

The challenges posed by the quantum-AI synergy surpass traditional international governance models. Therefore, an effective response requires a combination of international institutions, innovative arms control agreements, inclusive capacity-building programs, strong ethical principles, and multi-stakeholder cooperation models. If these efforts fail, quantum-AI technologies risk deepening global inequalities and increasing geopolitical tensions.

In this context, the safe and fair governance of quantum-AI technologies on a global scale is not only a technological necessity but also vital for preserving international stability and securing human rights. Without effective governance and inclusive cooperation, the potential benefits of these technologies will not be fully realized, and at the same time, risks will increase uncontrollably.

6. CONCLUSION

The strategic synergy between quantum technologies and artificial intelligence (AI) is emerging as a paradigmatic area of influence that is radically transforming the landscape of 21st-century international relations and security. This book chapter shows that the intersection of these two technologies is not merely a technical innovation; it is a multidimensional phenomenon that is reshaping the fundamental dynamics of the international system, such as power, security, deterrence, and sovereignty. In this context, quantum-AI integration harbors both opportunities and risks for national and international actors and is determining the nature of geopolitical competition.

In the security dimension, quantum technologies and AI are redefining the concept of national security through the breakability of current cryptographic systems and the capacity of sensor technologies to change the military balance. While quantum-based cryptography provides high security in information transfer, it reduces the validity of classical encryption methods and forces states to develop new defense measures. On the other hand, quantum sensors and AI-supported detection systems make it possible to make faster and more predictable decisions in the planning and implementation of military strategies. This situation is of critical importance, especially in nuclear deterrence and early warning systems; it reveals the necessity of reducing false alarm risks, restructuring crisis management and communication protocols.

In the economic dimension, the quantum-AI synergy has the potential to increase productivity and solve complex problems. Its capacity to produce solutions to global problems such as climate change, the energy crisis, and new material design encourages technological innovation and economic prosperity. However, the imbalance in the global distribution of technological developments creates an inequality problem called the "quantum divide." This divide reinforces the technological superiority of developed countries while causing developing countries to fall into a disadvantaged position in global competition and security issues. Therefore, technological advancement not only provides economic benefits but also makes the re-evaluation of international justice and equality principles mandatory.

In the normative dimension, the dual-use nature of quantum and AI technologies brings ethical and legal dilemmas. Autonomous weapon systems, individual surveillance technologies, and algorithmic decision support systems require the reinterpretation of international law and ethical norms. The proliferation of these technologies makes it mandatory to establish international standards within the framework of human rights, transparency, and accountability principles. The expansion of normative models like the EU's "Trustworthy AI" approach to include quantum technologies is considered an important step in establishing a global ethical framework.

In the strategic dimension, hybrid threats and algorithmic decision support systems are reshaping the concepts of war and peace. The use of autonomous systems is transforming traditional conflict models and creating a new element of uncertainty in states' strategic planning. At the same time, the advantages brought by the quantum-AI synergy make the need for international cooperation inevitable. The existential risks and global impacts of the technology increase the importance of interstate cooperation and multi-stakeholder governance models. In this context, measures such as the ban on lethal autonomous weapons, the integration of quantum-based threats into common defense doctrines, and the strengthening of crisis management protocols are of critical importance for the future stability of the international security architecture.

The opportunities offered by the quantum-AI synergy for humanity materialize in its capacity to create innovation and prosperity. Advanced quantum computing and AI applications can provide groundbreaking results in drug discovery, climate modeling, and complex engineering problems. Furthermore, open science and multi-stakeholder governance models can strengthen global cooperation and contribute to reducing inequalities through technology transfer and education programs. However, existential threats and dystopian surveillance risks show that these technologies have great destructive potential in the wrong hands. If cooperation fails, negative scenarios such as digital authoritarianism, social inequality, and global instability will be inevitable.

Future projections reveal the short, medium, and long-term effects of the quantum-AI synergy. In the short term (2025–2035), US-China competition will intensify, post-quantum cryptography applications will gain momentum, and quantum sensors will become widespread in the military field. In the medium term (2035–2050), quantum computers will become practical in commercial applications, and innovative technological products offering solutions to humanity's fundamental problems will emerge. In the long term (post-2050), if cooperation is successful, quantum-AI could lay the foundations for a Golden Age of humanity; otherwise, the race spiraling out of control will lead to a world order where digital authoritarianism is globalized.

In conclusion, the synergy between quantum technologies and artificial intelligence can be defined as a deep and multidimensional transformation with the potential to reshape the international system. The US-China competition, the EU's normative initiatives, the balancing strategies of other actors, and the inequalities faced by the Global South are determining the outlines of future geopolitics. In this case, three fundamental conclusions stand out: first, technological superiority is now an inseparable part of military and economic power, and quantum-AI is at the center of this superiority; second, existential risks make international cooperation a necessity, not a choice; and third, humanity must choose whether to use these powerful technologies for a dystopian future or for a more just and prosperous world. Therefore, in the quantum-AI age, ultimate success will belong not to those who develop the most powerful algorithm, but to those who possess the wisdom to govern this technology for the common benefit of humanity.

REFERENCES

AbuGhanem, M., & Eleuch, H. (2024). Full quantum tomography study of Google's Sycamore gate on IBM's quantum computers. *EPJ Quantum Technology*, *11*(1), 36. Advance online publication. DOI: 10.1140/epjqt/s40507-024-00248-8

Alvarado-Valiente, J., Romero-Álvarez, J., Moguel, E., García-Alonso, J., & Murillo, J. (2024). Orchestration for quantum services: The power of load balancing across multiple service providers. *Science of Computer Programming*, *237*, 103139. DOI: 10.1016/j.scico.2024.103139

Ashok, M., Madan, R., Joha, A., & Sivarajah, U. (2022). Ethical framework for Artificial Intelligence and Digital technologies. *International Journal of Information Management*, *62*, 102433. DOI: 10.1016/j.ijinfomgt.2021.102433

Bansal, R., Khanna, M., & Rajput, N. K. (2024). A Qualitative Evaluation of Multiple Quantum Computing Frameworks. *2024 2nd International Conference on Advances in Computation, Communication and Information Technology (ICAICCIT)*, *1*, 1296-1302. DOI: 10.1109/ICAICCIT64383.2024.10912413

Bernstein, D., & Lange, T. (2008). Post-quantum cryptography. *Nature*, *549*(7671), 188–194. DOI: 10.1038/nature23461 PMID: 28905891

Boretti, A. (2024). Technical, economic, and societal risks in the progress of artificial intelligence driven quantum technologies. *Discover Artificial Intelligence*, *4*(1), 67. DOI: 10.1007/s44163-024-00171-y

Can, M., & Vieira, A. (2022). The Chinese Military-Civil Fusion Strategy: A State Action Theory Perspective. *The International Spectator*, *57*(3), 85–102. DOI: 10.1080/03932729.2022.2080262

Chahri, S. (2021). Artificial intelligence act.

Chakraborty, C., Bhattacharya, M., Pal, S., & Agoramoorthy, G. (2023). India's Quantum Move: From Budget Allocation, Action and Future Challenges. *Molecular Biotechnology*, •••, 1–13. DOI: 10.1007/s12033-023-00975-w PMID: 38095823

Çokgüçlü, Y. (2022). Asya Pasifik ve Hint Pasifik'te ABD Öncülüğünde Geliştirilen İttifakların (Aukus- The Quad) ABD-Çin İlişkilerine Etkisi. *The International Journal of Social Sciences (Islamabad)*, *6*(25), 326–347. Advance online publication. DOI: 10.52096/usbd.6.25.21

Costa, F., & Rodrigues, M. (2020). Industry. *Technological Progress and Development: The Case of Southeast Asia.*, *9*(6), 1–7. DOI: 10.31270/IJAME/v09/i06/2020/1

Cyriac, R., Eswaran, S., & Selvarajan, S. (2024). Quantum Computing in Cryptographic Systems. *International Journal of Advanced IT Research and Development.* DOI: 10.69942/1920184/20240101/03

Derian, J. D., & Wendt, A. (2020). 'Quantizing international relations': The case for quantum approaches to international theory and security practice. *Security Dialogue, 51*(5), 399–413. DOI: 10.1177/0967010620901905

Devitt, S. (2016). Performing Quantum Computing Experiments in the Cloud. *Physical Review. A, 94*(3), 32329. DOI: 10.1103/PhysRevA.94.032329

Dhiman, J. S. (2025). *CHIPS and Science Act: A Catalyst for US Semiconductor Industry.* INTERANTIONAL JOURNAL OF SCIENTIFIC RESEARCH IN ENGINEERING AND MANAGEMENT., DOI: 10.55041/IJSREM38266

Dunjko, V., & Briegel, H. (2018). Machine learning & artificial intelligence in the quantum domain: A review of recent progress. *Reports on Progress in Physics, 81*(7), 074001. Advance online publication. DOI: 10.1088/1361-6633/aab406 PMID: 29504942

Elliott, C., Colvin, A., Pearson, D., Pikalo, O., Schlafer, J., & Yeh, H. (2005). *Current status of the DARPA Quantum Network.* Storage and Retrieval for Image and Video Databases.

Evsikov, K. (2022). Information Security of the Digital State in the Quantum Era. *Courier of Kutafin Moscow State Law University (MSAL)).* DOI: 10.17803/2311-5998.2022.92.4.046-058

Fedorov, A., Akimov, A., Biamonte, J., Kavokin, A., Khalili, Y., Kiktenko, E., Kolachevsky, N. N., Kurochkin, Y. V., Lvovsky, A. I., Rubtsov, A. N., Shlyapnikov, G. V., Straupe, S. S., Ustinov, A. V., & Zheltikov, A. (2019). Quantum technologies in Russia. *Quantum Science and Technology, 4*(4), 040501. Advance online publication. DOI: 10.1088/2058-9565/ab4472

Gercek, A., & Seskir, Z. (2024). Navigating the Quantum Divide(s). *IEEE Engineering Management Review.* Advance online publication. DOI: 10.1109/EMR.2025.3547927

Gitonga, C. (2025). The Impact of Quantum Computing on Cryptographic Systems: Urgency of Quantum-Resistant Algorithms and Practical Applications in Cryptography. *European Journal of Information Technologies and Computer Science.* DOI: 10.24018/compute.2025.5.1.146

He, Govoni, M., & Galli, G. (2020). Quantum simulations of materials on near-term quantum computers. *npj Computational Materials, 6*, 1-8. DOI: 10.1038/s41524-020-00353-z

Hildebrandt, M. (2020). The Artificial Intelligence of European Union Law. *German Law Journal, 21*(1), 74–79. DOI: 10.1017/glj.2019.99

Horowitz, M. (2019). When speed kills: Lethal autonomous weapon systems, deterrence and stability. *The Journal of Strategic Studies, 42*(6), 764–788. DOI: 10.1080/01402390.2019.1621174

Hughes, C., Finke, D., German, D.-A., Merzbacher, C., Vora, P. M., & Lewandowski, H. J. (2021). Assessing the Needs of the Quantum Industry. *IEEE Transactions on Education, 65*(4), 592–601. DOI: 10.1109/TE.2022.3153841

Jang, B., Choung, J., & Kang, I. (2022). Knowledge production patterns of China and the US: Quantum technology. *Scientometrics, 127*(10), 5691–5719. DOI: 10.1007/s11192-022-04478-4

Joseph, D., Misoczki, R., Manzano, M., Tricot, J., Pinuaga, F. D., Lacombe, O., Leichenauer, S., Hidary, J., Venables, P., & Hansen, R. (2022). Transitioning organizations to post-quantum cryptography. *Nature, 605*(7909), 237–243. DOI: 10.1038/s41586-022-04623-2 PMID: 35546191

Kantsepolsky, B., Aviv, I., Weitzfeld, R., & Bordo, E. (2023). Exploring Quantum Sensing Potential for Systems Applications. *IEEE Access : Practical Innovations, Open Solutions, 11*, 31569–31582. DOI: 10.1109/ACCESS.2023.3262506

Kathala, K. C. R., & Palakurthi, S. (2024). AI Literacy Framework and Strategies for Implementation in Developing Nations. *Proceedings of the 2024 the 16th International Conference on Education Technology and Computers*. DOI: 10.1145/3702163.3702449

Kgoale, T., & Odeku, K. (2023). *An analysis of the international and European Union legal instruments for holding artificial intelligence accountable*. Juridical Tribune., DOI: 10.24818/TBJ/2023/13/3.06

Krelina, M. (2021). Quantum technology for military applications. *EPJ Quantum Technology, 8*(1), 1–53. DOI: 10.1140/epjqt/s40507-021-00113-y

Lindsay, J. (2020). Demystifying the Quantum Threat: Infrastructure, Institutions, and Intelligence Advantage. *Security Studies, 29*(2), 335–361. DOI: 10.1080/09636412.2020.1722853

Lippert, B., & Perthes, V. (2020). Strategic rivalry between United States and China: causes, tragectories, and implications for Europe. 53. DOI: 10.18449/2020RP04

Liu, J. (2024). Artificial Intelligence and International Law: The Impact of Emerging Technologies on the Global Legal System. *Economics. Law & Policy*, *7*(2), p73. Advance online publication. DOI: 10.22158/elp.v7n2p73

Lu, C., Cao, Y., Peng, C.-Z., & Pan, J. (2022). Micius quantum experiments in space.

Maathuis, C., & Cools, K. (2025). Risks and Control Measures for Building Trustworthy Autonomous Weapon Systems. *International Conference on Cyber Warfare and Security*. DOI: 10.34190/iccws.20.1.3191

Menon, V., & Adhikari, M. (2023). Quantum computing in India: Recent developments and future. *IET Quantum Communication*, *4*(2), 93–95. DOI: 10.1049/qtc2.12056

Nesadurai, H. (2008). The Association of Southeast Asian Nations (ASEAN). *New Political Economy*, *13*(2), 225–239. DOI: 10.1080/13563460802018588

Orszag, M., Retamal, J., Saavedra, C., & Wallentowitz, S. (2007). Quantum Optics III. *Journal of Physics: Conference Series*, *84*, 11001. DOI: 10.1088/1742-6596/84/1/011001

Parker, E. (2021). Commercial and Military Applications and Timelines for Quantum Technology. DOI: 10.7249/RRA1482-4

Pfister, R., Schubert, G., & Kröll, M. (2023). Transfer of Logistics Optimizations to Material Flow Resource Optimizations using Quantum Computing. 32-42. DOI: 10.1016/j.procs.2024.01.004

Possati, L. (2023). Ethics of Quantum Computing: An Outline. *Philosophy & Technology*, *36*(3), 48. Advance online publication. DOI: 10.1007/s13347-023-00651-6

Raymer, M., & Monroe, C. (2019). The US National Quantum Initiative. *Quantum Science and Technology*, *4*(2), 020504. Advance online publication. DOI: 10.1088/2058-9565/ab0441

Riedel, M., Kovács, M., Zoller, P., Mlynek, J., & Calarco, T. (2019). Europe's Quantum Flagship initiative. *Quantum Science and Technology*, *4*(2), 020501. Advance online publication. DOI: 10.1088/2058-9565/ab042d

Roco, M. (2020). Possibilities for global governance of converging technologies. *Journal of Nanoparticle Research*, *10*(1), 11–29. DOI: 10.1007/s11051-007-9269-8

Sahu, S. K., & Mazumdar, K. (2024). State-of-the-art analysis of quantum cryptography: Applications and future prospects. *Frontiers in Physics (Lausanne)*, *12*, 1456491. Advance online publication. DOI: 10.3389/fphy.2024.1456491

Schmalz, S. (2024). Varieties of Digital Capitalism and the US–China Rivalry: The Rise of Competing Technological Spheres. *Critical Sociology*. Advance online publication. DOI: 10.1177/08969205241291645

Sharikov, P. (2024). International Regulations of Lethal Autonomous Weapons Systems: Transatlantic Security Dialogue. *World Economy and International Relations*. DOI: 10.20542/0131-2227-2024-68-12-38-48

Sharma, M. (2018). Decrypting China's Quantum Leap. *China Journal (Canberra, A.C.T.)*, *80*, 24–45. DOI: 10.1086/697232

Shoaib, M., Wang, Z., Ahvanooey, M. T., & Zhao, J. (2023). Deepfakes, Misinformation, and Disinformation in the Era of Frontier AI, Generative AI, and Large AI Models. *2023 International Conference on Computer and Applications (ICCA)*, 1-7. DOI: 10.1109/ICCA59364.2023.10401723

Singh, S., & Kumar, D. (2024). Enhancing Cyber Security Using Quantum Computing and Artificial Intelligence: A Review. *International Journal of Advanced Research in Science. Tongxin Jishu*, 4–11. Advance online publication. DOI: 10.48175/IJARSCT-18902

Smuha, N. (2019). The EU Approach to Ethics Guidelines for Trustworthy Artificial Intelligence. *Computer Law Review International*, *20*(4), 97–106. DOI: 10.9785/cri-2019-200402

Tom, J., Anebo, N., Onyekwelu, B., Wilfred, A., & Eyo, R. (2023). Quantum Computers and Algorithms: A Threat to Classical Cryptographic Systems. *International Journal of Engineering and Advanced Technology*. Advance online publication. DOI: 10.35940/ijeat.E4153.0612523

Tung, R., Zander, I., & Fang, T. (2023). The Tech Cold War, the multipolarization of the world economy, and IB research. *International Business Review*, *32*(6), 102195. Advance online publication. DOI: 10.1016/j.ibusrev.2023.102195

Turan, A. (2024). External Factors Affecting Türkiye-Russia Rivalry in the Second Karabakh War. *European Journal of Transformation Studies*, *12*(2), 172–195.

Wang, P.-H., Chen, J.-H., Yang, Y.-Y., Lee, C.-S., & Tseng, Y. (2023). Recent Advances in Quantum Computing for Drug Discovery and Development. *IEEE Nanotechnology Magazine*, *17*(2), 26–30. DOI: 10.1109/MNANO.2023.3249499

Willoughby, K., & Seskir, Z. (2021). Global innovation and competition in quantum technology, viewed through the lens of patents and artificial intelligence. *International Journal of Intellectual Property Management*. DOI: 10.1504/IJIPM.2021.10044326

Wu, F., Lu, C., Zhu, M.-L., Chen, H., Zhu, J., Yu, K., Li, L., Li, M., Chen, Q., Li, X., Cao, X., Wang, Z., Zha, Z., Zhuang, Y., & Pan, Y. (2020). Towards a new generation of artificial intelligence in China. *Nature Machine Intelligence*, *2*(6), 312–316. DOI: 10.1038/s42256-020-0183-4

Yamin, M., Ullah, M., Ullah, H., & Katt, B. (2021). Weaponized AI for cyber attacks. *Journal of Information Security and Applications*, *57*, 102722. DOI: 10.1016/j.jisa.2020.102722

Yesina, M. V., Ostrianska, Y. V., & Gorbenko, I. (2022). *Status report on the third round of the NIST post-quantum cryptography standardization process*. Radiotekhnika., DOI: 10.30837/rt.2022.3.210.05

Yin, J., Cao, Y., Li, Y., Liao, S., Zhang, L., Ren, J.-G., Cai, W.-Q., Liu, W.-Y., Li, B., Dai, H., Li, G.-B., Lu, Q.-M., Gong, Y.-H., Xu, Y., Li, S.-L., Li, F.-Z., Yin, Y.-Y., Jiang, Z.-Q., Li, M., & Pan, J.-W. (2017). Satellite-based entanglement distribution over 1200 kilometers. *Science*, *356*(6343), 1140–1144. DOI: 10.1126/science.aan3211 PMID: 28619937

Chapter 3
Artificial Intelligence in Diplomacy

Ashwini Basavaraju
https://orcid.org/0009-0009-9541-599X
Dayananda Sagar College of Arts, Science, and Commerce, India

K. R. Gopalan
https://orcid.org/0000-0002-3277-759X
Saveetha School of Law, Saveetha Institute of Medical and Technical Sciences, India

P. Selvakumar
https://orcid.org/0000-0002-3650-4548
Department of Science and Humanities, Nehru Institute of Technology, Coimbatore, India

T. C. Manjunath
https://orcid.org/0000-0003-2545-9160
Rajarajeswari College of Engineering, India

Gundepogu Venugopalarao
CVR College of Engineering, India

Sumanta Bhattacharya
https://orcid.org/0000-0003-2563-2787
Asian International University, India

ABSTRACT

The 21st century has ushered in an era of profound technological transformation, marked most notably by the rapid evolution of artificial intelligence (AI). Once confined to the realm of science fiction, AI has become an integral part of daily life and global industry, revolutionizing sectors from healthcare and finance to transportation and education. As nations grapple with the economic and societal implications of this digital revolution, AI is also increasingly finding its way into the traditionally human-centric domain of international diplomacy. This intersection of cutting-edge technology and global governance represents both an unprecedented opportunity and a complex set of challenges for statecraft, international relations, and the preservation of global norms. Diplomacy, as one of the oldest instruments

DOI: 10.4018/979-8-3373-4937-4.ch003

of statecraft, has historically relied on human intelligence, negotiation, subtlety, and strategic communication. From ancient emissaries sent between kingdoms to modern-day foreign service officers and multilateral institutions.

1. INTRODUCTION

The 21st century has ushered in an era of profound technological transformation, marked most notably by the rapid evolution of artificial intelligence (AI). Once confined to the realm of science fiction, AI has become an integral part of daily life and global industry, revolutionizing sectors from healthcare and finance to transportation and education. As nations grapple with the economic and societal implications of this digital revolution, AI is also increasingly finding its way into the traditionally human-centric domain of international diplomacy. This intersection of cutting-edge technology and global governance represents both an unprecedented opportunity and a complex set of challenges for statecraft, international relations, and the preservation of global norms. Diplomacy, as one of the oldest instruments of statecraft, has historically relied on human intelligence, negotiation, subtlety, and strategic communication. From ancient emissaries sent between kingdoms to modern-day foreign service officers and multilateral institutions, diplomacy has always required a nuanced understanding of cultures, political systems, and interpersonal dynamics.

However, the advent of AI technologies is reshaping the mechanics and possibilities of diplomacy. Today, AI-powered systems are being deployed to analyze massive volumes of diplomatic communication, model conflict scenarios, forecast political developments, and even simulate negotiation outcomes. These tools offer the potential to enhance decision-making, improve the efficiency of diplomatic operations, and provide deeper insights into complex international issues. The use of AI in diplomacy takes many forms, ranging from natural language processing (NLP) tools that translate and analyze multilingual diplomatic texts in real time, to machine learning algorithms that detect disinformation campaigns or predict geopolitical shifts. Governments and international organizations are investing in AI to better understand the rapidly changing global landscape, monitor compliance with international agreements, and manage crises. For instance, AI can be used to track troop movements via satellite imagery, identify violations of climate accords through environmental data, or detect early warning signs of political instability using social media trends.

1.1. The Role of AI in Modern Diplomacy

The 21st century has ushered in an era of profound technological transformation, marked most notably by the rapid evolution of artificial intelligence (AI). Once confined to the realm of science fiction, (Zaorski-Sikora et al, 2024) AI has become an integral part of daily life and global industry, revolutionizing sectors from healthcare and finance to transportation and education. As nations grapple with the economic and societal implications of this digital revolution, AI is also increasingly finding its way into the traditionally human-centric domain of international diplomacy. This intersection of cutting-edge technology and global governance represents both an unprecedented opportunity and a complex set of challenges for statecraft, international relations, and the preservation of global norms. Diplomacy, as one of the oldest instruments of statecraft, has historically relied on human intelligence, negotiation, subtlety, and strategic communication. From ancient emissaries sent between kingdoms to modern-day foreign service officers and multilateral institutions, diplomacy has always required a nuanced understanding of cultures, political systems, and interpersonal dynamics. However, the advent of AI technologies is reshaping the mechanics and possibilities of diplomacy. (Zaorski-Sikora et al, 2024) Today, AI-powered systems are being deployed to analyse massive volumes of diplomatic communication, model conflict scenarios, forecast political developments, and even simulate negotiation outcomes. These tools offer the potential to enhance decision-making, improve the efficiency of diplomatic operations, and provide deeper insights into complex international issues.

The use of AI in diplomacy takes many forms, ranging from natural language processing (NLP) tools that translate and analyse multilingual diplomatic texts in real time, to machine learning algorithms that detect disinformation campaigns or predict geopolitical shifts. Governments and international organizations are investing in AI to better understand the rapidly changing global landscape, monitor compliance with international agreements, and manage crises. For instance, AI can be used to track troop movements via satellite imagery, identify violations of climate accords through environmental data, or detect early warning signs of political instability using social media trends. (Uwizeye et al, 2024) In these ways, AI is becoming an indispensable part of the diplomatic toolkit. Yet, the integration of AI into diplomacy also raises significant ethical, legal, and strategic concerns. AI systems, while powerful, are only as good as the data they are trained on and the objectives they are programmed to achieve. Biases in data, opaque decision-making processes, and the potential for algorithmic manipulation all pose risks to the integrity and fairness of diplomatic engagements. (Uwizeye et al, 2024) Moreover, the rise of autonomous technologies in international relations, such as autonomous weapons or AI-driven surveillance, introduces new dimensions of conflict and accountability. Diplomats and policymakers must therefore grapple with how to regulate and govern AI technologies in a way that upholds international law, human rights, and democratic principles.

1.2. AI Applications in Diplomacy

Artificial Intelligence (AI) is increasingly becoming a critical force in reshaping the foundations of modern diplomacy, not merely as a supporting tool but as a transformative agent. (Iqbal et al, 2025) Diplomacy, long reliant on personal relationships, cultural intuition, negotiation acumen, and political foresight, is now being infused with advanced computational capabilities that enhance these human elements rather than replace them. AI's ability to analyse vast amounts of data in real time, detect patterns, forecast outcomes, and automate routine tasks is proving to be a force multiplier for diplomatic efficiency and strategic depth. (Fitsilis et al, 2024) This transformation is most evident in how AI is assisting diplomats in understanding complex global developments, managing crises, enhancing communication, combating misinformation, and negotiating international agreements. One of the most significant contributions of AI to diplomacy is its role in data analysis and decision support. Modern diplomacy generates and consumes vast volumes of information, including diplomatic cables, policy reports, news articles, social media posts, satellite imagery, and intelligence briefings. Human decision-makers, no matter how experienced or knowledgeable, are limited in their capacity to process and interpret such enormous and heterogeneous data sets within tight timeframes. (Iqbal et al, 2025) AI tools, especially those leveraging machine learning (ML) and natural language processing (NLP), allow for rapid synthesis of multilingual texts, detection of thematic trends, sentiment analysis, and the identification of anomalies that could indicate emerging geopolitical risks. (Fitsilis et al, 2024) For instance, AI can scan global media for early signs of civil unrest, identify shifting public sentiments during international negotiations, or track the evolution of political discourse across different regions.

In conflict prevention and crisis management, AI is increasingly being used to anticipate flashpoints and provide early warnings. Predictive analytics can integrate diverse datasets, such as economic indicators, environmental conditions, troop movements, and social media activity, to assess the likelihood of conflicts, humanitarian crises, or political instability. Governments and international organizations can then deploy diplomatic efforts proactively rather than reactively. For example, the UN's Global Pulse initiative uses AI to detect patterns in public communications and digital behaviour that may signal distress or disruption, enabling faster responses in fragile contexts. Similarly, AI-enabled satellite analysis can track environmental degradation or human displacement, contributing to the timely activation of diplomatic or humanitarian missions. AI also enhances the efficiency of diplomatic missions by automating routine tasks and supporting decision-making. Virtual assistants powered by AI can manage scheduling, document translation, and preliminary drafting of diplomatic notes, freeing human diplomats to focus on high-value strategic activities. NLP-based tools allow embassies to monitor local media in multiple languages simultaneously, identify narratives relevant to national interests, and respond promptly. Moreover, AI chatbots are being developed to provide consular services to citizens abroad, offering real-time responses to inquiries about travel advisories, visa regulations, and emergency assistance. These tools increase accessibility, reduce administrative burdens, and strengthen the public service dimension of diplomacy.

2. DATA-DRIVEN DECISION-MAKING: LEVERAGING AI FOR INFORMED DIPLOMACY

The applications of Artificial Intelligence (AI) in diplomacy have expanded rapidly in recent years, redefining traditional diplomatic practices and introducing new tools that support more agile, (Holmes et al, 2024) data-driven, and responsive engagement at both bilateral and multilateral levels. As global politics becomes increasingly complex, AI offers diplomats and foreign policy institutions a broad suite of capabilities that streamline operations, improve communication, analyse vast datasets, predict emerging threats, and facilitate strategic decision-making. From automating administrative tasks to providing deep geopolitical insights, AI is emerging as an indispensable component of modern diplomacy. This overview categorizes and explores the most significant areas in which AI is currently being applied within the diplomatic sphere, highlighting both its practical uses and the strategic advantages it offers. One of the most fundamental applications of AI in diplomacy is in data analysis and intelligence synthesis. Diplomacy involves processing immense amounts of information daily, from diplomatic cables, policy papers, and media reports to open-source intelligence and social media content. AI, especially through Natural Language Processing (NLP), enables diplomats and analysts to automatically extract key themes, entities, and sentiments from this data across multiple languages. Machine learning algorithms can be used to identify patterns, assess risks, and visualize trends over time. For instance, AI-driven media monitoring systems can flag relevant news articles and social media posts that signal political instability, conflict escalation, or disinformation campaigns. (Holmes et al, 2024) Tools like IBM Watson, Google Cloud NLP, and various custom AI solutions are being used by foreign ministries and international organizations to reduce information overload and focus attention on emerging issues that require diplomatic action.

Predictive analytics and early warning systems represent another transformative AI application in diplomacy. These systems use AI models to forecast developments in fragile states, anticipate conflict hotspots, and monitor conditions that may lead to mass displacement, famine, or unrest. (Silva et al, 2024) By aggregating data from diverse sources such as economic indicators, satellite imagery, and humanitarian reports, AI can help international actors identify early signals of crisis. For example, the United Nations' Global Pulse initiative and the European Commission's Joint Research Centre use AI-based modelling tools to provide early alerts about potential crises, thereby enabling preventive diplomacy and humanitarian planning. These capabilities enhance a diplomat's situational awareness and allow for more proactive, rather than reactive, engagement. In the realm of strategic communication and public diplomacy, AI is revolutionizing how states communicate with global audiences. Governments increasingly rely on AI-powered sentiment analysis tools to gauge public opinion and media narratives in foreign countries. (Silva et al, 2024) These insights help craft targeted messaging that is culturally sensitive and aligned with strategic objectives. Additionally, chatbots and virtual assistants powered by AI are used to engage with citizens and foreign publics on embassy websites and social media platforms, answering FAQs, sharing real-time travel advisories, and correcting misinformation. AI algorithms can also track how narratives evolve across digital platforms, helping diplomats understand the spread and impact of both legitimate messaging and disinformation. This is especially critical during global crises such as pandemics or wars, where accurate information and trust-building are essential for effective diplomacy.

2.1. Forecasting Diplomatic Outcomes

In the realm of international relations, where timing, accuracy, and strategic foresight are paramount, data-driven decision-making has emerged as a transformative force in modern diplomacy. (Mirahmadi et al, 2024) At the heart of this transformation is artificial intelligence (AI), which enables diplomatic institutions to harness data at an unprecedented scale and speed. Traditionally, diplomacy relied heavily on qualitative judgments, anecdotal evidence, and the experiential wisdom of seasoned diplomats. While these human insights remain irreplaceable, they are now increasingly augmented by vast streams of real-time data and the computational intelligence required to process, analyse, and interpret it. AI-powered tools are equipping policymakers and diplomats with actionable insights, enabling more informed, agile, and predictive decision-making processes across the entire spectrum of diplomatic activity, from conflict resolution and economic negotiations to climate diplomacy and public communication. One of the most powerful uses of AI in data-driven diplomacy lies in real-time information processing and situational awareness. In an age of big data, diplomats are overwhelmed by the sheer volume of information generated daily through global news outlets, social media platforms, intelligence reports, satellite imagery, and digital correspondence. (Mirahmadi et al, 2024) AI enables the automatic ingestion and analysis of this information to extract relevant signals from noise. Natural Language Processing (NLP) algorithms can scan thousands of diplomatic cables or news reports in multiple languages, identify recurring themes, detect sentiment changes, and summarize key developments. These insights allow foreign ministries to track the evolution of complex geopolitical events, assess the tone of international media coverage, and better understand the positions of foreign governments or non-state actors. For example, AI-driven tools can detect subtle shifts in language or tone in official statements from rival states, signalling a potential change in policy that warrants pre-emptive engagement or recalibration of strategy.

Moreover, AI enhances forecasting capabilities, offering diplomats a proactive edge in anticipating future developments. Through machine learning, predictive models can be trained on historical and current data to identify early warning signs of instability, such as economic distress, electoral tensions, environmental degradation, or refugee flows. These models are particularly valuable in fragile states or conflict-prone regions, where timely intervention may prevent escalation. (Suresh et al, 2025) The application of AI in conflict forecasting is exemplified by tools developed by organizations like the United Nations Global Pulse, which integrates social, economic, and environmental data to model scenarios that help guide diplomatic interventions. Similarly, AI systems are used by humanitarian agencies and development institutions to forecast famine or disease outbreaks, facilitating coordinated diplomatic responses and resource mobilization in advance. Data-driven diplomacy also plays a crucial role in policy formulation and impact assessment. (Suresh et al, 2025) AI models allow decision-makers to test various policy options through simulations and scenario analysis, projecting likely outcomes and unintended consequences. For example, when negotiating trade agreements or sanctions, diplomats can use AI to model economic impacts across different sectors and demographic groups, both domestically and abroad. In climate diplomacy, AI tools are used to simulate the environmental effects of different emission reduction targets and assess compliance pathways for international agreements like the Paris Accord. These evidence-based simulations enable negotiators to base their decisions not only on political judgment but also on robust quantitative analysis. This enhances the credibility and effectiveness of policy proposals while also fostering transparency and trust among negotiation partners.

2.2. AI-Powered Risk Assessment

As the complexity of international relations continues to deepen, the need for accurate, timely, and forward-looking insights in diplomacy has never been greater. Predictive analytics, an advanced application of artificial intelligence (AI) and data science, has emerged as a powerful tool for forecasting diplomatic outcomes and informing strategic decision-making. (Kommineni et al, 2025) Traditionally, diplomacy has relied on the instincts and experience of diplomats, along with historical analogies and qualitative assessments of political environments. While these human attributes remain essential, the dynamic nature of modern geopolitics, driven by rapidly shifting alliances, globalized economies, digital disruption, and non-state actors, requires more robust, evidence-based methodologies. Predictive analytics fills this gap by enabling diplomats and foreign policy analysts to identify trends, model scenarios, anticipate crises, and evaluate the probable consequences of different courses of action. At its core, predictive analytics refers to the use of statistical techniques, machine learning algorithms, and historical data to estimate future events. In the context of diplomacy, this includes forecasting political instability, conflict escalation, election outcomes, treaty success, and diplomatic behaviour of state and non-state actors. By aggregating and analysing structured and unstructured data, ranging from economic indicators and security metrics to social media posts and diplomatic communications, AI systems can uncover patterns and correlations that may not be visible to human observers. (Kommineni et al, 2025) These insights allow decision-makers to make more proactive, calculated interventions and reduce the risks of surprise, miscalculation, or policy failure.

One of the most impactful uses of predictive analytics in diplomacy is conflict prevention and crisis forecasting. (Sreekanthaswamy et al, 2025) AI models are increasingly deployed by governments, international organizations, and research institutions to anticipate the onset of violence or social unrest in fragile or volatile regions. For example, predictive tools developed by the U.S. Agency for International Development (USAID) and the United Nations Global Pulse initiative have been used to detect early signs of conflict by analysing a combination of local media reports, economic stress signals, commodity prices, migration flows, and weather patterns. These models can generate risk scores and timelines for potential flashpoints, enabling diplomatic actors to deploy preventive measures, mobilize mediation teams, or initiate backchannel negotiations. In regions such as the Sahel, the Horn of Africa, or Southeast Asia, predictive models have become a key part of early warning systems that inform diplomatic, military, and humanitarian responses. Predictive analytics also contributes significantly to electoral diplomacy, especially in monitoring the risks surrounding elections in transitional democracies. (Sreekanthaswamy et al, 2025) By examining voter registration patterns, campaign rhetoric, past voting behaviour, online discourse, and potential indicators of fraud or coercion, AI models can assess the likelihood of election-related violence or post-election disputes. This allows foreign ministries, election observers, and international mediators to prepare contingency plans, issue pre-emptive diplomatic statements, or send fact-finding missions. During the 2020 elections in several African and South Asian nations, predictive tools were used to monitor tensions, social media manipulation, and disinformation campaigns in real time, providing valuable intelligence that shaped diplomatic engagement and crisis mitigation strategies.

2.3. Breaking Language Barriers in Diplomacy

Artificial Intelligence (AI) has become an indispensable tool in the realm of international diplomacy, particularly in the domain of risk assessment. As global events become increasingly interconnected and volatile, (Limbore et al, 2025) the capacity to identify, evaluate, and respond to diplomatic risks in a timely and strategic manner is more critical than ever. AI-powered risk assessment systems are transforming how governments, foreign ministries, and international organizations perceive and prepare for threats to diplomatic stability, national interests, and international cooperation. (Limbore et al, 2025) These systems enable a shift from reactive crisis management to proactive risk mitigation, enhancing strategic foresight across all dimensions of foreign policy, from geopolitical tensions and cyber threats to misinformation campaigns and economic sanctions. At its core, AI-powered risk assessment involves the collection, integration, and analysis of diverse datasets to evaluate potential hazards that may impact diplomatic operations or international relations. Unlike traditional risk assessment methods that rely heavily on static models and human intuition, AI systems can continuously ingest real-time data from a wide array of sources, including news media, satellite imagery, economic reports, diplomatic cables, social media platforms, and open-source intelligence. Using advanced machine learning algorithms, these systems detect emerging patterns, identify anomalies, and generate risk scores based on both historical trends and predictive analytics. This capability allows diplomats to spot subtle indicators of instability or tension long before they escalate into full-blown crises.

One of the most important applications of AI in diplomatic risk assessment is in geopolitical threat detection. Machine learning models are trained to recognize warning signs associated with political unrest, military mobilization, electoral volatility, or diplomatic breakdowns. For example, by analysing social media sentiment in a particular country, AI can detect rising discontent that may precede demonstrations, riots, or coups. Similarly, satellite imagery analysed by computer vision algorithms can identify changes in military activity, such as increased troop deployments, construction of new bases, or the movement of weapon systems, that may signal potential aggression or defense posturing. These insights help diplomats prepare talking points, dispatch envoys, issue alerts, or initiate preventive negotiations with local counterparts. Another critical area where AI enhances risk assessment is cybersecurity and cyber diplomacy. (Tamilarasi et al, 2025) As digital infrastructure becomes an increasingly contested domain, the risks posed by state-sponsored cyberattacks, espionage, and infrastructure disruption have grown exponentially. AI-based threat detection systems can monitor cyber activity for suspicious patterns, such as phishing campaigns targeting diplomatic missions, malware propagation in government systems, or coordinated digital misinformation campaigns. (Tamilarasi C. et al, 2025) These tools can trace the origin and vectors of attacks, flag emerging vulnerabilities, and suggest mitigation strategies in near real-time. Furthermore, AI is used to assess the diplomatic ramifications of cyber incidents, helping policymakers determine whether a cyberattack constitutes an act of aggression, an intelligence-gathering operation, or a rogue non-state act, thereby informing proportional diplomatic responses.

3. AI-GENERATED CONTENT: ENHANCING DIPLOMATIC MESSAGING

In the increasingly interconnected landscape of international diplomacy, language remains both a bridge and a barrier. Effective communication across linguistic and cultural divides is essential for building trust, reaching agreements, and promoting mutual understanding among states and non-state actors. However, traditional translation and interpretation processes are often time-consuming, costly, and limited by human capacity, especially in real-time or high-volume diplomatic contexts. In recent years, the emergence of Artificial Intelligence (AI)-driven automated translation tools has revolutionized how diplomacy is conducted across languages. (Dahiya et al, 2025) These systems, powered by advances in Natural Language Processing (NLP) and deep learning, are enabling faster, more accessible, and increasingly accurate communication in multilingual environments. Automated translation is no longer a convenience, it is becoming a strategic asset in modern diplomacy, breaking down long-standing language barriers and democratizing access to international dialogue. At the heart of this transformation are neural machine translation (NMT) systems such as Google Translate, Microsoft Translator, Amazon Translate, and DeepL. (Dahiya et al, 2025) These AI-powered platforms utilize large-scale neural networks trained on multilingual corpora to translate text and speech between dozens, and sometimes hundreds, of languages. Unlike earlier rule-based or statistical translation systems, NMT models learn from vast amounts of bilingual data, capturing complex grammar structures, context-specific meanings, idiomatic expressions, and cultural nuances. This allows for more fluent and accurate translations that closely approximate human-level quality in many language pairs, particularly those with abundant training data. As a result, diplomats, negotiators, analysts, and consular staff can now translate official documents, correspondence, speeches, and legal texts within seconds, accelerating the pace of diplomatic work and improving accessibility for linguistically diverse audiences.

One of the most significant benefits of automated translation in diplomacy is real-time multilingual communication. In international forums such as the United Nations, European Union, ASEAN, or African Union, where representatives from dozens of countries convene, simultaneous interpretation has traditionally relied on professional interpreters working in dedicated booths. (Chib et al, 2025) While human interpreters remain indispensable for high-stakes negotiations and nuanced dialogue, AI-powered tools are supplementing these efforts through real-time speech translation applications. Platforms like Zoom, Google Meet, and Microsoft Teams have integrated automated captioning and translation features, allowing diplomats to follow meetings, webinars, or briefings in their preferred language. In fast-paced or emergency situations, such tools can facilitate immediate understanding and participation without the logistical delay of arranging interpreters. Furthermore, automated translation is enhancing public diplomacy and global outreach by enabling embassies and foreign ministries to communicate with broader audiences in local languages. Government websites, press releases, social media posts, and policy documents can be instantly translated to reach citizens, diaspora communities, civil society groups, and foreign publics. (Chib et al, 2025) This linguistic inclusivity strengthens trust, fosters transparency, and counters perceptions of elitism or exclusivity in diplomatic communication. For instance, embassies operating in multilingual regions can maintain websites with dynamic, AI-generated multilingual content, ensuring that local populations receive timely updates on visas, travel advisories, cultural events, and emergency services. This is particularly valuable in crisis situations such as natural disasters, pandemics, or civil unrest, where language-agnostic communication can save lives and reduce confusion.

3.1. Using AI to Track Diplomatic Sentiment

As diplomacy becomes increasingly digital, the ability to craft compelling, clear, and culturally resonant communication has never been more essential. In this rapidly evolving landscape, artificial intelligence (AI)-generated content is emerging as a transformative force in diplomatic messaging, fundamentally reshaping how governments, diplomats, and international organizations communicate with foreign publics, partner states, and global stakeholders. (Kaur et al, 2025) Leveraging advances in natural language generation (NLG), machine learning, and large language models (LLMs), AI is enabling the creation of high-quality, context-aware content across multiple formats, including speeches, press releases, social media updates, policy briefs, and public diplomacy campaigns. This new capability enhances both the efficiency and effectiveness of diplomatic communication, making it more adaptive, inclusive, timely, and scalable. At the heart of AI-generated content are LLMs such as GPT (Generative Pre-trained Transformer), Claude, LLaMA, and others, which are trained on vast corpora of multilingual text and fine-tuned for specific tasks. These models can generate fluent, coherent, and contextually appropriate text based on minimal prompts, allowing diplomats and communication teams to rapidly produce drafts of official documents, briefing notes, Q&A responses, and other written materials. This is especially valuable in time-sensitive or resource-constrained situations, such as responding to international crises, issuing public statements on fast-moving developments, or preparing for diplomatic engagements across time zones. (Kaur et al, 2025) AI accelerates the content creation process by providing reliable first drafts that human diplomats can review, refine, and approve, dramatically reducing turnaround time without compromising message quality.

One of the most significant advantages of AI-generated content in diplomacy is its role in strategic communication and narrative shaping. Effective diplomacy is not only about the policies a state pursues, but also about how those policies are framed, explained, and perceived by international audiences. (Samal et al, 2025) Through AI, foreign ministries can rapidly generate customized messaging tailored to different regions, cultures, or demographic groups. For example, a statement on climate cooperation can be framed with distinct emphasis depending on whether the audience is from the Global South, industrialized nations, or youth climate movements. (Samal et al, 2025) AI tools can generate localized content versions that reflect regional concerns, tone preferences, and communication styles, thus improving resonance and receptivity. In public diplomacy and digital engagement, AI-generated content enables embassies and missions to maintain a consistent and engaging presence across social media platforms, websites, and news outlets. Content can be automatically generated and scheduled for multiple channels, translated into local languages, and optimized for search engines or social media algorithms. AI can assist with crafting tweets, LinkedIn posts, Instagram captions, or even video scripts aligned with a mission's diplomatic priorities, whether it's promoting cultural exchanges, celebrating bilateral anniversaries, countering misinformation, or showcasing development assistance. Embassies often operate with limited communication staff; AI-generated content allows them to scale their outreach without stretching their human resources thin.

3.2. AI-Powered Chatbots

In the era of digital diplomacy, social media has emerged as both a platform for communication and a barometer of public sentiment. From heads of state tweeting foreign policy positions to citizens voicing real-time reactions to diplomatic events, social media has become a central stage for international discourse. (Hossain et al, 2024) As this digital transformation accelerates, artificial intelligence (AI)-powered social media monitoring is increasingly being used to track diplomatic sentiment, providing foreign ministries, embassies, and international organizations with actionable insights into how policies, statements, and international developments are being received across the globe. By analysing vast amounts of real-time social media data, AI tools allow diplomats to engage more responsively, gauge reputational standing, detect early signs of unrest, and craft targeted messaging that resonates with specific populations. (Hossain et al, 2024) At the core of AI-driven social media monitoring is the use of machine learning algorithms and natural language processing (NLP) to collect, filter, and interpret text, images, and video content from platforms like Twitter/X, Facebook, TikTok, Instagram, YouTube, Reddit, and regional networks such as VKontakte or Weibo. These AI tools sift through billions of posts in dozens of languages to identify patterns, measure sentiment (positive, negative, neutral), detect emerging narratives, and assess the reach and impact of diplomatic communications. Crucially, they also analyse the context in which content is shared, identifying influential voices, sentiment trends across regions, and how specific hashtags or keywords trend during diplomatic events such as summits, conflicts, elections, or bilateral meetings.

Figure 1. India as the Emerging Hub for AI Diplomacy

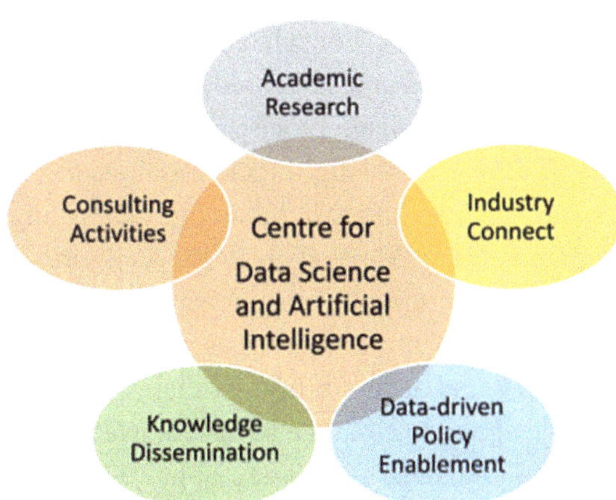

One of the most valuable applications of AI in this domain is sentiment analysis, which allows foreign ministries to measure the public response to diplomatic initiatives or international developments. (Soundariya et al, 2025) For example, after the announcement of a new trade agreement, an AI tool can scan millions of online comments to gauge public approval or concern in both signing and third-party countries. These insights help policymakers understand not only whether a policy is well received but also why, pinpointing the language, framing, or provisions that resonate or provoke resistance. This allows for tailored communication strategies to reinforce positive narratives or address specific misunderstandings and fears. In crisis diplomacy, real-time social media monitoring becomes especially critical. Whether during a natural disaster,. military conflict, political upheaval, or public health emergency, people increasingly turn to social media as a source of news, emotional expression, and protest. AI-powered systems can detect spikes in activity, identify emerging flashpoints, and highlight shifts in sentiment before they escalate into offline unrest or diplomatic backlash. For instance, during a regional border skirmish, monitoring online discussions can reveal how populations in both countries are interpreting events, what nationalist rhetoric is being mobilized, and whether misinformation is fuelling escalation. (Soundariya et al, 2025) Armed with these insights, diplomatic missions can engage more effectively, correct falsehoods, and influence narratives to reduce tensions.

3.3. Streamlining Diplomatic Communication

In the evolving landscape of 21st-century diplomacy, artificial intelligence (AI) is no longer a futuristic concept, it is a present-day enabler of more efficient, responsive, and inclusive foreign engagement. Among the most promising and immediately impactful tools are AI-powered chatbots, which have begun to transform how governments, embassies, consulates, and international organizations communicate with foreign publics and stakeholders. These conversational agents, driven by advances in natural language processing (NLP), machine learning, and large language models (LLMs), allow diplomatic missions to provide real-time assistance, disseminate information, and foster dialogue across linguistic and cultural boundaries. (de la Puente Pacheco M. A. et al, 2025) As digital diplomacy expands beyond formal statecraft to include public outreach, crisis response, and people-to-people engagement, chatbots are emerging as a key instrument in enhancing diplomatic service delivery and accessibility. At their core, AI-powered chatbots are automated systems designed to simulate human conversation via text or speech interfaces. Integrated into websites, messaging apps (e.g., WhatsApp, Facebook Messenger, Telegram), and government portals, these bots can answer frequently asked questions, provide guidance on consular procedures, issue travel advisories, schedule appointments, and even conduct preliminary screening for visa or asylum applications. (Pacheco et al, 2025) Their availability 24/7 is particularly valuable for embassies that operate in different time zones or face staffing constraints. For citizens abroad, diaspora communities, and foreign nationals seeking services, the ability to get accurate, up-to-date responses without navigating bureaucratic systems or waiting in long queues significantly improves the experience of engaging with diplomatic institutions.

One of the most powerful applications of diplomatic chatbots is in consular services and citizen assistance. (Lips et al, 2025) Embassies and consulates receive a massive volume of inquiries daily, from passport renewals and visa requirements to lost documents and emergency evacuations. Chatbots streamline this process by automating responses to routine questions, freeing up human staff to focus on complex or sensitive cases. For example, a chatbot can guide a user through the steps of renewing a passport, including required documents, fees, and available appointment slots. It can also handle inquiries in multiple languages, increasing inclusivity for non-native speakers and those with limited literacy. In emergency situations, such as natural disasters, civil unrest, or pandemics, chatbots can rapidly disseminate real-time updates, safety instructions, and contact information, providing a lifeline for citizens in distress. (Lips et al, 2025) Beyond service provision, chatbots are enhancing public diplomacy and strategic communication. Governments use chatbots to broadcast information about cultural events, development projects, bilateral initiatives, and national policies. These bots can be embedded in embassy websites or social media pages to proactively engage foreign publics with curated, interactive content. For instance, a chatbot might offer users a guided exploration of a country's foreign aid contributions in their region, answer questions about study abroad programs, or provide historical context for diplomatic decisions. Unlike static web pages or press releases, chatbots create dynamic, personalized experiences, encouraging dialogue rather than just one-way communication.

4. AI-FACILITATED NEGOTIATION: ENHANCING DIPLOMATIC EFFECTIVENESS

In the increasingly complex and fast-paced world of international relations, effective communication stands as a cornerstone of successful diplomacy. (Turianskyi et al, 2025) The advent of artificial intelligence (AI) has introduced powerful tools that enable diplomats and foreign service institutions to communicate with greater efficiency, precision, and adaptability. Among these tools, AI-powered virtual assistants have emerged as vital assets in streamlining diplomatic communication. Virtual assistants, advanced AI systems designed to understand, interpret, and respond to human language, are transforming how diplomatic missions manage internal coordination, external outreach, and decision-making processes. By automating routine tasks, providing real-time information, and facilitating seamless interaction across languages and time zones, virtual assistants enhance the operational capacity of diplomatic entities and contribute to more agile, informed, and responsive foreign policy execution. (Turianskyi et al, 2025) Virtual assistants in diplomacy are sophisticated AI agents, often equipped with natural language processing (NLP), machine learning, and contextual awareness. Unlike simple chatbots, which primarily respond to predefined queries, virtual assistants can engage in complex dialogues, proactively offer relevant information, schedule meetings, summarize documents, and integrate with various communication platforms. Their role extends beyond public-facing services to include internal support for diplomats, policy advisors, and administrative staff. This multi-dimensional functionality makes them uniquely suited to the intricate requirements of diplomatic environments, where timely, accurate, and secure communication is critical.

One of the primary ways virtual assistants streamline diplomatic communication is through enhancing internal coordination within foreign ministries and embassies. Diplomatic missions typically handle a large volume of communications daily, from interdepartmental memos and policy briefs to scheduling meetings with foreign counterparts and managing confidential correspondence. (Lazarus et al, 2025) Virtual assistants can automate many administrative and logistical tasks, such as organizing calendars, sending reminders, prioritizing emails, and drafting responses. For instance, a virtual assistant might summarize lengthy diplomatic cables, extract key action points from meeting minutes, or prepare briefing notes ahead of negotiations. By reducing the time diplomats spend on routine tasks, these assistants free up valuable human resources to focus on substantive policy analysis and interpersonal engagement. Moreover, virtual assistants help overcome language and cultural barriers that frequently challenge international communication. (Lazarus et al, 2025) Equipped with advanced translation capabilities and contextual understanding, they facilitate multilingual exchanges by instantly translating incoming and outgoing messages while preserving tone and diplomatic nuance. This is especially valuable in multilateral forums or bilateral settings involving diverse linguistic backgrounds. Virtual assistants can also provide cultural briefings or protocol guidelines tailored to specific countries or regions, helping diplomats avoid faux pas and navigate complex etiquette. This support enhances both the clarity and appropriateness of diplomatic communication, strengthening relationships and mutual respect between states.

4.1. Challenges of AI in Diplomacy

Negotiation has long been the cornerstone of diplomacy, serving as the primary mechanism through which states and international actors resolve conflicts, forge agreements, and advance mutual interests. Traditionally reliant on human skill, intuition, and experience, diplomatic negotiation is an inherently complex, multifaceted process influenced by political, cultural, economic, and psychological factors. In recent years, artificial intelligence (AI) has begun to revolutionize this domain by introducing new tools and methodologies that augment human capabilities and enhance the overall effectiveness of diplomatic negotiations. AI-facilitated negotiation leverages advanced computational techniques, including machine learning, natural language processing, data analytics, and decision-support systems, to assist diplomats in preparing for, conducting, and concluding negotiations with greater precision, efficiency, and strategic insight. (Uunona et al, 2025) This technological evolution promises to transform traditional diplomatic practices by enabling data-driven approaches, predictive modelling, scenario analysis, and real-time support that collectively improve outcomes and reduce risks. At the core of AI-facilitated negotiation is the ability of AI systems to process and analyse vast quantities of structured and unstructured data far beyond human cognitive limits. Diplomatic negotiations are increasingly data-intensive, drawing on historical records, treaties, political statements, economic indicators, and social media trends, among other sources. AI tools can synthesize this heterogeneous data to provide negotiators with comprehensive situational awareness and contextual understanding. For example, machine learning algorithms can analyse patterns in previous negotiation rounds, identify key stakeholders' priorities, and highlight areas of potential compromise or contention. (Uunona et al, 2025) Such insights help diplomats develop evidence-based negotiation strategies and anticipate opponents' moves, thereby enhancing their bargaining position and fostering more constructive dialogue.

One significant advantage of AI-facilitated negotiation lies in its ability to support pre-negotiation preparation and strategy development. By integrating data from multiple domains, including geopolitical risk assessments, trade statistics, public sentiment analysis, and legal frameworks, AI platforms can generate detailed profiles of negotiation counterparts and simulate potential negotiation trajectories. These simulations allow diplomats to test different approaches, forecast the outcomes of various concessions, and identify optimal negotiation tactics under diverse scenarios. This capability reduces uncertainty, mitigates cognitive biases, and improves the quality of decision-making before negotiations even begin. Furthermore, AI-driven tools can assist in drafting negotiation proposals, identifying mutually beneficial clauses, and ensuring compliance with international laws and standards, thereby expediting the drafting and review processes. (Hanita et al, 2025) During negotiations themselves, AI technologies can function as real-time decision-support systems, providing diplomats with timely recommendations based on ongoing developments. Natural language processing (NLP) enables AI to analyse conversation transcripts, extract key points, and detect changes in tone, sentiment, or emphasis. For instance, sentiment analysis can alert negotiators to shifts in emotional stance, such as increased hostility or willingness to compromise, allowing for agile adjustments in negotiation tactics. (Hanita et al, 2025) AI can also track commitments, deadlines, and unresolved issues dynamically, helping diplomats maintain situational awareness and avoid misunderstandings. These capabilities are especially useful in high-stakes multilateral negotiations or protracted peace talks, where complexity and information overload often challenge human negotiators.

4.2. Opportunities for AI in Diplomacy

The integration of artificial intelligence (AI) into the realm of diplomacy offers transformative opportunities but also introduces significant challenges that must be carefully navigated to safeguard the integrity, effectiveness, and ethical foundation of international relations. Among the most pressing concerns are issues related to bias, ethics, and transparency, each of which has profound implications for how AI technologies are designed, deployed, and managed in diplomatic contexts. (Christou et al, 2025) These challenges, if left unaddressed, risk undermining the trust, fairness, and accountability that underpin diplomatic engagement, potentially exacerbating geopolitical tensions, social inequities, and mistrust between states. Understanding these challenges is essential for policymakers, technologists, and diplomats alike to harness AI's benefits responsibly and ensure that the technology aligns with the core values of diplomacy. (Christou et al, 2025) One of the foremost challenges is the problem of bias embedded in AI systems. AI algorithms, particularly those driven by machine learning, rely heavily on data to "learn" patterns and generate outputs. However, data is often a reflection of historical, social, and institutional biases, conscious or unconscious, that permeate the environments from which it is collected. For example, diplomatic data sources may include official documents, media reports, social media content, and intelligence briefs, each carrying inherent biases related to culture, ideology, geopolitical perspectives, and power structures. When AI models are trained on such data without adequate scrutiny or correction, they risk perpetuating or even amplifying these biases. This can manifest in diplomatic AI applications through skewed risk assessments, inaccurate sentiment analysis, or unfair representation of actors and events, potentially influencing decision-making in ways that favour certain interests or perspectives over others.

Bias in AI systems is particularly problematic in diplomacy because decisions often have high-stakes consequences affecting international peace, security, and cooperation. For instance, if an AI system disproportionately flags certain countries or groups as risks based on biased data, it may lead to unwarranted suspicion, escalation of tensions, or discriminatory policy decisions. Similarly, bias in automated translation or content generation tools can distort meanings and cultural nuances, jeopardizing mutual understanding. (Luoma-aho et al, 2025) Furthermore, diplomatic AI systems used in negotiation or conflict resolution that operate with biased assumptions can reinforce existing power imbalances or exclude marginalized voices, undermining the legitimacy and inclusivity of diplomatic processes. (Luoma-aho et al, 2025) Addressing bias therefore requires rigorous data curation, algorithmic fairness techniques, continuous monitoring, and inclusion of diverse viewpoints in AI development teams. Closely linked to bias are broader ethical challenges posed by the use of AI in diplomacy. Diplomacy inherently involves sensitive judgment calls about values, interests, and rights, often under conditions of uncertainty and conflicting priorities. The introduction of AI raises critical questions about responsibility, accountability, and the moral limits of machine involvement in diplomatic affairs. For example, who is accountable if an AI-generated recommendation leads to diplomatic missteps, conflict escalation, or violations of international law? How can AI systems be programmed to respect principles of sovereignty, non-intervention, and human rights, especially when operating across diverse legal and cultural frameworks? The delegation of decision-making to AI also risks diminishing human empathy, intuition, and ethical reasoning, qualities that are essential in building trust and resolving conflicts peacefully.

5. EMERGING TRENDS AND TECHNOLOGIES IN AI AND DIPLOMACY

The advent of artificial intelligence (AI) in the diplomatic arena marks a transformative phase in international relations, presenting unparalleled opportunities to enhance both the effectiveness and efficiency of diplomacy. (Yawar et al, 2025) As the global landscape becomes increasingly complex, with multifaceted geopolitical challenges, rapid information flows, and heightened public scrutiny, traditional diplomatic processes face mounting pressures to adapt and innovate. AI technologies, encompassing machine learning, natural language processing, predictive analytics, and automated decision-support systems, offer powerful tools that can augment human capabilities, streamline workflows, and enable more informed, timely, and nuanced diplomatic actions. (Yawar et al, 2025) Exploring these opportunities reveals how AI can fundamentally reshape diplomatic practice, improve strategic outcomes, and strengthen global cooperation. One of the most significant opportunities AI presents is the enhancement of data processing and analysis capabilities. Diplomacy today generates and depends on vast volumes of data from diverse sources including intelligence reports, international treaties, economic indicators, media coverage, social media trends, and public opinion polls. Processing this complex and dynamic data manually is not only time-consuming but also prone to human error and cognitive overload. AI-powered algorithms excel at rapidly synthesizing and interpreting large datasets, identifying patterns, extracting relevant insights, and generating actionable intelligence. This capacity allows diplomats to gain comprehensive situational awareness, anticipate emerging trends, and make evidence-based decisions with greater confidence. By transforming raw data into meaningful knowledge, AI empowers diplomats to navigate uncertainty more effectively and respond proactively to international developments.

Beyond data analysis, AI facilitates predictive modelling and scenario planning that enhance strategic foresight in diplomacy. Machine learning models can simulate a wide range of political, economic, and social scenarios, forecasting potential outcomes of diplomatic initiatives or geopolitical events. For example, predictive analytics can assess the likely impact of sanctions, trade agreements, or peace negotiations by analysing historical precedents and current variables. (Obioha Val et al, 2025) This foresight enables diplomats to weigh risks and benefits more accurately, craft contingency plans, and tailor negotiation strategies to optimize results. Additionally, AI-driven simulations can serve as training tools, helping diplomats rehearse complex negotiations or crisis responses in virtual environments. These capabilities reduce uncertainty and increase the probability of successful diplomatic engagements, fostering more stable and predictable international relations. AI also offers opportunities to streamline routine diplomatic tasks and administrative processes, thereby improving operational efficiency. (Obioha Val et al, 2025) Many diplomatic functions, such as document translation, scheduling, protocol management, and information dissemination, are repetitive and resource-intensive. Natural language processing (NLP) technologies enable automated translation of documents and speeches with increasing accuracy, breaking down language barriers and facilitating smoother communication among diverse stakeholders. AI-driven virtual assistants can manage calendars, draft correspondence, organize meetings, and monitor deadlines, freeing diplomats to focus on substantive policy issues and relationship-building. By automating administrative burdens, AI reduces costs, accelerates workflows, and enhances the overall productivity of diplomatic missions.

5.1. Harnessing the Power of Technology for Effective Diplomacy

As artificial intelligence (AI) continues to evolve at an unprecedented pace, its intersection with diplomacy is poised to reshape the landscape of international relations in profound and multifaceted ways. (Miskimmon et al, 2025) The future of AI in diplomacy will be characterized not only by the refinement of existing technologies but also by the emergence of innovative applications and new paradigms that can enhance diplomatic practice, address complex global challenges, and transform how states and non-state actors interact on the world stage. Understanding these future directions involves exploring cutting-edge trends such as advanced machine learning models, quantum computing, autonomous systems, and the integration of AI with other frontier technologies, alongside the evolving governance frameworks and ethical considerations that will guide their deployment. This forward-looking perspective illuminates how diplomacy can harness AI's transformative potential while navigating the risks and uncertainties inherent in technological change. (Miskimmon et al, 2025) One of the most significant future trends is the rise of explainable and trustworthy AI systems designed specifically for diplomatic use. The current challenge of opacity in AI decision-making models has spurred intense research into explainable AI (XAI), which aims to make AI outputs transparent, interpretable, and justifiable to human users. In diplomacy, where trust, accountability, and clarity are paramount, XAI will enable diplomats and policymakers to better understand the rationale behind AI-generated insights, predictions, and recommendations. This transparency will foster confidence in AI tools, facilitate informed decision-making, and help identify and mitigate potential biases or errors. As XAI techniques mature, they will become integral components of AI-powered diplomatic platforms, improving collaboration between human and machine intelligence and enhancing the legitimacy of AI-assisted diplomacy.

Another promising future direction is the integration of quantum computing with AI to exponentially increase computational power and problem-solving capacity. Quantum computing's ability to process vast amounts of data simultaneously through quantum bits (qubits) holds transformative potential for complex diplomatic challenges, such as cryptography, secure communications, and modelling intricate geopolitical scenarios. Quantum-enhanced AI could significantly improve encryption methods, making diplomatic communications more secure against cyber threats, which are increasingly central to national security and international stability. Moreover, quantum AI could enable more accurate simulations of international crises and negotiations, providing diplomats with deeper insights and more robust predictive analytics. While practical quantum computing remains in developmental stages, its future convergence with AI represents a frontier that could redefine the technological toolkit available to diplomats. (Kirilkina et al, 2025) The future will also see advances in autonomous systems and robotics supporting diplomatic functions. Autonomous drones, robots, and unmanned vehicles equipped with AI capabilities are already used in surveillance, reconnaissance, and humanitarian missions. In diplomacy, these technologies may evolve to assist in peacekeeping operations, monitor compliance with treaties, or deliver aid in conflict zones, providing real-time, reliable data while minimizing human risk. Additionally, virtual and augmented reality (VR/AR) technologies combined with AI will offer immersive environments for diplomatic training, negotiations, and public diplomacy, enabling stakeholders to engage in realistic simulations or cultural exchanges regardless of geographic distance. (Kirilkina et al, 2025) These innovations promise to expand the scope and reach of diplomacy, facilitating more dynamic, inclusive, and effective interactions.

6. CONCLUSION

As we look toward the horizon of international relations, the future of diplomacy is increasingly intertwined with the rapid advancement and integration of artificial intelligence (AI) technologies. AI holds the promise of fundamentally transforming how diplomatic actors engage with one another, respond to global challenges, and shape the international order. The potential of AI to augment human intelligence, enhance analytical capacities, and automate routine processes opens new pathways for more effective, efficient, and adaptive diplomacy. However, harnessing this power requires thoughtful foresight, strategic investment, and a commitment to ethical and inclusive innovation. This discussion explores the future prospects of AI in diplomacy, examining how emerging technologies will redefine diplomatic practice, influence global governance, and contribute to a more interconnected and peaceful world. One of the most profound shifts in future diplomacy will stem from AI's ability to process and analyse massive datasets in real time, providing diplomats with unprecedented insights into complex global dynamics. Diplomatic decision-making often depends on timely, accurate information drawn from diverse sources including intelligence, economic indicators, social media, environmental data, and historical archives. Advanced AI systems equipped with machine learning and natural language processing will enable diplomats to rapidly synthesize this information, detect emerging trends, and anticipate geopolitical shifts before they fully materialize. This heightened situational awareness will improve strategic foresight, enabling more proactive and preventive diplomacy rather than reactive crisis management. As AI algorithms become more sophisticated, they will also help identify hidden patterns and subtle signals that might elude human analysts, offering a significant advantage in navigating an increasingly volatile international environment. The future will also witness the rise of AI-driven predictive analytics and scenario modelling, which promise to revolutionize how diplomats prepare for negotiations, manage conflicts, and design policy interventions. By simulating a range of possible futures based on a multitude of variables, AI can forecast the likely consequences of diplomatic actions with greater precision. These models will assist negotiators in identifying optimal strategies, assessing risks, and crafting more durable agreements. For instance, AI-enabled simulations might analyse the potential impacts of trade agreements on global markets, forecast the consequences of sanctions on political stability, or evaluate peacebuilding efforts in post-conflict zones. The ability to test diplomatic scenarios in virtual environments will enhance decision quality, reduce uncertainty, and increase the likelihood of peaceful outcomes. Another key prospect lies in AI's capacity to automate routine diplomatic functions, freeing human diplomats to focus on complex, strategic, and relational dimensions of their work. Administrative tasks such as document translation, protocol management, scheduling, and information dissemination are essential but time-consuming. AI-powered virtual assistants and automated workflows will streamline these functions, increase operational efficiency and reduce the risk of human error. Advanced natural language processing will further facilitate cross-cultural communication by enabling real-time, context-aware translations that preserve nuance and cultural sensitivities. By lowering language barriers and accelerating bureaucratic processes, AI will make diplomatic engagements smoother and more inclusive, particularly in multilateral settings involving diverse stakeholders.

REFERENCES

Chib, S., Mehta, A. K., Selvakumar, P., Saravanan, A., Mishra, B. R., & Manjunath, T. C. (2025). Mental Health Challenges and Solutions in High-Pressure Work Environments. In Harriott, S. (Ed.), *Innovative Approaches to Managing Conflict and Change in Diverse Work Environments* (pp. 247–272). IGI Global Scientific Publishing. DOI: 10.4018/979-8-3693-9556-1.ch011

Christou, G., Meyer, T., & Fanni, R. (2025). The European union: Assessing global leadership through actorness in artificial intelligence. *Journal of European Integration*, *47*(3), 383–401. DOI: 10.1080/07036337.2024.2377200

da Silva, J. B.Jr, Valdez, M. L., Sealey-Thomas, R., Galiano, S. G., Garcia-Saisó, S., Huerta, P., & D'Agostino, M. (2024). Digital health diplomacy and universal health coverage. *Bulletin of the World Health Organization*, *103*(2), 174. PMID: 39882492

Dahiya, R., & Selvakumar, P. Vidyadhara, & Manjunath, T. C. (2025). Design and Aerodynamics: Principles and Advances. In M. Mellal (Ed.), Innovations and Developments in Unmanned Aerial Vehicles (pp. 145-170). IGI Global Scientific Publishing.

de la Puente Pacheco, M. A., Torres, J., Blanco Troncoso, A. L., Guzmán Murillo, H. J., & Carrascal, J. X. M. (2025). Enhancing Critical Thinking and Argumentation Skills in Colombian Undergraduate Diplomacy Students: ChatGPT-Assisted and Traditional Debate Methods. *Journal of Political Science Education*, *21*(4), 1–11. DOI: 10.1080/15512169.2025.2449936

Fitsilis, F., & de Almeida, P. G. R. (2024). Artificial intelligence and its regulation in representative institutions. In *Research Handbook on Public Management and Artificial Intelligence* (pp. 151–166). Edward Elgar Publishing. DOI: 10.4337/9781802207347.00019

Hanita, M., & Daryanto, E. (2025). Digital Diplomacy Strategy to Win Indonesian Papuan Opinion for National Resilience. Journal of Law. *Politic and Humanities*, *5*(3), 1486–1496. DOI: 10.38035/jlph.v5i3.1226

Holmes, M., & Wheeler, N. J. (2024). The role of artificial intelligence in nuclear crisis decision making: A complement, not a substitute. *Australian Journal of International Affairs*, *78*(2), 164–174. DOI: 10.1080/10357718.2024.2333814

Hossain, M. A., Azim, K. S., Jafor, A. H. M., Shayed, A. U., Nikita, N. A., & Khan, O. U. (2024). AI and Machine Learning in International Diplomacy and Conflict Resolution. AIJMR-Advanced International Journal of Multidisciplinary Research, 2(5).

Iqbal, B. A., & Rahman, M. N. (2025). Digital Diplomacy Among BRICS Countries. In Innovations and Tactics for 21st Century Diplomacy (pp. 383-396). IGI Global.

Kaur, M., Selvakumar, P., & Dinesh, N. Mohit, Chandel, P. S., & Manjunath, T. C. (2025). Reconstruction and Preservation Strategies for Cultural Heritage. In S. Oflazoğlu & M. Dora (Eds.), Preserving Cultural Heritage in Post-Disaster Urban Renewal (pp. 385-412). IGI Global Scientific Publishing.

Kirilkina, I., & Karochkin, S. (2025). The impact of the expansion of artificial intelligence on modern diplomacy in countries worldwide. *Journal of Countries Studies*, *2*(4), 535–557.

Kommineni, M., Chundru, S., Maroju, P. K., & Selvakumar, P. (2025). Ethical Implications of AI in Sustainable Development Pedagogy. In Chinedu, C., Mafarja, N., Hussein, M., & Saleem, A. (Eds.), *Rethinking the Pedagogy of Sustainable Development in the AI Era* (pp. 17–36). IGI Global Scientific Publishing. DOI: 10.4018/979-8-3693-9062-7.ch002

Lazarus, A., & Fatehi, F. (2025). The Diplomat Within: Leading with Unity in a Multipolar World. *Leader to Leader*, *2025*(115), 32–38. DOI: 10.1002/ltl.20861

Limbore, N. V., Anute, N., Ahluwalia, G. K., Chordiya, P. B., Kalshetti, P., & Selvakumar, P. (2025). Ethical Leadership and Corporate Responsibility. In Harriott, S. (Ed.), *Innovative Approaches to Managing Conflict and Change in Diverse Work Environments* (pp. 193–218). IGI Global Scientific Publishing. DOI: 10.4018/979-8-3693-9556-1.ch009

Lips, K. R., & Gore, M. L. (2025). Science diplomacy: Using global environmental change as an opportunity for public diplomacy. In *Handbook on Public Diplomacy* (pp. 310–322). Edward Elgar Publishing. DOI: 10.4337/9781803926568.00035

Luoma-aho, V., & Badham, M. (2025). Future roles for communicators in digital media-arenas: Boxturners and global diplomats. *Corporate Communication Review*, *1*(1), 31–39. DOI: 10.63904/ccr.v1i1.9

Mirahmadi, S., & Omidi, A. (2024). Applications of Artificial Intelligence in Foreign Policy Decision-Making: Capacities and Challenges. *Political Strategic Studies*, *13*(50), 259–300.

Miskimmon, A., & O'Loughlin, B. (2025). Strategic narrative and public diplomacy: What artificial intelligence means for the endless problem of plural meanings of plural things. In Handbook on Public Diplomacy (pp. 34-46). Edward Elgar Publishing.

Obioha Val, O., Olaniyi, O. O., Gbadebo, M. O., Balogun, A. Y., & Olisa, A. O. (2025). Cyber Espionage in the Age of Artificial Intelligence: A Comparative Study of State-Sponsored Campaign. Oluwaseun Oladeji and Gbadebo, Michael Olayinka and Balogun, Adebayo Yusuf and Olisa, Anthony Obulor, Cyber Espionage in the Age of Artificial Intelligence: A Comparative Study of State-Sponsored Campaign (January 22, 2025).

Samal, A., & Misra, L. I. Mohit, Pougajendy, S., Chandel, P. S., Manjunath, T. C., & Selvakumar, P. (2025). Musealization and Tourism Practices. In S. Oflazoğlu & M. Dora (Eds.), Preserving Cultural Heritage in Post-Disaster Urban Renewal (pp. 115-142). IGI Global Scientific Publishing.

Soundariya, A., Behera, N. K., Selvakumar, P., Chandel, P. S., Gupta, S., & Manjunath, T. C. (2025). AI and Environmental Ethics: The Role of AI in Addressing Climate Change Ethical Considerations in AI-Driven Environmental Solutions. In Chakraborty, S. (Ed.), *Human Values, Ethics, and Dignity in the Age of Artificial Intelligence* (pp. 321–346). IGI Global Scientific Publishing. DOI: 10.4018/979-8-3693-9035-1.ch013

Sreekanthaswamy, N., Anitha, S., Singh, A., Jayadeva, S. M., Gupta, S., Manjunath, T. C., & Selvakumar, P. (2025). Digital Tools and Methods. In Çela, E., Paliktzoglou, V., Sengar, S., Eappen, P., & Vajjhala, N. (Eds.), *Enhancing School Counseling with Technology and Case Studies* (pp. 25–48). IGI Global Scientific Publishing. DOI: 10.4018/979-8-3693-8392-6.ch002

Suresh, R. V., Selvakumar, P., Naresh Babu, K., Nithya, G., Manjunath, T. C., & Kartigeyan, J. (2025). Best Practices and Practical Applications. In Çela, E., Paliktzoglou, V., Sengar, S., Eappen, P., & Vajjhala, N. (Eds.), *Enhancing School Counseling with Technology and Case Studies* (pp. 341–362). IGI Global Scientific Publishing. DOI: 10.4018/979-8-3693-8392-6.ch013

Tamilarasi, C., Sowmiya, K., Vignesh, G. D., Jasmine, R. L., Nehru, P., & Selvakumar, P. (2025). AI in Renewable Energy Education: Teaching the Future of Sustainable Power Systems. In Chinedu, C., Mafarja, N., Hussein, M., & Saleem, A. (Eds.), *Rethinking the Pedagogy of Sustainable Development in the AI Era* (pp. 133–152). IGI Global Scientific Publishing. DOI: 10.4018/979-8-3693-9062-7.ch007

Turianskyi, Y., & Wekesa, B. (2025). Conceptual and pragmatic perspectives on African digital diplomacy. In *Handbook on Public Diplomacy* (pp. 134–147). Edward Elgar Publishing. DOI: 10.4337/9781803926568.00021

Uunona, G. N., & Goosen, L. (2025). Navigating Ethical Consideration of Artificial Intelligence and the Metaverse in Scientific Research. In Navigating AI and the Metaverse in Scientific Research (pp. 213-236). IGI Global Scientific Publishing. DOI: 10.4018/979-8-3373-0340-6.ch011

Uwizeye, J., Asbaş, C., & Tuzlukaya, Ş. E. (2024). Exploring the Intersection of Cyber Security and Digital Diplomacy: Perspectives and Challenges. Perspectives on Innovation and Technology Transfer in Managing Public Organizations, 38-51.

Yawar, M. E., Sharify, J. A., & Sadat, S. A. (2025). Artificial Intelligence and International Peace and Security. *Acta Globalis Humanitatis et Linguarum*, *2*(2), 49–61. DOI: 10.69760/aghel.02500205

Zaorski-Sikora, Ł., Braniewicz-Zaorska, O. E., & Olaosebikan, O. (2024). Challenges in artificial intelligence management–selected aspects. Zarządzanie Innowacyjne w Gospodarce i Biznesie, (2/39), 13-26.

Chapter 4
Narrative Diplomacy and Strategic Communication

Arun Thapar
https://orcid.org/0009-0000-1484-8860
Indian Institute of Information Technology, Bhopal, India

Anshita Thapar
Tara Sadan Higher Secondary School, India

ABSTRACT

In this chapter, we discuss how narrative diplomacy has emerged as an International Relations characteristic in a period of artificial intelligence and digital transformation. It positions storytelling and strategic communication as the heart of international relations where governments, international organizations, and non-state actors are increasingly putting algorithm-based platforms as a means to shape world problems, cover policy justification, and sway opinion. With an interdisciplinary approach invoking non-traditional disciplinary themes that incorporate foreign relations and media studies and AI ethics, the chapter deciphers how narratives are developed, challenged, and reformulated in major international diplomatic forums namely the Munich Security Conference, the Raisina Dialogue, and the United Nations General Assembly.

1. INTRODUCTION

In this chapter, we discuss how narrative diplomacy has emerged as an International Relations characteristic in a period of artificial intelligence and digital transformation. It positions storytelling and strategic communication as the heart of international relations where governments, international organizations, and non-state

DOI: 10.4018/979-8-3373-4937-4.ch004

actors are increasingly putting algorithm-based platforms as a means to shape world problems, cover policy justification, and sway opinion. With an interdisciplinary approach invoking non-traditional disciplinary themes that incorporate foreign relations and media studies and AI ethics, the chapter deciphers how narratives are developed, challenged, and reformulated in major international diplomatic forums namely the Munich Security Conference, the Raisina Dialogue, and the United Nations General Assembly.

The discussion underscores the two-fold character of the AI-enabled communication: on the one hand, it increases the scope, accuracy and swiftness of diplomatic communications; on the other hand, it creates a certain amount of unease regarding manipulation, legitimacy, and accountability. A cross-case analysis indicates the theme strength of concerns digital sovereignty, climate change, and international security where narratives continue to underpin institutional power and influence multilateral agreement. In analyzing the latter, the chapter highlights the performative capabilities of diplomacy as a narrative practice and assesses the challenges that such capacity poses to institutional legitimacy and the development of global governance architecture. Both conceptual and empirical, this effort leads to the possibility of conceptualizing the future of the narrative diplomatic process in the age of AI-driven world and provides researchers, policymakers, and practitioners with a framework with which to contend with an increasingly fraught and technologically-mediated realm of international communication.

1.1. Defining Narrative Diplomacy in Contemporary Global Affairs

The development of a narrative diplomacy has emerged as a major instrument of international relation management as more people are becoming aware that influence is no longer exercised solely through material power as stories are now used to frame and explain and justify state actions. Narratives in diplomacy have the capacity to act not as simply a set of signifiers but as a self-sustaining system of meaning which enables actors to project their identities, establish legitimacy, and exert control over the state government and its external audience members in convincing them that they have done the right thing. As opposed to a more diplomatic mode that privileged negotiation and the transfer of official messages between government entities, narrative diplomacy places a stronger emphasis on persuasion by means of storytelling, framing and the contextualization of nondescript events into larger interpretative patterns. This type of communication has attained relevance right now in the world of global affairs since states and non-state actors find themselves struggling to determine the way the international issues are framed and resolved.

Narrative diplomacy becomes especially important when there is a crisis or change in the world order and the world struggles or is experiencing change. Institutions, as shown by Manfredi-Sanchez and Smith (2023) in their text on the strategic narratives of the European Union, wish to maintain a consistent image, and as such, use narratives to control their public face in times of crisis, presenting events in ways that support their legitimacy. Narratives, therefore, become an instrument in dealing with uncertainty and appearing like leaders. Likewise, Saliu (2023) notes that in the post-truth world where falsehood and competing truths are proliferated, the role of the post-truth world is different; now they are concerned with the struggle to win credibility. In this kind of environment, strategic storytelling is a must-have to avoid the losses in power, as well as a means to retain legitimacy in the international community.

Figure 1. Evolution of Diplomatic Narratives in the Digital Age

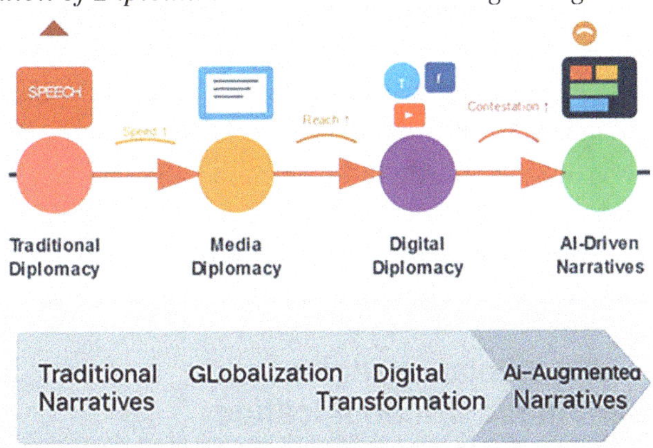

The figure shows the evolution of narrative diplomacy through four distinct phases. The first phase can be described as Traditional Diplomacy in which such narratives were mostly created in speeches, treaties, and official communique. The second phase is the rise of Media Diplomacy whereby the medium of television, reports, and broadcastings prevailed in guiding the world, especially the Cold War and the Cold War era. The third phase is Digital Diplomacy which saw the spread of the narrative strategies in the internet era and the ability to directly engage with the international audiences. Lastly is the fourth stage AI-Driven Diplomacy, where algorithmic technologies, data analytics and micro-targeting displace story-making, amplification and defense. The figure highlights how the established element of narration is still in the process of evolution and the technological shift has increased the pace, breadth, and the strategic dimensions of the process of narrative diplomacy.

As well as having a communicative aspect, narrative diplomacy is also relational: it is not merely about what message is conveyed, but also about how it is conveyed to various audiences, who may accept, resist or reinterpret the narratives they hear. This observation is consistent with the theory of framing advanced by Chong and Druckman (2007) who believes that issues are defined by the presentation done by political actors as a competitive arena. Narrative wars in diplomacy take place at several fronts; however, the same aspect witnessed by various parties is described in different lights to serve self-interests. Along these lines, Xin and Matheson (2018) point to the competing metaphors in the Belt and Road Initiative by highlighting how the various interpretations of the same project present confrontation over global authority and legitimacy.

In this sense, narrative diplomacy is not a variation of propaganda, but a formalized pattern of engaging in world-discourse. Narratives offer foreign policies coherence, a connection of the individual policies with national values, and elaborate on national strategies as a story acceptable to the rest of the world. An aspect of how and why certain frames are used is considered too. According to Arceneaux (2024), the creation of value in international communication may be based on the organizational story-telling, which leads to the creation of a feeling of trustworthiness, competence, and adherence to the values held by the audience. There are high stakes: those who manage to dominate the narratives in place can set terms of international debates, shape coalitions, and justify interventions.

1.2. The Role of Artificial Intelligence in Reshaping Diplomatic Communication

AI-enhanced communication reshapes diplomacy in several ways. First, it allows for precision in message delivery. Through the study of audience behavior and sentiments, AI can help diplomats create narratives that will have stronger appeal to the intended audiences. Clementson (2020) shows the relation between narrative persuasion and the aspects of identification and perceptions of trustworthiness, indicating that elaborated narratives to suit the perception more specifically are more effective due to the perception of belief. This fact is essential in a digital environment where communities are disjointed and growing less trusting of conventional sources of power.

Second, AI changes the visibility and velocity of narratives. Algorithmic curation favours particular contents in the social media, thus raising some diplomatic voices and drowning others. According to Fetterlof, Mordecai, and Wike (2020), the international perception of the United States when it comes to how it manages the COVID-19 crisis rapidly changed in a survey that indicated that the country experienced a drastic decrease in its image globally. AI in the media environment therefore increases the pressure to control narratives: a narrative can go global in a short period of time, but equally that narrative can be destroyed in hours by others or discredited by other evidence.

Third, AI challenges traditional notions of authenticity in diplomacy. In the AI era, Cook (2007) stated that authenticity and connectedness are growing as the central values in communication and this has come true. On the one hand, AI tools increase the capabilities of creating interesting, personalized messages; on the other hand, they leave manipulation, trust, and transparency questions. Plainly speaking, diplomats who overuse algorithmically created stories might lose credibility when understood by audiences as artificial or something unauthentic. This conflict highlights the ethical aspect of AI-enabled diplomacy, in which the component of strategic power and direct dialogue is still debatable.

Last but not least, AI changes the ratio of the actors in the field of narrative diplomacy. According to White (2015), corporations that operate in the private sector have an influence in determining and structuring of public diplomacy and this has increased in the digital era. Technology companies that design and run AI platforms now play the role of gatekeepers of international communication and determine which narrative is visible and which is marginalized. Such redistribution of power in the area of communication complicates the usual structure of diplomatic relationships by adding new comers, the commercial interest of which overlap the geopolitical interests.

1.3. Research Problem, Objectives, and Chapter Roadmap

The key issue that is determined in this chapter is the way narrative diplomacy operates in a time when AI technologies that drive communications complicate the possibilities and problems of storytelling in international relations. Narratives are not new to diplomacy but due to digital transformation, they have become prominent and far more complex than earlier. The combination of diplomacy, media, and AI begs the following questions: Mobile narratives deployed by states and non-state actors Where can global issues and events be framed by states and non-state actors? How does AI change narrative creation, distribution and reception? What do all these changes mean to the legitimacy of institutions and multilateral governance?

The objective of the chapter is threefold. First, it attempts to define the notion of narrative diplomacy and place it in the framework of strategic communication and international relations in general. Second, it explores the potential of AI in transforming the practices of narrative, specifically, by examining how AI-enhanced platforms can rein in, distort, or challenge diplomatic narratives. Third, it has empirical elements by including case studies of such international forums as Munich Security Conference, the Raisina Dialogue, and the United Nations General Assembly to trace the way the narratives of security, digital sovereignty, and transforming climate are constructed and contested. Along with such conceptual analysis, this chapter seeks to contribute to understanding through conducting empirical research about how narratives are used in modern diplomacy.

This chapter is structured in terms of the following themes. The second section lays the conceptual groundwork through an engagement with ideas of strategic communication, soft power, and framing in international relations. This is followed by an analysis of the AI augmented narrative ecosystem, which looks at how digital technologies change the communicative infrastructure of diplomacy. The Anatomy of Narrative Diplomacy the empirical core of the chapter is composed of the case studies that give tangible exemplification of narrative diplomacy at work. The second section synthesizes the results in order to draw patterns of narrative performance and contestation, and the third concludes by discussing implications of this evidence in the context of multilateralism and institutional legitimacy. The chapter ends with some considerations of what is to be done with narrative diplomacy in a world further disrupted by artificial intelligence and how this will open up new possibilities as well as create new challenges.

2. CONCEPTUAL FOUNDATIONS: DIPLOMACY, NARRATIVE, AND STRATEGIC COMMUNICATION

2.1. Literature Review

Narrative diplomacy as a genre of study has been inspired by the awareness that global politics is not only about the clash of material resources, but also of meaning. States, institutions, and non-state actors make use of stories to explain their actions, examine their policies, and gather support. These narratives, be they strategic narratives, discursive or symbolic performances have been found to be vital in how international relations are perceived and acted upon. This sense of narrative diplomacy links the communicative aspect of diplomacy to processes of soft power and strategic communication more broadly.

The most outstanding case of narrative diplomacy at work can be traced in the speeches of political leaders. Hobbs, Li, Huang, and Desmoulins (2025) reveal the way President Xi Jinping has employed storytelling as the way of expressing the grand strategy of China on the international scene. Putting national interests into the wider discourses of peace, development, and mutual benefit, Xi can articulate policy in the form of a story that can be heard globally. It is such an instance that can be considered narrative diplomacy as this enables the nexus between state identity and foreign policy goals to be joined through communicative practices towards legitimizing their various aims.

The significance of narrative diplomacy is also relevant to the process of strategic narrative wars where adversaries attempt to conquer the discursive domain. Mitić (2024) explores the Serbian context and demonstrates how different actors domestic and international shape the same issues in different ways in order to influence both, the opinion of the population and the foreign policy of the country. These kinds of disagreements underscore the idea that narrative diplomacy is no impartial procedure; it is a field of struggle over legitimacy. In that respect, the notion of narrative diplomacy intersects with the concept of strategic communication as taken by these authors: the setting of conscious efforts with the intent of a desired perception, attitude and behavior change through acts of communication.

Strategic communication is broader than traditional public diplomacy. According to Akman (2024), it has a broad range of practices including secret diplomacy and intelligence sharing as well as the open persuasion using the media and cultural programs. Its strategic communication then is a major one through which states are able to control their information environments. In the increasingly globalized world, narrative diplomacy can be seen as just such a variety of strategic communication, namely one in which the power of narrative to influence legitimacy is recognized and the power of narrative to shape how we all come to understand each other.

Soft power theory provides another dimension to this discussion. Joseph Nye coined the term soft power to define the potential of a state to obtain what they want by attractions as opposed to coercion. Narratives emerge as one of the strongest tools of soft power as they position a state as credible, trustworthy, and as one sharing similar values. As Snow (2023) demonstrates, such a pattern is characteristic of strategic communication conducted in the Indo-Pacific region by Japan, which focuses on the importance of partnership and reliability in the area of public diplomacy. Japan has taken a softer and kinder stance by creating narratives of friendship and collaboration, which helps it create a stable ally which leads to soft power.

Meanwhile, the technological shift in communications has made it difficult to use soft power. Ventura (2025) demonstrates that Ukraine has used visual narratives on Instagram to support international solidarity in times of war. Through the use of visual images and symbols together with emotional appeal, digital diplomacy of Ukraine provides an example of how a narrative can generate empathy and muster support on an ongoing basis. Practices that incorporate elements of soft power reach into the digital worlds where mediums of control are more and more disputable.

Lastly, narrative diplomacy is intimately connected with strategies of hybridity. ul Haq (2025) examines the case of Russian digital diplomacy and cyber governance:

in this example, strategic narratives are employed in conjunction with the tactics of hybridity to shape perception worldwide. The example of the Russian practice demonstrates the danger of narrative diplomacy when used in an adversarial environment: the narratives can be used to legitimize but, at the same time they can be used to delegitimize others, misinform or disrupt institutions. In this vein, narrative diplomacy acquires power of attraction as well as the means of disruption.

2.2. Theoretical Intersections

Narrative diplomacy can no longer be considered in solely international relation terms, but needs to be interdisciplinarity approached by studying the topics of media and AI ethics. The question of how--or whether--ideas, norms, and discourses contribute to the making of global politics has long been debated by international relations theory. The schools Constructivist, for example, focus on social construction of reality, or the importance of narratives that people share, which shapes identities, institutions, and policies. Both Hobbs et al. (2025) and Aoi (2024) refer to the role of narratives in the development of geopolitical concepts like the Indo-Pacific, which in their turn are not geographic but discursive. By defining the Indo-Pacific as a strategic region, policymakers and diplomats increase the reality to change the alliances, threat perception, and policy priorities.

The studies of media enable the individuals to understand how the narratives are produced, circulated and consumed. As Ventura (2025) testifies, visual communication coming in the form of images, memes, and videos can be just as influential as speeches when it comes to making perceptions. The information war is becoming a fight on hybrid areas where the use of both traditional media and digital media and social media meet. Proto, Lamoso-Gonzalez, and Garcia (2025) demonstrate how the European Union has re-contextualized its communication policy in the war on disinformation, and indeed what they call the FIMI Turn (Fight against Information Manipulation and Interference). Their examples show how media ecosystems provide not only the context of existence but thoroughly reconfigure the course of diplomatic stories.

The ethics of AI comes into play as systems driven by algorithms now allow mediation in the visibility and credibility of narratives. Algorithms determine what narratives are brought to the fore and which voices are neutralized and how exactly diplomatic messages come into contact with the general population. Kadyan and Singh (2025), discussing business intelligence in the HR discipline, point out that data-informed decisions are currently defined more by the Darwinians than the Evolutionists: the former group points to the ability of algorithms to create insight but the latter to the way the instruments create biases. Corresponding ethical issues appear in diplomacy: who owns the information, what narratives should be given relevance, and to what extent do practices involving manipulation undermine the principle of democratic accountability.

Those views in combination imply that the narrative diplomacy exists in the vicinity of world politics, technological media, and ethical dilemmas. It is not merely the question of the deliberate shaping of stories but also how they are supported or organized structurally (technologically, institutionally, normative) to jump or translate, to resonate or circulate.

2.3. Framework for Understanding Legitimacy

In order to make narrative diplomacy make sense, it is worth developing a framework outlining three interconnected facets: legitimacy, identity and framing. These ideas enable us to examine not only what is in a story, but also how this story may have political consequences.

Table 1. Key Theoretical Perspectives on Narrative Diplomacy

Perspective	Core Argument
Narrative Diplomacy	Stories provide coherence to foreign policy and legitimacy to state actions.
Strategic Communication	Deliberate efforts to influence perceptions through communicative practices.
Soft Power	Attraction and credibility shape outcomes through non-coercive influence.
Visual Narratives	Images and digital media amplify emotional and symbolic communication.
Hybrid Narratives	Narratives are combined with disinformation or cyber tactics.
Media Ecosystem Shifts	Platforms and algorithms restructure the flow of narratives.
Identity Construction	Narratives define self/other and frame geopolitical roles.
Legitimacy and Authority	Narratives legitimize institutional roles and global leadership.

Legitimacy is acceptation of power and the feeling that things are being done rightfully and it is acceptable. Diplomatic discourses usually attempt to justify state behavior in terms of wider narratives of justice or peace or shared values. To give a specific example, Hobbs et al. (2025) demonstrate how the speeches of Xi Jinping indeed justify the emergence of China as a peaceful and cooperative actor instead of a threatening one. In another example of such a narrative, Snow (2023) reports about how the establishment of Japan and its place in the Indo-Pacific occurs by allowing it to position itself as a reliable partner, friend, and strategist. Legitimacy then is as narrative as it is material argument.

Identity concerns the construction of self and other. The thing about diplomacy is that it feeds on narratives to establish who we are and who they are. One can find this process of identity formation in the work of Aoi (2024) about the Indo-

Pacific, when states in the region are trying to position themselves as belonging to the same strategic community and distinguishing themselves from their rivals. This is because the identity narratives give a sense of unity in foreign policy wherein the self-understandings given at home can be connected to the roles abroad. This is complemented by the research of Ventura (2025) that demonstrates how in Ukraine the discourse of digital stories builds a strong sense of nation, rousing support both internally and internationally.

Framing is a process that renders issues in a manner that brings out some elements over others. The concept of framing ties events to larger narratives that can influence how the publics reading them think about them. ul Haq (2025) reveals that Russia framed its strategies on cyber governance as being defensive and legitimate, but critics framed the similar activities as aggressive and destabilizing. Proto et al. (2025) point out how the EU re-interprets the effects of disinformation as a systematic danger to democracies, thus institutional responses were warranted. These cases demonstrate the major role of framing to global politics through contention of meaning.

By combining the concepts of legitimacy, identity, and framing, the framework focuses on the idea that a narrative diplomacy is more than just persuasion but the impetus behind creating things realities. It allows states to place themselves in international discourses, displace competing interpretations, and forge groupings. Meanwhile, it shows how weak narratives are, always prone to reinterpretation and counter criticism in the digital public sphere.

3. DIGITAL TRANSFORMATION AND THE AI-AUGMENTED NARRATIVE ECOSYSTEM

3.1. Algorithmic Platforms and Data-Driven Message Construction

The dynamic changes in digital technologies and artificial intelligence (AI) have significantly shifted the paradigm in the production and the outsourcing of diplomatic narratives. In earlier forms of diplomatic interaction, use was made of vast speeches and press releases, and policy documents were produced with a lot of care. In the contemporary context, however, much of the discursive struggle occurs in the algorithmically-mediated sphere where platforms, at least as much as governments, come to decide the presence and prominence of messaging. Algorithms curate, prioritize and promote the material and therefore develop an information context where specific discourses are overheard and others are silenced. The technological mediation also makes narrative diplomacy different through changing its opportunities as well as the risks.

In her article, Johnson (2023) observes that any subject matter of global security, such as nuclear strategy, has been inundated with algorithmic decision-making, adding that the logic underlying military risk management also regulates communication flows. Applied to diplomacy, algorithmic platforms reproduce the role of invisible forces that affect the global discussion with the emphasis on specific frames. Alpeda (2024) finds social media algorithms to be of critical importance to foreign policy communication by affecting the way a government communicates in aligning its messages to the algorithmic discovery. These adaptations incorporate issues such as framing them to provoke user interaction, making the content relevant to some discourses that are currently gaining popularity and using paid promotion to guarantee coverage to the digital population.

Data-driven message construction is another hallmark of AI-augmented diplomacy. Zhou and van der Meer (2024) assert that computational strategic communication is based on the gathering and processing of massive data on audience to ensure optimum message structure. Sophisticated analytic tools are now available to diplomats and the foreign ministry, enabling them to profile audience clusters and gauge reader/listener/viewer emotional responses and are able to anticipate what types of narratives will work. This results in a feedback loop that has never been seen before: messages do not only get constructed but are also continuously changed in response to the data insights. Mirza, Shah, Tamour, Hussain, and Khan (2025) emphasize the fact that the social media analytics now serve active intelligence to international political rhetoric construction, allowing governments to track their real-time sentiment changes and react to them timely.

This development has revolutionised diplomatic story-telling as it was previously a one-way issue compared to nowadays where the process is iterative with data enriched. Nonetheless, according to Gombar (2025), the possibility of cognitive warfare through algorithmic manipulation could be a problem because the narratives are constructed to be informed but also affect the subconscious. Such obscuring of communication and psychological influence have posed questions regarding international legitimacy and trust, and has raised issues to do with ethical use of AI in diplomacy.

Figure 2. AI-Augmented Ecosystem of Diplomatic Narratives

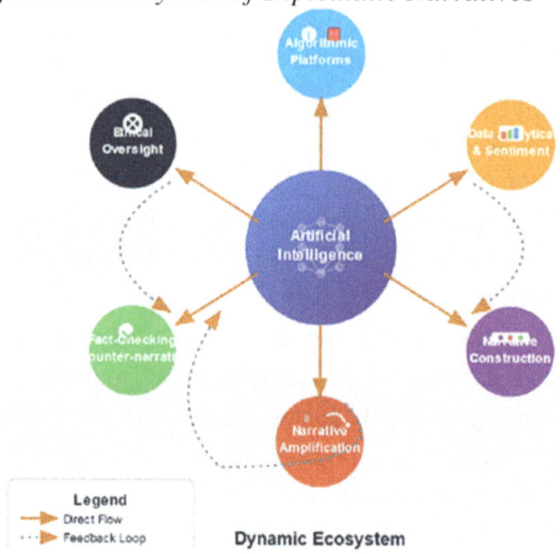

This figure represents the setting surrounding AI that transforms the diplomatic discourse. In the middle are algorithmic platforms, which can be seen as the mediating infrastructures between different actors. Around the core one can find nodes of diplomats, institutions, media organizations, and the publics and non-state actors. The arrows are used to show how information flows in multiple directions between diplomats and institutions, the platforms on which information is filtered and distributed, and the people who perceive, resist, or disperse this information. The figure also emphasizes the place of AI-based analytics, e.g. sentiment tracking and predictive modelling, that can generate feedback loops which can shape further narrative building. Such an ecosystem reveals the relational and dynamic quality of digital diplomacy as narratives constantly change through the interaction of actors and technologies.

3.2. Micro-Targeting, Sentiment Tracking, and Narrative Amplification

The potential impact of AI on diplomacy is therefore likely to result in micro-targeting; the capacity to convey specific messages to a particular group of people with accuracy. Applying the logic of politics and commercial marketing to the affairs of diplomacy, the segmentation of the general audience has become closer to the foreign affairs that are divided into several groups according to the data focused on the demographics, behaviour, and psychographic analysis. Erhiyanto and Santoso (2025) examine how American public diplomacy has resorted to AI powered political advocacy strategies that enable the diplomats to communicate to individuals and groups with messages that match with their existing ideas or anxieties. Such personalization augments the effectiveness of messages, but also runs the risk of atomizing the public sphere, where diverse audiences are receiving radically divergent versions of the same diplomatic discourse.

Sentiment tracking is another innovation reshaping diplomacy. Governments are able to review real-time response to their communication efforts by analysing social media interactions, search information and online discourse. Devanny (2024) observes that AI and its ability to process data means governments have strong cyber potential, which goes beyond security and dominating information. In diplomatic terms, sentiment monitoring can enable states to see the narratives that are being adopted and which ones are floundering. These data could then be used to help modify speeches, campaigns or diplomatic efforts. To illustrate, Mallick, 2024, focuses on the idea that sentiment analysis capabilities to predict the response of the masses is a vital asset in the contemporary state politics, as it enables the state to predict an adverse reaction and adjust its message to prevent such an event.

Narrative amplification involves an amplification of specific discourses due to the practices of AI driven platforms providing an algorithmic advantage to engagement. Emotional stories are those that elicit feelings of anger, fear, or empathy, and as such, they were more inclined to be promoted by algorithms. As Latif, Rooh, Malik, and Samad (2025) show, digital diplomacy and disinformation are related issues because the people implementing disinformation usually cut across the functionality and definitions of digital diplomacy because serious actors intentionally design emotional messages that will be amplified by the algorithm to influence global opinion. As much as amplification enhances the extent of strategic communications, this also creates loopholes as malevolent forces can use the same process to disseminate counter-narratives or disinformation geared towards their ends. According to Unver (2023), technology has become an essential device of information manipulation that impacted the ability of states and non-state actors to distort the debate in the public space and disrupt diplomatic work.

According to Fasinu, Olaniyan, and Afolaranmi (2024), the described dynamics are especially prominent with regards to the crisis communication where stable or destabilizing of diplomatic relations can be achieved through rapid amplification. Charles (2024) notes that algorithmically augmented communication can be used by small states, in order to garner a disproportional amount of visibility. Through the construction of narratives that are easy to disseminate in the digital space, small states can contribute to the debates and establish their relevance in the face of the lack of material power. This would imply that AI can change the communication power in international relations by creating chances of inclusion and threats of control.

3.3. Ethical Challenges: Transparency, Manipulation, and Digital Divides

But although these algorithmic platforms and data-driven approaches provide strong instruments of narrative diplomacy, at the same time they are bringing a lot of moral issues to the table. Transparency is a core concern. In explaining why accountability in the algorithms process is lacking, Zhou and van der Meer (2024) aver that the muddiness of communication channels within the algorithms system makes it difficult to hold any individual accountable. The lack of transparency makes the appreciation of diplomatic legitimacy more difficult, as it is possible that its success transformed into an algorithm algorithmic privilege rather than narrative credibility. These concerns of accountability are said to have to be faced in the context of digital diplomacy in case it is to be a force of peace, as digital diplomacy adds a layer of technologically mediated interaction that might interfere with the principles of open dialogue and fair representation (Lisenco 2025).

Table 2. AI-Enabled Tools in Narrative Diplomacy (Applications and Risks)

AI-Enabled Tool	Application in Diplomacy	Associated Risks
Algorithmic Platforms	Filtering and prioritizing diplomatic messages for visibility	Opaqueness of algorithms, lack of accountability
Data Analytics	Identifying audience clusters and tailoring messages	Privacy concerns, data misuse
Sentiment Tracking	Monitoring real-time reactions to speeches, campaigns, and policies	Over-reliance on volatile public opinion
Micro-Targeting	Delivering personalized narratives to segmented audiences	Fragmentation of public sphere, ethical concerns
Narrative Amplification	Enhancing reach of emotionally resonant content	Exploitation by disinformation campaigns
Automated Bots	Disseminating messages rapidly across platforms	Spread of propaganda, erosion of trust
Predictive Modeling	Anticipating responses to diplomatic initiatives	Risk of self-fulfilling or manipulative strategies

Manipulation is a second ethical concern. Gombar (2025) emphasizes the attribute of cognitive warfare wherein the use of algorithmic tools is employed to prey on the psychological weaknesses. In the diplomatic circle, this calls into concern the boundary between persuasion and manipulation. As discussed by Erhiyanto and Santoso (2025), the advocacy powered by AI is likely to undermine the values of democracy in case it prioritizes efficiency over truth. Latif et al. (2025) further state that disinformation campaigns make use of the same amplification mechanism as genuine diplomatic narratives thus, the borderline between soft power and information warfare mugginess. In these circumstances, the authenticity of diplomatic communication gets eroded because of the assumption of a manufactured story as opposed to inspiring one.

A third ethical issue is a continued existence of digital divides. Because the most technologically equipped states and institutions can use such AI tools to boost their power to tell a narrative, the less equipped actors can be pushed to the sidelines. Roy (2024) knows that AI creates imbalances in global communication where only influential players can talk and the others barely can understand and be considered. Brovina, Gashi, and Kabashi (2024) make a similar point by noting that digital diplomacy and national security are two-sided coins: on the one hand, digital tools can be used to increase the exposure, on the other hand, they complicate the situation and open vulnerabilities to states lacking effective technological infrastructures. Such divisions carry the risk of institutionalising inequalities within global governance where access to AI-based tools would become a factor of influence over narratives.

Scholars and practitioners in dealing with these ethical challenges insist that there is a need to introduce new governance frameworks. Mallick (2024) and Roy (2024) believe that ethical considerations will be the key to the future of diplomacy in the way that AI systems are designed and used. In the absence of such precautions, AI-enhanced diplomacy risks being compromised by manipulation, and mistrust and exclusion. Following Lisenco (2025), digital diplomacy also needs to be reconceptualized not only as a control mechanism, but also as a means of encompassing the world into a responsible, global dialogue.

4. CASE STUDIES

4.1. Munich Security Conference

Munich Security Conference (MSC) also represents one of the most influential scenarios of the global setting, where security narratives are produced and challenged. From the discussions of Track 1.5 platforms, forums such as the MSC play a critical role as these platforms involve both official state participation and inclusion of think tanks and participants of the private sector (see Longhini and Zimmerman (2021)). The result is an elite-driven but discursively permeable form of narration. The MSC offers a platform where visions of international security and partnerships are contested, and such confrontations have become more prominent in the digital space where addresses and interventions are widely broadcast and circulated through the world media.

Solidarity, trust, and deterrence are pursued as frames of international security framed predominately at the MSC. The article by Manfredi-Sanchez and Smith (2023) shows that crisis narratives can be used by the European Union, in this example to show that it is resilient and united in its call. Such narratives are magnified by the MSC, which helps to fix the perception of the EU as a trustworthy party in the provision of security. In line with this, constructions of alliance solidarity are dominant: the repetitive references to NATO solidarity and the transatlantic relationship portray the alliance not only as a military organization, but also as a community of shared values.

Yet the MSC also reveals contestation. Hansson, Madisson, and Ventsel (2023) explain the Russian penchant to employ counter-narratives, especially on technological topics, such as 5G, to dismiss the idea of the Western side, and portray themselves as victims of Western disinformation campaigns. This points to what Saliu (2023) refers to as the erosion of soft power in the post-truth era: namely, in which narratives are no longer taken at face-value but rather confronted with scepticism, competing truths, and catching blame. The MSC therefore illustrates the two-fold role of security narratives as both a means to cement unions and as an element of challenge.

Digitization stretches the visibility of these narratives. According to Stry and Lockyer (2022), the concept of a small story in digital diplomacy is that small portions of the discourse transmitted on social platforms such as Twitter do become part of a greater strategic narrative. The MSC is an example of this as portions of the addresses are shared online and become spread out with a life of their own, or out of the control of the initial speaker. In this respect, the MSC exemplifies how algorithmic amplification (described in Section 3) comes in direct contact with the sphere of high-level diplomacy and produces not only opportunities of influence but also risks of distortion.

4.2. Raisina Dialogue

The Raisina Dialogue in India has been a platform where the question of governance of the emerging technology and the politics of digital sovereignty is raised. In contrast to the MSC that mainly emphasizes the security partnerships, a lot of attention is paid to the intersections of technology, development and geopolitics in Raisina Dialogue. In the review of existing publications, Basu and Nachiappan (2023) point out that a lot of attention is paid to the issue of cybersecurity and hybridity, which is understandable since India is both a neo-digital power and a state that finds itself at the forefront of efforts to strike a balance between openness and regulating the global cyber sphere.

Digital sovereignty also functions as a framework in the narratives at Raisina and is defined as the ability to dictate the terms and conditions of engagement with information technology, on which national independence depends. This framing is of special interest with respect to the power termination of American and Chinese tech companies in the global discussion. The emphasis on sovereignty allows India and other states to convey the messages of not being constrained in digital architecture by external powers and at the same time they position themselves as proponents of inclusive and equitable systems of governance. This account corresponds with what Moral (2023) cites as reputation building practices in digital diplomacy whereby actors take advantage of the platforms such as Twitter to salvage or improve credibility in times of geopolitical contestation.

The Raisina Dialogue goes on to show how non-state actors can be utilized in narrative diplomacy. There are active acceptance and inclusion of technology companies, civil society and academic experts in discussions consequently creating a hybrid environment of the narrative. As seen in Tran (2024), social media dynamics affect international relations in diplomacy and even in situations like the relationships between China and France; this aspect can be seen at Raisina where social media guarantees an extension of the discussion even when not on grounds. The emergence of additional stakeholders complicates narrative control, but on the other hand, it promotes the legitimacy of the diplomatic narrative by placing it in the multi-stakeholder framework.

Moving forward, Saliu (2023) asserts that narratives have to work extra hard to uphold trust in the post-truth world, particularly in times when conflicting narratives about technology control exist in the wilderness. In Raisina, the conceptual focus on sovereignty and governance combats the issue head on: through having the narrative underpin the discourse of rights and fairness, the needs of the parties involved become legitimate not merely as national principles, but as enshrined international principles. In so doing Raisina turns into the school of narrative invention where the technology of politics is redefined as an issue of equality and sovereignty.

4.3. The Climate Diplomacy

The most well-known arena of this diplomatic narration is the United Nations General Assembly (UNGA) where states attempt to share their ideas about how the world order should be. Such climate diplomacy manoeuvrings have become some of the most evident narrative themes at UNGA with climate change, as is understood, not purely an environmental challenge but also a geopolitical and developmental challenge. According to Gray and Baturo (2021), the UNGA is one of the best arenas to delegate rhetoric because the speeches allow the state heads, ministers, and representatives to project national identities and priorities through speeches.

Some of the terms most common with climate rhetoric in the UNGA are urgency, justice, and responsibility. Mao, Zhang, Liu, Hussain, and Cambria (2024) show that how metaphorical thinking in the Security Council debates influences the perceptions on climate and security concerns, and the same can be observed at the UNGA. The leaders use the metaphors of survival, stewardship, and solidarity to position climate change as a science survival challenge that requires collaborative effort. The example provided by Flinaldi, Faisol, Hadi, and Ilyas (2024) demonstrates that it is possible to decipher the performative tools that define the mode through which leaders, including King Salman, express the intent of strategic communication and incorporate legitimacy with the help of the rhetorical choices.

North-South dynamics of contestation in climate diplomacy is also highlighted by the UNGA. Developing nations often place climate discourse through the lens of justice and equity with an emphasis on past liability, and the necessity of financial assistance. Moral (2023) observes that the European Union has been implementing digital diplomacy as a method of repairing its reputation, positioning itself as a green leader. This discourse is however dogged by claims, which depict inadequate pledges or hypocrisy. According to Etl-Nadudvari (n.d.), it is impossible to study strategic narratives outside the framework of geopolitical conflicts since climate justice narratives occur within power disparities between a developed and a developing nation.

Digital diplomacy amplifies these dynamics. Even minor states can use new media to be sure their voices will be heard in the UNGA (Charles, 2024). Smaller actors can acquire this visibility since by using digital platforms to raise the profile of speeches, share soundbites or display symbolic gestures, they will have access to the crowds that would otherwise be inaccessible in an already saturated diplomatic space. This is in line with what Spry and Lockyer (2022) termed as small stories, in that even the smallest of interventions can be exponentially expanded into a significant story. The UNGA can, therefore, be regarded as a showcase of traditional multilateral practices combined with new digital-era storytelling, which is why it can also be referred to as narrative diplomacy.

5. COMPARATIVE INSIGHTS INTO NARRATIVE STRATEGIES, ACTORS, AND THEMES

The three forums draw different patterns of narrative diplomacy. Discursive themes at the Munich Security Conference include unity in alliance and securitisation of threats, but also reading into them discourses of culpability and fake news. The Raisina Dialogue is run on technologies of governance and digital sovereignty a predisposition of a world of data and infrastructure. At the UNGA, climate diplomacy is a clear example of how a discourse of justice, responsibility, and survival determines the legitimacy of the global order. Though these differences exist, a common trend reveals itself: narratives are increasingly co-constructed by both state and non-state actors and enhanced by the digital arena.

The three forums discussed through the lens of legitimation, identity and framing. Manfredi-Sanchez and Smith (2023) say that crises required coherent narratives to maintain institutional legitimacy, an aspect that is clear in security debates, technology, and climate discourses. As Saliu (2023) points out, soft power is especially vulnerable in the post-truth era as seen in contested narratives across all three forums. The digital technologies, as Spry and Lockyer (2022) point out, increase the scale as well as the instability of narratives and make the very notion of strategic storytelling continuous and dynamic. All of this indicates that narrative diplomacy is not a marginal aspect of world politics but a central modality in which global challenges can be and must be interpreted.

Table 3. Comparative Analysis of Narrative Strategies in Three Case Studies

Forum	Central Themes	Narrative Strategies	Key Actors Involved
Munich Security Conference	Security, alliances, deterrence	Framing solidarity; countering blame narratives	States, NATO, EU, Russia, think tanks
Raisina Dialogue	Digital sovereignty, governance, cyber	Sovereignty framing; multi-stakeholder legitimation	India, tech firms, civil society, global South actors
United Nations General Assembly	Climate change, justice, global order	Metaphorical cognition; appeals to justice/responsibility	Global North/South states, UN institutions, NGOs

6. IMPLICATIONS FOR MULTILATERALISM AND INSTITUTIONAL LEGITIMACY

6.1. Narrative Control and Consensus-Building in Global Governance

Narrative diplomacy is central to the operations of multilateralism since global governance not only relies on negotiating the rules but on establishing common meaning. The international organizations like the United Nations, European Union, or regional organizations cannot operate without narratives that explain problems and a just action and convince different actors to agree to collective action. Framing threats to wring approval of its own policies is a central style, as Köhler (2019) points out, of justification through approval of the politicians, and in a multilateral environment of policy justification this style of framing has to appeal across different cultures and political systems. Narratives therefore serve as tools of control as they lead the way to interpreting the crises and determining how to act as a community.

The analysis of discourse has been able to depict the control of narrative in multilateral situations. As stated by Huckin, Andrus, and Clary-Lemon (2012), the ideology portrayed in discourse indicates that institutional writings and speeches incorporate the assumptions about legitimacy and authority. The same can be said regarding contradictions in discourse that occur when institutions simply pretend to be united with something going on in the background (Hodge, 2012). Narrative control in global governance balances perspectives, however, it should be coherent. The capacity to qualify one coherent narrative that may bring together disparate forces can ease the fostering of a consensus, whereas the inability to do so is likely to lead to the disintegration and stagnation.

Marschlich (2022) postulates that states are not the only actors to strive toward organizational legitimacy; multinational corporations also engage in organizational legitimacy quest through what the author refers to as corporate diplomacy. This understanding is being more pertinent since, the involvement of the multilateral governance is increasingly being found in the participation of the private actors. Other institutions with competing discourses are introduced by the corporations, non-governmental and civil society organizations. These narratives have to be reinforced or opposed. The task of consensus-building therefore lies beyond governments and institutions must operate in a multi-actor environment characterized by the distributed and manifestation of legitimacy.

Stories on solidarity, justice, and responsibility are of specific concern to consensus-building. As Lakoff (2004) reminds us, language creates social realities by determining how the social is perceived as either fair or inclusive. In the multilateral negotiations on climate change, the common but differentiated notion of responsibility has enabled the negotiating states of vastly different interests to find a common solution in form. Without such narrative frames, multilateral consensus would remain elusive. Langer (2023) shows how the construction of a geopolitical role through language helped the EU and the U.S. to become coherent in the approaches toward Venezuela, despite the fundamental differences in the reasons invested in it. These show that narrative control is a fundamental aspect of the operation of multilateral governance.

Table 4. Implications of Narrative Diplomacy for Multilateral Institutions

Dimension	Implication for Institutions
Narrative Control	Essential for framing crises and enabling consensus-building
Consensus-Building	Requires inclusive narratives balancing diverse perspectives
Credibility Diplomacy	Institutional legitimacy depends on consistent and authentic narratives
Algorithmic Mediation	AI-driven platforms reshape visibility and contestation of narratives
Resistance and Counter-Narratives	Institutions must engage with rather than suppress competing narratives
Future Adaptation	Narrative literacy and digital adaptation needed for legitimacy

The narrative credibility of multilateral institutions displays itself in the digital age when formal authority is not enough to establish the legitimacy of the institutions. According to Jones and Collins (2006), ideology tends to be encoded in communication and institutions have a continual need to prove that what they are saying is not a mere rhetoric. Narrative credibility comes in when viewers believe there has to be some sense of continuity, genuineness, and equity in institutional messaging. In the virtual space, however, where information is distributed based on AI, such credibility has become very difficult.

Increasingly, I technologies make the scope and instability of institutional discourses greater. The algorithmic mediation presented by Sahmeni and Afifah (2019) in their analysis of media discourse can either reveal or modulate the intended meaning of the messages. Institutions that previously dictated their channels of communication do so in an environment where their stories will be refiltered, recontextualized and questioned in real-time across digital platforms. Rho Yoonsup, Adilla, Sutjiatmi and Afrizal (2023) also underline the importance of media-driven framing in political discourse, proving that it can be altered quite quickly due to the ways in which it is narrated and disseminated. In the case of multilateral institutions, credibility will depend not just on what the stories comprise, but also on the ability to withstand the digital media environment that is fractious at best.

Kazemian and Hashemi (2014) emphasize the role of rhetoric strategy in building credibility and analyse the specific examples of the speeches of Barack Obama that use the systemic functional linguistics to strengthen authority. In the same way, importation of rhetorical coherence into institutional speech at the UN or EU has to present legitimacy. However, as shown by Hart (2018), event-framing can have a strong implication on the process of assigning blame, thus, making institutional narratives instantly lose credibility when they appear to be unfair or partisan. This is echoed in the case of Israel as Khalidi (2014) discovers that Israeli policies present a certain picture of repression as represented in institutional discourse that undermines its viability in international forums. In the case of multilateral institutions, credibility stakes become inseparable with the resonance of narratives with contested global publics.

In this context, storytelling legitimacy is one type of the soft power of institutions. Irimiea (2017) views professional discourse as a social practice and points out that legitimacy is achieved in the course of the everyday interactions. In the case of such institutions as the UN legitimacy is not a virtual quality but an outcome of a certain uniformity in the performance of narrative: speeches, resolutions, symbolic acts that all build authority. Knoblock (2020) shows how different actors were given legitimacy based on discourses of Ukrainian crisis with key role being played by the institutions in structuring the parameters of debate. Otherwise, institutions attempt to regain their anchoring as arbiters of international order that has lost out on narrative credibility.

7. CONCLUSION

The discussion of the narrative diplomacy in the context of the current international venues shows that storytelling has not only become an additional tool to diplomacy but one of the practices of this profession. In the era of the digital transformation and artificial intelligence, narratives act as a glue between power, legitimacy, and global governance. They justify acts, generate popular concern, build coalitions, and put questions in a possible crisis formulation. Yet, they are also the loci of contest and the arena where power is disputed and contrary stagings unfold in such a way that they shift the discourse. The conclusions made on the basis of this work draw both opportunities of narrative diplomacy in an AI-driven world and the challenges of this type of diplomacy.

As the exploration of the phenomena of narrative diplomacy is completed, several key findings can be mentioned. First, stories have changed with the change in technology with the digital world and those enhanced with AI replacing the traditional diplomatic communication scenarios. Not only has it increased the pace of storytelling, it has also diversified the reach of the actors. Every now person governments, international organizations, corporations, civil society, and even other individuals can now take part in the construction of diplomatic discourse. Consequently, narrative diplomacy is now more pluralistic than ever before in addition to becoming more fragmented and explosive.

Second, narratives are created, disputed and redefined continuously. The process story revealed that legitimacy can never be absolute but can only be supported by means of adaptation. The success in the narrative diplomacy does not actually rely on the initial construction of a convincing narration but rather on the capacity to handle contestation and reacts against counter-narrations. This fact comprises a necessity of principle in dynamic nature of narrative power in world politics.

Third, narrative diplomacy is thematically diverse as seen by case studies of the Munich Security Conference, Raisina Dialogue and United Nations General Assembly. Ensuring security is central to the transatlantic discourse, technology sovereignty is critical in Asia, and justice on climate change is on centre stage of the multilateral body. In all these examples, however disparate, legitimacy stands out as the key concept: the narratives that strike their particular chords are those which can be explained as advancing interests within a perceived system which itself has consistency with more general values, be that justice or solidarity or responsibility. Where narratives fall short in this alignment, this may spell doom in the form of rejection or delegitimization.

Fourth, using artificial intelligence in narrative diplomacy can be vast. In reinventing I reshapes not only the processes of production of narratives but also the processes of circulation and reception of the narratives. Algorithmic platforms amplify certain discourses while marginalizing others. Narratives can also be micro-targeted and constantly calibrated owing to data analytics. The availability of sentiment tracking allows for real-time loops during diplomacy, which can be more responsive but also more dangerous at the same time. These dynamics indicate that AI is not a technology that is external to international communication anymore but is an internal mediator of international communication.

Finally, the implications for institutions are clear. Multilateral organisations should understand that their mandate is increasingly based on their narrative legitimacy. A successful global governance does not just rely on the existence of agreements and regulations but on compelling narratives, which can harmonize the actors. Institutions that are unable to adjust to the narrative environment will become obsolete whereas those innovative with their narrative practices will be at the centre of the international order.

Theoretically, the chapter adds and enhances the knowledge on diplomacy as discursive and performative practice. By combining the knowledge in the fields of international relations, media studies, and AI ethics, it proves that narrative power is a very important aspect of soft power and legitimacy. Narratives are not secondary but central to global politics because they help structure perceptions and indeed establish the patterns of multilateral rule. The theoretical framework of legitimacy, identity, and framing designed below can be seen as a way of analysing how the narratives work in a practical sense.

To exercise, the conclusions are of the significance of narrative literacy by the diplomats and the communicators. As we have seen, storytelling has become a centric competency in international relations. Diplomats have to be capable of creating coherent discourses, predict counter-discourses, and recontextualise messages to respond to counter-discursive as well as counter-narrative measures. They also need to know the technologies within which the narratives navigate, such as social media algorithms and AI-based analytics. Narrative diplomacy in the present day relies not just upon the potential of rhetoric, but also technological savvy.

On a policy point of view, ethical governance of AI in diplomacy is needed as highlighted in the analysis. Although AI makes available a useful tool of amplification and streamlining of stories, there are dangers of encoding and compromise, as well as exclusion. Policy designers need to develop rules that bring a sense of transparency, accountability, and fairness in the AI-mediated communications. The institutional-level policy responses must lead to inclusivity in the narrative building process, whereby lack of representation of small states and those underrepresented should not be imposed by technologically skewed discourse landscape. Narrative equity is threatening to take after resource equity in global governance.

The future means that active adaptation will be needed by those practicing narrative diplomacy. To diplomats, the need to hone the skill of adaptive storytelling would be a priority. This is not only the training of set-piece oratory but the perfection of methods of immediate response to contestation cycles as they have become characteristic of the digital age. The main attributes contributing to more credible narrative are flexibility, coherence, and authenticity. Diplomats also have to adopt the use of multi-channel communications, and make sure their story is coordinated, regardless of the mediums of communications (speeches, social media, informal encounters).

In the case of communicators especially those working in the areas of governments and international organizations, we should focus on narrative coherence and resonance. The communicators should also learn to communicate complex policies in the most appealing narratives that will get the attention of different people. They should also observe and evaluate the reception of narratives with data analytics to not only use the tool to ensure optimization factors but also as a type of diagnostic to assess legitimacy. The strategies used should be underpinned by effectiveness of communication transparency in order to prevent the sense of manipulation that has been associated with the mistrust to AI-elevated messages.

The burden of these international organisers of forums such as the Munich Security Conference, Raisina Dialogue and the United Nations General Assembly is to cue up an environment in which these narratives can be realised, engaged and integrated in a positive way. Organizers need to bear in mind that, forums are not only negotiating halls but storytelling. The inclusion of the diverse voices, including digital participation, and fair representation of different views will increase the legitimacy of such platforms. The potential organizers should also invest in the technologies that can help provide the dialogue environment on the one hand and withstand the manipulation on the other.

Another recommendation is the creation of narratives resilience interventions. Institutions make plans against cyber-threats, military crises, and must make plans against narrative-crises, when their legitimacy is threatened by disinformation, or counter-narratives, or when they fail to communicate effectively. The development of resilience entails the growth of trust and varied lines of communication and incorporation of narratives into larger systems of credibility. Institutions and states who prepare in anticipation of narrative disruptions are also likely to be in a better position of maintaining legitimacy in challenging landscapes.

This figure provides a vision of future of the narrative diplomacy based on a roadmap that might dictate future tendencies of this type of diplomacy. It highlights three major branches. The first branch, Technological Transformation, has such evolutions as generative AI, immersive digital diplomacy, and predictive analytics that will open up the spaces of narrative world-creation and distribution. The second branch Global Governance is devoted to institutional adaptation revealing how multilateral institutions need to improve on the credibility of the narrative they provide, build less exclusive communication, and overcome issues of power symmetry in digital participation. The third category is Ethical Challenges, which points out the danger of manipulation, bias, and marginality, and therefore the necessity of rules on transparency, accountability, and fairness. The branches are connected via arrows, to indicate that they are interdependent, with technological change therefore having effects on the other levels and vice versa. The figure emphasizes that narrative diplomacy of the future will not follow one trajectory but the interaction of these moving dimensions.

Lastly, the practitioners should also become pro-active and be able to be ahead of the developments in terms of anticipating the directions that narrative diplomacy take. With the further evolution of AI technologies, the possibilities of narrative mediation will be extended, to such methods as generative content and immersive virtual diplomacy. Preparing for these changes requires both innovation and caution. Practitioners will need to embrace the possibilities of technology as long as their integrity does not interfere with the legitimacy of tradition (authenticity), equity (fairness), and inclusiveness (inclusivity), which are deemed to be hallmarks of legitimate diplomacy.

REFERENCES

Akman, M. K. (2024). Secret Diplomacy and Information Rights: interdisciplinary analyses through strategic intelligence, public relations and international security.

Aoi, C. (2024). The Indo-Pacific, Geopolitics, and Strategic Communications: Construction of 'the Indo-Pacific'. *Defence Strategic Communications*, *14*(14), 26–67.

Arceneaux, P. (2024). Value creation through organizational storytelling: Strategic narratives in foreign government public relations. *Public Relations Review*, *50*(2), 102433. DOI: 10.1016/j.pubrev.2024.102433

Basu, A., & Nachiappan, K. (2023). Will India Negotiate?. Hybridity, Conflict, and the Global Politics of Cybersecurity, 189.

Brovina, N., Gashi, B., & Kabashi, D. (2024). The Impact of Digital Diplomacy On National Security: Navigating The Positive and Negative Aspects.

Charles, J. (2024). Rethinking diplomacy: how small states can leverage new media for the conduct of diplomacy in the digital age (Master's thesis, University of Malta).

Chong, D., & Druckman, J. (2007). A theory of framing and opinion formation in competitive elite environments. *Journal of Communication*, *57*(1), 99–118. DOI: 10.1111/j.1460-2466.2006.00331.x

Clementson, D. E. (2020). Narrative persuasion, identification, attitudes, and trustworthiness in crisis communication. *Public Relations Review*, *46*(2), 101889. DOI: 10.1016/j.pubrev.2020.101889

Cook, F. (2007). It's a small world after all: Multiculturalism, authenticity, connectedness among trends to watch in next 50 years. *The Public Relations Strategist*, *13*(1), 30–33.

Devanny, J. (2024). Artificial Intelligence and Cyber Power.

Fasinu, E. S., Olaniyan, B. J. T., & Afolaranmi, A. O. (2024). Digital Diplomacy in the Age of Social Media: Challenges and Opportunities for Crisis Communication. *African Journal of Social Sciences and Humanities Research*, *7*(3), 24–38. DOI: 10.52589/AJSSHR-0TOOED5F

Gombar, M. (2025). Algorithmic Manipulation and Information Science: Media Theories and Cognitive Warfare in Strategic Communication. *European Journal of Communication and Media Studies*, *4*(2), 1–11. DOI: 10.24018/ejmedia.2025.4.2.41

Gray, J., & Baturo, A. (2021). Delegating diplomacy: Rhetoric across agents in the United Nations General Assembly. *International Review of Administrative Sciences, 87*(4), 718–736. DOI: 10.1177/0020852321997560

Hansson, S., Madisson, M. L., & Ventsel, A. (2023). Discourses of blame in strategic narratives: The case of Russia's 5G stories. *European Security, 32*(1), 62–84. DOI: 10.1080/09662839.2022.2057188

Hart, C. (2018). Event-frames affect blame assignment and perception of aggression in discourse on political protests: An experimental case study in critical discourse analysis. *Applied Linguistics, 39*(3), 400–421.

Hobbs, M., Li, M., Huang, Z. A., & Desmoulins, L. (2025). Storytelling and grand strategy in public diplomacy: A case study of the speeches of president Xi Jinping. *Public Relations Review, 51*(4), 102594. DOI: 10.1016/j.pubrev.2025.102594

Hodge, B. (2012). Ideology, identity, interaction: Contradictions and challenges for critical discourse analysis. Critical Approaches to Discourse Analysis across Disciplines, 5(2).

Huckin, T., Andrus, J., & Clary-Lemon, J. (2012). Critical discourse analysis and rhetoric and composition. College Composition & Communication, 64(Special Issue: Research Methodologies), 107-129.

Irimiea, S. B. (2017). Professional discourse as social practice. *European Journal of Interdisciplinary Studies, 3*(4), 108–119. DOI: 10.26417/ejis.v9i1.p108-119

Johnson, J. (2023). *AI and the bomb: Nuclear strategy and risk in the digital age.* Oxford University Press. DOI: 10.1093/oso/9780192858184.001.0001

Jones, P. E., & Collins, C. (2006). Political analysis versus critical discourse analysis in the treatment of ideology: Some implications for the study of communication. *Atlantic Journal of Communication, 14*(1-2), 28–50. DOI: 10.1080/15456870.2006.9644768

Kadyan, P., & Singh, R. (2025). Smart HRM: Unleashing the Power of Business Intelligence for Workforce Excellence. In Harnessing Business Intelligence for Modern Talent Management (pp. 275-308). IGI Global Scientific Publishing.

Kazemian, B., & Hashemi, S. (2014). Critical discourse analysis of Barack Obama's 2012 speeches: Views from systemic functional linguistics and rhetoric. [TPLS]. *Theory and Practice in Language Studies, 4*(6), 1178–1187. DOI: 10.4304/tpls.4.6.1178-1187

Khalidi, R. I. (2014). From the editor: Israel: A carceral state. Journal of Palestine Studies, 43(4), 5-10.

Knoblock, N. (Ed.). (2020). *Language of conflict: Discourses of the Ukrainian crisis*. Bloomsbury Publishing. DOI: 10.5040/9781350098633

Köhler, I. (2019). *Framing the threat: How politicians justify their policies*. Walter de Gruyter GmbH & Co KG. DOI: 10.1515/9783110626056

Lakoff, R. T. (2004). *Language and woman's place: Text and commentaries* (Vol. 3). Oxford University Press.

Langer, A. (2023). Geopolitical role construction through language: A critical discourse analysis of EU and US policy statements towards Venezuela (2017-2019).

Latif, M. A., Rooh, S., Malik, M. F., & Samad, A. (2025). Digital Diplomacy and Disinformation: Reshaping Global Public Opinion. [DSSR]. *Dialogue Social Science Review, 3*(5), 150–169.

Lisenco, V. (2025). Digital diplomacy for peace: A new frontier in international relations. Revista Moldovenească de Drept Internaţional şi Relaţii Internaţionale, (1), 39-52.

Longhini, A., & Zimmerman, E. (2021). Regional security dialogues in Europe and in Asia: The role of Track 1.5 forums in the practice of international security. *European Journal of International Security*, *6*(4), 481–502. DOI: 10.1017/eis.2021.14

Manfredi-Sánchez, J. L., & Smith, N. R. (2023). Public diplomacy in an age of perpetual crisis: Assessing the EU's strategic narratives through six crises. *Journal of Communication Management (London)*, *27*(2), 241–258. DOI: 10.1108/JCOM-04-2022-0037

Mao, R., Zhang, T., Liu, Q., Hussain, A., & Cambria, E. (2024). Unveiling diplomatic narratives: Analyzing United Nations Security Council debates through metaphorical cognition. In *Proceedings of the Annual Meeting of the Cognitive Science Society* (Vol. 46).

Marschlich, S. (2022). *Corporate diplomacy: How multinational corporations gain organizational legitimacy: A neo-institutional public relations perspective*. Springer Nature. DOI: 10.1007/978-3-658-36818-0

Mirza, S. J., Shah, E. A., Tamour, F. A., Hussain, H., & Khan, M. B. (2025). The Role of Social Media Analytic in Crafting International Political Narrative. *The Critical Review of Social Sciences Studies*, *3*(2), 2456–2468. DOI: 10.59075/gft9jn19

Mitić, A. (2024). Global Strategic Narrative Wars: The Battle for Serbia.

Moral, P. (2023). Restoring reputation through digital diplomacy: the European Union's strategic narratives on Twitter during the COVID-19 pandemic.

Proto, L., Lamoso-González, P., & García, L. B. (2025). The EU's FIMI Turn: How the European Union External Action Service Reframed the Disinformation Fight. *Media and Communication*, *13*, 13. DOI: 10.17645/mac.9474

Sahmeni, E., & Afifah, N. (2019). Using critical discourse analysis (CDA) in media discourse studies: Unmask the mass media. REiLA. *Journal of Research and Innovation in Language*, *1*(2), 39–45. DOI: 10.31849/reila.v1i2.2764

Saliu, H. (2023). Narratives of public diplomacy in the post-truth era: The decline of soft power. *Communicatio Socialis.*

Snow, N. (2023, February). A Reliable Friend and Strategic Partner in the Indo-Pacific Region: Japan's Strategic Communications and Public Diplomacy. In William & Mary Global Research Institute/Gates Forum Paper.

Spry, D., & Lockyer, K. (2022). Large data and small stories: A triangulation approach to evaluating digital diplomacy. *Place Branding and Public Diplomacy*, *18*(3), 272–286. DOI: 10.1057/s41254-021-00248-w

Tran, E. (2024). Twitter, public diplomacy and social power in soft-balancing China–France relations. *Journal of Contemporary China*, *33*(146), 267–294. DOI: 10.1080/10670564.2023.2193150

ul Haq, S. (2025). Russia's Digital Diplomacy and Cyber Governance: Strategic Narratives, Hybrid Tactics, and Global Implications (2000 2025). ASSAJ, 3(02), 1287-1302.

Ünver, A. (2023). *The role of technology: new methods of information manipulation and disinformation*. ResearchGate.

Ventura, S. (2025). War and its imagery: The visual narrative of the Ukrainian state's Instagram account Ukraine. Ua as a tool of digital public diplomacy. *International Journal of Strategic Communication*, *19*(3), 379–403. DOI: 10.1080/1553118X.2024.2395407

White, C. L. (2015). Exploring the role of private-sector corporations in public diplomacy. *Public Relations Inquiry*, *4*(3), 305–321. DOI: 10.1177/2046147X15614883

Wike, R., Fetterlof, J., & Mordecai, M. (2020, November 15). U.S. image plummets international as most say country has handled coronavirus badly. Pew Research Center.

Xin, J., & Matheson, D. (2018). One Belt, competing metaphors: The struggle over strategic narrative in English-language news media. *International Journal of Communication*, *12*(1), 4248–4268.

Zhou, A., & van der Meer, T. G. (2024). Computational strategic communication in a data-driven world. *Public Relations Review*, *50*(102496), 102496. DOI: 10.1016/j.pubrev.2024.102496

Chapter 5

AI in Media Framing, Public Diplomacy, and Diplomatic Influence

Geetali Tilak
https://orcid.org/0000-0002-1933-6159
Tilak Maharashtra Vidyapeeth, India

P. Selvakumar
https://orcid.org/0000-0002-3650-4548
Department of Science and Humanities, Nehru Institute of Technology, Coimbatore, India

T. C. Manjunath
https://orcid.org/0000-0003-2545-9160
Rajarajeswari College of Engineering, India

Datla Ganesh
CVR College of Engineering, India

S. Pougajendy
https://orcid.org/0009-0002-6988-7343
Sri Manakula Vinayagar Engineering College, India

Mallikarjuna Badiger
https://orcid.org/0009-0004-0192-304X
Dayananda Sagar Business Academy, India

ABSTRACT

In the rapidly evolving digital age, Artificial Intelligence (AI) has emerged as a transformative force across numerous sectors, profoundly reshaping how information is created, disseminated, and interpreted. Among the most impacted domains are media and diplomacy, two fields historically reliant on human judgment, nuanced communication, and complex decision-making. AI's integration into media and diplomacy is no longer a futuristic concept but an unfolding reality, presenting unprecedented opportunities while simultaneously surfacing significant challenges. The rise of AI technologies—from machine learning algorithms and natural language processing (NLP) systems to advanced data analytics and autonomous agents—has

DOI: 10.4018/979-8-3373-4937-4.ch005

revolutionized traditional processes, enabling new modes of interaction, insight generation, and influence. In the realm of media, AI is redefining the landscape of journalism, content creation, and audience engagement.

1. INTRODUCTION

In the rapidly evolving digital age, Artificial Intelligence (AI) has emerged as a transformative force across numerous sectors, profoundly reshaping how information is created, disseminated, and interpreted. Among the most impacted domains are media and diplomacy, two fields historically reliant on human judgment, nuanced communication, and complex decision-making. AI's integration into media and diplomacy is no longer a futuristic concept but an unfolding reality, presenting unprecedented opportunities while simultaneously surfacing significant challenges. The rise of AI technologies, from machine learning algorithms and natural language processing (NLP) systems to advanced data analytics and autonomous agents, has revolutionized traditional processes, enabling new modes of interaction, insight generation, and influence. In the realm of media, AI is redefining the landscape of journalism, content creation, and audience engagement. Automated content generation, personalized news feeds, real-time sentiment analysis, and sophisticated fact-checking tools have begun to transform the way media organizations operate. AI-powered algorithms now curate personalized information streams tailored to individual preferences, increasing user engagement but also raising questions about echo chambers and misinformation. The ability of AI to analyse vast datasets allows media outlets to identify trending topics, predict audience behaviour, and optimize distribution strategies with a precision previously unattainable. However, this technological advancement is a double-edged sword. While AI can enhance efficiency and democratize access to information, it also poses risks such as the proliferation of deepfakes, synthetic media, and algorithm-driven bias, which can undermine public trust and distort democratic discourse.

Diplomacy, a field traditionally characterized by human negotiation, cultural sensitivity, and strategic communication, is also undergoing a paradigm shift with the incorporation of AI. Governments and international organizations increasingly deploy AI tools to process massive quantities of geopolitical data, monitor global events in real-time, and simulate diplomatic scenarios. AI facilitates improved decision-making by offering predictive analytics that can assess the potential outcomes of diplomatic initiatives or conflicts. Additionally, AI-powered translation and communication tools help overcome language barriers, fostering more inclusive and effective dialogue among diverse actors on the international stage. The application of AI in cyber diplomacy and security further highlights its critical role in protecting national interests and maintaining global stability in an interconnected world. Yet, the use of AI in diplomacy introduces ethical dilemmas and strategic uncertainties. The opacity of AI decision-making processes, potential manipulation by malicious actors, and the risk of escalating conflicts through autonomous systems challenge existing diplomatic norms and frameworks. The confluence of AI, media, and diplomacy reflects broader societal transformations driven by digital technologies, making it imperative to carefully examine both the opportunities and challenges posed by AI. On one hand, AI enhances the speed, accuracy, and reach of communication, enabling media outlets and diplomats to respond swiftly to emerging issues, engage with diverse populations, and shape public opinion or international policies more effectively. On the other hand, the integration of AI raises critical questions about accountability, transparency, and ethical governance. These questions underscore the complex interplay between technology, society, and governance in the age of AI.

1.1. Media Framing and Public Diplomacy: Understanding the Role of AI

In the rapidly evolving digital age, Artificial Intelligence (AI) has emerged as a transformative force across numerous sectors, profoundly reshaping how information is created, disseminated, and interpreted. Among the most impacted domains are media and diplomacy, two fields historically reliant on human judgment, nuanced communication, and complex decision-making. (Atad E. et al, 2023) AI's integration into media and diplomacy is no longer a futuristic concept but an unfolding reality, presenting unprecedented opportunities while simultaneously surfacing significant challenges. The rise of AI technologies, from machine learning algorithms and natural language processing (NLP) systems to advanced data analytics and autonomous agents, has revolutionized traditional processes, enabling new modes of interaction, insight generation, and influence. In the realm of media, AI is redefining the landscape of journalism, content creation, and audience engagement. Automated content generation, personalized news feeds, real-time sentiment analysis, and sophisticated fact-checking tools have begun to transform the way media organizations operate. AI-powered algorithms now curate personalized information streams tailored to individual preferences, increasing user engagement but also raising questions about echo chambers and misinformation. (Atad et al, 2023) The ability of AI to analyse vast datasets allows media outlets to identify trending topics, predict audience behaviour, and optimize distribution strategies with a precision previously unattainable. However, this technological advancement is a double-edged sword. While AI can enhance efficiency and democratize access to information, it also poses risks such as the proliferation of deepfakes, synthetic media, and algorithm-driven bias, which can undermine public trust and distort democratic discourse.

Diplomacy, a field traditionally characterized by human negotiation, cultural sensitivity, and strategic communication, is also undergoing a paradigm shift with the incorporation of AI. Governments and international organizations increasingly deploy AI tools to process massive quantities of geopolitical data, monitor global events in real-time, and simulate diplomatic scenarios. (Bano et al, 2023) AI facilitates improved decision-making by offering predictive analytics that can assess the potential outcomes of diplomatic initiatives or conflicts. Additionally, AI-powered translation and communication tools help overcome language barriers, fostering more inclusive and effective dialogue among diverse actors on the international stage. The application of AI in cyber diplomacy and security further highlights its critical role in protecting national interests and maintaining global stability in an interconnected world. Yet, the use of AI in diplomacy introduces ethical dilemmas and strategic uncertainties. The opacity of AI decision-making processes, potential manipulation by malicious actors, and the risk of escalating conflicts through autonomous systems challenge existing diplomatic norms and frameworks. The confluence of AI, media, and diplomacy reflects broader societal transformations driven by digital technologies, making it imperative to carefully examine both the opportunities and challenges posed by AI. On one hand, AI enhances the speed, accuracy, and reach of communication, enabling media outlets and diplomats to respond swiftly to emerging issues, engage with diverse populations, and shape public opinion or international policies more effectively. On the other hand, the integration of AI raises critical questions about accountability, transparency, and ethical governance. (Bano et al, 2023) Who is responsible when AI systems propagate misinformation or make erroneous predictions influencing diplomatic decisions? How can the media ensure fair representation and avoid reinforcing biases embedded in AI algorithms? How do diplomats adapt to AI's disruptive potential while preserving human-centric negotiation and empathy? These questions underscore the complex interplay between technology, society, and governance in the age of AI.

1.2. Diplomatic Influence in the Digital Age

Media framing is a pivotal concept in communication studies, referring to the way media sources select, emphasize, and present particular aspects of events, issues, or actors to shape public perception and discourse. It is the process by which the media organizes reality into meaningful narratives by highlighting certain elements while omitting or downplaying others, thereby influencing how audiences interpret and respond to information. In the context of public diplomacy, the strategic use of communication by states or non-state actors to influence foreign publics and foster mutual understanding, media framing becomes an essential mechanism for shaping international images, building narratives, and advancing diplomatic objectives. (Chernobrov, 2022) With the advent of Artificial Intelligence (AI), the traditional dynamics of media framing and public diplomacy are undergoing profound changes, offering new opportunities for strategic communication while also posing complex challenges regarding control, authenticity, and influence. At its core, media framing functions by constructing interpretive frameworks that guide audience cognition and emotional response. Frames can shape the public's understanding by attributing causes and consequences, assigning responsibility, and suggesting appropriate solutions or reactions. For example, coverage of a conflict might be framed through lenses such as human rights violations, national security, or economic interests, each generating different implications and policy support. Public diplomacy actors rely on framing to craft narratives that resonate with target audiences abroad, promoting positive images of their country, values, and policies. The framing of issues like climate change, migration, or geopolitical conflicts in international media can significantly affect public opinion and diplomatic relations. (Chernobrov, 2022) Traditional media gatekeepers, editors, journalists, broadcasters, have historically held the power to determine dominant frames through editorial decisions, narrative choices, and agenda-setting.

AI technologies, however, are fundamentally reshaping how media framing operates in the contemporary communication ecosystem. Automated content generation, natural language processing, sentiment analysis, and machine learning algorithms enable unprecedented scale, speed, and precision in framing media narratives. AI tools can analyse massive volumes of news, social media posts, and public discourse in real-time to detect dominant frames, emerging trends, and audience sentiment across different cultural and linguistic contexts. This empowers public diplomacy practitioners to tailor their messaging with granular accuracy, adapting frames to maximize resonance and influence. AI-driven personalization can deliver customized narratives to specific demographic segments, enhancing engagement and persuasive power. Moreover, (Chib et al, 2025) AI algorithms embedded in social media platforms and search engines play a crucial role in reinforcing or altering media frames by controlling what content users see, effectively shaping collective perceptions on a global scale. This rise of AI-powered media framing offers significant strategic advantages in public diplomacy. Governments and diplomatic actors can employ AI to monitor international media landscapes for frame shifts, detect misinformation campaigns, and respond swiftly to crises with targeted messaging. AI facilitates scenario modelling and predictive analytics, helping diplomats anticipate how different frames might influence foreign publics and diplomatic outcomes. Additionally, AI's capacity to generate synthetic media, such as automated video summaries or chatbot dialogues, introduces novel avenues for immersive storytelling and interactive diplomacy. Such technologies allow for more dynamic, culturally sensitive, and multilingual public diplomacy campaigns that can penetrate diverse information environments and counter hostile narratives. (Chib et al, 2025) The ability to harness AI for framing thus represents a potent tool for advancing national interests, fostering dialogue, and building soft power in an increasingly interconnected world.

1.3. AI-Generated Content

The concept of diplomatic influence has undergone a profound transformation in the digital age, propelled by the rapid advancement and integration of Artificial Intelligence (AI) technologies. (Dahiya et al, 2025) Traditionally, diplomatic influence was exercised through formal negotiations, statecraft, cultural exchanges, and carefully crafted messaging mediated by human diplomats operating within established channels. However, the emergence of digital communication platforms, big data analytics, and AI-powered tools has fundamentally altered the mechanisms and scale through which states and non-state actors exert influence on the global stage. AI, in particular, stands out as a pivotal force reshaping the nature of diplomatic influence by augmenting capabilities in information gathering, strategic communication, decision-making, and crisis management, while also introducing new complexities that challenge conventional diplomatic paradigms. Diplomatic influence in the digital era is increasingly defined by the ability to control narratives, shape perceptions, and mobilize public opinion across vast and diverse audiences. (Dahiya et al, 2025) AI technologies enable unprecedented extraction, analysis, and synthesis of information from enormous datasets, social media streams, and digital communications, allowing diplomats to gain real-time insights into global public sentiment, political trends, and emerging risks. Machine learning algorithms can identify patterns that human analysts might miss, offering predictive capabilities to anticipate geopolitical shifts and craft proactive diplomatic strategies. This enhanced situational awareness empowers states to fine-tune their foreign policy messaging, tailor public diplomacy initiatives, and engage more effectively with foreign publics and key stakeholders. The integration of AI into diplomatic practice thus amplifies influence by enabling more informed, agile, and data-driven decision-making.

Moreover, AI facilitates the automation and personalization of communication at scale, revolutionizing how diplomatic messages are disseminated and received. Through natural language processing, chatbots, and AI-driven content generation, diplomatic missions can engage with global audiences in multiple languages, cultural contexts, and formats, fostering deeper connections and understanding. (Fasinu et al, 2024) Personalized digital campaigns powered by AI allow for targeted outreach that resonates with specific demographic groups, increasing the effectiveness of public diplomacy efforts. AI also enhances cyber diplomacy capabilities by providing advanced tools for monitoring and countering disinformation, protecting critical infrastructure, and managing digital security risks that could undermine diplomatic credibility and influence. The ability to deploy AI in both offensive and defensive diplomatic operations marks a new frontier in international relations, where information dominance becomes a critical form of power projection. However, the impact of AI on diplomatic influence is accompanied by significant challenges and ethical considerations. One fundamental concern is the potential erosion of human judgment and diplomatic intuition as AI systems assume greater roles in analysing complex situations and recommending courses of action. AI's reliance on data quality and algorithmic design raises questions about biases, transparency, and accountability in diplomatic decision-making. There is a risk that overreliance on AI could lead to misinterpretations or escalations, especially in high-stakes situations where nuanced cultural and political understanding is crucial. Furthermore, the proliferation of AI-generated misinformation, deepfakes, and cyber influence operations complicates the information environment, making it more difficult for diplomats to maintain credible narratives and build trust with foreign publics. (Fasinu et al, 2024) These challenges necessitate the development of robust governance frameworks and ethical guidelines to ensure that AI enhances rather than undermines diplomatic integrity and global stability.

1.4. The Role of AI in News Production

The advent of Artificial Intelligence (AI)-generated content represents one of the most profound shifts in the media landscape, fundamentally transforming the way information is produced, framed, and consumed. AI-generated content, ranging from text, images, audio, to video, employs sophisticated algorithms such as natural language processing (NLP), generative adversarial networks (GANs), and deep learning to autonomously create media material with minimal human intervention. (Ingenhoff & Chariatte, 2025) As AI content generation matures, it increasingly influences media framing by shaping narratives, controlling the flow of information, and constructing realities that engage or manipulate audiences at scale. This new paradigm presents both exciting opportunities for innovation and significant challenges concerning authenticity, ethics, and the nature of truth in public discourse. Media framing, the process by which information is organized and presented to shape perception, has traditionally been controlled by human editors, journalists, and content creators who decide which facts to highlight, which voices to amplify, and which contexts to provide. AI-generated content disrupts this dynamic by enabling the automated creation and distribution of framed narratives at speeds and volumes previously unimaginable. (Ingenhoff & Chariatte, 2025) News articles, social media posts, editorial summaries, and even opinion pieces can now be generated algorithmically, often tailored to specific audience preferences, languages, or cultural contexts. For example, AI-powered systems can generate personalized news feeds that adapt the framing of stories to individual user profiles, emphasizing certain aspects while downplaying others to maximize engagement and emotional impact. This capability significantly amplifies the reach and influence of particular frames, making AI a powerful tool in shaping public opinion and discourse.

One of the key advantages of AI-generated content in media framing is its ability to enhance efficiency and scalability in content production. News organizations and media outlets face constant pressure to deliver timely, relevant, and diverse content across multiple platforms. AI tools can automate routine reporting tasks, such as summarizing financial reports, sports results, or weather updates, freeing human journalists to focus on investigative and in-depth reporting. Beyond automation, AI can also assist in uncovering new frames by analysing vast datasets to identify emerging trends, public sentiments, and underreported perspectives. By integrating AI into editorial workflows, media organizations can experiment with innovative framing strategies that better resonate with their audiences while maintaining high content volume and velocity. (Jha & Kumar, 2023) This symbiosis of human creativity and AI efficiency promises to enrich media diversity and responsiveness in an increasingly competitive digital environment. However, the rise of AI-generated content also raises profound ethical and practical concerns regarding media framing. One of the foremost challenges is the potential erosion of authenticity and trust. AI-generated texts or images, especially those produced by generative models like GPT or GANs, can be indistinguishable from human-created content, leading to "deepfake" phenomena and synthetic narratives that can manipulate public perception. Malicious actors might exploit AI to craft disinformation campaigns, propaganda, or biased frames that serve specific ideological, political, or commercial interests, undermining the credibility of traditional media and democratic processes. The automation of framing risks amplifying existing biases encoded in training data or algorithms, perpetuating stereotypes or marginalizing minority voices unintentionally. (Jha & Kumar, 2023) Moreover, the opacity of AI decision-making processes makes it difficult to trace accountability for misleading or harmful content, complicating efforts to regulate and govern AI-generated media ethically.

2. SENTIMENT ANALYSIS: UNDERSTANDING PUBLIC OPINION THROUGH AI

Automated journalism, also known as algorithmic or robot journalism, represents a transformative development in the field of news production, driven by advances in artificial intelligence (AI), machine learning, and natural language generation (NLG). This technology enables the automatic generation of news content by computers with minimal or no human input, using data sets and predefined templates to produce coherent and often highly readable articles. (Ju et al, 2023) Initially applied to routine news coverage, such as sports scores, weather reports, financial earnings, and election results, automated journalism has since expanded in scope, application, and sophistication. As media organizations increasingly adopt AI tools to meet the growing demand for rapid, high-volume content production in a 24/7 digital media environment, automated journalism is reshaping editorial workflows, newsroom dynamics, and even the broader ethics and economics of journalism itself. One of the primary motivations behind the development and implementation of automated journalism is efficiency. Traditional journalism can be labour-intensive and time-consuming, especially when dealing with large volumes of repetitive or data-heavy stories. AI systems, by contrast, can instantly process raw data, such as statistics from a sports game or quarterly financial reports, and transform it into well-structured narratives at a scale and speed unattainable by human reporters. News agencies such as the Associated Press, Reuters, Bloomberg, and The Washington Post have embraced automated journalism to supplement their coverage. For instance, the Associated Press has used AI to expand its coverage of corporate earnings reports from a few hundred companies to thousands, dramatically increasing the breadth of reporting while freeing human journalists to focus on more in-depth and investigative stories. This shift demonstrates how AI can enhance newsroom productivity without necessarily replacing human journalists, provided the integration is done thoughtfully.

Beyond efficiency, AI offers consistency, scalability, and data accuracy. AI-generated content is often less prone to typographical errors or miscalculations, assuming the underlying data is reliable. Automated systems also ensure consistency in tone and format across multiple stories, which is particularly useful for outlets managing large volumes of similar content. Moreover, AI tools can operate across multiple languages, time zones, and platforms, making it possible to deliver real-time updates to diverse global audiences. This scalability is especially valuable in contexts such as live event coverage, crisis reporting, and local news reporting, where traditional resources may be limited (Ju et al, 2023). AI-powered systems can also generate updates in real time, offering news consumers immediate access to information as it becomes available, thus enhancing the relevance and timeliness of journalism in a fast-moving digital world. However, the growing role of AI in news production is not without its challenges, particularly concerning journalistic quality, ethics, and accountability. One of the key concerns is the potential erosion of editorial judgment. Human journalists bring context, critical analysis, empathy, and ethical consideration to the news production process, qualities that AI, despite its sophistication, still lacks. While automated systems can produce fact-based reports, they struggle with complex narratives that require interpretation, cultural sensitivity, or investigative depth. This limitation means that AI-generated stories may miss nuances, oversimplify complex issues, or fail to consider the broader implications of the data they process. Additionally, there is the risk of unintentional bias in automated content, as AI systems learn from existing data and language corpora, which may reflect societal prejudices or unbalanced perspectives. Without rigorous oversight, such biases can be perpetuated and amplified, undermining journalistic integrity and public trust.

2.1. AI-Powered Engagement

Sentiment analysis, also known as opinion mining, is a powerful subfield of natural language processing (Kaur et al, 2025) (NLP) that uses Artificial Intelligence (AI) to identify, extract, and quantify subjective information in text data. By analysing language patterns, tone, and contextual cues, sentiment analysis algorithms are capable of determining the emotional valence, positive, negative, or neutral, of written or spoken content. In the digital age, where public discourse increasingly unfolds on online platforms such as social media, forums, news websites, and customer reviews, sentiment analysis has emerged as an indispensable tool for governments, businesses, media organizations, and (Kaur et al, 2025) researchers seeking to understand public opinion at scale. It provides a window into collective mood, attitudes, and reactions, offering actionable insights that inform decision-making, communication strategies, and policy development. As AI models become more advanced and context-aware, the scope and precision of sentiment analysis are expanding dramatically, reshaping how institutions engage with and respond to public sentiment in real time. At its core, sentiment analysis operates by parsing large volumes of text data, tweets, comments, articles, transcripts, etc., and applying machine learning or deep learning techniques to classify the sentiment expressed. This process often begins with text pre-processing, which includes tokenization, lemmatization, and removal of stop words to prepare raw text for analysis. Next, algorithms may use lexicon-based approaches (relying on dictionaries of known sentiment-laden words) or machine learning models trained on annotated datasets to identify sentiment patterns. More sophisticated techniques involve deep neural networks such as recurrent neural networks (RNNs), long short-term memory networks (LSTMs), and transformer-based models like BERT or GPT, which capture contextual relationships between words and better understand nuances such as sarcasm, ambiguity, or cultural idioms. The outputs typically assign sentiment scores or labels to text units, ranging from individual phrases to entire documents, allowing analysts to track sentiment trends over time, across regions, or among different demographic groups.

In the context of public opinion analysis, sentiment analysis serves as a critical bridge between raw textual data and meaningful sociopolitical insights. Governments and political institutions use AI-driven sentiment analysis to monitor citizen responses to policies, speeches, events, and crises. (Kommineni et al, 2025) By examining social media chatter or news commentary, they can detect approval, criticism, concerns, or polarization, which aids in adjusting public messaging, anticipating protests, or measuring the impact of political campaigns. Similarly, corporations use sentiment analysis for brand monitoring, product feedback, and reputation management, responding to consumer sentiment with greater agility and personalization. Media organizations, too, use sentiment analytics to assess audience engagement and understand how news coverage influences public attitudes. In academia and social research, sentiment analysis has become a cornerstone method for studying phenomena such as political polarization, cultural trends, misinformation, and public health behaviours. (Kommineni M. et al, 2025) One of the most transformative aspects of AI-driven sentiment analysis is its scalability and real-time responsiveness. Traditional public opinion polling is resource-intensive, time-bound, and often limited in scope or frequency. In contrast, AI enables continuous monitoring of vast, diverse, and unstructured data streams, producing sentiment insights almost instantaneously. (Li & Wake, 2024) For example, during a national election or a public health emergency, sentiment analysis can track the evolving mood of the population, identify regional variations, and highlight key topics of concern, all in real time. This dynamic capability empowers decision-makers to respond swiftly, deploy targeted interventions, and engage more effectively with the public. In diplomacy and international relations, sentiment analysis is increasingly used to gauge foreign public opinion toward a country's policies or actions, supporting strategic communication and soft power initiatives. (Li & Wake, 2024) By understanding how foreign populations perceive bilateral relations, global events, or cultural exchanges, diplomats can tailor their outreach and narrative framing to enhance international trust and cooperation.

2.2. Using AI to Track Public Opinion

In the evolving landscape of global communication, Artificial Intelligence (AI) has emerged as a transformative force in public diplomacy, fundamentally reshaping how states and diplomatic actors engage with foreign publics. AI-powered engagement refers to the use of machine learning, natural language processing (NLP), data analytics, and predictive modelling to enable more targeted, personalized, and interactive diplomatic outreach. (Limbore V. et al, 2025) Traditionally, public diplomacy, defined as the practice by which a country communicates with and influences foreign audiences, relied on cultural exchanges, broadcasting, and interpersonal relationships to build soft power and foster mutual understanding. Today, with the ubiquity of digital platforms and social media, and the proliferation of user-generated content, diplomats are turning to AI-driven technologies to effectively navigate and influence this complex, fast-paced, and data-rich information environment. At the core of AI-powered engagement is the ability to understand, segment, and interact with audiences at scale and in real time. AI enables the analysis of massive volumes of social media data, news content, blogs, comments, and other digital footprints to identify public sentiments, emerging narratives, and influential individuals or communities. By leveraging sentiment analysis, topic modelling, and network analysis, diplomats can map out the contours of public opinion in foreign societies, track shifts in attitudes, and identify moments of opportunity or crisis. (Limbore V. et al, 2025) This situational awareness allows diplomatic missions to tailor their communication strategies with unprecedented granularity, crafting messages that resonate with specific groups based on language, cultural context, interests, or emotional tone. Such targeted communication increases the relevance and effectiveness of public diplomacy campaigns, allowing states to foster goodwill, counter misinformation, and influence discourse in ways that are more subtle, strategic, and adaptive.

Figure 1. Corporate Diplomacy Strategy and Instruments

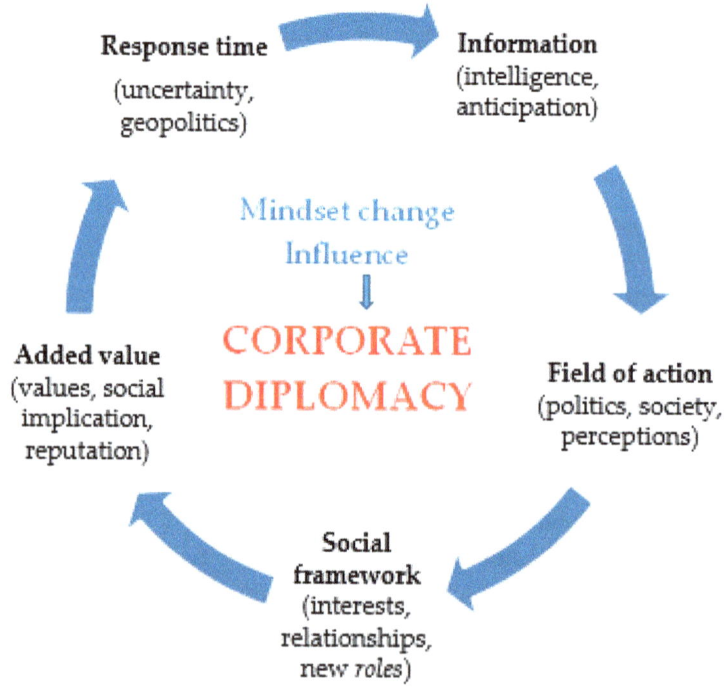

AI also enables two-way engagement by powering conversational agents, such as multilingual chatbots or virtual assistants, that allow diplomatic missions to interact with foreign publics in a more dynamic and responsive manner. These AI tools can answer questions about a country's policies, provide visa and travel information, facilitate cultural exchange opportunities, or even offer real-time translation services. By being available 24/7 and capable of operating across multiple platforms and languages, these systems significantly expand the reach and inclusivity of diplomatic communication. More importantly, they create interactive touchpoints that help demystify foreign cultures, build empathy, and reduce barriers to dialogue. (Manfredi-Sánchez et al, 2023) This level of engagement, powered by AI, reflects a shift from one-way broadcasting to participatory diplomacy, where mutual understanding is cultivated through continuous, responsive, and personalized interaction. Furthermore, AI enhances strategic decision-making in public diplomacy by offering predictive insights and performance analytics. Machine learning algorithms can analyse historical and real-time data to forecast public reactions to diplomatic initiatives, simulate the impact of different messaging strategies, or assess the effectiveness of past campaigns. For example, by analysing engagement metrics, such as likes, shares, comments, and sentiment, AI systems can determine which types of content are most effective in promoting a country's image or clarifying its foreign policy. These insights can guide future content creation, channel selection, and timing, making public diplomacy more evidence-based and goal-oriented. (Manfredi-Sánchez et al, 2023) Additionally, anomaly detection algorithms can identify sudden spikes in negative sentiment or misinformation, enabling proactive countermeasures before narratives spiral out of control. In this way, AI serves as both a radar and a compass, helping diplomats navigate complex communication environments and align their strategies with evolving public sentiment.

2.3. Leveraging AI to Understand Cultural Nuances

In the age of digital communication, social media has emerged as one of the most powerful platforms for public discourse, transforming how individuals express opinions, share experiences, and engage with political, cultural, and social issues. With billions of users generating content daily across platforms like Twitter (X), Facebook, Instagram, TikTok, Reddit, and YouTube, the sheer scale and velocity of online dialogue have made traditional methods of public opinion analysis insufficient. (Marschlich et al, 2022) Enter Artificial Intelligence (AI), a transformative force in the field of social media monitoring. AI-powered social media monitoring involves using advanced algorithms and machine learning models to collect, process, and analyse large-scale digital conversations in real time, allowing organizations to gain deep insights into the attitudes, behaviours, concerns, and emotional states of diverse populations. (Marschlich et al, 2022) Whether in the context of public diplomacy, marketing, crisis response, or political campaigns, AI-driven monitoring tools are now essential for interpreting the digital pulse of society. In practice, (Massa et al, 2024) AI-enhanced social media monitoring is used extensively across the public and private sectors to support decision-making and policy development. Similarly, (Massa et al, 2024) NGOs and civil society organizations leverage AI monitoring to detect grassroots mobilization, understand public engagement with advocacy issues, and inform outreach strategies. In the commercial world, businesses use social media intelligence for brand monitoring, customer sentiment analysis, product development, and crisis management. The ability to track real-time feedback empowers companies to be more responsive to customer needs and reputational risks, ensuring agility in a highly competitive market landscape.

3. PREDICTIVE ANALYTICS: FORECASTING DIPLOMATIC OUTCOMES

In an increasingly interconnected world, understanding and respecting cultural differences is not just an asset, it is a necessity. Cultural intelligence (CQ), defined as the capability to relate and work effectively across cultures, has become a critical skill for diplomats, multinational corporations, international organizations, and even automated systems that interact with global audiences. (Miskimmon et al, 2025) Traditionally cultivated through human experience, exposure, and education, cultural intelligence is now being enhanced by artificial intelligence (AI), which offers new opportunities to decode, interpret, and respond to cultural nuances at scale. AI-powered systems, integrating natural language processing (NLP), machine learning, computer vision, and sentiment analysis, are being developed to help machines and decision-makers better understand the subtleties of cultural behaviour, communication styles, values, symbols, and social norms across diverse regions and populations. This marriage of technology and cultural understanding is paving the way for more effective cross-cultural communication, diplomacy, marketing, (Miskimmon et al, 2025) content localization, and global strategy development. AI's capacity to process massive volumes of data makes it a powerful tool for recognizing cultural patterns and trends. Social media posts, blogs, online news, and multimedia content from around the world provide a real-time reflection of how different societies think, feel, and communicate. AI algorithms can analyse linguistic cues, emotional expressions, idiomatic phrases, and contextual references to detect cultural differences in attitudes, preferences, humour, taboos, and conflict resolution styles. For instance, what constitutes politeness, assertiveness, or irony can vary widely across cultures, and AI systems trained on localized data can be designed to account for these distinctions. In digital diplomacy or customer engagement platforms, such cultural sensitivity can mean the difference between forging trust or sparking misunderstanding. By leveraging cultural data sets and training AI models in region-specific communication norms, organizations can ensure their messaging resonates appropriately with diverse target audiences.

3.1. AI-Driven Decision-Making

In an era characterized by complex international relations, rapidly shifting geopolitical landscapes, and information overload, the application of predictive analytics in diplomacy is reshaping how policymakers anticipate and respond to global events. Predictive analytics, powered by artificial intelligence (AI), machine learning (ML), and big data, is the process of using historical data, real-time information, and statistical algorithms to forecast future trends, behaviours, or outcomes. In the realm of diplomacy, predictive analytics is increasingly being deployed to model diplomatic behaviour, assess conflict risks, (Pamment et al, 2025) forecast treaty viability, analyse negotiation dynamics, and anticipate the outcomes of international interventions. By transforming vast and unstructured data into actionable intelligence, predictive analytics enhances strategic foresight and enables more proactive, data-informed diplomacy. At its core, predictive analytics involves several key components: data collection, data processing, model building, and outcome prediction. Diplomatic data can take many forms, official records of past negotiations, economic indicators, media sentiment, social media trends, military movements, humanitarian data, travel patterns, cyber activity, and more. These data points, once aggregated, are analysed using AI and machine learning models that detect patterns, correlations, and anomalies. (Pamment et al, 2025) For instance, supervised learning models may be trained on historical data sets of successful and failed treaties to predict the likelihood of future diplomatic agreements succeeding under specific conditions. Natural language processing (NLP) can be used to analyse the tone and content of diplomatic communications, speeches, or social media posts by state officials, revealing shifts in attitude or strategy. Unsupervised learning models might cluster countries by behavioural similarities in voting at the United Nations or their response patterns in times of conflict, providing insight into emerging alliances or fault lines.

One of the most compelling uses of predictive analytics in diplomacy lies in conflict forecasting. By integrating satellite imagery, refugee flows, social media unrest indicators, economic volatility, and historical conflict data, AI systems can identify regions at high risk of escalation. These systems can forecast potential triggers, such as contested elections, water scarcity, ethnic polarization, or cross-border incursions, weeks or even months in advance. Organizations such as the United Nations, International Crisis Group, and governmental foreign ministries are increasingly using such tools to guide early warning systems and preventive diplomacy. (Pavón-Guinea et al, 2024). Diplomatic actors can use these insights to optimize their bargaining positions, adjust timelines, and prioritize agenda items. (Pavón-Guinea et al, 2024) For instance, if predictive models suggest that a proposed arms control treaty will fail due to an impending election in one of the participating states, negotiators might adjust their approach or delay key discussions. Similarly, predictive tools can be employed to assess the receptivity of foreign publics to diplomatic initiatives, such as cultural exchanges, trade agreements, or climate partnerships, by analysing sentiment trends across digital and traditional media.

3.2. Digital Diplomacy

The integration of artificial intelligence (AI) into the decision-making processes of modern diplomacy is ushering in a paradigm shift in how states and international organizations conduct foreign affairs. (Samal et al, 2025) As international relations become increasingly complex, shaped by global interdependence, technological acceleration, and data proliferation, AI-driven decision-making offers a powerful mechanism to enhance diplomatic effectiveness. By leveraging machine learning, data analytics, natural language processing (NLP), and decision support systems, diplomats and foreign policy strategists can analyse vast and multifaceted data streams, simulate scenarios, anticipate outcomes, and make more agile, evidence-based decisions. (Samal et al, 2025) Far from replacing human agency, AI is redefining the conditions under which diplomacy is practiced, bringing new speed, precision, and strategic depth to negotiations, policy formulation, crisis management, and public engagement. AI-driven decision-making in diplomacy begins with data, its collection, structuring, and interpretation. Modern diplomacy relies on processing massive amounts of information: from real-time news feeds, social media activity, and economic indicators to satellite imagery, classified intelligence, and diplomatic cables. Traditional human-led analysis, while valuable, is often overwhelmed by the volume, velocity, and variety of this information.

One significant advantage of AI-driven decision-making is its ability to enhance strategic foresight through scenario modelling and simulation. Machine learning models, trained on historical data and contextual variables, can simulate the likely outcomes of various policy options. (Song et al, 2023) For example, if a government is considering imposing economic sanctions on a state for human rights violations, AI can estimate the probable economic, political, and public opinion impacts both domestically and abroad. These predictive insights can help diplomats weigh the costs, benefits, and risks of alternative strategies. AI-based simulation platforms, often coupled with game-theoretical approaches, can also model the reactions of adversaries, allies, or neutral parties, enabling more comprehensive risk assessments and better anticipation of second- and third-order effects. This capacity is particularly crucial in time-sensitive or high-stakes situations such as nuclear negotiations, cyber incidents, or humanitarian crises. AI also enhances decision-making by supporting more targeted and responsive diplomatic engagement. Through advanced audience segmentation and sentiment analysis, (Song et al, 2023) AI tools can help tailor diplomatic messages to specific foreign publics, increasing their resonance and reducing the risk of cultural or political missteps. In public diplomacy, chatbots and conversational AI systems can engage with foreign citizens, answer policy questions, and clarify misinformation, operating around the clock and in multiple languages. AI can further aid in real-time crisis communication, providing up-to-date insights into how a diplomatic message is being received, which channels are most effective, and how narratives are evolving across platforms. This level of granularity allows foreign ministries and embassies to shift from broad, one-size-fits-all messaging to precise, adaptive communication strategies informed by live feedback.

4. CHALLENGES OF AI IN MEDIA AND DIPLOMACY

In the 21st century, diplomacy has undergone a profound transformation, evolving from a largely behind-the-scenes practice among elites to a dynamic, public-facing enterprise influenced by global connectivity and digital engagement. This evolution, commonly referred to as "digital diplomacy", reflects the increasing reliance of foreign ministries, international organizations, and diplomats on digital platforms to conduct foreign policy, shape narratives, and engage foreign publics directly. (Soundariya et al, 2025) As global audiences shift their attention from traditional media to social media, mobile platforms, and online communities, digital diplomacy has become a core element of soft power, information strategy, and reputation management. At the heart of this transformation lies artificial intelligence (AI), which plays a critical role in shaping, measuring, and responding to public opinion. AI enables diplomatic actors not only to monitor real-time sentiment across digital ecosystems but also to craft targeted messages, detect disinformation, and anticipate shifts in public mood, thereby enhancing both the reach and impact of their diplomatic efforts. Digital diplomacy, in its broadest sense, refers to the use of digital technologies, including social media, websites, virtual communication tools, and now AI, to support diplomatic functions such as public engagement, crisis communication, cultural exchange, and international negotiations. It allows states and institutions to bypass traditional gatekeepers like the press and engage audiences directly, whether through official Twitter accounts, Facebook pages, YouTube channels, or interactive campaigns. Digital diplomacy can be used to explain foreign policy decisions, promote national values, offer consular assistance, counter hostile narratives, or build cultural ties with foreign citizens. (Soundariya et al, 2025) However, as digital platforms have grown more complex and fragmented, and as information warfare and misinformation have proliferated, traditional communication strategies have proven insufficient. This is where AI steps in, offering scalable, real-time tools for data analysis, content generation, behaviour prediction, and audience engagement.

One of AI's most important contributions to digital diplomacy is in understanding and shaping public opinion. (Sreekanthaswamy et al, 2025) Through natural language processing (NLP), sentiment analysis, and machine learning algorithms, AI can process vast amounts of online content, tweets, posts, blogs, comments, forum discussions, and media articles, to gauge how the public perceives specific events, policies, or actors. This allows diplomats to track the digital pulse of foreign populations in real time and tailor their communication strategies accordingly. For example, if sentiment analysis reveals a rise in negative sentiment toward a country following a controversial military deployment, public diplomacy officials can craft messages aimed at clarification, reassurance, or soft power engagement. By recognizing not only the tone but also the themes and values underlying public opinion, AI tools help ensure diplomatic communication is more nuanced, timely, and culturally appropriate. AI also plays a central role in strategic content dissemination. (Sreekanthaswamy et al, 2025) Using predictive analytics and audience segmentation, AI can identify which groups are most likely to be receptive to specific diplomatic messages, and which platforms or influencers are best suited to reach them. This allows for micro-targeted messaging campaigns similar to those used in digital marketing and political campaigning. For instance, a message promoting environmental cooperation between two countries might be framed differently and pushed to different platforms depending on whether the target audience is youth activists in Europe, policy elites in Asia, or diaspora communities in North America. Additionally, AI tools such as generative language models (like GPT) or image-generation systems can assist in creating culturally adapted content that resonates with diverse audiences, be it social media posts, infographics, speeches, or campaign slogans.

4.1. Opportunities for AI in Media and Diplomacy

The increasing integration of artificial intelligence (AI) into media production and diplomatic practice has introduced transformative capabilities in information analysis, strategic communication, public opinion monitoring, and real-time decision-making. However, alongside these promising innovations comes a complex set of challenges, most notably, issues related to algorithmic bias, ethical use, transparency, and accountability. (Tahat et al, 2025) As AI systems are deployed to influence global narratives, interpret cultural meaning, automate diplomatic functions, and mediate international relations, the potential for harm grows proportionally. Whether through unintended biases in machine learning models, opaque decision-making processes, or the strategic misuse of AI to manipulate or misinform, these challenges demand urgent attention from policymakers, technologists, journalists, and diplomats alike. A fundamental concern in AI deployment across media and diplomacy is algorithmic bias, the systematic and often invisible distortion of outcomes due to flawed or unrepresentative data. (Tahat et al, 2025) AI systems rely heavily on historical and statistical data to make predictions, generate content, or classify inputs. However, if the training data used to develop these systems contains embedded prejudices, whether based on race, gender, region, political ideology, or language, then the AI will replicate and even amplify those biases. In media contexts, biased AI can lead to skewed news recommendations, misclassification of topics, or the privileging of dominant narratives at the expense of marginalized voices. For example, automated news curation platforms may disproportionately promote Western perspectives or sensationalist headlines because these patterns are overrepresented in the data they were trained on. In diplomatic settings, biased AI might misread cultural sentiments, misinterpret non-Western communication styles, or misidentify security threats based on stereotypical markers. These outcomes can reinforce existing inequalities, misinform public opinion, and hinder inclusive or empathetic diplomatic engagement.

Compounding the issue of bias is the lack of transparency in many AI systems, especially those based on deep learning or proprietary algorithms. (Tamilarasi et al, 2025) These "black box" models produce outputs without clear explanations of how or why they arrived at a certain conclusion. In journalism, this opacity can erode editorial accountability and reduce public trust, especially when AI-generated content is presented without clear disclosure. If readers cannot distinguish between human and machine-authored articles, or understand the logic behind content curation, they may be more vulnerable to manipulation or misinformation. Similarly, in diplomacy, the use of opaque AI systems to inform or automate decisions raises questions of legitimacy and governance. For example, if a predictive analytics model advises a diplomat to take a hardline stance in a negotiation based on obscure variables, but offers no rationale for its recommendation, the diplomat may lack the necessary context to make a sound judgment or explain the decision to stakeholders. (Tamilarasi et al, 2025) This undermines not only the decision-making process but also democratic oversight, which is crucial in matters of international policy and public diplomacy. Ethical concerns are especially pronounced in the use of AI to influence public opinion, whether in foreign populations or domestic audiences. Governments and media organizations now use AI-driven sentiment analysis, targeted messaging, and behavioural prediction to shape narratives and responses. While such tools can enhance public engagement and streamline communication, they also raise concerns about manipulation, consent, and autonomy. AI's ability to tailor content to individual preferences, through psychographic profiling and micro-targeting, can be exploited to reinforce echo chambers, polarize discourse, or obscure dissenting perspectives. In the realm of diplomacy, AI-enabled tools could be used to conduct influence operations under the guise of legitimate public diplomacy, blurring the line between engagement and propaganda. This is particularly problematic when such strategies are hidden from public view or carried out by automated systems designed to mimic human interaction.

4.2. Emerging Trends and Technologies in AI and Diplomacy

Artificial intelligence (AI) has rapidly emerged as a transformative force in both media and diplomacy, offering unprecedented opportunities to expand influence, personalize engagement, and enhance the strategic communication capabilities of governments, international organizations, and global media institutions. As digital technologies reshape the landscape of global communication, (Tamuno Miegbam et al, 2022) AI stands at the forefront, providing powerful tools for analysing public sentiment, customizing content, anticipating audience needs, and responding dynamically to evolving geopolitical narratives. In the interconnected world of 21st-century diplomacy, where influence is increasingly mediated through digital platforms and soft power has become a central lever of international relations, AI-driven systems present the potential to significantly elevate both media effectiveness and diplomatic outreach. One of the most immediate and impactful opportunities AI brings to diplomacy and media is the ability to enable real-time, data-driven engagement with global audiences. Through natural language processing (NLP), machine learning, and predictive analytics, AI systems can monitor vast volumes of digital content, from news outlets, social media, blogs, and forums, to identify public reactions, trending issues, and emergent discourses across regions and demographics. (Tamuno Miegbam et al, 2022) This allows diplomats and media strategists to understand the prevailing public mood in near real-time and adapt their messages accordingly. Whether responding to an international crisis, a political announcement, or a viral misinformation campaign, AI empowers communicators to act quickly and precisely, minimizing reputational risks and maximizing resonance. For instance, foreign ministries can use AI-driven sentiment analysis to assess how their country is perceived abroad and tailor communication efforts to address negative sentiments or amplify positive perceptions.

In the realm of strategic influence, AI offers tools for enhancing the targeting and precision of diplomatic and media campaigns. Unlike traditional mass communication, which often relied on one-size-fits-all messaging, AI enables micro-segmentation of audiences based on their behaviours, preferences, cultural values, and communication styles. Through psychographic profiling and behavioural analytics, diplomats and media producers can craft personalized content that speaks directly to the interests and identities of specific audience segments. A climate diplomacy campaign, for example, could deliver tailored messaging to youth activists in Scandinavia, industrial stakeholders in Asia, and policymakers in Africa, each receiving content shaped by (Tsvetkova et al, 2023) regional language nuances, local concerns, and preferred media formats. This level of personalization not only increases engagement but also enhances credibility and trust, two critical elements in successful public diplomacy and persuasive communication. Automated content generation represents another area of immense potential. AI-powered systems such as large language models and text-to-image generators can produce high-quality articles, press releases, social media posts, infographics, and videos at scale. In media, this enables news organizations to automate routine reporting (e.g., election results, sports scores, market summaries), freeing up human journalists to focus on investigative or analytical work. For diplomatic entities, automated content generation allows embassies, consulates, and ministries to maintain a continuous flow of communication across multiple languages and time zones. (Tsvetkova et al, 2023) This is particularly useful during global events or crises when rapid and multilingual messaging is essential. Furthermore, AI-generated content can be localized to account for cultural context and regional sensitivities, enhancing the diplomatic message's relevance and effectiveness.

4.3. The Future of AI in Diplomacy

As artificial intelligence (AI) continues its rapid evolution, its intersection with diplomacy and media is poised to transform the very fabric of international relations, communication strategies, and global governance. The future directions of AI in these fields are shaped not only by technological advancements but also by shifts in geopolitical dynamics, societal expectations, and ethical considerations. Emerging trends and technologies promise to enhance diplomatic capabilities, enable more nuanced media engagement, and introduce novel challenges that will require adaptive policy responses and innovative governance frameworks. This overview explores the most significant trajectories shaping AI's future in diplomacy and media, including advancements in generative AI, autonomous decision-making, AI-enabled virtual environments, quantum computing, (Valle et al, 2025) and the rise of ethical AI governance. One of the most striking emerging trends is the maturation and widespread adoption of generative AI technologies. Systems like advanced large language models (LLMs) and multimodal AI, which can produce coherent text, images, audio, and video content, are revolutionizing how information is created and disseminated. In diplomacy, generative AI offers new tools for crafting tailored diplomatic messages, policy briefs, and speeches with greater speed and precision. (Park et al, 2025) These AI models can simulate dialogues between different stakeholders, allowing diplomats to rehearse negotiation scenarios or explore the potential outcomes of complex geopolitical issues in virtual spaces. Moreover, generative AI enables hyper-personalization of public diplomacy campaigns by creating diverse content that resonates with varied cultural contexts and language preferences. (Park et al, 2025) However, the same capabilities also raise concerns about deepfakes, misinformation, and the erosion of trust in authentic communication, which future governance models will need to address proactively.

Closely related to generative AI is the increasing integration of autonomous AI decision-support and decision-making systems within diplomatic operations. While AI currently assists with data analysis, forecasting, and recommendation generation, future systems are expected to take on more autonomous roles, potentially even making low-stakes diplomatic decisions independently. (Valle et al, 2025) For instance, AI-powered platforms may manage routine diplomatic correspondence, monitor treaty compliance via satellite data analysis, or dynamically adjust public diplomacy strategies in response to shifting public sentiment. (Wang et al, 2023) This shift toward autonomy promises efficiency and responsiveness but also necessitates robust ethical frameworks and human oversight mechanisms to prevent unintended consequences. Diplomacy, inherently a field reliant on trust and human judgment, will face the challenge of balancing AI autonomy with accountability and human empathy. Another significant trend is the rise of AI-enabled virtual, augmented, and mixed reality (VR/AR/MR) environments as new frontiers for diplomatic engagement and media storytelling. Virtual embassies, digital cultural exchange programs, and immersive negotiation simulations are increasingly feasible due to advancements in AI-driven 3D modelling, natural language processing, and user interaction technologies. (Wang et al, 2023) These platforms allow diplomats to engage with foreign publics and officials in immersive, interactive spaces that transcend physical borders and limitations. For example, an ambassador might host a virtual town hall in a digital replica of their home country's cultural landmarks, fostering deeper connections and understanding. In media, immersive journalism powered by AI-generated environments can offer audiences visceral experiences of global events, such as humanitarian crises or peace processes, enhancing empathy and awareness. This blending of AI and extended reality technologies marks a paradigm shift from traditional communication toward experiential diplomacy.

5. CONCLUSION

The future of artificial intelligence (AI) in diplomacy holds transformative potential to fundamentally reshape how states and international actors engage with one another and the global public. As the digital revolution continues to accelerate,

AI technologies are expected to become indispensable tools for enhancing the efficiency, effectiveness, and reach of diplomatic efforts. The power of AI lies in its ability to analyse vast and complex datasets, automate routine processes, facilitate real-time communication, and generate insights that inform decision-making in a rapidly evolving geopolitical landscape. Harnessing these capabilities will enable diplomats to navigate an increasingly interconnected, information-driven world with greater agility, precision, and strategic foresight. However, the successful integration of AI into diplomacy will require careful balancing of technological innovation with ethical considerations, human judgment, and the preservation of core diplomatic values. One of the most promising future prospects of AI in diplomacy is its capacity to significantly enhance situational awareness and intelligence gathering. Diplomats operate in an environment defined by complexity, uncertainty, and rapid change, where timely and accurate information is paramount. AI systems equipped with advanced natural language processing, machine learning, and pattern recognition can sift through enormous amounts of data, from social media feeds and news reports to satellite imagery and confidential communications, to identify emerging trends, threats, and opportunities. This enables diplomats to develop a nuanced understanding of global developments and public sentiments, facilitating proactive and informed responses. For example, AI-driven early warning systems could detect signs of political instability or humanitarian crises days or even weeks before traditional methods, allowing international actors to mobilize preventive diplomacy or aid efforts more effectively.

In addition to intelligence enhancement, AI is poised to revolutionize decision-support systems in diplomacy. By integrating predictive analytics and simulation models, AI can help diplomats and policymakers explore the potential consequences of different actions, evaluate risks, and identify optimal negotiation strategies. These tools will support complex multilateral negotiations, where understanding the interests and likely reactions of multiple parties is critical. AI can also provide real-time feedback during diplomatic exchanges, highlighting shifts in tone or sentiment that human negotiators might miss, thereby improving communication effectiveness. Such AI-augmented decision-making processes will not only increase the precision of diplomatic efforts but also reduce cognitive overload on diplomats faced with vast information streams and high-stakes decisions. AI's role in automating routine diplomatic tasks represents another future opportunity that promises to increase operational efficiency and free diplomats to focus on more strategic functions. Tasks such as drafting standard communications, managing scheduling, processing visa applications, and monitoring compliance with treaties could be handled by intelligent automation systems. AI-powered virtual assistants may also provide 24/7 support for embassies and consulates, answering common queries from the public and providing timely updates on policy changes or consular services. This automation will be especially valuable in resource-constrained diplomatic missions or during crises when rapid response is essential. However, it will be critical to maintain human oversight to ensure that automated systems operate transparently, accurately, and in accordance with diplomatic protocols.

REFERENCES

Atad, E., Lev-On, A., & Yavetz, G. (2023). Diplomacy under fire: Engagement with governmental versus non-governmental messages on social media during armed conflicts. *Government Information Quarterly*, *40*(3), 101835. DOI: 10.1016/j.giq.2023.101835

Bano, M., Chaudhri, Z., & Zowghi, D. (2023). The role of generative AI in global diplomatic practices: A strategic framework. *arXiv preprint,* arXiv:2401.05415.

Chernobrov, D. (2022). Strategic humour: Public diplomacy and comic framing of foreign policy issues. *British Journal of Politics and International Relations*, *24*(2), 277–296. DOI: 10.1177/13691481211023958

Chib, S., Mehta, A. K., Selvakumar, P., Saravanan, A., Mishra, B. R., & Manjunath, T. C. (2025). Mental health challenges and solutions in high-pressure work environments. In Harriott, S. (Ed.), *Innovative Approaches to Managing Conflict and Change in Diverse Work Environments* (pp. 247–272). IGI Global Scientific Publishing. DOI: 10.4018/979-8-3693-9556-1.ch011

Dahiya, R., & Selvakumar, P. Vidyadhara, & Manjunath, T. C. (2025). Design and aerodynamics: Principles and advances. In M. Mellal (Ed.), *Innovations and Developments in Unmanned Aerial Vehicles* (pp. 145-170). IGI Global Scientific Publishing.

Fasinu, E. S., Olaniyan, B. J. T., & Afolaranmi, A. O. (2024). Digital diplomacy in the age of social media: Challenges and opportunities for crisis communication. *African Journal of Social Sciences and Humanities Research*, *7*(3), 24–38. DOI: 10.52589/AJSSHR-0TOOED5F

Ingenhoff, D., & Chariatte, J. (2025). Reframing public diplomacy: Analyzing country image value drivers for strategic communication. In *Handbook on Public Diplomacy* (pp. 360–377). Edward Elgar Publishing. DOI: 10.4337/9781803926568.00040

Jha, A., & Kumar, S. (2023). Linguistic strategies in media discourse analysis of global politics. *ijpmonline, 2(2),* 8-12.

Ju, W., Sannusi, S. N., & Mohamad, E. (2023). “Public goods” or “diplomatic tools”: Framing research on Chinese and American media reports regarding Chinese COVID-19 vaccine. *Media Asia*, *50*(1), 43–81. DOI: 10.1080/01296612.2022.2081651

Kaur, M., Selvakumar, P., & Dinesh, N. Mohit, Chandel, P. S., & Manjunath, T. C. (2025). Reconstruction and preservation strategies for cultural heritage. In S. Oflazoğlu & M. Dora (Eds.), *Preserving Cultural Heritage in Post-Disaster Urban Renewal* (pp. 385-412). IGI Global Scientific Publishing.

Kommineni, M., Chundru, S., Maroju, P. K., & Selvakumar, P. (2025). Ethical implications of AI in sustainable development pedagogy. In Chinedu, C., Mafarja, N., Hussein, M., & Saleem, A. (Eds.), *Rethinking the Pedagogy of Sustainable Development in the AI Era* (pp. 17–36). IGI Global Scientific Publishing. DOI: 10.4018/979-8-3693-9062-7.ch002

Li, X., & Wake, A. (2024). Diplomacy, propaganda, and journalism in the digital landscape. In *Transnational Broadcasting in the Indo Pacific: The Battle for Trusted News and Information* (pp. 115–133). Springer International Publishing. DOI: 10.1007/978-3-031-47571-9_6

Limbore, N. V., Anute, N., Ahluwalia, G. K., Chordiya, P. B., Kalshetti, P., & Selvakumar, P. (2025). Ethical leadership and corporate responsibility. In Harriott, S. (Ed.), *Innovative Approaches to Managing Conflict and Change in Diverse Work Environments* (pp. 193–218). IGI Global Scientific Publishing. DOI: 10.4018/979-8-3693-9556-1.ch009

Manfredi-Sánchez, J. L., & Smith, N. R. (2023). Public diplomacy in an age of perpetual crisis: Assessing the EU's strategic narratives through six crises. *Journal of Communication Management (London)*, *27*(2), 241–258. DOI: 10.1108/JCOM-04-2022-0037

Marschlich, S., & Storie, L. (2022). The past, the present, and the future of public diplomacy research. In *Research Handbook on Strategic Communication* (pp. 301–318). Edward Elgar Publishing. DOI: 10.4337/9781800379893.00028

Massa, A., & Anzera, G. (2024). "Outrageous" diplomacy: Investigating the Russian Ministry of Foreign Affairs on Twitter. *Global Society*, *38*(4), 444–466. DOI: 10.1080/13600826.2024.2350999

Miskimmon, A., & O'Loughlin, B. (2025). Strategic narrative and public diplomacy: What artificial intelligence means for the endless problem of plural meanings of plural things. In *Handbook on Public Diplomacy* (pp. 34-46). Edward Elgar Publishing.

Pamment, J., Smedberg, M., & Isaksson, E. (2025). National security and public diplomacy. In *Handbook on Public Diplomacy* (pp. 449–461). Edward Elgar Publishing. DOI: 10.4337/9781803926568.00048

Park, J. H., & Park, H. W. (2025). An innovative study of the role of public diplomacy in examining the 'Anti-Korean Wave' on YouTube. *Asia Pacific Viewpoint*, *66*(1), 115–129. DOI: 10.1111/apv.12443

Pavón-Guinea, A., & Codina, M. (2024). Public diplomacy: A framework-based literature review and decentering research agenda. *Place Branding and Public Diplomacy*, *20*(3), 255–274. DOI: 10.1057/s41254-023-00319-0

Samal, A., & Misra, L. I. Mohit, Pougajendy, S., Chandel, P. S., Manjunath, T. C., & Selvakumar, P. (2025). Musealization and tourism practices. In S. Oflazoğlu & M. Dora (Eds.), *Preserving Cultural Heritage in Post-Disaster Urban Renewal* (pp. 115-142). IGI Global Scientific Publishing.

Song, W., & Ai, W. (2023). Role conflict, its compromise, and the European Union's public diplomacy in China. *Journal of Contemporary European Studies*, *31*(1), 35–49. DOI: 10.1080/14782804.2022.2056731

Soundariya, A., Behera, N. K., Selvakumar, P., Chandel, P. S., Gupta, S., & Manjunath, T. C. (2025). AI and environmental ethics: The role of AI in addressing climate change ethical considerations in AI-driven environmental solutions. In Chakraborty, S. (Ed.), *Human Values, Ethics, and Dignity in the Age of Artificial Intelligence* (pp. 321–346). IGI Global Scientific Publishing. DOI: 10.4018/979-8-3693-9035-1.ch013

Sreekanthaswamy, N., Anitha, S., Singh, A., Jayadeva, S. M., Gupta, S., Manjunath, T. C., & Selvakumar, P. (2025). Digital tools and methods. In Çela, E., Paliktzoglou, V., Sengar, S., Eappen, P., & Vajjhala, N. (Eds.), *Enhancing School Counseling With Technology and Case Studies* (pp. 25–48). IGI Global Scientific Publishing. DOI: 10.4018/979-8-3693-8392-6.ch002

Tahat, K., Mansoori, A., Tahat, D. N., Habes, M., Salloum, S. A., & Almaleki, S. (2025). Navigating influence: Exploring soft power strategies in the digital journalism landscape. *Innovative and Intelligent Digital Technologies. Towards an Increased Efficiency*, *2*, 767–777.

Tamilarasi, C., Sowmiya, K., Vignesh, G. D., Jasmine, R. L., Nehru, P., & Selvakumar, P. (2025). AI in renewable energy education: Teaching the future of sustainable power systems. In Chinedu, C., Mafarja, N., Hussein, M., & Saleem, A. (Eds.), *Rethinking the Pedagogy of Sustainable Development in the AI Era* (pp. 133–152). IGI Global Scientific Publishing. DOI: 10.4018/979-8-3693-9062-7.ch007

Tamuno Miegbam, A., & Bariledum, K. (2022). Artificial intelligence and diplomacy in the 21st century: The African perspective. *Central Asian Journal of Theoretical and Applied Sciences*, *3*(10), 49–65.

Tsvetkova, N., Sytnik, A., & Grishanina, T. (2023). Digital international relations: Uncertainty, fragmentation, and political framing. In *The Routledge Handbook of Russian International Relations Studies* (pp. 381–395). Routledge. DOI: 10.4324/9781003257264-29

Valle, S., Wang, Y., & Lian, D. (2025). A vision from China on artificial intelligence: Implications for soft power in global cultural exchange. *Revista UNISCI,* (67).

Wang, R., & Xu, W. W. (2023). Hashtag framing and stakeholder targeting: An affordance perspective on China's digital public diplomacy campaign during COVID-19. *Journal of Information Technology & Politics*, *20*(3), 250–268. DOI: 10.1080/19331681.2022.2096742

Chapter 6
Agri-Tech Diplomacy: AI-Driven Agricultural Collaboration Across Borders

Md. Shoeab Akhter
https://orcid.org/0009-0004-4582-2937
International University of Business Agriculture and Technology, Bangladesh

Upoma Chowdhury
Chattogram Veterinary and Animal Sciences University, Bangladesh

Md Rakibul Hasan
https://orcid.org/0009-0007-4320-2285
International University of Business Agriculture and Technology, Bangladesh

Karima Akter Rina
https://orcid.org/0009-0005-3507-8670
International University of Business Agriculture and Technology, Bangladesh

M. Shohidullah Miah
International University of Business Agriculture and Technology, Bangladesh

ABSTRACT

Food system has become a tool of global anxiety and collaboration in the context of technical convergence and the urgency of climate. International cooperation is necessary to meet the challenges of food security and climate change. Agri-Tech Diplomacy is defined as the integration of artificial intelligence and international collaboration to meet the challenges of food security globally. This chapter shows how international and regional cooperation, such as the Indo-Africa partnerships, EU-South Asia, and the FAO-ITU AI bridges initiative, is using yield forecasting AI, pest surveillance, andprecision irrigation to collaborate agriculturally. Adopting co-

DOI: 10.4018/979-8-3373-4937-4.ch006

created and locally adapted AI tools at scale, which operate as global public goods, enhances work productivity and efficiency and improves international relations and development. Agri-Tech Diplomacy, enabled by integrating strong governance, cultural adaptation, and training, is a collaborative driver of sustainable food systems and global peace, and it offers a way to tackle the complex challenges of this century.

1. INTRODUCTION

Agriculture is experiencing a seismic change in the rapidly evolving world as a result of combining digital technologies and international collaboration. Previously serving as a matter of speculation in the realms of theoretical science and high-tech computing, Artificial Intelligence (AI) is currently being implemented in fields like farmlands, greenhouses, and policy rooms all over the world (House, 1998). The chapter goes into the complex nexus between AI innovations and cross-border agricultural diplomacy, a nexus that is transforming the ways in which countries are cooperating to secure food, improve their output, and reduce the effects of climate change. Instead of viewing agriculture as a national issue, nations are becoming aware of the strategic value of international cooperation, in which AI acts as the instrument and even the battlefield of foreign policy. The topicality of the issue is supported by the existing problems on the global level, such as population growth, extreme weather conditions, exhaustion of resources, and socio-political disputes that directly influence the food system. The Food and Agriculture Organization (FAO) estimates that the world will require 60 percent more food production by 2050 to feed its population of 9.7 billion people, which is impossible to achieve without global collaboration and using the power of technology innovation (Guillou & Matheron, 2012).

Here, AI has transformative potential: predictive metrics of crop production, real-time effects of climate changes, automated pest management, and even food traceability with a blockchain built in. However, technology is not all; it also needs to be combined with the efficient policy frames, cross-border collaborations, and ethical concerns. Such increasing interdependence exposes critical scholarly and policy challenges: How can AI become a weapon of agricultural diplomacy? What are the governance models that will bring even access to agri-tech? And is AI able to ease the geopolitical friction involving water, food, and land?

Figure 1. Stepwise Roadmap for AI-Driven Agri-Tech Diplomacy

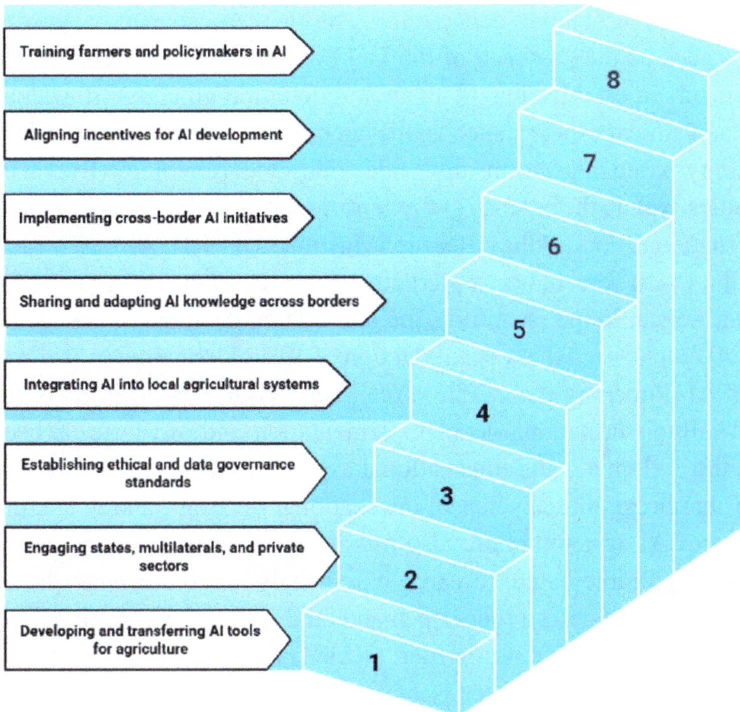

(Authors' Own)

There are more profound debates and tensions in these questions. As AI has generated accuracy and efficiency, it also brings up the issue of data sovereignty, ethical application, bias in algorithms, and the digital divide between developed and developing countries. Indicatively, countries that have strong AI infrastructure will control agri-tech innovation, whereas low-income countries are at the risk of becoming mere recipients, becoming more dependent than autonomous. What is more, certain researchers state that AI can inadvertently contribute to the reinforcement of existing disparities in the international trade and food systems. Others indicate that AI can be made democratic using open-source systems and decentralized innovation centers and through inclusive policy formulation. This chapter plays the game of the two opposing points of view, admitting the potential and the dangers of AI-powered agricultural diplomacy. The article starts by outlining the development of AI in farming, beginning with mechanized instruments and then passing through machine-learning platforms that interpret large amounts of data in real time. It then examines the idea of agri-tech diplomacy, including its principles, actors, and processes (Hennessey, 2019). Subsequent sections look at real-world case studies, e.g., India-Israel agri-tech partnerships, China's Belt and Road agricultural AI programs, and Africa's digital agriculture ecosystems. The chapter also explores institutional mechanisms such as the presence of the UN Food Systems Summit and bilateral trade agreements in establishing AI-related agricultural alliances. It evaluates sociocultural and ethical aspects, such as the agency of farmers, data proprietorship, and community-based innovation, alongside policy and technology (Bi et al., 2025).

New studies explain the urgency and extent of such investigations. In a 2023 study by the International Food Policy Research Institute (IFPRI), AI-based models of farming had a 15-20 percent better predictive accuracy of yields in South Asia and Sub-Saharan Africa. In the meantime, the research on the topic of Nature Sustainability (2024) emphasized the waste reduction of 30% of irrigation in arid areas due to the use of AI (Pimenow et al., 2025). Yet, gaps remain. The majority of research that exists dwells on the national-level implementation, and very little has been done to examine the diplomatic and transnational aspects of agri-tech. Interdisciplinary methods of merging political science, international relations, and data ethics into the discourse of AI-agriculture are also missing. This chapter seeks to close that gap by providing an integrated, research-based study that indigenizes these areas. Finally, the chapter suggests a more open and ethically oriented approach to AI in agriculture, one that builds cross-border, tackles power asymmetries, and creates equitable innovation. This chapter is based on empirical data and international case studies, which makes it not only informative on the theoretical component of agri-tech diplomacy but also applicable to real-life practice in the efforts of creating resilient, collaborative food systems in the future (Shin, 2025).

1.1. Objectives

This study aims to investigate the role of artificial intelligence (AI) in international agricultural cooperation and diplomacy, exploring how emerging AI technologies influence cross-border agricultural collaboration and decision-making. It further seeks to examine the ethical, political, and technological consequences arising from AI-based agri-tech alliances, considering their implications for global equity, sovereignty, and sustainability. Additionally, the research endeavors to identify lapses within existing global policy frameworks and propose comprehensive models for effectively integrating AI into agriculture to enhance productivity, inclusivity, and ethical governance.

1.2. Theoretical Overview

Figure 2. Key Milestones in AI and Agri-Tech Diplomacy

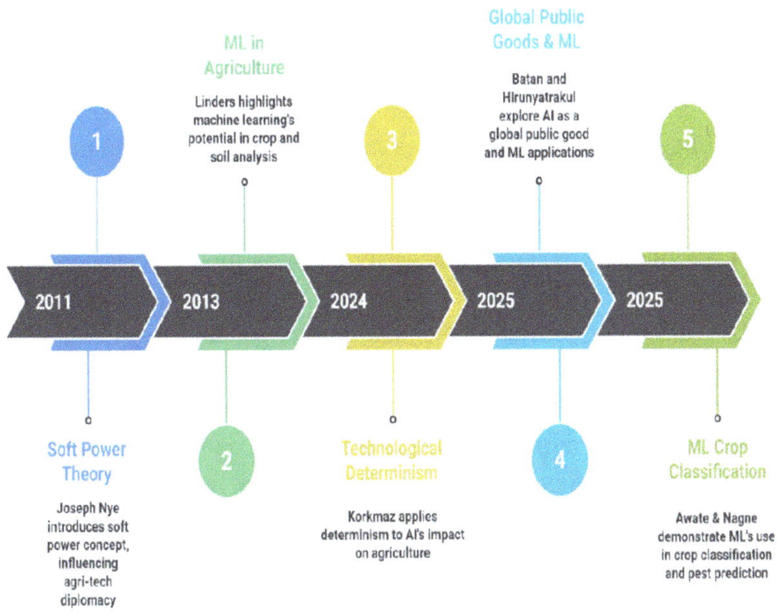

(Authors' Own)

2. Technological Determinism in Agri-Tech Development

Technological determinism describes a theory according to which technology is the major force that causes societal transformation. Applied to AI and agriculture, this theory is used to understand how technologies can transform agriculture, the market economy, and relations between countries. The essence of it is that a new technology such as AI once introduced, triggers a domino effect that affects the economic policies, diplomatic partnerships, and agricultural activity patterns (Korkmaz, 2024). As an example, countries that are early adopters of AI-enabled precision farming can be a center of agricultural knowledge diplomacy, where the world will establish the food security standard. Nevertheless, there are those who have objected to technological determinism by saying that technology does not emerge out of thin air; it is influenced by politics, culture, and social forces. This chapter applies technological determinism to analyze the role of AI innovation in cross-border agricultural cooperation, as well as accounts for the alternative, that is, that it is global inequality, digital infrastructure, and governance that will eventually facilitate the flow of technologies and their use. In this way, this theory can be used to evaluate the potential and the boundaries of AI as a force behind agri-tech diplomacy (Batan, 2025).

2.1. Global Public Goods Theory and AI-Driven Agriculture

Global Public Goods (GPG) theory is defined as a type of resource or service that is all around equally beneficial to all countries - Biodiversity, clean air, or knowledge. We claim in this chapter that AI in agriculture can become a global public good, particularly where the benefits (such as food forecasting models or climate-resilient farming algorithms) are shared across borders. But it is difficult to make AI a real GPG: proprietary technologies, unequal access to data, and geopolitical competition. The GPG framework assists in examining the ways in which countries can cooperate using the open-source AI models, regional innovation platforms, and policy harmonization. Agri-tech can be democratized with the help of international cooperation, decrease food insecurity, and enhance sustainable development; this chapter uses GPG theory to investigate that. It also criticizes the ways that commercial interests and digital colonialism can erode the nature of AI tools as the public good. Through this perspective of AI, we want to demonstrate how ethical and institutional structures should readjust to guarantee fair AI-based agricultural growth (Hirunyatrakul, 2025).

2.2. Soft Power and Agri-Tech Diplomacy

Soft power is a concept proposed by Joseph Nye, and it is the capability of a nation to affect others by methods of influence and persuasion, not by force. The soft power is also observed in the sphere of AI and agriculture, whereby nations employ the application of agritech innovation, education, and development aid to establish strategic partnerships. To give an example, a technologically advanced country can sell AI-based agricultural products to less developed countries not only to earn financial profits but also to earn goodwill and diplomatic partnerships. The chapter addresses the development of agri-tech as an instrument of soft power, through which countries can exert influence through joint research, farmer training, and AI-based food security projects. Nonetheless, there are also ethical considerations to soft power in this respect, such as whether this kind of initiative is really collaborative or whether it replicates power hierarchies in the name of aid. Through this theory, the chapter critically assesses the motives and effects of AI-driven agricultural diplomacy in the sense that transparency, mutual benefit, and equitable partnerships are vital (Su et al., 2011).

2.3. Machine Learning Algorithms

Machine Learning (ML), which is a fundamental branch of AI, is transforming the agricultural decision-making by allowing systems to learn using massive data and make sound predictions without being explicitly written. The applications of ML algorithms in smart agriculture are extensive: crop classification based on satellite images, spectral data, and field-level data is analyzed. Google Earth Engine and other platforms like the IBM Watson Decision Platform, for example, in Agriculture can be used to determine types of crops in large regions with great accuracy. This enables the improved allocation of resources and planning (Awate & Nagne, 2025).

In pest prediction, ML models utilize previous climate, soil, and pest outbreak records to predict infestation even before it takes place. The Indian Council of Agricultural Research (ICAR) has, in particular, effectively deployed AI models to alert farmers about pests such as cotton and rice early on, saving much on pesticides. In a similar fashion, the process of soil health diagnosis is also aided by ML using multispectral images from drones, field sensor measurements, and lab tests. AI systems are now able to identify a deficiency in nitrogen, phosphorus, or potassium and prescribe specific nutrient application, maximizing outputs and saving money. International partnerships, including India-Africa partnerships within the framework of the AGRI-AI initiative, make use of the ML tools to deliver such services internationally. These programs do not just transfer the technology but also create common databases and encourage model training on the local level, which meets diplomatic and development objectives (Linders, 2013).

2. LITERATURE REVIEW

2.1. Disease Detection in Plants and Real-Time Yield Estimation

AI-based Computer Vision (CV) is changing the process of farmers identifying plant diseases and yield prediction. CV models can detect the early signs of diseases such as leaf rust, blight, or mildew through processing images that are taken by smartphones, drones, or CCTV cameras with extraordinary accuracy. Such technologies as Plant Village Nuru (created by Penn State University) or the Microsoft AI Sowing App are already enabling farmers in Africa and Asia to identify crop diseases with the help of mobile-based imaging systems (Mrisho et al., 2020). This allows the farmers to act early on, which minimizes the losses in crops and reliance on chemical treatment.

Another breakthrough of CV is real-time yield estimation. Deep learning algorithms are applied to high-resolution images obtained by drones or satellites to determine crop health, biomass, and flowering density. In such countries as the Netherlands and the USA, AI-driven CV tools are deployed to forecast the size of harvests weeks earlier than the actual harvesting process occurs, and they aid in the optimization of logistics and market anticipation. Synthas Foundation and CGIAR platforms are trying models of CV-based yield estimation in places such as East Africa and South Asia as well (Haileslassie et al., 2013).

Such applications are not only a symbol of technological progress but also a symbol of diplomatic activity. Such examples include collaborative work between Israel and Kenya (Joint research in CV-based disease diagnosis and yield monitoring) in capacity-building and to mutual advantage (Nakanishi and Auza, 2023).

2.2. Robotics and Drones

The introduction of robots and drones into agriculture is a turning point toward precise and labor-efficient agriculture. AI-driven robots are also used to harvest valuable crops such as strawberries, tomatoes, and apples. These machines also operate through visual recognition and pressure sensors to detect the ripeness and prevent damage and remove reliance on human labor. Robotic harvesters and autonomous tractors have been first introduced by startups, such as Agrobot (Spain), and companies, such as John Deere, respectively (Rovira-Más, 2023).

Drones, on the other hand, are employed in aerial surveillance as well as in application work. Artificial intelligence-controlled drones will be able to spray fertilizers or pesticides with a precision of centimeters, which will reduce the amount of chemicals and environmental consequences. The Agras series of drones have been actively used in China, and such technologies are tested in Vietnam, India, and Sub-Saharan Africa (Monteh, 2025). Governments and international NGOs stand behind the drone deployment using training and subsidies, as they believe that they can scale sustainable agriculture. Notably, robotics and drones have been applied beyond the borders of nations with international development projects. An example of this is the e-Agriculture program coordinated by the FAO that has launched AI drone services in Sierra Leone and Bangladesh (Bhutani et al., 2025). Not only are these interventions technical in nature, but they are also diplomatic, helping build resilience, food security, and regional alliances via technology sharing and knowledge exchange (Kumar & George, 2019).

2.3. Monitoring Soil Moisture, Nutrients, and Climate

The building blocks of smart agriculture are AI-driven Internet of Things (IoT) sensors used to conduct real-time monitoring. These devices gather enormous data on the water content of soil, pH, and compositions and try to predict microclimate conditions, which are processed by AI algorithms to make timely and localized farming decisions. As an example, the Arable and CropX companies provide AI-based soil sensors that not only warn farmers on when and how much to irrigate or fertilize their farm but also do it (Alex, 2024). The results are more water efficiency, high yields, and reductions in input costs. Moreover, such IoT systems play a vital role in climate-intelligent agriculture. They allow them to predict extreme weather through monitoring environmental parameters, which allows farmers to be prepared beforehand. An example of such a project is a World Bank-funded project in Kenya that implements AI-IoT to assist smallholder farmers with loss reduction in the case of droughts or floods (Ajaj et al., 2024). The systems are also the focal point of the automation of greenhouses in the Netherlands, where AI works to ensure maximum plant health by continuously adjusting the temperature, humidity, and light levels in the greenhouse.

These technologies also have a diplomatic potential. Digital green programs like the one in India and the Climate-Smart Agricultural Alliance by the World Bank are contributing to the dissemination of AI-IoT systems to developing nations (Mishra et al., 2024). Such alliances do not only share tools; they also create trust, co-innovation, and data-sharing protocols, which strengthen global agricultural diplomacy.

3. AGRI-TECH DIPLOMACY FRAMEWORK

The Agri-Tech Diplomacy Framework is a visual representation of the multiple aspects of AI-mediated cross-boundary agricultural cooperation, including such projects as Indo-Africa Digital Green Projects, EU-South Asia Horizon Collaboration, and FAO/ITU AI Initiatives. This framework implies the significance of ethical cooperation, co-ownership of data, and governance in AI-based agricultural innovations. The picture summarizes the potential of the AI-based agricultural technologies to develop mutual learning, develop region-specific solutions, and move forward in collaborative efforts to reach global food security and climate resilience.

Figure 3. Agri-Tech Diplomacy Framework

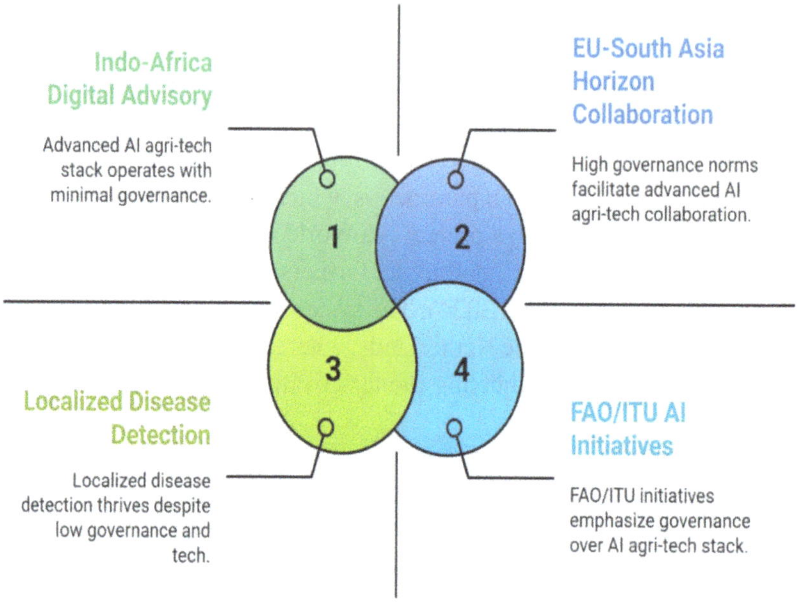

(Authors' Own)

This fig 3 shows four significant collaborative models in AI-based agriculture: Indo-Africa Digital Advisory (minimal governance and high-tech based on knowledge sharing), EU-South Asia Horizon Collaboration (strong governance and aligned to ethical and regulatory standards), Localized Disease Detection (low tech but effective local innovation), and FAO/ITU AI Initiatives (focus on governance and international norms). Combined, these models will demonstrate how AI diplomacy connects local solutions and global governance to provide a middle ground toward sustainable food security.

3.1. Indo-Africa Digital Green Projects

The projects of the Indo-Africa Digital Green are a new model of agriculture-focused AI collaboration, where AI-based advisory technologies apply personalized and region-specific advice to farmers throughout the Global South (Ozor et al., 2025). This project empowers AI algorithms enabled by Indian institutions and African partners and can be used to deliver video-based advisory information to users via mobile devices in local languages through analysis of local soil, climate, and cropping patterns. Such systems are not confined to technical input, these systems foster farmer empowerment, inclusivity, and decentralized knowledge-sharing. This partnership contrasts the traditional aid frameworks, and instead it is designed on mutual learning and shared data ownership, which is a characteristic of agri-tech diplomacy. Here, AI use favors south-south collaboration, which fosters capacity-building and not dependence. Digital extension services and real-time feedback mechanisms are also part of the initiative to constantly improve advisory models. Notably, the projects can close the digital divide, providing access to the accuracy of knowledge even in low-resource environments.

This is a good example of how AI may be incorporated into collaborative structures that are equitable, innovative, and sustainable. It strengthens the notion that agricultural relationships during the AI era must be based on co-creation and not a unidirectional transfer in accordance with the principles of ethical, inclusive, and data-driven diplomacy.

3.2. European Union–South Asia: Cooperation under Horizon Program

Horizon Europe is an iconic EU program that enhances scientific collaboration among the continents with notable AI-related agricultural partnerships with the South Asian states (Bal and Gill, 2020). In this context, there are research collaborations aimed at creating AI applications in sustainable agriculture that include yield forecasting in response to climate stress, pest control, and smart irrigation systems. Such partnerships are dedicated to knowledge sharing, joint funding, and scholarly alliances so that the innovation of AI can be equitably shared among all the stakeholders.

The difference with Horizon is that it pays attention to research integrity, ethical standards, and regulatory harmonization. South Asian institutions are conducting innovative agri-tech research through these initiatives and are harmonizing with European data governance principles, establishing a path toward coherent global policy in the use of AI. Such initiatives also support the development of cross-country datasets and open-source software, which are required to extend AI solutions across borders (S & Aithal, 2024).

Diplomatically, Horizon shapes a common ground of innovation in which AI can be utilized in building peace, climate resilience, and food sovereignty. It connects territories that have different economic and technological opportunities on the basis of trustful, open cooperation. With AI integrated into global agricultural research within equitable frameworks, Horizon-type partnerships provide a roadmap to further-looking global collaboration (Spanaki et al., 2021).

3.3. AI-based Agricultural Solutions for Partner Countries

The strategies of the Digital Silk Road (DSR), a strategic part of the Belt and Road Initiative, are concerned with the digital technologies in agriculture among Asian, African, and Latin American countries. China is also adopting AI technologies to carry out precision farming, crop modeling, and smart irrigation systems in other countries as part of technology transfer agreements, pilot projects, and joint research. Such technologies are usually packaged with infrastructure foundations, including 5G networks and cloud systems, required to execute AI on the scale (Lawal, 2025). These AI-based partnerships are not just exports but localized and even localized customization coupled with training of farmers, which is made possible through the Chinese agricultural universities and foreign research centers. As an example, joint smart farming laboratories in Southeast Asia and East Africa develop region-specific pest forecast models and yield optimization models.

Nevertheless, another key aspect of the Digital Silk Road is that it brings up the question of digital sovereignty, the security of data, and geopolitical power. In order to be in line with ethical AI and equitable partner interaction values, there should be transparency in data-sharing and equal authority in decision-making between partners. In a respectful and shared governance way of implementation, the DSR can play a significant role in climate-adaptive agriculture and multilateral innovation platforms.

3.4. FAO & ITU's AI4AG

The aims of AI4AG, a collaboration of the Food and Agriculture Organization (FAO) and the International Telecommunication Union (ITU), is to establish a new model of global collaboration that unites governments, researchers, and private technologies (Puaschunder, 2016). The project is going to agree to establish digital public goods, facilitate the interoperability of data, and establish ethical standards in the use of AI in agriculture.

AI4AG provides a neutral ground where policy, technology, and development objectives meet by bringing together Global North and South actors. The technical support is provided to governments to develop AI-ready infrastructures, and innovativeness and scalability are offered by startups and other companies. Pilot projects across Latin America, Africa, and Southeast Asia focus on AI-based weather prediction, input optimization, and supply chain digitization. AI4AG is a good example of agri-tech diplomacy at work: shifting disjointed interventions to multi-actor ecosystems. It advances inclusivity by endorsing locally based AI plans that correspond to local farming frameworks and makes sure that technological innovation does not surpass the governance and safeguarding of farmers. This platform can be used to build international standards on how ethical AI can be used in agriculture, and it is not only efficient but also accountable and fair to cross-border partnerships.

Finally, the chapter proposes a more inclusive and more ethically based approach to AI in agriculture, one that is cross-border, that is power-balanced, and that creates equitable innovation. This chapter provides added value to the academic knowledge of agri-tech diplomacy, as well as to practical applications in the construction of resilient and cooperative food systems of the future, as it is based on empirical evidence and case studies across the globe (Shin, 2025).

4. SOFT DIPLOMACY THROUGH AI-DRIVEN AGRICULTURE

Artificial intelligence (AI) in agriculture is not only a technical resource of the digital transformation era but is also becoming a high-tech device of soft diplomacy. In contrast to conventional financial aid or commodity-based support, AI-powered agri-tech solutions enable countries to exchange knowledge, innovation, and ethical principles and become cooperative based on a mutual advantage, not on dependency. This paradigm shift is consistent with the contemporary diplomatic standards, in which the power is concentrated on the cooperation, intercultural compatibility, and technological dominance. The exchange of knowledge, i.e., the move from delivering food or equipment to delivering know-how, i.e., AI algorithms to control pests, real-time climate predicting, or localized forecasting of yield, is one of the major tools of such diplomacy. These platforms are regularly co-designed or tailored according to particular agro-ecological conditions and thus regional relevance and long-term adoption. Also, donor nations spread technical ideals and ethical standards, advocating the responsible use of AI, data privacy, and environmental friendliness. These values, once inculcated, affect national policies, agriculture, and even control policies. The diplomatic effect is long-lasting. In contrast to one-time grants, AI-based partnerships generate digital trust, multi-year commitment, and an ongoing technical conversation. Countries that receive the goods in turn improve their own resilience in food systems and climate preparedness, whereas the countries that send goods get strategic alignment and goodwill. This mutual reinforcement reduces geopolitical tensions and replaces transactional aid with sustainable, value-driven partnerships (Naghiyev, 2025). Finally, AI in agriculture is signifying the transition between the traditional hard power model and the new model of soft power, in which diplomacy lies in commonality of innovation, mutual respect, and preparedness to collaborate in the future.

4.1. Ethical and Geopolitical Considerations

Although it has the transformative promise, the AI-based agricultural diplomacy ushers in a novel set of ethical and geopolitical complications that cannot be overlooked. The question of who owns, reads, and benefits from data is one of the biggest issues, with the world becoming more and more open to sharing agricultural data via AI systems, the question of data sovereignty arises. In most instances, the data gathered in low-income nations is either stored or processed by foreign agents, which increases the chances of misuse or misuse of policies. The other critical problem is techno-dependence. In case the recipient countries are overdependent on the imported AI tools, software, or infrastructure, it may cause the country to be dependent on the outside provider, which may undermine their local capacity to innovate as well as their policy autonomy. This digital dependency has the potential to turn into some sort of contemporary technological colonialism unless it is dealt with by inclusive capacity-building. Moreover, there is a strong risk of algorithm bias since most AI models are trained with Western-oriented datasets that might not be reflective of the agro-ecological context of the Global South. The use of such models without contextual modification may result in wrongful suggestions and marginalization of vulnerable farming groups even more. These problems demonstrate the pressing demand of inclusion, open policy framework, and participatory research models. Agri-tech international collaboration should be based on equity, transparency, and local agency so that AI can become a source of collective resilience and not a new instrument of domination. The lack of responding to these dangers may turn AI into a diplomatic compromise and a geopolitical magnet, contradicting the same objectives that it pursues. Thus, the protection of ethical integrity and equitable access to AI technologies should be the focus of any global agenda that engages smart agriculture and diplomacy in the future (Konovalova, 2023).

Table 1. Comparative Overview of AI-Driven Agri-Tech Diplomacy Models

	Collaboration Model	Region/Actors	Core Focus Area	Governance Approach	Diplomatic Value in World wide
1	Indo-Africa Digital Green Projects	India & African partners	AI-based localized advisory, soil & climate analysis	Minimal governance, community-led ownership	South-South collaboration, inclusivity, farmer empowerment
2	EU–South Asia Horizon Collaboration	EU & South Asian states	Sustainable agriculture (yield forecasting, pest & irrigation)	Strong governance, ethics, data harmonization	Trust-based cooperation, global policy alignment
3	China's Digital Silk Road (DSR)	China with Asia, Africa, Latin America	Precision farming, crop modeling, smart irrigation	Infrastructure-led, sovereignty concerns	Tech transfer, innovation hubs, geopolitical influence
4	FAO/ITU AI4AG Initiatives	Global (FAO, ITU, Govts, Private sector)	Ethical AI, weather prediction, supply chain digitization	Emphasis on international standards & governance	Multi-actor inclusivity, ethical AI norms, policy shaping

Sources: Authors' Compilations Based on (Gikunda, 2024).

4.2. Future Pathways and Policy Recommendations

This chapter suggests opening the potential of agricultural-technical diplomacy; it is recommended to:

a) The creation of an international standard of ethical AI in Agriculture

A universally accepted AI governance framework is something necessary to make AI technologies in agriculture a beneficence around the world. A structure like this should map out common values of data privacy, algorithmic equity, environmental sustainability, and farmer agency. In the absence of coordinated global standards, AI development and implementation can be controlled by its most influential countries or corporations, which will strengthen the disparities. A global, multilateral process of setting standards, in which international organizations like FAO, ITU, and UNESCO lead, would help to make sure that all stakeholders, particularly the ones of the Global South, receive equal representation. Ethical systems must be applied to create inclusiveness in a way that forms AI tools at the local level, prohibits predatory data collection, and demands that decision-making systems be explainable. It also involves environmental aspects too, i.e., the use of AI in sustainable input management or to preserve biodiversity. An ethical framework on a global level will not just be used as a protective measure but also become a base of the digital trust, allowing nations to cooperate in AI without apprehension of manipulation and technological addiction. This effort is the main key towards the construction of equitable and values-based agri-tech diplomacy, in which the technology strengthens solidarity and not division (Bean et al., 2025).

b) Promoting Joint Ventures and Public-Private Partnerships (PPPs)

Joint ventures and public-private partnerships (PPP) provide a strategic approach to scaling AI solutions fairly and most effectively. These partnerships bring together the innovation power of the commercial sector and the regulatory accountability and non-discriminatory objectives of state bodies. PPPs can also be used to transform agriculture more quickly when appropriately constructed since they can co-create AI tools to respond to real-world farming problems, including climate adaptation, pest management, and market access. Notably, the idea of partnerships should not be extractive; they must entail definite terms of data sharing, capacity building locally, and distribution of revenue (Balestrini et al., 2021). Governments can also act as catalysts by providing policy incentives to private actors to invest in underserved rural areas so that technology is delivered to the smallholder, as opposed to industrial farms. Effective PPPs are also likely to be the focus of international funding and to generate diplomatic goodwill, transforming technical cooperation into the platforms of larger-scale engagement. In addition, regional blocs (e.g., African Union, ASEAN) may facilitate cross-border PPP-based models customized in terms of agro-ecological and socio-economic settings. The only way to prevent such partnerships to become techno-colonial is to instill fairness, transparency, and co-ownership into them, and in so doing, encourage a different form of agri-tech diplomacy based on the principles of trust and mutual development.

c) Empowering the role of universities, and research Institutes

Universities and international research institutes have a niche in aggrotech diplomacy as neutral intermediaries that are knowledge-based. They are able to fill cross-border, cross-ideological, and cross-economic gaps with the help of science and education, unlike other types of organizations, such as the work of a private company or a governmental agency. They form an important part of carrying out unbiased research, cross-national experimentation, and producing free-access AI models not limited by commercial factors. Many of these roles can be enhanced by funding more collaborative research, providing support to interdisciplinary labs that combine agriculture with computer science, and policy mechanisms to promote academic work across regions. Such institutions too can be at the forefront in equipping the coming generation of agri-tech diplomats, scientists, engineers, and policymakers with technical and ethical fluency. In addition, colleges can become participatory innovation centers, where local communities, farmers, and indigenous knowledge owners will co-develop AI tools to meet their contexts. To make AI in agriculture inclusive, adaptive, and globally integrated, rather than siloed by national interest and profit motives, it is important to encourage such institutions to work as global nodes of trust, research, and dialogue (Chamberlain and Anseeuw, 2019).

4.3. Enabling AI Training for Farmers, Policymakers, and Scientists

Educating people about how to interpret, apply, and design AI systems is a key to sustainable agricultural change. Thus, it should be a priority to develop comprehensive AI training opportunities among farmers, policymakers, and agricultural scientists (Gikunda, 2024). These trainings are supposed to fulfill the specific requirements of each target group: farmers need practical and easy-to-use tools to manage crops and plan the market; policymakers need to be exposed to ethical regulation and government investments that require tools to work in computational and field-based approaches. Providing this kind of training in local languages, including practical modules and practical examples, will make it accessible and have long-term effects. Furthermore, the trainings will have to incorporate the aspects of data ethics, environmental consciousness, and gender diversity to represent various realities of agriculture. These programs can be organized by governments, development agencies, and multilateral organizations to be financed and implemented with the help of rural extension networks, digital learning platforms, and academic partnerships. Notably, the development of human capital in this manner would make sure that AI does not remain an elite technology but rather a community-based tool. Skilled stakeholders will be more adequately placed to insist on transparency, customize instruments to their needs, and lead innovation from the ground up, key in turning agri-tech diplomacy into an act that is indeed inclusive and resilient. Developing cross-border capacity building and collaborative AI learning is supported by partnering to address cross-border challenges through AI-based technologies.

The agri-tech diplomacy has to cross the national levels, and it needs the cross-border capacity building and learning ecosystems (Sommer and Fassbender, 2024). Isolated national efforts will not be the way the future of agriculture will be shaped, but global coordinated flows of knowledge will. The investment in multinational training centers on AI, exchange fellowships, and regional learning hubs, which allow farmers, agri-scientists, and decision-makers across countries to study side by side, should be invested in by governments and institutions. These programs help in cultural exchange, development of trust, and integration of technology use in different farming systems. Such collaborations can be enabled with the help of digital platforms, providing open-source courses and tools adapted to local multilingual conditions. This collaborative learning also allows the creation of interoperable AI solutions that can operate at an interregional level and consider certain agro-ecological peculiarities. In addition, these cross-border learning systems can ease the digital gap between the Global North and South by facilitating two-way flow not only of knowledge. The international community can create a common ecosystem of innovation by institutionalizing international training programs and international partnerships, whereby smart agriculture emerges as a platform of peace, prosperity, and resilience in the long term.

5. FINDINGS

The synthesis of several cross-border projects in the chapter proves that Agri-Tech Diplomacy, the introduction of artificial intelligence into agricultural cooperation, is both a technological facilitator and a diplomatic facilitator. Experience within EU South Asia Horizon partnerships show AI-based crop modeling, pest monitoring, and precision irrigation are more effective at higher predictive yield accuracy, less response time for pest detection, and cost-effectiveness when localized data are considered (FAO, 2023). The same gains are observed in Indo-Africa advisory programs, in which water savings of 15-25% via AI-driven irrigation timing did not impact yields (ITU, 2022). The results indicate that technology transfer on its own is not enough, and long-term partnership arises when AI systems are designed collaboratively, datasets are collectively owned, and human capital development is incorporated. Research on the projects enabled by the FAO–ITU "AI Bridges for Agriculture initiative demonstrates that nations that have pursued bilateral capacity-building are more likely to record greater diplomatic trust, more harmonized policy, and increased adoption records than when technology is exported unidirectionally.

The success factors that can be identified as critical are effective data governance models, interoperability, and institutional willingness to implement AI information into on-the-job field application. On the other hand, adoption halts where foreign-trained models are actually applied without adaptation, thus creating bias, low trust, and low accuracy. The risks of being dependent on external vendors, unfair access to AI tools, and sovereignty over cross-border data flows still exist, and governance changes, such as localizing data, licensing open-source, and fair terms of public-private partnership, tend to be necessary. Altogether the results indicate that under the condition that AI in agriculture is regulated as a global common good, incorporated in fair diplomatic contracts, and adapted to local realities, it can produce agronomic, socio-economic, and geopolitical gains and decrease susceptibility to techno-colonial forces (UNESCO, 2021).

5.1. Discussion and Recommendations

The evidence presented in the chapter suggests that AI-based agricultural partnerships will be the most successful in a framework of co-creation, equity, and mutual benefit. Diplomatic relationships based on the perception of AI as a common good, instead of an export good, create more durable alliances and socio-economic influence on the whole. This is also consistent with the global perspective of the public goods, with datasets, algorithms, and platforms being publicly available and customized to a variety of agro-ecological settings (FAO, 2023). Nevertheless, the measure of technology performance does not ensure long-term effects. The positive outcomes of localization-focused programs like Indo-Africa digital advisory services demonstrate the importance of localization quality, i.e., transparently trained AI models use region-specific data, are presented in local languages, and thus use farmer feedback loops. Without this, trust and utility can be compromised due to prejudice and imprecision. It is further worth mentioning that the findings caution on the dangers of geopolitical imbalance, where, in the case of smaller countries, influential players dominate the primary AI infrastructure and create reliance and dependence, which makes them less autonomous. This needs to be addressed by having transparent governance mechanisms, vendor diversification, and capacity-building programs, which would allow the development of local AI.

To ensure equitable and sustainable advancement of AI in agriculture and other critical sectors, it is essential to institutionalize co-creation models and mandate joint ownership of AI tools and datasets within cross-border agreements. Governments and international organizations should apply open standards and promote interoperability and open licensing to prevent vendor lock-in and ensure inclusive access to technological innovation. At the same time, efforts must be made to strengthen data governance by embedding farmer-centric mechanisms that uphold consent, privacy, and data sovereignty. It is also vital to localize AI solutions by prioritizing region-specific training datasets and culturally adapted user interfaces that reflect local languages, practices, and socio-economic realities. To sustain these systems, stakeholders should build human capital through comprehensive AI literacy programs for farmers, extension agents, and policymakers alike. Establishing regional AI hubs can further serve as centers for research and development, testing, and policy dialogue. Moreover, robust resilience safeguards should be integrated into AI frameworks, including fallback operational clauses in the event of system failure. Finally, the use of multilateral platforms such as FAO, ITU, and UNESCO should be expanded to harmonize international standards, facilitate cross-border cooperation, and enable the equitable sharing of knowledge and resources.

6. CONCLUSION

The conclusion of this chapter is that Agri-Tech Diplomacy is an increasingly significant nexus of technology, governance, and international relations, with AI as a source of agricultural innovation and as a nexus of geopolitical collaboration. The cases considered indicate that the most effective results, i.e., better yield, resource optimization, and enhanced diplomatic relationships, can be achieved when AI tools are developed and adapted locally and regulated through fair frameworks that consider them as common goods of the world. However, the threats of dependency, bias, and sovereignty disagreements indicate that proactive governance and capacity-building are necessary. Integrating AI implementation into open and transparent and co-owned systems is a way in which countries can reduce these risks and increase mutual advantages. AI-enhanced agricultural diplomacy is not the technical transfer of technology but rather building trust, exchanging knowledge, and a cross-border digital commons. With climate pressures increasing and food systems becoming more and more interrelated, the principles in this chapter provide a guide in changing AI in agriculture into a competitive edge instead of a collaborative tool to enhance global resilience and sustainability.

REFERENCES

Ajaj, R., Buheji, M., & Hassoun, A. (2024). Optimizing the readiness for industry 4.0 in fulfilling the Sustainable Development Goal 1: Focus on poverty elimination in Africa. *Frontiers in Sustainable Food Systems*, *8*, 1393935. Advance online publication. DOI: 10.3389/fsufs.2024.1393935

Alex, K. (2024). *Agriculture and Aquaculture Applications of Biosensors and Bioelectronics*. IGI Global.

Awate, P. L., & Nagne, A. D. (2025). Satellite Imagery and GIS Applications in Precision Agriculture. In Rani, S., Dutta, S., Rocha, Á., & Cengiz, K. (Eds.), *AI and Data Analytics in Precision Agriculture for Sustainable Development* (pp. 185–206). Springer Nature Switzerland., DOI: 10.1007/978-3-031-93087-4_11

Bal, R., & Gill, I. S. (2020). *Policy Approaches to Artificial Intelligence Based Technologies in China, European Union and the United States* (SSRN Scholarly Paper No. 3699640). Social Science Research Network. DOI: 10.2139/ssrn.3699640

Balestrini, M., Kotsev, A., Ponti, M., & Schade, S. (2021). Collaboration matters: Capacity building, up-scaling, spreading, and sustainability in citizen-generated data projects. *Humanities & Social Sciences Communications*, *8*(1), 169. DOI: 10.1057/s41599-021-00851-5

Batan, A. (2025). Assessing the Role of Public-Private Partnerships in Advancing Sustainable Development Goals Through Agri-Tech and Renewable Energy Solutions. *Transactions on Social Innovation, Digital Inclusion, and Ethical AI*, *15*(2), 1–11.

Bean, E., Burleigh, C., Haskell, C., Burris-Melville, T., Payne, J., & Pathak, B. (2025). Eavesdropping on UNESCO AI Policy, Leadership, and Ethics. *Journal of Leadership Studies*, *18*(4), 98–110. DOI: 10.1002/jls.70007

Bhutani, V., Bahadur, P. S., & Sansaniwal, S. K. (2025). Leveraging Technology for Ethical and Sustainable Global Development. In *Bridging Technology and Development for Sustainable Innovation and Geopolitical Dynamics* (pp. 279–302). IGI Global Scientific Publishing., DOI: 10.4018/979-8-3693-9072-6.ch011

Bi, S., Yuan, X., & Ni, W. (2025). *Building Sustainable and Trustworthy Indigenous Knowledge Preservation Ecosystem* (No. arXiv:2504.17281). arXiv. https://doi.org//arXiv.2504.17281DOI: 10.48550

Chamberlain, W., & Anseeuw, W. (2019). Inclusive businesses in agriculture: Defining the concept and its complex and evolving partnership structures in the field. *Land Use Policy*, *83*, 308–322. DOI: 10.1016/j.landusepol.2019.02.008

Gikunda, K. (2024). *Harnessing Artificial Intelligence for Sustainable Agricultural Development in Africa: Opportunities, Challenges, and Impact* (No. arXiv:2401.06171). arXiv. https://doi.org//arXiv.2401.06171DOI: 10.48550

Guillou, M., & Matheron, G. (2012). *The World's Challenge: Feeding 9 Billion People*. Editions Quae.

Haileslassie, A., Craufurd, P. Q., Blummel, M., Gumma, M. K., Palanisami, K., & Nageswara Rao, V. (2013). *Drivers and major changes in agricultural production systems in drylands of South Asia: Assessing implications for key environmental indicators and research needs*. 11th International Conference on Dryland Development : "Global Climate Change and its Impact on Food & Energy Security in the Dry lands," Beijing, China. https://oar.icrisat.org/7145/

Hennessey, E. (2019, February 1). *What is science diplomacy? | EBSCOhost.* https://openurl.ebsco.com/contentitem/gcd:135719927?sid=ebsco:plink:crawler&id=ebsco:gcd:135719927

Hirunyatrakul, P. (2025). Intersection Thesis and Pathways for AI-Prosperity Alignment in the Global South: An Examination of AI for Good in Thailand [Doctoral, UCL (University College London)]. In *Doctoral thesis, UCL (University College London).* (pp. 1–275). https://discovery.ucl.ac.uk/id/eprint/10207371/

House, R. J. (1998). A brief history of GLOBE. *Journal of Managerial Psychology, 13*(3–4), 230–240. DOI: 10.1108/02683949810215048

Konovalova, M. (2023). AI AND DIPLOMACY: CHALLENGES AND OPPORTUNITIES. *Journal of Liberty and International Affairs, 9*(2), 520–530. DOI: 10.47305/JLIA2392520k

Korkmaz, S. C. (2024). Emerging Technologies and Power Asymmetry in International System: An Analysis over Artificial Intelligence. In *Artificial Intelligence*. CRC Press. DOI: 10.1201/9781003483571-7

Kumar, N., & George, J. (2019). Regional Cooperation for Sustainable Food Security in South Asia: An overview and policy lessons. In *Regional Cooperation for Sustainable Food Security in South Asia*. Routledge India.

Lawal, Y. (2025). AI and IoT-Based Smart Irrigation: A Review of Challenges and Future Trends. *International Congresses of Turkish Science and Technology Publishing*, 770–776.

Linders, D. (2013). Towards open development: Leveraging open data to improve the planning and coordination of international aid. *Government Information Quarterly, 30*(4), 426–434. DOI: 10.1016/j.giq.2013.04.001

Mishra, R., Devi, M. P., Gupta, S., & Kumar, D. (2024). Smart Farming Beyond Boundaries: Global Collaboration and Innovation. In *Agriculture 4.0*. CRC Press. DOI: 10.1201/9781003570219-20

Monteh, R. N. (2025). The Origin and Evolution of Military Drone (UAVs) Technology in Warfare Equipment in Africa. *Political Science and Security Studies Journal*, *6*(2), 20–36. DOI: 10.33445/psssj.2025.6.2.3

Mrisho, L., Mbilinyi, N., Ndalahwa, M., Ramcharan, A., Kehs, A., McCloskey, P., Murithi, H., Hughes, D., & Legg, J. (2020). Evaluation of the accuracy of a smartphone-based artificial intelligence system, PlantVillage Nuru, in diagnosing of the viral diseases of cassava (p. 2020.01.26.919449). *bioRxiv*. DOI: 10.1101/2020.01.26.919449

Naghiyev, N. I. (2025). *The EU's Response to China's Growing Influence in Central and Eastern Europe* [Thesis]. http://dspace.khazar.org/handle/20.500.12323/7987

Nakanishi, Y. J., & Auza, P. M. (2023). Connected Vehicles and Driving Automation Systems. In Nof, S. Y. (Ed.), *Springer Handbook of Automation* (pp. 1079–1113). Springer International Publishing., DOI: 10.1007/978-3-030-96729-1_50

Ozor, N., Nwakaire, J., Nyambane, A., Muhatiah, W., & Nwobodo, C. (2025). Enhancing Africa's agriculture and food systems through responsible and gender inclusive AI innovation: Insights from AI4AFS network. *Frontiers in Artificial Intelligence*, *7*, 1472236. Advance online publication. DOI: 10.3389/frai.2024.1472236 PMID: 39917548

Pimenow, S., Pimenowa, O., Prus, P., & Niklas, A. (2025). The Impact of Artificial Intelligence on the Sustainability of Regional Ecosystems: Current Challenges and Future Prospects. *Sustainability (Basel)*, *17*(11), 4795. DOI: 10.3390/su17114795

Puaschunder, J. M. (2016). *Global Alliance for Information and Communication Technologies and Development (GAID) as an International Platform for Cross-Sectoral Solution Finding and Policy Dialogue on Information and Communication Technologies for Development* (SSRN Scholarly Paper No. 2726399). Social Science Research Network. https://papers.ssrn.com/abstract=2726399

Rovira-Más, F. (2023). Agricultural Robotics. In *Encyclopedia of Digital Agricultural Technologies* (pp. 34–46). Springer., DOI: 10.1007/978-3-031-24861-0_147

Shin, D. (2025). *Debiasing AI: Rethinking the Intersection of Innovation and Sustainability*. Routledge., DOI: 10.1201/9781003530244

Sommer, U., & Fassbender, F. (2024). Environmental Peacebuilding: Moving beyond resolving Violence-Ridden conflicts to sustaining peace. *World Development*, *178*, 106555. DOI: 10.1016/j.worlddev.2024.106555

Spanaki, K., Karafili, E., & Despoudi, S. (2021). AI applications of data sharing in agriculture 4.0: A framework for role-based data access control. *International Journal of Information Management*, *59*, 102350. DOI: 10.1016/j.ijinfomgt.2021.102350

Su, H., Fang, S., & Young, C. (2011). Relationship transparency for partnership enhancement: An intellectual capital perspective. *Journal of Business and Industrial Marketing*, *26*(6), 456–468. DOI: 10.1108/08858621111156449

Chapter 7
AI in Digital Communication Practices:
The Reconstruction of Symbolic Capital Within Digital Diplomacy

Oğuz Han Öztay
Van Yüzüncü Yıl University, Turkey

Hasan Yurdakul
https://orcid.org/0000-0002-5606-6469
Bağımsız Araştırmacı, Turkey

ABSTRACT

The primary objective of this study is to investigate the role of artificial intelligence (AI) in generating symbolic capital in the era of digital diplomacy. Focusing on the role of communication technologies in this transformation, this research examines the impact of AI-supported public diplomacy activities on the struggle for prestige, legitimacy, and recognition in the international arena within the context of Pierre Bourdieu's theory of capital. Conducted using a qualitative research strategy, the study concludes that AI accelerates the process of transforming economic, cultural, and social capital into symbolic capital, thereby expanding the diplomatic spheres of influence of states. Examples such as the Antalya Diplomacy Forum, the United Arab Emirates' (UAE) virtual ambassador application, and South Korea's metaverse diplomacy reveal how critical communication and technological competence are in the process of creating symbolic power. However, this process also deepens existing inequalities between technologically advanced and developing countries.

DOI: 10.4018/979-8-3373-4937-4.ch007

1. INTRODUCTION

In the global arena, power relations and diplomatic conflicts are rooted not only in military and economic factors but also in the symbolic dominance that countries establish over one another. In the international public sphere, nations compete for recognition across various classifications and categories at the state level, such as being peaceful, ethical, democratic, and technologically advanced. This competition can be linked to Pierre Bourdieu's concept of "symbolic capital." The expression of symbolic capital depends on a strong and influential framework of recognition, prestige, and legitimacy (Swartz, 2013). In fact, acquired symbolic capital is viewed as a legitimate authority rather than an overt display of power in the international public sphere. Therefore, utilizing symbolic capital in diplomacy confers privileges and prestige upon those who wield it in the global arena (Bourdieu, 2022, pp. 104-106).

When Bourdieu's concept of symbolic capital is considered in the context of diplomacy, it aligns with states' struggles to be recognized as legitimate, respected, and reputable actors in the international arena. Indeed, public diplomacy is essentially evaluated as a series of public relations and communication strategies pursued by states within specific frameworks in order to gain recognition. Public diplomacy, which is typically conducted through traditional forms of communication, media, cultural events, and representations of leaders, is now being carried out with AI-supported strategic communication and data analytics, alongside technological advancements. Therefore, the application of technological advancements in public diplomacy has introduced a new dimension to communication processes and plans, and the technological context has become a distinct point of differentiation in the international arena (Garakhanova, 2023). Thus, AI-supported public diplomacy activities have also become central to the production of symbolic capital.

Technological advancements and the integration of artificial intelligence (AI) into diplomacy have shifted recognition and reputation processes beyond traditional metrics to include data-driven performance. AI now functions as both an instrument and a domain for generating symbolic capital. States are increasingly leveraging AI tools to organize forums, summits, and social media campaigns on digital platforms, thereby enhancing their diplomatic influence and prestige. AI-supported content production, strategic discourse analysis, and audience segmentation exemplify the new mechanisms for producing symbolic capital. Digital representation, algorithmic reputation, and the deployment of digital ambassadors and virtual representatives have become central to the contemporary struggle for international recognition.

AI applications, driven by technological progress, have evolved from being mere technical tools to serving as indicators of a country's international standing. Consequently, AI-supported public diplomacy now constitutes a significant dimension in the production of symbolic capital. Countries are increasingly focusing on technological competence, digital adaptation, and data literacy to maintain their legitimacy and prestige. However, this emphasis on technology exacerbates existing inequalities in the international system. The integration of AI into public diplomacy has transformed the field into a performative arena, where states utilize technological initiatives to project values such as modernity, advancement, and strategic vision.

The pursuit of recognition, legitimacy, and prestige now extends beyond physical boundaries into the digital domain. As a result, the concept of diplomacy is being redefined, with countries engaging in new technologically driven power relations. This study analyzes the implementation of AI-supported public diplomacy through the lens of Bourdieu's theory of symbolic capital. Diplomatic competition is expected to intensify in technological and symbolic domains, in addition to traditional political and economic arenas. Accordingly, this research offers a significant contribution to the academic literature.

In this study, the role of AI in diplomatic processes will be discussed through Pierre Bourdieu's concept of symbolic capital. In today's digital age, diplomacy is shaped not only by traditional means of communication but also by values such as recognition, reputation, legitimacy, and respect. States go beyond traditional diplomatic tools and address the global public, positioning themselves through algorithms, data analytics, automated content generation, sentiment analysis, and artificial intelligence. This transformation reshapes diplomacy as a field of symbolic struggle.

This study posits that public diplomacy has transformed into a competition for legitimacy, increasingly shaped by technological performance and digitalization. It examines cases including the Antalya Diplomacy Forum, the United Arab Emirates' virtual ambassadors, and South Korea's metaverse diplomacy. To navigate these developments, both scholars and practitioners in diplomacy require an analytical perspective informed by AI technologies to develop effective strategies.

1.1. Theoretical Framework

The study is primarily based on three theoretical frameworks. The first is the theory of public diplomacy. Specifically, within the framework of Nye's soft power and communication-based public diplomacy approach, the transition to network-based and interactive diplomacy in the modern era is examined, and the role of artificial intelligence (AI) applications in public diplomacy is discussed. The second theoretical framework of the study is based on Bourdieu's concept of symbolic capital. In particular, the relationship between symbolic power and social networks is evaluated in terms of how it is reshaped by digital environments and artificial intelligence applications. Finally, the production of symbolic capital in the public diplomacy process, particularly in the context of artificial intelligence (AI) and digital interaction, is emphasized. When AI is used in the diplomatic field to produce new narratives, construct positions, and develop visibility strategies, its potential to generate high amounts of symbolic capital for actors and the resulting scale of new inequalities in the international arena are re-examined in light of the literature.

1.2. Public Diplomacy

As a type of political and strategic communication, public diplomacy can be defined as the process of influencing the ways of thinking of different countries and societies internationally through direct communication with them (Gilboa, 2008). Yun (2022) offers a similar definition, approaching public diplomacy as communication established by the state with actors in the international arena and emphasizing that this communication process aims to convey the country's image, values, and policies to target audiences. Therefore, the understanding that "there is no diplomacy without communication" (Jönsson, 2016, p. 79) prevails in public diplomacy. Public diplomacy is often expressed as a "soft power" tool, carried out by various civil society organizations and diverse fields, ranging from cultural elements to academic actors (Nye, 2023a). Thus, public diplomacy is not only a political and strategic form of communication conducted by states through official channels, but also, as expressed in Nye's concept of "soft power," a strategy to influence international public opinion through non-state actors (culture, education, media, NGOs, etc.) (Fitzpatrick, 2017). In this context, public diplomacy, unlike classical diplomacy, focuses on mutual dialogue and establishing long-term relationships rather than being a one-sided communication process.

In public diplomacy discussions, Nye's concept of soft power has paved the way for a paradigm shift. In his 1991 work, Bound to Lead: The Changing Nature of American Power, Nye questioned the role of military and economic power in public diplomacy, bringing dialogic interaction, civil society organizations, and long-term perception management to the forefront. In other words, he argued that communication-focused elements in the public diplomacy process are more appealing than traditional persuasion (Sevin, 2015). In this context, soft power, defined as the ability to persuade others to want the results you want through appeal and persuasion, is defined as a communication strategy that establishes direct communication with foreign populations to support strategic goals (Nye, 2005). From this perspective, as Nye also points out, soft power is a long-term investment and requires consistency (Kalın, 2011, p. 28). The approach referred to as soft power in public diplomacy uses the persuasiveness and concept of persuasion provided by communication rather than coercion (Nye, 2021, p. 199). This situation also shows similarities with Antonio Gramsci's concept of hegemony. Gramsci (2014) introduced the concept of "consent-based power" in his work, Prison Notebooks. In other words, powerful structures and classes increase their appeal and dominance not only through coercion or forceful elements, but also through social consent. In this respect, Nye's soft power approach strongly overlaps with Gramsci's concept of hegemony.

Gramsci, particularly when explaining how class domination is established in the domestic political process, defines a similar form of hegemonic influence in international relations as a form of power based on attraction rather than coercion, as Nye does. We see that the central concept for both thinkers is persuasion and the production of consent. Indeed, the arguments for this process in both thinkers are communication, education, media, and ideological content production. These arguments are the source of both soft power and hegemony. The role of communication is clear and important in both Nye's soft power approach and Gramsci's concept of hegemony. The development of communication technologies and the widespread use of mass media have shifted the relationships between societies and states to a more abstract level. In the public diplomacy process, the credibility of content shared through communication tools has become a crucial source of appeal and influence (Nye, 2023b, p. 57). Furthermore, the ability of powerful countries to set the international agenda has also increased with the advent of communication tools.

According to McCombs & Shaw (1972), agenda setting determines what the public thinks about through mass communication tools. Examining agenda setting from the perspective of soft power, the public diplomacy process, which Nye refers to as strategic communication, reveals a connection between communication tools and perception management. For example, Hollywood films and BBC news serve as elements of soft power in shaping the global agendas of the US and the UK. Indeed, according to Nye (1991), these elements represent a country's capacity to influence others through the attractiveness of its culture, ideology, and policies, in other words, its power to set the agenda. In other words, it is seen that media and cultural diplomacy support soft power through agenda setting (Nye, 2021). For example, Entman (2008) theoretically examined the role of the media in the US's public diplomacy and soft power strategies in his study titled "Theorizing Mediated Public Diplomacy: The U.S. Case." In this study, Entman attempts to empirically explain the communicative link between agenda setting and soft power in public diplomacy, proposing the "Cascading Activation Model." This communicative model explains how media messages spread through interactions between the government, elites, media, and public opinion, and demonstrates how the effect of soft power in public diplomacy operates through a cascading process. Another example is Wang's (2016) study, "Offensive for Defensive: The Belt and Road Initiative and China's New Grand Strategy." This study also highlights the link between international communication and power struggles by showing how soft power strategies can be reframed by the media. Indeed, these examples are effective in consolidating soft power because they not only determine what is important in public diplomacy through mass media but also how it will be interpreted (Scheufele & Tewksbury,

2007). Thus, powerful states that control communication tools increase their symbolic power and capital through these tools, attributing themselves a more important place in the international public sphere. Especially in the 21st century, transformations in communication technologies, technological innovations such as satellite broadcasting, digitalization, and mobile communication have transformed communication strategies and diversified soft power arguments by taking soft power relations in public diplomacy to a new dimension.

Technological advancements and digitalization have led to significant changes and transformations in various areas, particularly in the field of communication. Indeed, soft power (Nye, 2023b, p. 58), which has gained greater importance in the information age, has transformed into "smart power" with the development of communication technologies (Nye, 2021, p. 203). In this context, Nye states that technological developments, reductions in communication costs, and the instantaneous nature of communication have enabled countries' cultural and ideological influence to reach wider audiences than ever before. In this sense, information-rich actors have gained power in the international arena. Thus, the connection between different content and information is shaped particularly by new communication technologies (Guo & McCombs, 2011). Indeed, this situation is proof that public diplomacy has also transformed in the context of technology. Furthermore, it is understood that capital-rich countries and actors are information-rich actors in this transformation. First, economic capital is needed to possess information power and the tools to disseminate this power. Then, a cultural capital accumulation is required to create content. Therefore, the information wealth expressed by Nye is based on economic and cultural capital resources in the background.

In the context of public diplomacy, Castells (2007) argues that the transformation of soft power is closely linked to the concepts of the information society and the network society. When Castells discusses the information society, he refers to the power of producing, processing, and disseminating information to shape the economic, political, and cultural lives of societies. In the network society, he asserts that individuals and institutions are interconnected through digital networks, and power relations are now shaped by these networks. Indeed, in his work "Soft Power: The Evolution of a Concept" (2021), Nye emphasizes the importance of new media and communication technologies, stating that the technologically changing world of fiber-optic cables, satellites, social media, and digital platforms accelerates the spread of information and culture, creating paradigms in the distribution of power. With the development of communication technologies, power in the international arena and in the process of public diplomacy is now assessed not only by the military and economic capacity of states, but also by the appeal of cultural content disseminated through information and networks, as defined by Castells. Thus, hegemony is established through symbols produced and disseminated on digital platforms, as in Gramsci's civil society.

Today, technological advancements have accelerated digital transformation, making Artificial Intelligence (AI) tools an integral part of everyday life. Indeed, this change has impacted numerous areas and structures, particularly economic and cultural ones. In this context, states' public diplomacy strategies are also transforming their relations with each other by incorporating many elements into the process, such as AI-based communication, data analysis, and targeted messages. For example, the work of J. Wang & Dubbins (2024) emphasize that AI applications create valuable opportunities for increasing efficiency and maximizing impact in public diplomacy. It is stated that AI applications have a revolutionary impact on the management of influential public diplomacy processes, particularly in content creation, developing new strategies, facilitating the analysis and synthesis of large volumes of information, overcoming language barriers very quickly through the use of AI-supported translation tools, and improving operational processes. On the other hand, AI applications are also noteworthy for their potential to play an active role in critical processes, such as consular services, crisis management, and diplomatic planning (Mostafaei et al., 2025). Therefore, it is also crucial for public diplomacy actors to integrate into the digital transformation, understand new technologies, and utilize AI applications in this process (Konovalova, 2023).

AI is rapidly transforming how states interact with the world. Public diplomacy, once defined by cultural exchange and state-sponsored media, is now influenced by algorithmic precision, data-driven strategy, and digital persuasion (Collective, 2025). The use of digital technologies and AI applications in public diplomacy creates tremendous opportunities to build stronger, more diverse, and more enduring bridges between offline and online communities (Bjola et al., 2019, p. 83). However, these innovations inevitably bring with them transparency, security, and new types of risks. For example, Hlihor (2024) highlights the potential for AI applications to be manipulative in the public diplomacy process. It is emphasized that actors seeking to misinform and manipulate public opinion, particularly in democratic societies, may resort to AI applications. In this regard, while the use of AI applications in public diplomacy is seen as revolutionary, the dangers and risks it creates appear too dangerous to be ignored.

With the global adoption of AI applications, it can be said that competition in public diplomacy has already begun. A full-fledged quest for groundbreaking technology in the field of AI is taking place between the US, China, and more recently, the EU, Korea, Japan, Russia, and India, and it is inevitable that the winners will establish economic and geopolitical dominance in the future (Feijóo et al., 2020, p. 3). In other words, the effective and strategic use of AI applications in the public diplomacy process strengthens the position of states that master these applications internationally (Varela, 2024, p. 172) and turns them into a valuable asset. Therefore, it can be seen that countries possessing technology and AI have an advantage over others in the public diplomacy process. In other words, while the investments made by countries with technological capital in AI applications make them more attractive internationally, it can be said that inequalities between countries have become increasingly apparent. Countries and societies that are ahead in terms of technological competence and digital capital accumulation are exacerbating international inequalities by leveraging AI applications in public diplomacy and integrating them into the process quickly. In other words, high integration into the digital sphere strengthens the prestige, status, and, in short, the symbolic capital of countries and societies on a global scale, just as it affects the social status of individuals in social life (Choi et al., 2020, p. 5; Yurdakul, 2025, p. 310). Therefore, investments in AI applications are expected to increase in the near future.

2. SYMBOLIC CAPITAL IN THE FIELD OF PUBLIC DIPLOMACY, BOURDIEU, AND ARTIFICIAL INTELLIGENCE

Public diplomacy, in its classical sense, refers to the strategies employed by countries and states to establish relationships in the international arena. When these relationship-building strategies are considered in the context of Bourdieu, they can be evaluated as one of the fields of symbolic struggle. Symbolic capital, one of Pierre Bourdieu's types of capital, emerges when individuals, institutions, or countries or states acquire values such as recognition, legitimacy, and prestige. Furthermore, symbolic capital can also be considered a result and reflection of economic, social, and cultural capital. Therefore, it is seen as the legitimized form of these types of capital and can constitute the implicit power mechanism of many relationships, primarily social relationships. Indeed, when approached from the perspective of public diplomacy, it represents how countries and states are defined in the international arena. In particular, countries' efforts to be recognized as legitimate, reputable, and developed actors are considered a struggle for symbolic capital.

According to Bourdieu, capital, regardless of its type and form, represents historical accumulation and labor (Bourdieu, 2011). He argues that capital possesses both tangible and intangible characteristics. Capital is noteworthy for its role in the emergence of hierarchies and divisions, both in the social space and in the international arena. The international arena, one of the areas of conflict, is the scene of power struggles between states, and the source of this power struggle is capital. Therefore, countries are evaluated based on the volume and structure of capital that represents them in the international arena (Jourdain & Naulin, 2020, p. 115).

Thus, capital is decisive in the struggles for recognition and prestige that countries experience in the international arena.

For Bourdieu, the concept of capital is a type of energy source that is valid in areas such as the social, cultural, and political spheres and can be concentrated in the hands of a small number of individuals, institutions, and states. This energy can be distributed, appropriated, and manipulated among people, societies, countries, and states (Bourdieu, 2022, p. 389). Thus, gains in certain areas, such as economic accumulation, advanced educational opportunities, technological proficiency, and military superiority, can secure the power and prestige of states in the international arena. This demonstrates that capital not only provides accumulation and value in economic terms, but can also be accumulated and utilized in various areas.

Bourdieu defines capital in four distinct types: economic, cultural, social, and symbolic capital (Jourdain & Naulin, 2020, pp. 106-107). The first of these is economic or financial capital, which is the source of other types of capital. This type of capital refers to economic resources. Cultural capital represents the goods and practices associated with the enlightened culture in society. Social capital is the use of acquaintance relationships within a society. Symbolic capital, on the other hand, is prestige in the social field. Indeed, according to Bourdieu, these types of capital can be converted into one another (Bourdieu, 2011). In fact, according to him, the basic logic of how capital works is that one type of capital can be converted into a different type of capital within a space. Bourdieu's types of capital are the source of determining an individual's position in the social field and the emergence of these positions. When Bourdieu's capital typology is evaluated from the perspective of public diplomacy, we encounter the strategic use of these types of capital by states and international actors to strengthen their positions in the global field or to enter a new position in the competitive landscape. This is because, according to Bourdieu, strategy involves the use of specific types of capital to pursue interests within a given field (Bourdieu, 2016, p. 104). In other words, strategy represents actions taken in pursuit of one's own interests and attempts to gain access to the field of power using accumulated capital (Bourdieu, 2018, p. 113). From this perspective, economic capital in public diplomacy encompasses investments in organizations, such as the mobilization of material resources, funding for cultural events, and the execution of media campaigns. Cultural capital, on the other hand, encompasses initiatives aimed at promoting a country's history, art, language, and cultural heritage on a global scale. Social capital in public diplomacy encompasses activities such as establishing two-way relationships and expanding diplomatic networks. Symbolic capital, on the other hand, constitutes perhaps the most visible but also the most abstract aspect of public diplomacy. A country's recognition for qualities such as being peaceful, reliable, technologically advanced, or respectful of human rights gives it prestige, legitimacy, and reputation-based power in the international arena.

The state is the most important producer of symbolic capital (Bourdieu, 2014). From this perspective, in terms of public diplomacy, the state legitimately transfers symbolic resources to the international arena. By transferring the legitimate discourses, it constructs internally, such as human rights, emphasis on democracy, and achievements in technology, to the international arena, the state can present them as elements of soft power. Thus, these discourses enable the strategic construction of meaning at the international level, allowing it to enter into power struggles. All of this legitimizes the state's symbolic power and the elements arising from this power in the international arena as well.

When approaching public diplomacy from Bourdieu's perspective, it is possible to say that public diplomacy is not only a communicative process but also a struggle and transformation of capital (Ertem-Eray, 2023, p. 289). This can also be seen as a means of gaining legitimacy in the international arena. In particular, the use of abstract forms of capital as a public diplomacy strategy in the international arena represents sources of power that are invisible in diplomatic practice but have a profound impact (Kuus, 2015, p. 368). Therefore, symbolic power in the international arena affects a country's recognition, legitimacy, status, and visibility in the diplomatic sphere (Adler-Nissen, 2011, pp. 327-330). Symbolic power also facilitates the deepening of public diplomacy communication strategies (Edwards, 2009) and the attainment of status in the international arena. For example, states use their cultural elements, economic resources, or bilateral relations—that is, capital accumulations that can generate legitimacy in the social sphere—to gain symbolic power (Zamorano, 2016). In other words, economic, cultural, and social capital accumulations are the source of symbolic power. Therefore, as Bourdieu mentions in his field theory, the field of public diplomacy must also be considered as a set of fields that are valid in the global arena (Bourdieu, 1989). The use of different fields alongside different types of capital also constitutes the capital of that field. International prestige, legitimacy, and reputation are built with symbolic capital, as required by the nature of the diplomatic role. Thus, symbolic power is an integral part of public diplomacy.

Technological developments, digitalization, and the legitimizing discourse of artificial intelligence applications in the international arena —i.e., becoming one of the new sources of symbolic power —are decisive in the transformation of public diplomacy and the context in which communication strategies will take shape. In particular, states and actors that possess substantial amounts of the types of capital described by Bourdieu have seen their appeal and prestige in the international arena increase in recent years. Since prestige represents a kind of sovereignty (Freud, 2023, p. 20), symbolic capital can be considered a silent power in creating and maintaining power relations. In today's public diplomacy process, the symbolic power of countries that possess Artificial Intelligence (AI) capital and the technological accumulation that constitutes this capital is increasingly gaining credibility and legitimacy in the international community.

The development of technology-based applications, such as Artificial Intelligence (AI), is one indicator of both states' interest in new areas (Taylor, 2012, p. 210) and where capital investments are beginning to accumulate (Yurdakul, 2024, p. 327). This situation is causing AI to grow rapidly and its areas of use to spread. In other words, AI is not only an economic investment tool, but it is also redefining the volume of capital accumulation that affects global life and the struggles within that life (Suskind, 2022, p. 33). The relationship between AI and productivity (Byrnjolfsson, 2022; Nachman, 2022) also shapes the relationships between capital and struggles. As Bourdieu points out, the concentration of capital in the hands of a small number of individuals, institutions, or countries has led to a similar concentration of technological knowledge and capacity in the field of artificial intelligence, concentrated in the hands of only a few countries and states (Acemoğlu, 2022, p. 24), providing these actors with a powerful strategic advantage.

AI applications, which have become an important part of capital accumulation and strategic communication (Fox, 2024, p. 519), are also deepening international relations. Thus, public diplomacy, a crucial element of international relations, is also evolving, and countries' positions are being reassessed according to new criteria. While the international maneuverability of countries possessing AI capital increases, this situation provides them not only with technological superiority but also with symbolic capital, which confers prestige, recognition, and legitimacy on a global scale, as defined by Bourdieu. Thus, these countries become more persuasive and effective actors in public diplomacy activities. Indeed, countries lacking technological power – given that these countries also have weak classical capital accumulation and insufficient capital stocks in the technological and digital fields (Ericson et al., 2024, p. 307) - experience a lack of AI applications in the public diplomacy process, which can gradually weaken their impact in the international arena.

The digital transformation in public diplomacy, along with technological developments, has reshaped diplomatic norms, values, and working practices (Manor & Huang, 2022, p. 167). The rapid integration of AI applications into this digitalization process, in particular, can bring together material, immaterial, and intellectual capital within its own structure and, in this respect, can transform into a broader and more inclusive type of capital (Luo & Yu, 2022, p. 157). Indeed, from Bourdieu's perspective, AI is one of the areas where economic, cultural, social, and symbolic capital intersect or merge. On the other hand, AI also functions as a meta-capital that facilitates the transformation of these forms of capital into one another. Thus, states that possess AI technologies gain an advantage not only in terms of technical capacity but also in terms of prestige, influence, and agenda-setting power in the international arena.

3. ARTIFICIAL INTELLIGENCE AND PUBLIC DIPLOMACY IN THE PRODUCTION OF SYMBOLIC CAPITAL

Bourdieu states that classical forms of capital, such as economic and cultural capital, are transformed into symbolic capital along with recognition and legitimacy, and this transformation is linked to the volume of original capital in a given field. The subtle elements of the field of diplomacy are structures where symbolic power is concentrated and visible. The digitization of diplomacy alongside technological developments, social platforms, visual communication forms, and network logic highlights "perceptual" values such as transparency, participation, and visibility (Manor & Huang, 2022). On the other hand, the effective use of AI in public diplomacy rapidly transforms classical capital accumulation into symbolic capital in the international arena. In other words, AI in public diplomacy creates an accelerating effect, as described by Bourdieu.

The use of AI in public diplomacy is not merely the transfer of a technological innovation to a field; it has also brought about a shift in understanding and perception within that field, leading to the emergence of a new discourse production mechanism. In other words, this situation highlights a tendency for a series of content and discourse engineering approaches, such as message modeling and sentiment analysis, to be applied according to mass segments, ultimately transforming into symbolic power (Edwards, 2009). Furthermore, recognition categories in the digital sphere, such as algorithmic visibility and metric values, have become the current form of diplomatic symbolic capital (Manor & Huang, 2022). Thus, AI applications increase the power of symbolic capital alongside metric power in public diplomacy.

The transition from public diplomacy based on the classical communication process to digital public diplomacy has opened up new areas of communication and interaction between states, countries, and societies. With the digitization of public diplomacy, soft power has also strengthened, and messages reach their target more quickly and effectively (Cull, 2013). At the same time, with digitization, the visibility of countries and actors has also become a source of symbolic capital gains. On the other hand, it is understood that digital platforms have opened up a new arena of competition in public diplomacy and that countries are also competing to produce symbolic power in this arena. At the same time, online interaction, user data, and feedback enhance legitimacy strategies by leveraging the concept of symbolic capital.

Based on Mazumdar's (2024) work, when we ask the question, "Is digital diplomacy a reproduction of traditional public diplomacy practices via the internet, or does it create a new type of public interaction?" we understand that digital diplomacy involves the creation of new practices. It is evident that practices such as developing diplomatic discourse through everyday life, supported by interactive content, and the rapid and accessible nature of responses, are effective in shaping power relations within public diplomacy. These new practices indicate that the production of symbolic capital has also become digital and is incorporated into everyday life practices. On the other hand, the easy and rapid integration of digitalized public diplomacy practices into AI applications can be expanded with automated content production, sentiment analysis, and micro-targeting. Thus, countries can increase the volume of their symbolic capital accumulation and strengthen their legitimacy in the public diplomacy process. In other words, both the use of the digital sphere and the shift towards AI applications in public diplomacy create new sources of symbolic capital.

Along with digital transformation, diplomatic norms, boundaries, and forms of interaction are being restructured. Social media, online platforms, and visual content, in particular, are creating new understandings and norms in the distribution of diplomatic messages. At the same time, the ways in which international actors participate in the field, their strategies for gaining legitimacy, and their expectations are undergoing a radical transformation (Kaljurand, 2019). Thus, a new style in public diplomacy, namely the digital habitus, has emerged. This has led to the transformation of the diplomatic sphere into a digital diplomatic sphere, a change in the framework of perception, and, along with these, the increasing power of digital symbolic capital, which is becoming more concrete and digitalized, has become the rising value of the international sphere.

The digitization of public diplomacy and the emergence of Artificial Intelligence as a key component of public diplomacy have added a new layer to existing inequalities in the international arena, making the boundaries of these inequalities increasingly apparent. When approached from a Bourdieuian perspective, particularly in relation to capital, these inequalities come to the fore. When it comes to digitalization, Bourdieu's approach focuses on the issue of digital capital (Addeo et al., 2023; Airoldi, 2022; Bannykh, 2020; Calderón Gómez, 2021; Calhoun, 2016; Ragnedda, 2017, 2018; Ragnedda et al., 2020; Yurdakul, 2025). Indeed, in these studies, digital capital is associated with digital skills, access to networks and infrastructure, online legitimacy and visibility, the ability to transform traditional capital accumulation, and accumulated capital of individuals, institutions, actors, states, and countries. Digital capital reshapes symbolic capital by opening up a new field of production through digital practices based on metric values. This situation creates digital and numerical divisions, as well as digital divides.

With the widespread use of AI, it can be said that inequalities linked to the accumulation of digital capital are deepening, particularly in the context of countries and their populations. The tendency to separate the roles of production (education) and consumption (distribution/application) in AI and to create power asymmetries within many fields, including diplomacy, is increasing day by day. In this context, AI not only accelerates the accumulation of symbolic capital but also monopolizes the production of legitimacy and visibility by unequally distributing the material and organizational infrastructure (Khanal et al., 2025). On the other hand, countries with strong technological resources and capital legitimize symbolic power and violence by directing international diplomacy through data colonialism (Couldry & Mejias, 2023). When read through Bourdieu's perspective of symbolic violence, platform metrics and the economy of visibility asymmetrically redistribute the legitimate right to speak. The transformation of public diplomacy into digital diplomacy silences and legitimizes inequality through the use of technology. Indeed, the digital capital accumulation of digital diplomacy actors places them in a central position in international diplomacy, granting them symbolic power (Arapov et al., 2017). In short, although digital diplomacy or AI diplomacy accelerates the production of symbolic capital, differences arising from many different factors, such as infrastructure, technological and digital skills, and access to language models, can create unequal intra-field distribution returns. In this case, it further deepens the distinctions and differences between countries in public diplomacy.

4. COMMUNICATION AND TECHNOLOGICAL TRANSFORMATION IN DIPLOMACY

This section of the study will focus on the importance of communication tools in public diplomacy, the transformation of public diplomacy practices by digitalization and new communication strategies, the general definition of AI, and the identification of points where it intersects with diplomacy. In particular, the role of AI in data analysis and strategic communication in diplomatic contexts, as well as its applications in automated content production and perception management, will be discussed with examples such as Türkiye's Antalya Diplomacy Forum events, the UAE's virtual ambassadors, and South Korea's metaverse diplomacy. Furthermore, Bourdieu's approach to capital and the concept of symbolic capital will be re-evaluated in this context.

4.1. The Relationship Between Media and Symbolic Capital in Public Diplomacy

Public diplomacy essentially encompasses a set of communication activities established by countries with other countries and peoples. In particular, countries seek to promote their foreign policies to other countries through both diplomatic channels and the media. From this perspective, the transmission of these policies is as important as the policies themselves, which are defined and implemented in public diplomacy. Therefore, it can be said that communication plays a central role in the public diplomacy process. Indeed, Gilboa's (1998) study defines the role of the media in public diplomacy as that of a mediator. According to him, public diplomacy is shaped by the triangle of states, media, and public opinion. In another study, Gilboa attempted to analyze the complex relationship between public diplomacy and the media by dividing it into two groups and using six conceptual models (Gilboa, 2000). The first group classifies public diplomacy messages according to their level of openness to the media and the public, while the second group focuses on the active roles of the media in the public diplomacy process. In another study, Gilboa draws attention to the concept of global communication and reopens the debate on the relationship between public diplomacy and communication (Gilboa, 2002).

In this study, Gilboa highlights both the limiting and facilitating aspects of global communication in public diplomacy. Indeed, the dominant role of the media in decision-making, the media's shift from a spectator role to becoming a mediator involved in the public diplomacy process, the formation of public opinion by actors through the media, and the steering of masses by strategic messages reveal the crucial role of communication in the public diplomacy process. Thus, communication tools can both determine the dynamics of the public diplomacy field and ensure the transformation of capital. In particular, the active role of the media in the public diplomacy process can be linked to its catalytic function in the production of symbolic capital by countries and actors. On the other hand, public opinion formed by the media also legitimizes symbolic capital. Thus, it will tend to expand the boundaries of symbolic capital in the international arena.

In the public diplomacy process, the role of the media within the field of diplomacy and the impact of media actors on the production of symbolic capital are more clearly revealed in the work of Kishan Thussu (2000). It shows how the global media, controlled by the US, guided international diplomacy by taking into account the geostrategic interests of the West during the 1999 Kosovo Crisis. It is understood that the media's news content and preferences were shaped with geographical interests in mind, the international discourse and agenda were reconstructed, the Kosovo intervention was framed as "humanitarian aid" rather than an "intervention against a sovereign state" to legitimize it, and this narrative contributed to the production of symbolic capital. Thus, in the public diplomacy process, symbolic violence is legitimized through the media, and the foreign policy discourses of certain countries are becoming widespread and accepted internationally. Entman (2008) explains this situation with the "cascading network activation" model.

The cascading network activation model posits that powerful countries craft their public diplomacy messages through the media, disseminate them through the media, and influence public opinion with the assistance of media elites. The narrative created by powerful countries through the media can generate international legitimacy and prestige, which in turn strengthens the symbolic capital that can be used in the international arena. The relationship between the media and the field of diplomacy points to the formation of networks between states and media elites. Thus, the media play an active role in shaping the dynamics of the field in the international space. All of this shows that the media is one of the mechanisms for the reproduction of symbolic power and symbolic violence. In other words, although the media appears to act independently of governments in the public diplomacy process, it has the potential to reproduce and promote the strategic agendas of states (Karl, 1982, p. 143).

4.2. Public Diplomacy, New Media, and Symbolic Capital

With the technological transformation of communication tools, public diplomacy is also changing and reshaping itself in terms of both content and form. In particular, the communication established by international actors and leaders with the global public opinion takes place more through digital communication channels than through traditional media. Today, conducting public diplomacy through traditional media is insufficient and ineffective. On the other hand, the positioning and ideological relationships of traditional media in the international arena constitute one of the most fundamental inequalities in public diplomacy. Public diplomacy, reshaped by digitalization, fills the gap between media diplomacy and public diplomacy on the one hand, while directly facilitating the diplomatic process on the other. An example of this is Ukrainian President Volodymyr Zelenskyy's direct address to foreign parliaments and the global public via digital platforms during the war (Saliu, 2022). In this example, Zelenskyy succeeded in capturing the world's attention with instant strategic messages via digital communication platforms and was able to mobilize international support. Indeed, this situation creates Zelenskyy's online visibility, legitimacy, and influence on the one hand; it has also ensured the production of symbolic prestige in the digital sphere. On the other hand, the field of diplomacy is being reshaped through social media platforms. Furthermore, Zelensky's diplomatic communication has given rise to a new language and discourse, shaping a diplomatic habitus. This language and discourse have been shaped by the nature and limitations of social media.

As can be seen from the example of Zelensky, public diplomacy has evolved beyond traditional propaganda tools to become a multi-actor, interactive communication process. Digital communication platforms offer opportunities for leaders, various actors, and states to actively engage in the field of diplomacy. Sevin & Ingenhoff (2018) analyze public diplomacy conducted through digital communication platforms in the context of network relations and content production. In this context, countries are encountering attempts to build their international image and attract the attention of the global public not only through official channels and diplomatic accounts, but also through the participation of civilian users. Thus, digital visibility, interaction power, and perception management transform into the digital form of symbolic capital. For example, examining the 2011 Arab Spring movement, it is possible to say that social media drew the attention of the international public. Indeed, this situation shows that new actors can be involved in public diplomacy. Thus, while it demonstrates that digital communication platforms facilitate the development of new digital networks that complement classical diplomatic networks, it also suggests that digital tools are employed strategically for political influence (Ociepka, 2012). This situation is evaluated within the context of the concept of strategic public management, which involves establishing strategic relationships and setting the agenda (Zhang, 2013). Therefore, digital communication platforms open the way for effective crisis management, setting a new agenda, strategic message management, and proactive and reactive interventions in public diplomacy.

With the rise of digitalization, public diplomacy has been conducted through digital communication platforms in recent years. Thus, public diplomacy creates its own language while also utilizing the language of digital communication platforms. In other words, retrofitted content can be more effective both nationally and internationally (Zhong & Lu, 2013). The rapid interaction and feedback provided by digitalization are effective in producing strategic messages in public diplomacy. Indeed, it is understood that digital communication platforms are a new medium in the development of public diplomacy. Moreover, digital communication platforms have now become a new form of diplomacy in their own right, rather than just an alternative communication channel in public diplomacy. This situation has led to the addition of new concepts to the public diplomacy literature. In this context, Su & Xu (2015) employ the concept of "Twitplomacy" to highlight the diplomatic communication practices of states, institutions, and individuals on social media. According to Su and Xu, "Twitplomacy" refers to the development of new strategies by powerful and competitive countries in the international arena to influence public opinion through the collection of concrete data on digital platforms. In this regard, Di Martino (2020) evaluates the use of digital communication platforms in the public diplomacy process in five different ways. A taxonomy has been developed to categorize how digital platforms are utilized in public diplomacy, encompassing classifications such as passively evaluating messages received by countries or actors through digital communication platforms, data-driven analysis and strategy updates, content development based on community demands, and image-based symbolic strategy production. This suggests that symbolic capital is closely tied to the active and effective use of digital communication platforms, thereby creating a new source of visibility, reputation, and prestige for state actors. On the other hand, it also shows that digital communication platforms are one of the new spaces of public diplomacy.

The introduction of digital communication tools in public diplomacy has also changed international competition. It is understood that social media platforms have become a virtual battlefield, where actors from different countries are in fierce competition for target audiences and information (Lin, 2024). In this regard, it is clear that network structure and time-dependent changes are very important in this process. When evaluated from a network perspective, it is now understood that not only shared content but also positioning within the network has come to the fore. In other words, certain nodes provide some actors with an advantage in shaping international public opinion. Lin's network-focused public diplomacy approach actually highlights that international capital is not only accumulated through messages but also produced through networks. Thus, digital communication platforms are becoming increasingly central to public diplomacy. On the other hand, these platforms are also becoming a powerful tool that transforms public participation in the public diplomacy process (Rachmawati et al., 2024). Consequently, these power relations also create inequalities in the digital world. In particular, the capital gap between developing and developed countries is also evident in the digitalization of public diplomacy. Indeed, according to Perdani et al. (2024), while developing countries are unable to utilize digital communication platforms effectively as a public diplomacy tool, developed countries are leveraging social media for national image building, perception management, and brand strategies. Therefore, the relationship between digital diplomacy strategies and countries' levels of development is becoming apparent. On the other hand, it is understood that the use of digital platforms in public diplomacy creates a historical and economic context, and thus requires a holistic approach.

4.3. Artificial Intelligence and the Reconstruction of Symbolic Capital in Public Diplomacy

Artificial Intelligence studies have a history spanning over 65 years. Artificial Intelligence (AI) is a digital technology designed and produced by humans (Fetzer, 1990, p. 3). AI is considered one of the disciplines that uses powerful algorithms capable of mimicking important aspects of human intelligence (Gomez et al., 2022, p. 3076). The simplest definition of artificial intelligence is framed by its disembodied nature, its control by a program, and its reliance on technological tools to function (Yurdakul, 2024, p. 329). Therefore, the disembodied nature of artificial intelligence increases its impact and power on social life (Dyer-Witheford et al., 2022, p. 21). Whether we are aware of it or not, AI has permeated our daily lives, taking on new roles in various areas, including industry, health, transportation, education, and society (Jiang et al., 2022). Artificial intelligence applications have become an integral part of life today, and humanity's relationship with the world is beginning to take shape through digital tools and algorithms (Reese, 2020, p. 51).

The relationship between AI and public diplomacy is one of the rapidly growing areas of debate and research, particularly in recent years, in both diplomatic circles and academia. In this relationship, two different assessments can be made, particularly in terms of opportunities and risks. Targeting and personalization, content production and translation, sentiment analysis and reputation management, as well as virtual and augmented reality, can be considered opportunities for AI in the public diplomacy process. On the other hand, bias, perception management, ethics, and data privacy pose risks in this process. Although AI has the potential to revolutionize public diplomacy, like any innovation, artificial intelligence carries its own risks.

AI applications can be integrated into the entire public diplomacy process. AI, particularly through big data analysis, can map the interests, concerns, and information habits of target audiences to develop data-driven diplomatic strategies; create content such as text, audio, and video; conduct monitoring and evaluation measurements; identify potential crises that could affect countries' images in advance; and rebuild soft power indicators with AI (Mostafaei et al., 2025, pp. 2-3). However, alongside these, algorithmic biases, transparency, and ethical dilemmas, as well as the digital divide, are also considered risks arising from AI (Bradshaw & Howard, 2018). For example, Saudi Arabia's decision to grant citizenship to robots is seen as one of the risks arising in terms of public diplomacy (Puaschunder, 2019). Thus, it is seen that the relationship between the role of countries in public diplomacy and strategic messages is becoming increasingly blurred.

Radanliev (2025) states that AI and similar tools add strategic depth to cyber diplomacy. These technological tools promise a new type of symbolic capital that generates visibility and credibility for states. In particular, competencies such as crisis foresight, data-driven policy-making, and increased diplomatic engagement function as sources of symbolic capital that strengthen the image and legitimacy of states (Hossain et al., 2024). Therefore, when evaluated within the framework of an approach from Bourdieu's perspective, AI technologies create not only technical competence but also reflexive power gained in the communication environment in the form of international legitimacy and prestige. AI applications used in the public diplomacy process also feed symbolic capital in areas such as text analysis, risk management, and social assessments. However, as Bourdieu also points out, structural differences and the inadequacy of classical capital stocks deepen international inequalities. In other words, the geographical and institutional monopolization in the development and distribution of these technologies may fuel new dynamics of inequality in the arena of digital diplomacy. When evaluated using Bourdieu's concepts, state actors with knowledge of and access to AI gain visible prestige in the field of digital diplomacy, while others may be relegated to a less visible position (Kirilkina & Karochkin, 2025).

Denmark's "Technology Diplomacy," launched in 2017, encompasses an innovation-focused approach involving a wide range of actors, including states, technology companies, international organizations, and civil society (Bjola & Kornprobst, 2025). This has added a new dimension to diplomatic theory through the concept of a multi-actor organization. Along with technology diplomacy, the use of AI tools, blockchain, and 5G technology in diplomatic processes represents the ability of states or actors to gain diplomatic prestige not only through information or communication power but also by producing innovation, seizing technological leadership in the international arena with an innovative image, and reassigning legitimacy. For example, the Antalya Diplomacy Forum (ADF)[1] can be considered a significant technological initiative that represents this innovative approach.

Since 2021, the ADF has been a highly participatory platform in Antalya, bringing together leaders, foreign policymakers, academics, businesspeople, and media actors from various fields. The forum's official manifesto is framed as opening a multi-actor space for "dialogue and norm production at a fragmented global level." While the theme for 2024 is "Advancing Diplomacy in Times of Turmoil," the theme for 2025 is "Reclaiming Diplomacy in a Fragmented World" (Akıllı, 2025). This framework illustrates Türkiye's objective of accruing legitimacy, prestige, and visibility in the international arena through digital technologies. In 2024, a special panel titled "AI and Diplomacy" was organized within the ADF. This panel initiated a discussion on the impact of AI on power, prosperity, and norms. Thus, the ADF has demonstrated its innovative capacity by bringing not only geopolitical topics but also technological diplomacy to the forefront. The implication of "technological competence" that this AI-themed content added to the forum brand has been an element that directly feeds symbolic capital.

According to Üste and Aydın (2022), the ADF represents innovation in the diplomacy paradigm. In particular, the multi-actor and network-based approach demonstrates that public diplomacy is conducted as a holistic process. The ADF is also effective in setting a diplomatic agenda. Şehitoğlu and Eren (2022) state that the ADF is a new type and concrete example of soft power. It provides Türkiye with symbolic prestige on the international stage, thereby granting it diplomatic legitimacy. Viewed through Bourdieu's concept of symbolic capital, the visibility, perceived legitimacy, and innovative diplomatic performance within ADF strengthen the state's position in the diplomatic arena. In the context of new media and technology diplomacy, the ADF combines conference diplomacy with digital agenda-setting capacity; for example, through AI-focused sessions and visibility on digital platforms, it demonstrates that symbolic capital is also produced digitally. With ADF, the field of diplomacy has become increasingly complex and multi-layered. In addition, Türkiye's visibility is increasing both internationally and in digital media. This not only gives Türkiye international prestige but also increases its authority. In other words, Türkiye has earned its authority. It also creates a network-based and multi-actor process of interactive habitus.

In technology-based diplomacy, the UAE's (United Arab Emirates) virtual ambassadors can be seen as one of the most striking and symbolic manifestations of the "Digital UAE" vision[2]. Indeed, this initiative can be considered one of the attempts to profoundly transform traditional diplomacy. In the UAE's digital diplomacy practice, the "virtual ambassador" utilizes AI-powered avatars/digital personas, or AI representatives of official institutions, to convey institutional messages, rather than accredited diplomats in the classical sense. The primary objectives are to provide 24/7 service, offer multilingual access, engage the public through storytelling, promote digital literacy, and generate symbolic prestige. While AI ambassadors make the UAE's innovation power visible, they also accelerate the production of symbolic capital by translating its claim to technological leadership into everyday communication.

The UAE's virtual representative initiatives employ AI-based public diplomacy across a wide range of areas, including government services, security, and city branding. This is a "staging" that accelerates the transformation of technical/cultural capital into symbolic capital, as seen from Bourdieu's perspective: innovation, power → visibility → legitimacy → prestige. However, without transparency, bias management, and accountability, this capital can remain fragile. It is also understood that the UAE uses technology as a soft power tool instead of traditional soft power tools (cinema, music).

Another example in this process is South Korea's "Metaverse Diplomacy." Digital New Deal 2.0 strategy[3] announced in 2022 aims to develop the metaverse ecosystem. In this context, four priority areas have been identified. These are the platform ecosystem, expert training, company support, and ethical/social norms. South Korea represents one of the rare state models that adopts the metaverse as a strategic public diplomacy tool and aims for sectoral leadership. Indeed, this initiative has the potential to transform cultural and technological capital into symbolic capital through the metaverse. On the other hand, it legitimizes digital public diplomacy with concrete projects. In terms of symbolic capital, this initiative enhances the visibility of cultural and technological innovation, thereby increasing the state's prestige, while metaverse campaigns generate symbolic legitimacy. Furthermore, it is understood that the concept of the metaverse has expanded the field of diplomacy. Consequently, state actors are adopting new diplomatic practices by developing strategies tailored to digital platforms.

5. CONCLUSION

This section examines, within a Bordieuan framework, how technological developments, digitalization, and AI applications play a transformative role in both practical public diplomacy and at the scientific level. In this context, while diplomacy, in its classical sense, refers to the political, economic, and cultural interactions of states in the international arena, digital diplomacy and AI-supported strategies have opened up a new field in the production of symbolic values such as legitimacy, prestige, and recognition. AI is not only a technical tool but also embodies the nature of meta-capital, which produces status, visibility, and prestige in international relations. Applications such as algorithms, data analytics, automated content generation, virtual ambassadors, and the metaverse are fundamentally transforming how states represent themselves in the global public sphere. This transformation is rapidly converting traditional forms of capital (economic, cultural, social) into symbolic capital.

Examples such as Türkiye's Antalya Diplomacy Forum, the UAE's virtual ambassadors, and South Korea's metaverse diplomacy strategy demonstrate that states embrace AI and digital technologies not only as a technical capacity indicator but also as a source of diplomatic prestige. Such initiatives strengthen countries' positions on the international stage while also contributing to the formation of new diplomatic norms and habits.

States that master AI and digital diplomacy tools gain the power to set the international agenda and position themselves as legitimate and reputable actors. In contrast, actors with weak technological capital become less visible on the global stage and are relegated to a disadvantaged position in diplomatic interactions. In this context, AI accelerates the production of symbolic capital while reinforcing international inequalities. This demonstrates that capital-based inequalities are not being eliminated by technological developments; rather, they are deepening, making it increasingly difficult to bridge the gap between countries.

Consequently, AI-supported public diplomacy has become a critical threshold in today's diplomatic competition. AI applications not only bring speed, efficiency, and accessibility to diplomacy but also become central to the production of symbolic power, legitimacy, and prestige. In this context, diplomacy in the future will be shaped not only by political and economic power struggles but also by technological capacity and digital capital. Therefore, it is inevitable that states wishing to play an effective role internationally will view AI technologies not merely as a tool but as a strategic source of symbolic capital production.

REFERENCES

Acemoğlu, D. (2022). Yapay zekayı yeniden tasarlamak (H. Dölkeleş, Çev.). In Cohen, J., & Chasman, D. (Eds.), *Yapay zekayı yeniden tasarlamak: Otomasyon çağında iş, demokrasi, adalet* (pp. 7–31). Elif Yayınevi.

Addeo, F., D'Auria, V., Delli Paoli, A., Punziano, G., Ragnedda, M., & Ruiu, M. L. (2023). Measuring digital capital in Italy. *Frontiers in Sociology, 8*, 1–12. DOI: 10.3389/fsoc.2023.1144657 PMID: 37274604

Adler-Nissen, R. (2011). On a field trip with Bourdieu. *International Political Sociology, 5*(3), 327–330. DOI: 10.1111/j.1749-5687.2011.00137_1.x

Airoldi, M. (2022). *Machine habitus: Toward a sociology of algorithms*. Polity Press.

Akıllı, E. (2025, Nisan). Rewiring diplomacy in the technopolar world | opinion. *Daıly Sabah.* https://www.dailysabah.com/opinion/op-ed/rewiring-diplomacy-in-the-technopolar-world

Arapov, S., Dadabaev, T., & Laumulin, C. (2017). The use of digital diplomacy as a tool for symbolic violence: Framing analysis of Russian–Turkish relations on Twitter. *Cambridge Journal of Eurasian Studies, 1*(41), 124–128. DOI: 10.22261/UZV32B

Bannykh, G. (2020, March). Digital capital and the labor market: Factors of mutual influence. In *International Scientific Conference" Far East Con"(ISCFEC 2020)* (pp. 2946-2953). Atlantis Press. DOI: 10.2991/aebmr.k.200312.420

Bjola, C., Cassidy, J., & Manor, I. (2019). Public diplomacy in the digital age. *Lahey Diplomasi Dergisi, 14*(1-2), 83–101. DOI: 10.1163/1871191X-14011032

Bjola, C., & Kornprobst, M. (2025). Studying tech diplomacy—Introduction to the special issue on tech diplomacy. *Global Policy, 0*, 1–8. DOI: 10.1111/1758-5899.70035

Bourdieu, P. (1989). Social space and symbolic power. *Sociological Theory, 7*(1), 14–25. DOI: 10.2307/202060

Bourdieu, P. (2011). The Forms of capital. In Szeman, I., & Kaposy, T. (Eds.), *Cultural Theory: An Anthology* (pp. 81–98). Wiley-Blackwell.

Bourdieu, P. (2014). *On the StateLectures at the College de France, 1989-1992* (D. Fernbach, Çev.). Polity Press.

Bourdieu, P. (2016). *Sosyoloji meseleleri* (F. Öztürk, B. Uçar, M. Gültekin, & A. Sümer, Çev.). Heretik Yayıncılık.

Bourdieu, P. (2018). *Bir pratik teorisi için taslak: Kabiliye üzerine üç etnoloji çalışması* (N. Ötken, Çev.). Bilgi Üniversitesi.

Bourdieu, P. (2022). *Genel sosyoloji: College de France dersleri (1981-1983)* (E. Emirosmanoğlu, Çev.). İletişim Yayınları.

Bradshaw, S., & Howard, P. N. (2018). The global organization of social media disinformation campaigns. *Journal of International Affairs, 71*(1.5), 23-32.

Byrnjolfsson, E. (2022). Sorun işler değil, ücretlerdir (H. Dölkeleş, Çev.). In Acemoğlu, D. (Ed.), *Yapay Zekayı Yeniden Tasarlamak: Otomasyon Çağında İş, Demokrasi Ve Adalet* (pp. 55–60). Elif Yayınevi.

Calderón Gómez, D. (2021). The third digital divide and Bourdieu: Bidirectional conversion of economic, cultural, and social capital to (and from) digital capital among young people in Madrid. *New Media & Society, 23*(9), 2534–2553. DOI: 10.1177/1461444820933252

Calhoun, C. (2016). Bourdieu sosyolojisinin ana hatları (G. Çeğin, Çev.). In Çeğin, G., Göker, E., Arlı, A., & Tatlıcan, Ü. (Eds.), *Ocak ve Zanaat Pierre Bourdieu Derlemesi* (pp. 77–131). İletişim Yayınları.

Castells, M. (2007). Communication, power and counter-power in the network society. *International Journal of Communication, 1*, 238–266.

Choi, J. R., Straubhaar, J., Skouras, M., Park, S., Santillana, M., & Strover, S. (2020). Techno-Capital: Theorizing media and information literacy through information technology capabilities. *New Media & Society*, •••, 1–23. DOI: 10.1177/1461444820925800

Collective, T. (2025, June 12). The role of artificial ıntelligence in shaping public diplomacy. *Tech Collective*. https://techcollectivesea.com/2025/06/12/artificial-intelligence-public-diplomacy/

Couldry, N., & Mejias, U. A. (2023). The decolonial turn in data and technology research: What is at stake and where is it heading? *Information Communication and Society, 26*(4), 786–802. DOI: 10.1080/1369118X.2021.1986102

Cull, N. J. (2013). The long road to public diplomacy 2.0: The internet in US public diplomacy. *International Studies Review, 15*(1), 123–139. DOI: 10.1111/misr.12026

Di Martino, L. (2020). Conceptualising public diplomacy listening on social media. *Place Branding and Public Diplomacy, 16*(2), 131–142. DOI: 10.1057/s41254-019-00135-5

Dyer-Witheford, N., Kjosen, A. M., & Steinhoff, J. (2022). *Yapay zeka ve kapitalizmin geleceği: İnsandışı bir güç* (B. Cezar, Çev.). İletişim Yayınları.

Edwards, L. (2009). Symbolic power and public relations practice: Locating ındividual practitioners in their social context. *Journal of Public Relations Research, 21*(3), 251–272. DOI: 10.1080/10627260802640674

Entman, R. M. (2008). Theorizing mediated public diplomacy: The U.S. case. *The International Journal of Press/Politics, 13*(2), 87–102. DOI: 10.1177/1940161208314657

Ericson, P., Dobbe, R., & Lindgren, S. (2024). Tracing class and capitalism in critical AI research. *TripleC, 22*(1), 307–328. DOI: 10.31269/triplec.v22i1.1464

Ertem-Eray, T. (2023). Extending the cultural-economic model of public relations through Bourdieu's theoretical lens to inform public diplomacy efforts. *Public Relations Inquiry, 12*(3), 271–291. DOI: 10.1177/2046147X231180862

Feijóo, C., Kwon, Y., Bauer, J. M., Bohlin, E., Howell, B., Jain, R., Potgieter, P., Vu, K., Whalley, J., & Xia, J. (2020). Harnessing artificial intelligence (AI) to increase wellbeing for all: The case for a new technology diplomacy. *Telecommunications Policy, 44*(6), 1–14. DOI: 10.1016/j.telpol.2020.101988 PMID: 32377031

Fetzer, J. H. (1990). What is artificial intelligence? J. H. Fetzer (Ed.), In *Artificial Intelligence: Its Scope and Limits* (pp. 3-27). Springer Netherlands. DOI: 10.1007/978-94-009-1900-6_1

Fitzpatrick, K. (2017). Public Diplomacy in the Public Interest. *The Journal of Public Interest Communications, 1*(1), 78. DOI: 10.32473/jpic.v1.i1.p78

Fox, N. J. (2024). Artificial ıntelligence and the black hole of capitalism: A more-than-human political ethology. *Social Sciences (Basel, Switzerland), 13*(10), 507. DOI: 10.3390/socsci13100507

Freud, S. (2023). *Kitle psikolojisi ve ego analizi* (E. Yıldırım, Çev.). Oda Yayınları.

Garakhanova, N. (2023). Yapay zekâ çağında kültürel diplomasi. In Çakmak, F. (Ed.), *Sosyal & beşerî bilimler alanında akademik çalışmalar* (pp. 77–114). Gece Kitaplığı.

Gilboa, E. (1998). Media diplomacy: Conceptual divergence and applications. *The Harvard International Journal of Press/Politics, 3*(3), 56–75. DOI: 10.1177/1081180X98003003005

Gilboa, E. (2000). Mass communication and diplomacy: A theoretical framework. *Communication Theory, 10*(3), 275–309. DOI: 10.1111/j.1468-2885.2000.tb00193.x

Gilboa, E. (2002). Global Communication and Foreign Policy. *Journal of Communication, 52*(4), 731–748. DOI: 10.1111/j.1460-2466.2002.tb02571.x

Gilboa, E. (2008). Searching for a theory of public diplomacy. *The Annals of the American Academy of Political and Social Science, 616*(1), 55–77. DOI: 10.1177/0002716207312142

Gomez, C., Guardia, A., Mantari, J. L., Coronado, A. M., & Reddy, J. N. (2022). A contemporary approach to the MSE paradigm powered by artificial intelligence from a review focused on polymer matrix composites. *Mechanics of Advanced Materials and Structures, 29*(21), 3076–3096. DOI: 10.1080/15376494.2021.1886379

Gramsci, A. (2014). *Hapishane Defterleri* (A. Cemgil, Çev.). Belge Yayınları.

Guo, L., & McCombs, M. (2011, May). Network agenda setting: A third level of media effects. In *annual conference of the International Communication Association, Boston, MA.*

Hlihor, E. (2024). Public diplomacy in the era of artificial intelligence – opportunities and challenges in promoting security in international politics –. *Romanian Military Thinking, 4*(4), 656–671. DOI: 10.55535/RMT.2024.4.42

Hossain, M. A., Azim, K. S., Jafor, A. H. M., Shayed, A. U., Nikita, N. A., & Khan, O. U.Mir Abrar HossainKazi Sanwarul AzimA H M JaforAzher Uddin ShayedNabila Ahmed NikitaObyed Ullah Khan. (2024). AI and machine learning in ınternational diplomacy and conflict resolution. *AIJMR - Advanced International. Journal of Multidisciplinary Research, 2*(5), 1–17. DOI: 10.62127/aijmr.2024.v02i05.1095

Jiang, Y., Li, X., Luo, H., Yin, S., & Kaynak, O. (2022). Quo vadis artificial intelligence? *Discover Artificial Intelligence, 2*(1), 1–19. DOI: 10.1007/s44163-022-00022-8

Jönsson, C. (2016). Diplomacy, communication and signalling. In Constantinou, C. M., Kerr, P., & Sharp, P. (Eds.), *SAGE Handbook of Diplomacy* (p. 79). SAGE Publications. DOI: 10.4135/9781473957930.n7

Jourdaın, A.,& Naulın, S. (2020). *Pierre Bourdieu'nün kuramı ve sosyolojik kullanımları* (Ö. Elitez, Çev.). İletişim Yayınları.

Kalın, İ. (2011). Soft power and public diplomacy in Türkiye. *Perceptions: Journal of International Affairs, 16*(3), 5–23.

Kaljurand, M. (2019). Diplomacy in the digital age. *The Fletcher Forum of World Affairs, 43*(1), 53–62.

Karl, P. A. (1982). Media diplomacy. *Proceedings of the Academy of Political Science, 34*(4), 143–152. DOI: 10.2307/3700976

Khanal, S., Zhang, H., & Taeihagh, A. (2025). Why and how is the power of Big Tech increasing in the policy process? The case of generative AI. *Policy and Society, 44*(1), 52–69. DOI: 10.1093/polsoc/puae012

Kirilkina, I., & Karochkin, S. (2025). The impact of the expansion of artificial intelligence on modern diplomacy in countries worldwide. *Journal of Countries Studies, 2*(4), 535–557. DOI: 10.22059/jcountst.2024.377065.1130

Kishan Thussu, D. (2000). Media wars and public diplomacy. *Javnost - The Public, 7*(3), 5-17. DOI: 10.1080/13183222.2000.11008747

Konovalova, M. (2023). AI and diplomacy: Challenges and opportunities. *Journal of Liberty and International Affairs, 9*(2), 520–530. DOI: 10.47305/JLIA2392520k

Kuus, M. (2015). Symbolic power in diplomatic practice: Matters of style in Brussels. *Cooperation and Conflict, 50*(3), 368–384. DOI: 10.1177/0010836715574914

Lin, Z. (2024). A virtual battlefield for embassies: Longitudinal network analysis of competing mediated public diplomacy on social media. *Political Communication, 41*(5), 808–836. DOI: 10.1080/10584609.2024.2312865

Luo, Y., & Yu, L. (2022). Capital or technology? Which is better at promoting the value of AI companies—Theoretical analysis and empirical test. *Systems, 10*(5), 152–174. DOI: 10.3390/systems10050152

Manor, I., & Huang, Z. A. (2022). Digitalization of public diplomacy: Concepts, trends, and challenges. *Communication and the Public, 7*(4), 167–175. DOI: 10.1177/20570473221138401

Mazumdar, B. T. (2024). Digital diplomacy: Internet-based public diplomacy activities or novel forms of public engagement? *Place Branding and Public Diplomacy, 20*(1), 24–43. DOI: 10.1057/s41254-021-00208-4

McCombs, M. E., & Shaw, D. L. (1972). The Agenda-Setting Function of Mass Media. *Public Opinion Quarterly, 36*(2), 176–187. DOI: 10.1086/267990

Mostafaei, H., Kordnoori, S., Ostadrahimi, M., & Banihashemi, S. S. A. (2025). Applications of artificial intelligence in global diplomacy: A review of research and practical models. *Sustainable Futures : An Applied Journal of Technology, Environment and Society, 9*, 1–15. DOI: 10.1016/j.sftr.2025.100486

Nachman, L. (2022). Salt Otomasyoncu Yaklaşımın Ötesinde (H. Dölkeleş, Çev.). In Acemoğlu, D. (Ed.), *Yapay Zekayı Yeniden Tasarlamak: Otomasyon Çağında İş, Demokrasi Ve Adalet* (pp. 60–64). Elif Yayınevi.

Nye, J. S. (1991). *Bound to Lead: The Changing Nature of American Power*. Basic Books.

Nye, J. S. (2005). Soft Power: The Means To Success. In *World Politics*. Public Affairs.

Nye, J. S. (2021). Soft power: The evolution of a concept. *Journal of Political Power, 14*(1), 196–208. DOI: 10.1080/2158379X.2021.1879572

Nye, J. S. (2023a). *Soft power and great-power competition: Shifting sands in the balance of power between the United States and China*. Springer. DOI: 10.1007/978-981-99-0714-4

Nye, J. S. (2023b). *Yumuşak Güç: Dünya Siyasetinde Başarının Araçları* (R. İnan-Aydın, Çev.). Serbest Akademi.

Ociepka, B. (2012). Impact of new technologies on international communication: The case of public diplomacy. *Informacijos Mokslai, 59*, 24–36.

Perdani, M. K., Afandi, R., Lusa, S., Sensuse, D. I., Putro, P. A. W., & Indriasari, S. (2024). Social media as an instrument of public diplomacy in the digital era: A systematic literature review. *Policy & Governance Review, 8*(3), 284–302. DOI: 10.30589/pgr.v8i3.976

Puaschunder, J. M. (2019). Artificial diplomacy: A guide for public officials to conduct artificial intelligence. *SSRN, 1*, 39–54. DOI: 10.2139/ssrn.3376302

Rachmawati, I., Kuncoro, H. R., Sari, D. L., & Tahalea, S. P. (2024, September). Digital diplomacy in the 21st century: The Transformative role of social media platforms in public engagement. In *2nd International Conference on Advance Research in Social and Economic Science (ICARSE 2023)* (pp. 567-576). Atlantis Press. DOI: 10.2991/978-2-38476-247-7_57

Radanliev, P. (2025). Cyber diplomacy: Defining the opportunities for cybersecurity and risks from Artificial Intelligence, IoT, Blockchains, and Quantum Computing. *Journal of Cyber Security Technology, 9*(1), 28–78. DOI: 10.1080/23742917.2024.2312671

Ragnedda, M. (2017). *The third digital divide a weberian approach to digital inequalities*. Routledge. DOI: 10.4324/9781315606002

Ragnedda, M. (2018). Conceptualizing digital capital. *Telematics and Informatics, 35*(8), 2366–2375. DOI: 10.1016/j.tele.2018.10.006

Ragnedda, M., Ruiu, M. L., & Addeo, F. (2020). Measuring digital capital: An empirical ınvestigation. *New Media & Society, 22*(5), 793–816. DOI: 10.1177/1461444819869604

Reese, B. (2020). *Yapay zeka çağı dördüncü çağ: Akıllı robotlar, bilinçli bilgisayarlar ve insanlığın geleceği* (M. Doğan, Çev.). Say Yayınları.

Saliu, H. (2022). Rethinking media diplomacy and public diplomacy towards a new concept: Digital media diplomacy. *Online Journal Modelling the New Europe, 39*, 4–24.

Scheufele, D. A., & Tewksbury, D. (2007). Framing, agenda setting, and priming: The evolution of three media effects models. *Journal of Communication, 57*(1), 9–20. DOI: 10.1111/j.0021-9916.2007.00326.x

Şehitoğlu, R.,& Eren, E. (2022). Konferans diplomasisi perspektifinde Antalya diplomasi forumu'nun uluslararası ilişkilerdeki rolü. *İletişim ve Diplomasi, 7*, 185-204. DOI: 10.54722/iletisimvediplomasi.1111491

Sevin, E. (2015). Pathways of connection: An analytical approach to the impacts of public diplomacy. *Public Relations Review, 41*(4), 562–568. DOI: 10.1016/j.pubrev.2015.07.003

Sevin, E., & Ingenhoff, D. (2018). Public diplomacy on social media. *International Journal of Communication, 12*, 3663–3685.

Su, S., & Xu, M. (2015). Twitplomacy: Social media as a new platform for development of public diplomacy. [IJEP]. *International Journal of E-Politics, 6*(1), 16–29. DOI: 10.4018/IJEP.2015010102

Suskind, D. (2022). Daha az iş olan bir dünya (H. Dölkeleş, Çev.). In Cohen, J., & Chasman, D. (Eds.), *Yapay zekayı yeniden tasarlamak: Otomasyon çağında iş, demokrasi ve adalet* (pp. 31–35). Elif Yayınevi.

Swartz, D. (2013). *Kültür ve iktidar: Pierre Bourdieu'nün sosyolojisi. (Çev. E. Gen).* İletişim Yayınları.

Taylor, T. (2012). *Yapay maymun: Teknoloji insan evrimini nasıl değiştirdi* (A. Muhaddisoğlu, Çev.). Alfa Bilim.

Üste, A. N., & Aydın, U. S. (2022). A New Era in Diplomacy: The Case of the Antalya Diplomacy Forum. *PERCEPTIONS: Journal of International Affairs, 27*(2), 197–217.

Varela, D. T. (2024). Navigating Cyber diplomacy in the governance of emerging AI technologies: Lessons from transatlantic cooperation. *Journal of Artificial Intelligence General science (JAIGS), 2*(1), 172-180. DOI: 10.60087/jaigs.v2i1.104

Wang, J., & Dubbins, A. (2024, August 12). *What Artificial Intelligence Means for Public Diplomacy*. USC Center on Public Diplomacy. https://uscpublicdiplomacy.org/blog/what-artificial-intelligence-means-public-diplomacy

Wang, Y. (2016). Offensive for defensive: The belt and road initiative and China's new grand strategy. *The Pacific Review, 29*(3), 455–463. DOI: 10.1080/09512748.2016.1154690

Yun, S.-H. (2022). Against the current: Back to public diplomacy as government communication. *International Journal of Communication, 16*, 3047–3064.

Yurdakul, H. (2024). Yapay zekâ, sermaye ve toplum. In Hülür, H., & Yaşin, C. (Eds.), *Yapay zeka, toplum ve kültür* (pp. 326–342). Ütopya Yayınları.

Yurdakul, H. (2025). *Tekno-i leti şi m çağinda di ji tal sermaye eşi tsi zli ği ni n gündeli k hayata yansimasi üzeri ne bi r alan araştirmasi* [Unpublished Doctoral Thesis]. Ankara Hacı Bayram Veli Üniversitesi.

Zamorano, M. M. (2016). Reframing cultural diplomacy: The ınstrumentalization of culture under the soft power theory. *Culture Unbound, 8*(2), 165–186. DOI: 10.3384/cu.2000.1525.1608165

Zhang, J. (2013). A strategic issue management (SIM) approach to social media use in public diplomacy. *The American Behavioral Scientist, 57*(9), 1312–1331. DOI: 10.1177/0002764213487734

Zhong, X., & Lu, J. (2013). Public diplomacy meets social media: A study of the US Embassy's blogs and micro-blogs. *Public Relations Review, 39*(5), 542–548. DOI: 10.1016/j.pubrev.2013.07.002

ENDNOTES

1 https://antalyadf.org/

2 https://www.baesystems.com/en/insight/the-art-of-digital-diplomacy

3 https://www.msit.go.kr/eng/bbs/view.do?sCode=eng&mId=4&mPid=2&pageIndex=&bbsSeqNo=42&nttSeqNo=626&searchOpt=ALL&searchTxt

Chapter 8
Digital Inclusion and AI Diplomacy:
Addressing Inequality Through Multilateral Forums

Hemendra Singh
https://orcid.org/0000-0003-1160-8284
Jindal Global Law School, O.P. Jindal Global University, Sonipat, India

ABSTRACT

This chapter critically examines the intersection of digital inclusion and artificial intelligence in contemporary multilateral diplomacy. It explores how AI tools are reshaping global negotiations, while also reinforcing structural inequalities in access, participation, and epistemic recognition. Framing digital inclusion as both a human rights concern and a prerequisite for sustainable development, the analysis interrogates algorithmic asymmetries and decision-making exclusions across leading diplomatic forums. Through a comparative study of the Raisina Dialogue, African Union Summits, the G20, and the Boao Forum, the chapter highlights divergent governance models and their impact on digital equity. It further investigates how Global South actors, civil society networks, and sub-state institutions innovate norms and strategies to challenge marginalisation and assert digital sovereignty. Concluding with a call for institutional redesign, the chapter advocates for participatory, rights-based approaches that embed inclusion into the normative core of global governance.

DOI: 10.4018/979-8-3373-4937-4.ch008

1. INTRODUCTION

Artificial intelligence is rapidly transforming the landscape of global diplomacy. From real-time policy simulations to data-driven decision support, AI tools are now integral to how multilateral institutions and states engage with complex global challenges. These technologies promise enhanced speed, precision, and analytical depth, offering new possibilities for early warning systems, climate negotiations, development financing, and peacebuilding strategies. However, the growing reliance on AI also brings to the forefront critical concerns about access, equity, and participation within the international system (Farahani & Ghasemi, 2024). As AI becomes a core infrastructure of diplomatic engagement, it is essential to interrogate who is included in shaping these tools and who remains on the margins.

Recent research by Mostafaei, Kordnoori, Ostadrahimi, and Banihashemi (2025) emphasizes how AI can support decision-making in international forums through predictive modelling and data aggregation, but also cautions that uneven technological capacities may deepen geopolitical divides. Similarly, Gehl Sampath (2021) provides a trenchant critique of how global AI governance structures often exclude actors from the Global South, both in norm-setting and implementation. Her analysis demonstrates that digital marginalization is not only a matter of infrastructure gaps but is rooted in broader political and economic asymmetries that determine whose values, data, and priorities are embedded in emerging AI systems.

While there is considerable discourse around digital inclusion, much of it remains narrowly defined in terms of connectivity and infrastructure. Such a framing overlooks the deeper issues of epistemic exclusion and structural inequality. For instance, many developing countries are asked to align with AI norms that they had little or no role in drafting, thereby participating in global processes without influencing their substantive direction (Demaidi, 2025). Multilateral forums often emphasize the importance of inclusion in principle, but in practice, they tend to relegate the voices of less technologically advanced states to the periphery. This dynamic undermines both the legitimacy and the effectiveness of AI-enhanced diplomacy.

Furthermore, the growing involvement of private technology corporations in diplomatic processes introduces additional complexities. These entities often set technical standards, provide platforms for diplomatic engagement, and shape the very architecture of AI tools. Yet they are driven by proprietary interests rather than public accountability. This raises serious questions about transparency, control, and democratic oversight in a field where decisions have global consequences. Diplomats and policymakers from underrepresented regions frequently encounter challenges in accessing the necessary technical expertise and negotiating power to advocate for their national or regional interests (Al Mokdad, 2025).

The question of digital inclusion must therefore be reframed. It is not enough to focus on extending digital infrastructure or increasing digital literacy. What is needed is a justice-oriented framework that centers the agency of historically marginalized actors and ensures meaningful participation in global AI governance. This requires investing in local knowledge systems, fostering regional innovation ecosystems and designing inclusive institutional mechanisms that go beyond tokenistic consultation.

This chapter seeks to examine the intersection of AI and diplomacy through the lens of global justice and sustainable development. It argues that without a deliberate shift in how digital inclusion is conceptualized and operationalized, AI-driven diplomacy may entrench existing inequities rather than mitigate them. By analysing the current state of multilateral engagement with AI, the chapter aims to identify both the structural barriers to inclusion and the normative possibilities for creating a more equitable digital order. It advocates for a multilateralism that is not only digitally enabled but also socially just, inclusive, and representative of the diverse realities and aspirations of all regions.

1.1. Research Question and Methodology

This chapter is guided by a central research question: How can AI-enhanced diplomatic processes contribute to meaningful digital inclusion in multilateral forums, and under what conditions do they risk reinforcing existing inequalities? The question arises from the recognition that digital inclusion in global governance is not merely a matter of technological access or connectivity, but a deeper issue of voice, representation, and institutional design. In multilateral arenas where decisions about digital futures are increasingly shaped by AI-driven tools, understanding who participates, who influences outcomes, and whose knowledge is considered legitimate becomes essential. This inquiry aims to illuminate how global governance structures can either enable or marginalize actors from the Global South and other historically underrepresented groups within AI diplomacy.

The methodology adopted is doctrinal and comparative in nature, with a strong normative orientation. It involves a close analysis of legal texts, institutional mandates, and governance frameworks that regulate or shape the use of AI in diplomatic contexts. Comparative case studies of selected multilateral platforms, such as interregional summits and global forums, will provide insight into varying degrees of inclusion and exclusion in practice. Attention will also be given to institutional processes, procedural openness, and the design features of AI tools used within these settings. The research adopts an evaluative lens that is attentive to power, procedural equity, and epistemic justice, thereby framing digital inclusion not only as an outcome but as a condition for the legitimacy and fairness of AI-enhanced diplomacy.

2. REFRAMING DIGITAL INCLUSION AS GLOBAL JUSTICE

The concept of digital inclusion has often been reduced to metrics of access, infrastructure, and connectivity, especially in the context of global development. However, in the evolving landscape of multilateral diplomacy where artificial intelligence technologies mediate decision-making and participation, such a narrow definition is no longer sufficient. Digital inclusion must be reinterpreted as a principle of global justice, one that interrogates whose voices are heard, whose knowledge is recognized, and whose interests are served. The deployment of artificial intelligence in diplomatic processes has implications that reach far beyond technological gaps. It raises foundational questions about institutional legitimacy, epistemic fairness, and equitable governance. This section introduces a justice-oriented framework to examine how digital inclusion operates in global forums and why it must be treated as a structural requirement for the legitimacy and effectiveness of AI-enhanced diplomacy.

2.1. A Multidimensional Concept of Digital Inclusion

The concept of digital inclusion has often been constrained by its association with mere access to technological infrastructure, such as internet connectivity, digital devices, and broadband coverage (Al-Muwil et al., 2019). While these elements are undeniably important, they form only the surface of a much deeper and more intricate terrain. Digital inclusion, especially in the context of diplomacy and international governance, must be reconceived as a layered and multidimensional construct that encompasses not only physical access but also the capacity to participate meaningfully, influence outcomes, and navigate the digital ecosystem with autonomy and legitimacy. Access without agency does not amount to inclusion. It may, in fact, mask structural inequalities under the guise of formal participation.

A multidimensional approach to digital inclusion must engage with the structural, cognitive, institutional, and cultural barriers that condition how actors enter and operate within digital spaces. These barriers are particularly acute for countries in the Global South, marginalized communities, and non-dominant knowledge systems. For instance, a nation may be digitally connected, but its diplomats may lack the technological literacy, data infrastructure, or institutional support to contribute effectively to artificial intelligence negotiations or cybersecurity protocols. In many multilateral forums, the language of digital governance is encoded in technical terms, bureaucratic formats, and regulatory models developed by powerful states and corporate actors. This creates a form of epistemic exclusion that operates even when procedural inclusion appears to exist.

Cultural and linguistic marginalization also undermines substantive participation. Many artificial intelligence systems used in diplomacy rely on training datasets and interface designs that are skewed toward dominant languages, predominantly English, and reflect cultural assumptions from North American or European contexts. This not only limits communicative clarity for others but also distorts the framing of issues, erasing alternative epistemologies, indigenous knowledge, and plural legal traditions. Digital tools may render participation more efficient, but they do not inherently democratize decision-making. On the contrary, when systems of artificial intelligence are introduced without corresponding institutional safeguards and representational checks, they tend to amplify existing power hierarchies and embed exclusion more deeply into the procedural architecture.

Furthermore, digital inclusion must be situated within a broader political economy. Unequal access to cloud infrastructure, data centres, encryption technologies, and digital development financing places severe constraints on the ability of less-resourced states and communities to shape or even understand the tools being used in diplomatic practice. The outsourcing of digital tools to large technology firms further complicates this landscape, as it creates dependencies that are neither transparent nor accountable to public norms. Inclusion in such contexts becomes conditional and contingent, mediated through platforms and protocols that operate outside democratic oversight. This raises urgent normative questions about who owns the digital spaces in which diplomacy unfolds, and on what terms participation is allowed.

A robust notion of digital inclusion must therefore be grounded in principles of distributive justice, epistemic fairness, and institutional pluralism. It should prioritize not only who is at the table, but also who sets the agenda, who writes the code, who owns the data, and whose values are embedded in the algorithms. Without confronting these deeper issues, the term digital inclusion risks becoming an empty signifier, used to validate processes that remain fundamentally exclusionary. To meet the demands of an equitable and just global order, inclusion must be treated not as a technical goal but as a political and legal imperative.

2.2. Epistemic Justice and Structural Inequality in AI Systems

The global deployment of artificial intelligence systems has brought to the fore a deeper crisis of epistemic inequality. While technological advancement often appears as a neutral or universally beneficial process, the production and deployment of AI systems are embedded within power-laden knowledge regimes that systematically privilege dominant actors. Epistemic justice, in this context, refers to the fair distribution of the capacity to know, interpret, and contribute to systems of meaning-making and decision-making (Cummings et al., 2023). In the realm of diplomacy, where decisions are shaped by data-driven insights and algorithmic models, epistemic injustices can lead to entire populations, communities, and even states being rendered invisible, misrepresented, or structurally excluded from deliberation.

At the heart of this problem lies the way AI systems are trained, validated, and deployed. Much of the data used in training large-scale AI systems is derived from sources that overrepresent particular languages, geographies, and social practices, typically rooted in the Global North. Consequently, AI models often fail to recognize, understand, or accurately interpret inputs from non-dominant regions. This form of structural epistemic exclusion manifests in diplomatic settings where AI-driven language translation tools, predictive analytics, and diplomatic advisory systems do not account for regional nuances, indigenous terms, or culturally specific norms. As a result, AI systems may produce outputs that distort or erase the lived realities and perspectives of marginalized actors.

Structural inequality is further reinforced when the power to design, modify, and govern AI tools is concentrated in a handful of corporations or nation-states. These entities determine not only the functionality of the tools but also the epistemic boundaries within which diplomatic engagement takes place. In such a context, knowledge production becomes a form of control, and participation in global governance becomes contingent upon alignment with dominant epistemologies. Actors from the Global South, even when present in multilateral forums, may find themselves unable to influence digital policies because the terms of engagement are already shaped by AI systems that do not accommodate their worldviews.

The epistemic injustice does not end with data. It extends into the norms and ontologies that undergird AI systems. For example, the prioritization of efficiency, quantifiability, and predictive certainty in AI design reflects a technocratic rationality that is often at odds with pluralistic or deliberative approaches to diplomacy. This epistemic narrowing limits the types of knowledge deemed valid and the modes of reasoning considered acceptable in digital forums. Traditional knowledge systems, oral traditions, and community-based epistemologies are often excluded by default because they do not fit the format or logic of dominant AI systems.

To address this, epistemic justice in AI diplomacy must go beyond diversifying datasets or improving representation in algorithms. It must involve rethinking the normative foundations of AI development and deployment. This includes incorporating participatory design methods that actively involve underrepresented stakeholders in the construction of AI tools used in governance. It also requires institutional reforms that allow for contestation, revision, and accountability in how AI is used in multilateral processes. Knowledge diversity should not be treated as an afterthought or a technical adjustment, but as a foundational element of equitable digital governance.

Finally, addressing epistemic inequality demands a commitment to transparency and reflexivity. Diplomatic institutions must be willing to interrogate the epistemic assumptions embedded in the AI tools they use and ask whose knowledge counts, whose voices are amplified, and whose experiences are ignored. Without such reflection, AI-enhanced diplomacy risks becoming a technocratic exercise that reproduces global hierarchies rather than challenging them. Epistemic justice offers a critical lens to ensure that digital inclusion is not merely about formal access, but about the substantive capacity to shape knowledge, influence decision-making, and participate in the construction of global futures on equal terms.

3. AI TOOLS IN DIPLOMACY: CAPABILITIES AND EXCLUSIONS

As artificial intelligence becomes increasingly embedded in the practice of international diplomacy, it is reshaping both the mechanics and the meaning of global engagement. AI tools such as real-time translation, automated negotiation simulations, and predictive analytics are now integral to how diplomats formulate positions, analyze scenarios, and even anticipate geopolitical developments (Pasupuleti, 2025). These innovations offer the promise of efficiency, enhanced coordination, and data-driven insight, but they also introduce structural asymmetries that exacerbate existing power imbalances. Not all countries or diplomatic actors possess the same technological infrastructure, institutional capacity, or access to sophisticated AI systems. As a result, the deployment of AI in diplomatic contexts risks reinforcing global hierarchies, where technologically dominant actors shape not only the tools of negotiation but the epistemological frames that define legitimate knowledge and strategic discourse. Far from being neutral instruments, AI systems reflect the interests, assumptions, and cultural biases of those who design and control them. Consequently, the rise of AI-enhanced diplomacy compels us to interrogate who is included in shaping multilateral decisions and whose voices are systematically marginalized in the digital conduct of diplomacy.

3.1. Key AI Functions in Multilateral Settings

Artificial intelligence is increasingly integral to the functioning of multilateral diplomacy, not only as a tool for automation and efficiency but as a structuring force that redefines how international institutions process information, make decisions, and mediate normative frameworks. In global and regional fora such as the United Nations, the European Union, the African Union, and the Organisation for Economic Co-operation and Development, AI systems are now embedded in a range of operational domains including data aggregation, policy forecasting, multilingual communication, and anticipatory governance. Machine learning algorithms enable these institutions to manage and interpret vast and heterogeneous datasets that would otherwise overwhelm human capacity. For instance, AI-driven platforms are used to detect early signs of climate disruption, food insecurity, or forced displacement by correlating satellite data, real-time sensor inputs, social media signals, and historical event patterns. These systems support early warning mechanisms and enhance strategic foresight, enabling a shift from reactive diplomacy to preventive intervention. In the context of conflict mediation or humanitarian crises, such capacities are especially significant, as they inform the rapid mobilisation of diplomatic resources, targeted financial assistance, or coordinated regional responses.

Natural language processing tools have likewise become essential in multilateral diplomacy, addressing longstanding issues of linguistic inequality and communicative asymmetry Hachkevych & Nykolyshyn, 2023). AI-powered translation systems now support real-time multilingual negotiations and document preparation, thereby widening participation among states with limited linguistic infrastructure. Automated transcription and summarisation tools aid in preserving institutional memory, especially during complex negotiations or committee proceedings where human note-taking may be error-prone or politically partial. In high-stakes negotiation settings, AI is also deployed for discourse sentiment mapping, allowing diplomats and mediators to track shifts in alignment, detect latent tensions, and recalibrate strategies accordingly. Importantly, AI is not merely performing technical functions but increasingly shaping the normative underpinnings of international cooperation. The use of large language models in drafting policy recommendations, summarising past agreements, and offering legally consistent alternatives introduces a new layer of computational interpretation that may subtly reframe the direction of debate and the scope of acceptable compromise.

Further, AI-based decision support systems are beginning to influence institutional agenda-setting by forecasting likely outcomes of proposed treaties or resolutions. These simulation tools allow multilateral actors to model negotiation scenarios, anticipate voting behaviours, and explore the geopolitical consequences of policy choices before they are tabled. Such applications introduce a new epistemic logic to diplomacy, privileging predictive analytics over deliberative uncertainty and potentially marginalising dissenting viewpoints that do not conform to dominant data-driven assumptions. As AI systems gain legitimacy within institutional workflows, questions arise regarding transparency, bias, and representational equity. Many multilateral institutions lack clear protocols for auditing algorithmic outputs or contesting automated suggestions, raising serious concerns about the accountability of decisions shaped by opaque digital infrastructures. Furthermore, the development and procurement of these AI tools are often outsourced to private entities or external governments, introducing questions of sovereignty, digital dependence, and epistemic outsourcing. In this evolving landscape, AI functions not as a neutral facilitator but as a co-producer of diplomatic knowledge and global norms, with profound implications for who sets the agenda, whose interests are prioritised, and how legitimacy is constructed in the governance of global affairs.

3.2. Asymmetries in Use and Impact

The integration of artificial intelligence into multilateral diplomacy has accentuated and, in some cases, institutionalised long-standing asymmetries between states. These asymmetries are most visible in the divergent capacities of countries to develop, access, deploy, and govern AI technologies within the diplomatic machinery of global governance. While AI promises to enhance efficiency, reduce bureaucratic delay, and improve access to large-scale data for informed policy deliberation, these benefits accrue disproportionately to states with mature digital ecosystems, robust data infrastructures, and the institutional expertise required to manage complex technologies. Wealthier countries in the Global North typically benefit from established partnerships with leading AI firms, academic institutions, and think tanks, allowing them to pilot experimental governance tools, shape ethical guidelines, and define global AI norms. These states can embed their strategic preferences within the technical design of diplomatic platforms, from document classification algorithms and real-time translation tools to predictive negotiation simulators and automated agenda-setting systems. By contrast, many countries in the Global South are systematically excluded from this process due to limited investment in foundational digital infrastructure, under-resourced foreign services, insufficient training in computational tools, and constrained access to the proprietary systems increasingly used by multilateral institutions (Wall, Saxena, & Brown, 2021). The resulting divide not only limits participation but also compromises epistemic autonomy, as states unable to interrogate or modify AI systems become passive recipients of their outputs.

This asymmetry is not just technological but also structural and epistemological. The underlying data models that power diplomatic AI tools are often trained on corpora dominated by Western linguistic, cultural, and policy references. Consequently, diplomatic styles, priorities, and historical narratives from the Global South are routinely underrepresented or mischaracterised in algorithmic processes. For example, AI systems that summarise country submissions or generate negotiation briefs might disproportionately highlight themes aligned with Euro-American policy paradigms, while overlooking or downplaying alternative framings rooted in indigenous knowledge, postcolonial justice, or regional developmental visions. These epistemic exclusions are further exacerbated by the procurement practices of global institutions. Increasingly, multilateral bodies rely on outsourcing AI solutions to transnational technology companies headquartered in a handful of powerful countries. These vendors often operate on commercial logic and deploy off-the-shelf solutions developed for entirely different socio-political contexts. When such tools are introduced into the high-stakes space of diplomacy, they bring embedded biases and design assumptions that shape outcomes in subtle but consequential ways. Localisation, if undertaken at all, is typically minimal and reactive. This raises the concern that algorithmic governance in diplomatic contexts can become a form of soft power projection, where dominant states indirectly institutionalise their normative frameworks through technical means.

Furthermore, the interface between AI and diplomacy is reshaping not only the mechanics of international negotiation but also the politics of credibility, legitimacy, and voice. In forums where AI tools are used to visualise policy trends, model future scenarios, or flag inconsistencies across country reports, states with technical proficiency and resources can strategically leverage these tools to advance their agendas, rebut criticism, and propose rule changes with an empirical veneer. In contrast, countries lacking the capacity to scrutinise these systems may find themselves unable to contest flawed outputs, challenge implicit assumptions, or even understand how decisions were reached. This creates an uneven playing field where influence is mediated by algorithmic legibility. The more data a state can generate, manage, and input into the system, the more visible and credible its diplomatic claims appear. As a result, traditional hierarchies of power based on geopolitical influence are now being layered with new digital hierarchies, where algorithmic fluency becomes a prerequisite for institutional relevance.

This dynamic has profound implications for the legitimacy of multilateralism. If AI tools continue to be deployed without meaningful input from all stakeholders, and if their inner workings remain opaque to the majority of participating states, the normative foundations of global cooperation risk being hollowed out. Technocratic decision-making may displace political negotiation, and automated systems may come to define what is considered rational, fair, or urgent. This shift would not only erode the principles of sovereign equality and inclusive participation but also deepen mistrust among states already sceptical of global governance frameworks. Therefore, addressing asymmetries in AI use and impact is not merely a technical challenge but a political imperative. It calls for a fundamental rethinking of how diplomatic technologies are designed, procured, and governed, ensuring that multilateralism in the AI era is not reduced to a data-driven echo chamber for the powerful but remains a genuinely deliberative and pluralistic space. Bridging these gaps will require targeted capacity-building, equitable technology transfers, institutional redesign, and most importantly, the political will to democratise the infrastructure of global diplomacy.

3.3. Algorithmic Marginalisation and Decision-Making Gaps

As artificial intelligence systems become embedded in the institutional practices of multilateral diplomacy, a critical and often underexplored consequence is the emergence of algorithmic marginalisation within decision-making processes. This marginalisation refers not only to the exclusion of certain actors from the design and interpretation of algorithmic systems, but also to the structural silencing of alternative political visions, priorities, and knowledge frameworks that do not conform to the dominant logic embedded in these systems. Unlike traditional forms of diplomatic exclusion, which may result from political marginalisation or lack of access to forums, algorithmic marginalisation is embedded in the infrastructure of decision support (Ghasemaghaei & Kordzadeh, 2024). It operates through data selection, problem framing, model construction, and the algorithmic prioritisation of information that determines which voices are amplified and which are rendered invisible. Multilateral institutions increasingly rely on AI to parse vast quantities of data, detect patterns, flag policy inconsistencies, and even propose compromise language. Yet these processes inevitably encode assumptions about relevance, rationality, and normative desirability that reflect the perspectives of those who design the systems rather than those most affected by their outcomes.

This phenomenon is particularly acute in the context of the Global South, whose diplomatic inputs are often fragmented, under-documented, or expressed through frames that AI tools are not calibrated to recognise. For instance, positions articulated through non-Western legal traditions, indigenous epistemologies, or region-specific environmental or cultural logics are frequently misrepresented or overlooked in automated analyses and outputs. As a result, countries that already experience political or economic marginalisation face a new layer of exclusion, where their contributions are not just ignored but systematically filtered out by processes perceived as objective or neutral. This creates a recursive cycle in which algorithmic outputs reinforce existing hierarchies and biases in global governance, thereby closing the space for meaningful participation and deliberation. It also raises serious questions about the transparency and contestability of diplomatic technologies. Many AI-driven tools used in international organisations function as black boxes, with limited opportunities for states or civil society to interrogate how conclusions are drawn, what data is omitted, or which interpretive frameworks are privileged. In such settings, decisions appear technocratic and data-driven, even when they are underpinned by deeply political judgments.

Moreover, algorithmic marginalisation does not only occur at the level of discourse or agenda setting. It affects material resource flows, access to technical assistance, and the allocation of institutional attention. For example, AI tools used to assess implementation of treaty obligations or to flag gaps in compliance may prioritise states with digitally robust reporting mechanisms while overlooking contextual barriers faced by countries with weaker data systems. This can lead to unequal scrutiny, misaligned interventions, and reputational harm that compounds structural inequalities. It also incentivises states to conform to a narrow digital template in order to remain visible and credible within institutional frameworks, often at the expense of local priorities and governance models. The danger here is not merely that AI tools introduce bias, but that they formalise it into systems of authority that are difficult to contest. The authority of data and algorithms becomes a new source of legitimacy, sidelining the pluralistic and dialogical foundations upon which multilateral diplomacy has historically rested.

The decision-making gaps created by algorithmic systems are also epistemic in nature. As AI increasingly informs issue prioritisation, scenario planning, and anticipatory governance within international bodies, it shapes the collective imagination of what is seen as possible, desirable, or threatening. If training data and model logic are skewed toward dominant geopolitical narratives or corporate policy paradigms, then diplomatic strategies are likely to converge around a narrow band of solutions, leaving less room for radical rethinking or emancipatory politics. This not only curtails the agency of marginalised states but also impoverishes the collective intelligence of the multilateral system. The absence of diverse viewpoints and consecratory knowledge weakens the adaptability and resilience of global governance structures in the face of complex and evolving crises. Thus, the political stakes of algorithmic marginalisation extend far beyond fairness or inclusion; they pertain to the very capacity of international institutions to govern justly, responsively, and democratically.

To counter this emerging form of exclusion, it is essential to advance principles of algorithmic pluralism, participatory design, and institutional accountability within multilateral forums. This entails not only technical reforms, such as ensuring transparency in model documentation and bias auditing, but also structural changes in how decisions about AI deployment are made. Marginalised states and non-state actors must be included in the governance of diplomatic technologies from the outset, not merely as users or beneficiaries but as co-designers and norm shapers (Inuwa-Dutse, 2023). A more deliberative and inclusive approach to algorithmic governance is crucial to prevent the consolidation of digital power in the hands of a few and to uphold the democratic ethos of multilateral diplomacy in the AI era. Without such measures, the promise of AI as a tool for enhancing global cooperation may instead entrench new forms of exclusion and render diplomacy less accountable to those it purports to serve.

4. COMPARATIVE FORUM ANALYSIS

Digital inclusion is increasingly framed as a key objective in global and regional diplomacy, yet its interpretation and implementation vary widely across forums. As artificial intelligence becomes central to governance and negotiation processes, disparities in access, representation, and normative priorities are becoming more visible. This section introduces a comparative analysis of multilateral platforms such as the Raisina Dialogue, African Union Summits, the G20, and the Boao Forum, to examine how digital inclusion is being articulated and acted upon. By focusing on these diverse spaces, the chapter reveals how structural inequalities, institutional cultures, and regional interests shape the way digital equity is pursued, negotiated, or sidelined within the evolving architecture of AI diplomacy.

4.1. Raisina Dialogue and India's Bridge Diplomacy

The Raisina Dialogue, held annually in New Delhi, has evolved into a leading global platform for diplomatic engagement on pressing international issues, especially those concerning digital governance and emerging technologies. India uses this venue not only to shape the conversation on global technology norms but also to position itself as a strategic intermediary between the digital priorities of advanced economies and the development needs of the Global South. Through the Raisina Dialogue, India articulates a vision of inclusive digital diplomacy grounded in principles of accessibility, sovereignty, and shared innovation.

Central to India's digital diplomacy is the idea of digital public infrastructure, which is consistently showcased at Raisina as a means of transforming state capacity and reducing inequality. India's experiences with platforms such as Aadhaar for identification, UPI for payments, and DigiLocker for digital documentation are presented as templates that can be adapted by other countries seeking low-cost and high-impact digital ecosystems. These initiatives are not only framed as national successes but are increasingly being offered as global public goods to partner countries in Africa, Southeast Asia, and Latin America. By fostering cross-border digital cooperation based on open standards and public purpose technology, India aims to lead by example and facilitate a more equitable distribution of digital benefits.

At the same time, the Raisina Dialogue provides a forum to engage with global tensions over data regulation, platform accountability, and AI ethics (Mahrenbach, 2024). India uses this space to advocate for a pluralistic model of data governance that respects national contexts while promoting innovation and individual rights. This model seeks to move beyond the dominant paradigms offered by the United States and China by offering a middle path rooted in sovereignty, inclusivity, and democratic values. India's repeated emphasis on ethical AI and responsible technology deployment reflects its growing role in shaping global digital norms while addressing the anxieties of developing nations.

Nevertheless, India's bridge diplomacy is not without internal contradictions. While the Raisina Dialogue projects a confident and forward-looking narrative, there remain significant domestic challenges in closing the digital divide, safeguarding personal data, and ensuring transparency in algorithmic decision making. Critics argue that without robust legal safeguards and participatory oversight, the promise of inclusive digital transformation risks being undermined by centralised control and uneven access. Despite these tensions, the Raisina Dialogue continues to serve as a key site where competing models of digital development are negotiated, and where the contours of a more inclusive and multipolar digital order are being imagined.

India's digital diplomacy at Raisina also invites comparison with the regional digital strategies advanced through other forums such as the African Union Summits. These gatherings reveal how regional bodies are asserting their own technological agency while confronting structural dependencies, a theme that deepens the broader inquiry into digital inclusion through multilateral processes.

4.2. African Union Summits and Regional Digital Sovereignty

The African Union (AU) Summits have become increasingly influential arenas where the contours of Africa's digital future are being shaped through regional coordination, agenda setting, and norm development. As the continent grapples with the complex implications of digital transformation, AU Summits provide a platform for articulating collective interests in data governance, infrastructure development, artificial intelligence, and digital rights. Unlike individual state efforts that often remain constrained by limited technical and financial resources, the AU framework enables African states to pool capacities and negotiate with external actors from a position of relative strength. This regional approach has been particularly vital in asserting what many African leaders refer to as digital sovereignty, a concept that extends beyond technical autonomy to encompass political and epistemic control over digital systems and standards (Ayodele, 2021).

At the heart of the AU's digital strategy is the Digital Transformation Strategy for Africa 2020 to 2030, which is frequently foregrounded at the Summits. This strategy envisions a digitally empowered Africa where technologies are harnessed to drive inclusive development, governance, and integration. It advocates for cross-border digital corridors, harmonised data protection laws, digital identity frameworks, and investment in local innovation ecosystems. These priorities are regularly endorsed at the Heads of State Summits, where leaders recognise that the digital domain is not merely a matter of technical policy but a critical vector for asserting continental agency in global affairs. The AU's emphasis on pan-African digital cooperation reflects a growing understanding that fragmented national responses are insufficient to counteract external dependencies and cyber vulnerabilities.

The African Union Summits have also created space for contesting the terms of Africa's engagement with global digital powers. While many African states rely heavily on infrastructure and platforms provided by external actors, including China's Digital Silk Road and Western technology firms, the Summits reveal a growing pushback against extractive models of digital engagement. Discussions have increasingly centred around the risks of data colonialism, surveillance partnerships, and the offshoring of digital decision making. By fostering continental guidelines and advocating for local data centres, open standards, and domestic talent pipelines, the AU seeks to anchor digital transformation within African political and ethical frameworks. This focus on self-determination is not only reactive to external threats but also proactive in generating new imaginaries of technological governance rooted in African knowledge systems, languages, and priorities.

Despite its promise, the regional project of digital sovereignty faces formidable challenges. Disparities in infrastructure, regulatory maturity, and political will across AU member states hinder uniform implementation of agreed strategies. Furthermore, external actors continue to exploit asymmetries in capacity by negotiating bilaterally with weaker states, thereby undermining regional coherence. Nonetheless, the Summits remain critical in setting collective expectations, building regional solidarity, and institutionalising African voices in global digital negotiations. They are also a reminder that digital inclusion in Africa cannot be achieved without structural reforms that address long-standing inequalities in connectivity, education, and civic participation.

As the AU advances its digital agenda through Summit diplomacy, it presents a compelling counterpoint to India's bridge diplomacy at the Raisina Dialogue. Whereas India seeks to mediate between global models and local needs, the AU attempts to build autonomous regional systems that resist external dependence. The contrast between these approaches underscores the diversity of pathways toward digital inclusion and offers fertile ground for comparative insights into how different multilateral actors navigate the interplay between technology, power, and justice in the digital age.

4.3. G20 and Boao Forum

The G20 and the Boao Forum for Asia represent two influential yet ideologically distinct platforms that shape global digital governance through multilateral coordination, norm articulation, and policy diffusion. While both forums bring together key global and regional actors to deliberate on the future of digital transformation, they differ significantly in terms of institutional design, governance orientation, and normative ambition. The G20, as a grouping of the world's major economies, offers a broad-based forum where digital issues intersect with economic growth, financial regulation, and geopolitical stability. In contrast, the Boao Forum, primarily focused on Asia, reflects China's vision of a cooperative digital order rooted in state-led development, technological sovereignty, and infrastructure-driven connectivity. A comparative engagement with these platforms reveals divergent strategies in addressing global digital inequalities and advancing inclusive digital multilateralism.

The G20's engagement with digital inclusion has evolved over time, particularly since the adoption of the Digital Economy Task Force and the annual release of Digital Economy Ministerial Declarations. These initiatives emphasise the importance of bridging digital divides, promoting interoperability, investing in digital skills, and ensuring that emerging technologies serve human-centred development. However, the G20's consensus-driven model, while inclusive in spirit, often results in vague formulations and diluted commitments due to the diverse interests of its members. The forum's reliance on voluntary guidelines and non-binding frameworks limits its ability to enforce digital equity measures in practice. Nonetheless, it remains a key space for norm-building and agenda-setting, particularly when it comes to data flows, artificial intelligence ethics, and regulatory interoperability. During India's presidency of the G20, there was a notable emphasis on digital public infrastructure (Rai, 2023), Global South perspectives, and the democratization of access, although persistent tensions between free market proponents and digital sovereignty advocates constrained more transformative outcomes.

In contrast, the Boao Forum for Asia operates within a more coherent normative framework that prioritises regional solidarity, infrastructure development, and the promotion of sovereign digital models. Backed by Chinese leadership and investment, Boao serves as a platform for showcasing regional digital cooperation projects, including cross-border e-commerce zones, digital silk road initiatives, and artificial intelligence partnerships. The forum promotes a narrative of technology as a tool for development and self-determination, often challenging dominant Western paradigms of digital liberalism. Within this context, digital inclusion is framed less in terms of access to open markets and more as a function of state capacity, policy alignment, and mutual recognition among partner states. While this model enables rapid deployment of infrastructure and policy convergence, it also raises concerns about the export of surveillance technologies, limited civic participation, and normative asymmetry in defining digital rights.

These contrasting approaches reflect broader geopolitical tensions that shape global digital governance. The G20 model, though inclusive and pluralistic, struggles with fragmentation and lack of enforcement. It relies heavily on the goodwill of members and the influence of rotating presidencies to prioritise digital equity. The Boao model, while more directive and cohesive, is closely tied to state interests and lacks the multistakeholder diversity that characterises more democratic digital governance regimes. As such, both forums represent partial solutions to the global challenge of digital inclusion. Their comparative trajectories highlight the difficulty of crafting governance structures that are both efficient and equitable, particularly in a rapidly evolving technological landscape marked by inequality, competition, and asymmetrical dependencies.

Together, the G20 and Boao Forum reveal how the future of digital inclusion is being shaped not only by technical standards and market access but also by underlying political philosophies and institutional architectures. Understanding the tensions and complementarities between these models is essential for scholars and policymakers seeking to navigate the complex terrain of digital multilateralism. It also invites further reflection on how inclusive digital futures can be designed in ways that balance sovereignty with cooperation, efficiency with accountability, and innovation with justice.

5. INCLUSION FROM THE MARGINS

As global digital governance evolves, actors from the Global South are increasingly asserting their presence in shaping multilateral diplomacy around artificial intelligence and digital inclusion. Moving beyond traditional roles as passive recipients of global norms, these states and civil society actors are actively advancing alternative frameworks that emphasize equity, historical context, and development justice. This section introduces their strategic interventions, highlighting how inclusion from the margins is redefining the terms and institutions of AI diplomacy.

5.1. Normative Innovation and Southern Diplomacy

States and civil society actors from the Global South are increasingly engaging in normative innovation to contest and reshape the prevailing digital governance landscape (Farhad, 2025). Normative innovation here refers to the generation of new principles, discourses, and institutional proposals that challenge dominant paradigms of AI governance which have largely been shaped by actors in the Global North. These interventions are not merely reactive but strategically forward-looking, seeking to embed values such as fairness, equity, contextual adaptability, and digital sovereignty into global and regional policy dialogues. The emphasis is on promoting frameworks that reflect the historical and structural inequalities that shape the experience of digital exclusion in the South, rather than accepting techno-legal solutions designed in contexts with vastly different institutional, economic, and infrastructural baselines.

One significant contribution has been the growing call for recognition of data as a collective and developmental resource rather than merely an economic asset subject to market extraction. Southern countries have argued for governance models that respect community rights over data, recognize differentiated national capacities, and allow for contextually grounded safeguards. Forums such as the African Union have called for continental-level data strategies and AI frameworks that promote local innovation, protect public interest, and ensure that digital ecosystems serve broader development goals. Similarly, the Latin American region has witnessed increased engagement in global norm-setting processes, with countries like Brazil and Mexico advocating for inclusive governance mechanisms that resist surveillance capitalism and reinforce democratic control over algorithmic systems.

Another area of normative innovation involves the articulation of digital sovereignty as a necessary condition for meaningful participation in global digital governance. Rather than interpreting sovereignty as isolationism, these actors emphasize it as a means to reclaim agency over technical infrastructure, knowledge production, and regulatory frameworks. This includes efforts to develop indigenous digital capabilities, establish public-interest technology alliances, and resist overdependence on proprietary platforms controlled by a handful of powerful transnational corporations. By foregrounding concerns over dependency, extraction, and asymmetry, Southern diplomacy has begun to reframe debates about ethics and regulation in AI in ways that compel multilateral institutions to confront the underlying structural inequalities embedded in the digital economy.

In essence, the Global South is not only asserting its voice but also reconfiguring the normative terrain on which digital inclusion is debated. These interventions challenge the idea that technical solutions alone can resolve issues of marginalisation. Instead, they insist on the co-production of norms that reflect diverse epistemologies, socio-political conditions, and visions of justice. Through regional coalitions, multilateral alliances, and participation in global AI forums, Southern actors are advancing a counter-narrative that links digital inclusion to broader struggles for postcolonial justice and equitable global governance.Bottom of Form

5.2. Role of Civil Society and Sub-State Actors

Civil society organizations, grassroots networks, academic institutions, and sub-state actors such as city governments and regional bodies have emerged as critical agents in advancing digital inclusion within the broader landscape of AI diplomacy. Their role has become especially vital in contexts where national-level interventions are either inadequate, structurally constrained, or oriented toward elite or corporate interests. These actors bring grounded perspectives, lived experiences, and alternative knowledge systems into diplomatic and regulatory processes, ensuring that AI-related decisions do not remain the sole domain of state representatives and technocratic elites. Their engagement underscores a bottom-up approach to global digital governance, one that foregrounds equity, participation, and accountability.

Civil society organizations often serve as watchdogs, policy innovators, and conveners of cross-border solidarity. They expose algorithmic harms that disproportionately affect marginalized populations, challenge opaque data practices, and campaign for rights-based regulatory standards. In countries across Africa, Latin America, and South Asia, civil society groups have documented discriminatory impacts of biometric systems, AI surveillance, and automated welfare delivery, bringing these issues into regional and global forums (Pagliaro, Michel, & Rafael, 2021). Their advocacy has shaped debates within the United Nations, the Internet Governance Forum, and regional institutions, calling for transparency, human rights safeguards, and meaningful public engagement in the design and deployment of AI systems. These interventions have often been crucial in reframing digital inclusion as a matter of justice, rather than charity or access alone.

At the same time, sub-state actors such as municipalities, regional parliaments, and provincial agencies are playing increasingly influential roles in modeling inclusive digital practices. Cities like Barcelona and Amsterdam have implemented public digital infrastructure projects rooted in democratic data governance, emphasizing transparency, participatory design, and community ownership. These localized experiments demonstrate viable alternatives to dominant platform-based models, particularly in urban governance and service delivery. In federated systems such as India, Brazil, and Nigeria, state and provincial governments have introduced digital policies that prioritize linguistic inclusion, local entrepreneurship, and digital literacy for historically excluded communities. These efforts not only supplement national initiatives but also challenge centralized digital development paradigms that may overlook subnational disparities and context-specific needs.

Furthermore, civil society and sub-state actors frequently collaborate through transnational networks to influence global AI policy. Initiatives such as the Cities Coalition for Digital Rights or the Global Data Justice project bring together actors across borders to formulate shared principles, exchange best practices, and push for institutional reforms in multilateral spaces. These networks amplify voices from the periphery and provide counterweight to dominant corporate and geopolitical interests. By participating in international standard-setting bodies, regional consultations, and AI ethics dialogues, these actors help embed concerns of equity, linguistic diversity, gender justice, and environmental sustainability into normative debates that often risk being technocratic or abstract.

Civil society and sub-state actors are indispensable to any meaningful agenda for digital inclusion. Their contributions transcend technical fixes and emphasize structural change, participatory governance, and the democratization of digital futures. They reassert the importance of local knowledge, social accountability, and inclusive institution-building within the multilateral architecture of AI diplomacy. In doing so, they are not only shaping policy outcomes but also redefining who gets to participate in the making of digital norms, and on whose terms.

5.3. Toward Institutional Redesign for Digital Equity

The pursuit of genuine digital inclusion in global AI diplomacy necessitates a fundamental redesign of existing institutional frameworks. Many of the current multilateral and regional bodies governing digital technologies operate within outdated mandates, centralized decision-making structures, and technocratic cultures that fail to accommodate the voices and realities of marginalized populations. These institutions often privilege dominant geopolitical and commercial interests, thereby reinforcing the structural exclusions that digital inclusion agendas seek to undo. As a result, institutional redesign must begin with a recognition that equity, pluralism, and participation are not peripheral concerns but foundational principles for the legitimacy and effectiveness of digital governance.

A first step toward redesign involves reconfiguring representation and participation mechanisms in key forums. Multilateral institutions must evolve beyond state-centric diplomacy and formally integrate civil society, subnational governments, indigenous groups, and historically underrepresented regions into deliberative and decision-making processes. This requires not just invitations to participate but structural guarantees of influence, including voting rights, agenda-setting powers, and access to technical resources and institutional memory. Forums such as the G20, World Summit on the Information Society, and the International Telecommunication Union should adopt inclusive governance models that reflect the diversity of digital experiences and needs, particularly from the Global South. Without such reforms, these bodies risk reproducing the very digital divides they are tasked with addressing.

Second, institutional redesign must promote epistemic diversity by integrating alternative knowledge systems, languages, and evaluative criteria into how AI is assessed, regulated, and deployed. Technical expertise must be complemented by social, legal, and ethical insights rooted in local contexts. This implies revising the composition of expert committees, establishing multilingual policy pipelines, and creating funding mechanisms to support research and innovation from under-represented regions. Such changes would allow global institutions to shift from a narrow focus on infrastructure and standards toward a more holistic understanding of digital justice. Inclusion must not only be about seats at the table but also about whose frameworks and values shape the rules of engagement.

Third, accountability and transparency mechanisms within digital governance institutions require strengthening. Many AI-related negotiations and regulatory processes remain closed to public scrutiny or are heavily shaped by corporate lobbying. To counter this, institutional reforms should mandate the publication of meeting transcripts, stakeholder submissions, and impact assessments, while also ensuring accessible grievance redress mechanisms for those adversely affected by digital policies. Embedding independent oversight bodies, public reporting obligations, and participatory audits would go a long way in restoring trust and legitimacy to global digital governance. These steps are especially vital in contexts where digital inclusion intersects with human rights, environmental harm, and algorithmic discrimination.

Finally, institutional redesign must support capacity building as a structural commitment rather than a secondary goal. Digital inclusion cannot advance without addressing the asymmetries in knowledge, infrastructure, and negotiation power that exist across regions. Institutions must invest in long-term training, digital literacy, policy support, and infrastructure development in underserved areas, especially in the Global South. Moreover, capacity building should be conceived as mutual and bidirectional, recognizing that innovation, ethics, and governance insights also emerge from the peripheries. The logic of solidarity must replace the logic of assistance, anchoring digital equity within a framework of shared responsibility and co-development.

Overall, institutional redesign for digital equity entails a profound shift in the norms, structures, and cultures of global AI governance. It demands reimagining institutions not just as administrative centres but as democratic spaces capable of responding to the complexities of a rapidly transforming digital world. This redesign must be grounded in justice, inclusion, and accountability, ensuring that digital diplomacy does not simply manage inequality but actively works to dismantle it. Only through such transformation can digital inclusion become a durable and meaningful pillar of global governance.

6. CONCLUSION

The legitimacy of multilateral governance in the digital age increasingly rests on the extent to which it embodies inclusive principles in both form and substance. In a world where artificial intelligence is reshaping diplomacy, policymaking, and global cooperation, the exclusion of large sections of the global population from decision-making processes raises critical concerns about the fairness and effectiveness of international institutions. Inclusion is no longer a rhetorical ideal but a foundational requirement for legitimacy. When governance structures fail to reflect the diversity of digital experiences, needs, and knowledge systems, they risk reinforcing systemic inequalities, losing public trust, and generating outcomes that lack moral or practical authority.

Multilateral institutions that aim to guide the ethical deployment of AI must therefore centre inclusion not only as a normative commitment but as a structural design principle. This involves rethinking who participates in setting agendas, who defines problems, who frames solutions, and who benefits from policy outcomes. In traditional diplomatic structures, legitimacy has often been derived from state sovereignty and consensus among powerful actors. However, as digital technologies permeate all aspects of life and affect individuals across borders, a broader basis for legitimacy becomes essential. It must now include responsiveness to affected communities, procedural fairness in governance, and recognition of historically marginalized voices.

Moreover, inclusion enhances institutional legitimacy by expanding the epistemic base of governance. Policies informed by a plurality of experiences and perspectives are more likely to be context-sensitive, equitable, and robust. For instance, incorporating perspectives from the Global South, from gender and disability rights advocates, and from indigenous knowledge systems enables more nuanced understandings of risk, access, and harm in AI systems. This, in turn, leads to more just and sustainable outcomes. Without such inclusion, multilateralism risks becoming a mechanism for reinforcing the status quo, dominated by a narrow set of geopolitical and commercial interests.

Importantly, inclusion as a basis for legitimacy must go beyond participation to encompass influence and accountability. Token representation or limited consultation processes do little to alter the power dynamics that shape AI governance. Legitimate multilateralism must create meaningful avenues for co-decision, resource sharing, and joint norm development. Institutional innovations such as rotating leadership, shared data stewardship, multilingual deliberation, and community-led audits can help embed inclusivity into the operational fabric of digital governance. These mechanisms contribute not only to ethical legitimacy but also to practical legitimacy by producing policies that are more likely to be accepted, implemented, and sustained across diverse contexts.

Ultimately, a multilateralism that fails to embrace inclusion will be perceived as illegitimate by those it marginalizes, and its policies will lack the authority needed for global cooperation in a rapidly changing digital landscape. By contrast, an inclusive multilateralism anchored in justice, transparency, and participation can offer a compelling model for AI governance, one that strengthens the moral and political foundations of global diplomacy. The chapter thus argues that inclusion is not an optional value but the cornerstone of legitimacy in the governance of emerging technologies.

Achieving equitable digital engagement through multilateral diplomacy requires concrete policy shifts that address structural disparities in access, influence, and capacity. While normative commitments to inclusion have become more common in international forums, they often remain unfulfilled without the institutional and policy mechanisms to operationalise them. Therefore, translating inclusion into action entails a reconfiguration of policy priorities, resource allocation, and governance practices that centre on equity, especially for historically underrepresented states and communities. Equitable digital engagement demands more than access to infrastructure or tools, it involves sustained participation in decision-making, ownership over data and digital assets, and the ability to shape norms and standards that govern the global digital commons.

One of the foremost policy imperatives is to establish funding mechanisms that reduce the digital capacity gap between Global North and Global South actors. Equitable engagement will remain aspirational if states and civil society groups in the Global South are systematically excluded due to resource constraints. Dedicated funds, capacity-building programs, and technology transfers - structured through fair and transparent international partnerships - are essential to enable meaningful engagement in digital diplomacy. Similarly, multilateral institutions must adopt procurement and agenda-setting policies that prioritize inclusive participation, including travel support, translation services, and equitable speaking slots in global forums. These operational measures are key to ensuring that diverse actors can participate fully and on equal footing.

Another critical pathway involves institutional reforms that enhance transparency and accountability in digital negotiations and norm-setting. Too often, key decisions in multilateral settings are taken in closed or informally constituted groups, limiting input from states with lower bargaining power or from non-state actors representing affected populations. Formalising stakeholder engagement through mandatory public consultation processes, publishing draft negotiation texts, and enabling civil society monitoring of AI and data governance can help reduce asymmetries in influence. These reforms would not only widen access but would also enhance the legitimacy of outcomes and reduce the perception that global digital governance is the preserve of powerful corporate or geopolitical actors.

Additionally, digital engagement must be grounded in multilingualism, cultural sensitivity, and recognition of diverse epistemologies. Current diplomatic and technical dialogues are heavily shaped by dominant linguistic and conceptual frameworks, often reflecting Euro-American legal traditions, corporate terminologies, or technocratic vocabularies that marginalise other ways of knowing and governing. Policy frameworks should institutionalise mechanisms that accommodate vernacular understandings of digital rights, plural ethical systems, and regionally specific data governance models. This also requires supporting locally-driven research and indigenous innovation, ensuring that technological solutions are co-created and not merely imposed.

Finally, equitable engagement requires ongoing evaluation and adjustment through inclusive monitoring and review systems. Multilateral institutions must establish mechanisms to periodically assess the inclusiveness and effectiveness of their digital policies, using both quantitative and qualitative indicators developed in collaboration with a broad set of actors. Feedback loops must be embedded into institutional design, allowing course correction when inclusion falters. In sum, policy pathways for equitable digital engagement must move beyond declarations to institutional and operational commitments that reshape how multilateral forums function. This transformation is essential if digital diplomacy is to respond to the realities of an interconnected yet unequal world, and if global governance is to embody the democratic values it seeks to uphold.

In conclusion, the legitimacy and future relevance of multilateral diplomacy in the age of artificial intelligence will depend on the extent to which it embraces inclusion as a structural imperative rather than a rhetorical gesture. This chapter has shown that digital inclusion must be understood in multidimensional terms, encompassing not only access to technology but also meaningful participation in decision-making, representation in agenda-setting, and the ability to shape the epistemic frameworks that govern AI systems. The comparative analysis of diplomatic forums and the role of Global South actors underscores that while significant asymmetries persist, there are also emerging strategies of resistance, innovation, and reconfiguration that point toward more equitable modes of engagement. For AI diplomacy to fulfil its transformative potential, global institutions must commit to redistributing not just digital resources but also authority, recognition, and voice. Only then can digital cooperation become a credible tool for justice and solidarity in a fractured world.

REFERENCES

Al Mokdad, A. (2025, July). *AI diplomacy in the Global South — strategy or afterthought?* Medium. Retrieved from: https://medium.com/@almokdadali1/ai-diplomacy-in-the-global-south-strategy-or-afterthought-fb63218bf109

Al-Muwil, A., Weerakkody, V., El-Haddadeh, R., & Dwivedi, Y. K. (2019). Balancing digital-by-default with inclusion: A study of the factors influencing e-inclusion in the UK. *Information Systems Frontiers*, *21*(3), 635–659. DOI: 10.1007/s10796-019-09914-0

Ayodele, O. (2021). The digital transformation of diplomacy: Implications for the African Union and continental diplomacy. *The South African Journal of International Affairs*, *28*(3), 379–401. DOI: 10.1080/10220461.2021.1968944

Cummings, S., Dhewa, C., Kemboi, G., & Young, S. (2023). Doing epistemic justice in sustainable development: Applying the philosophical concept of epistemic injustice to the real world. *Sustainable Development (Bradford)*, *31*(3), 1965–1977. DOI: 10.1002/sd.2497

Demaidi, M. N. (2025). Artificial intelligence national strategy in a developing country. *AI & Society*, *40*(2), 423–435. DOI: 10.1007/s00146-023-01779-x

Farahani, M., & Ghasemi, G. (2024). *Artificial intelligence and inequality: Challenges and opportunities*. Qeios., DOI: 10.32388/7HWUZ2

Farhad, S. (2025). Passengers in Flight: AI Governance Capacity in the Global South. *Digital Society : Ethics, Socio-Legal and Governance of Digital Technology*, *4*(2), 39. DOI: 10.1007/s44206-025-00195-6

Gehl Sampath, P. (2021). Governing artificial intelligence in an age of inequality. *Global Policy*, *12*(S6), 21–31. DOI: 10.1111/1758-5899.12940

Ghasemaghaei, M., & Kordzadeh, N. (2024). Understanding how algorithmic injustice leads to making discriminatory decisions: An obedience to authority perspective. *Information & Management*, *61*(2), 103921. DOI: 10.1016/j.im.2024.103921

Hachkevych, A., & Nykolyshyn, M. (2023). AI Toolkit for Diplomats. *International Science Journal of Jurisprudence & Philosophy*, *2*(3), 45–54. DOI: 10.46299/j.isjjp.20230203.03

Inuwa-Dutse, I. (2023). *FATE in AI: Towards algorithmic inclusivity and accessibility*. In *Proceedings of the 3rd ACM Conference on Equity and Access in Algorithms, Mechanisms, and Optimization (EAAMO '23)* (Article 13, pp. 1–14). Association for Computing Machinery. DOI: 10.1145/3617694.3623233

Mahrenbach, L. (2024). *Whose AI is it anyway? Moving global debates from 'mine' to 'ours'*. Observer Research Foundation. https://www.orfonline.org/expert-speak/whose-ai-is-it-anyway-moving-global-debates-from-mine-to-ours

Mostafaei, H., Kordnoori, S., Ostadrahimi, M., & Banihashemi, S. S. A. (2025). Applications of artificial intelligence in global diplomacy: A review of research and practical models. *Sustainable Futures : An Applied Journal of Technology, Environment and Society*, *9*, 100486. DOI: 10.1016/j.sftr.2025.100486

Pagliaro, H., Michel, R., & Rafael, S. (2021). The problem of automated facial recognition technologies in Brazil: Social countermovements and the new frontiers of fundamental rights. *Latin American Human Rights Studies*, *1*(1), 1. Advance online publication. DOI: 10.31261/LAHRS.2021.01.01

Pasupuleti, M. K. (2025). AI's role in global stability, diplomacy, and peacebuilding. *International Journal of Academic and Industrial Research Innovations*, *5*(2), 1–11. DOI: 10.62311/nesx/32268

Rai, V. (2023). *The G20 and India's digital public infrastructure*. Institute of South Asian Studies, National University of Singapore. https://www.isas.nus.edu.sg/papers/the-g20-and-indias-digital-public-infrastructure/

Wall, P. J., Saxena, D., & Brown, S. (2021). *Artificial Intelligence in the Global South (AI4D): Potential and risks*. In *Proceedings of the 1st Virtual Conference on Implications of Information and Digital Technologies for Development*. DOI: 10.48550/arXiv.2108.10093

Chapter 9
Bridging Nations Through Sports:
The Strategic Role of Sports Diplomacy in Global Relations

Yalin Aygun
https://orcid.org/0000-0002-1018-657X
Inonu University, Turkey

ABSTRACT

This chapter examines sports diplomacy as part of the twenty-first-century shift from traditional state-centered diplomacy to a multi-actor, multi-level practice spanning culture, economy, communication, and governance. It defines sports diplomacy through its links to soft power and public diplomacy, distinguishing it from broader sport–politics debates and nation branding. Tracing its evolution from the Olympic Truce to Cold War bridge-building and post-Cold War mega-events, the chapter highlights key actors such as states, federations, NGOs, athletes, and corporations. It also addresses issues like sportswashing, governance deficits, and human rights concerns, emphasizing the uneven and often temporary nature of soft power gains. Looking forward, it argues that the credibility of sports diplomacy depends on digital engagement, sustainability, inclusivity, and ethical governance aligned with global development goals.

1. INTRODUCTION

Sports diplomacy has emerged as one of the most dynamic and multifaceted forms of diplomacy in the twenty-first century (Abdi et al., 2018). Traditionally, diplomacy was understood as the exclusive preserve of state representatives con-

DOI: 10.4018/979-8-3373-4937-4.ch009

ducting formal negotiations behind closed doors (Pigman, 2014). However, contemporary diplomacy has become increasingly multidimensional, encompassing cultural, economic, scientific, and public dimensions (Garsten & Sörbom, 2023). Within this expanded diplomatic toolkit, sport has secured a prominent role due to its universal popularity, symbolic resonance, and ability to transcend linguistic, cultural, and political barriers (Grix & Brannagan, 2024; Ozsari, 2018).

Unlike conventional diplomacy, which often relies on formal protocols and elite-level engagement, sports diplomacy functions across multiple levels simultaneously. At the macro level, states strategically employ mega-events such as the Olympic Games or the FIFA World Cup to project soft power, showcase development, and reinforce nation branding (Kobierecki, 2023). At the meso level, governments and institutions use sports exchanges, training programs, and joint initiatives to foster cultural understanding and political cooperation. At the micro level, individual athletes, coaches, and grassroots organizations act as cultural ambassadors, building interpersonal bridges and fostering dialogue across communities (Grix et al., 2021).

Despite its growing salience, sports diplomacy remains conceptually contested. Scholars disagree on whether it is a form of soft power, a subtype of cultural diplomacy, or a broader set of practices situated at the intersection of politics, culture, and identity (Woodward, 2025). Moreover, while the positive potential of sports diplomacy is often highlighted, including its capacity to facilitate dialogue, reduce tensions, and promote international cooperation, critical perspectives emphasize its instrumentalization for political propaganda, "sportswashing," and image management by authoritarian regimes (Almeida & Ozdemir, 2024; Grix & Brannagan, 2024).

The importance of examining sports diplomacy lies in its dual nature: it is simultaneously a site of cultural attraction and a contested field of political struggle. This chapter addresses this complexity by (1) clarifying the conceptual foundations and theoretical frameworks underpinning sports diplomacy, (2) tracing its historical evolution from antiquity to the digital era, (3) mapping the key actors and mechanisms involved, (4) examining regional variations in strategies and practices, (5) analyzing challenges and critiques, and (6) considering future directions, particularly regarding sustainability, human rights, and digital media.

By synthesizing theoretical perspectives and empirical cases, the chapter provides a comprehensive framework for understanding sports diplomacy as both a soft-power resource and a contested arena where legitimacy, influence, and identity are negotiated. In doing so, it highlights the role of sport not merely as entertainment but as a strategic instrument of international relations.

2. CONCEPTUAL FOUNDATIONS

2.1. Defining Sports Diplomacy

At its core, sports diplomacy refers to the strategic use of sport, sporting events, organizations, and personalities for diplomatic purposes. It involves both state and non-state actors and operates across a wide spectrum of activities, from mega-events and bilateral exchanges to grassroots programs and athlete-led initiatives (Grix & Brannagan, 2024; Ozsari, 2018).

Unlike "sport and politics," which often denotes political interventions in sport (e.g., boycotts or sanctions), sports diplomacy emphasizes the deliberate deployment of sport to achieve diplomatic objectives such as improving bilateral relations, enhancing national image, fostering peace, or advancing trade and tourism (Na & Dallaire, 2022). Its scope extends from highly formal state-led strategies, such as the European Union's sports diplomacy framework, to more organic and informal interactions, such as athlete ambassadors engaging in intercultural dialogue.

2.2 Soft Power and Public Diplomacy

The most influential theoretical lens for sports diplomacy is soft power, as developed by Joseph Nye. Soft power refers to the ability of a state to influence others by attraction rather than coercion, drawing on cultural values, political ideals, and institutions (Abdi et al., 2018). Sport, with its universal appeal and emotional resonance, provides an exceptionally powerful vehicle for such attraction.

States incorporate sport into their public diplomacy strategies, aiming to reach foreign publics directly rather than exclusively through governments. International sporting success, mega-event hosting, and the export of sports culture (e.g., martial arts, professional leagues) contribute to a "politics of attraction" that fosters goodwill and shapes perceptions (Grix et al., 2021; Grix & Brannagan, 2024). Importantly, soft power is not exercised in isolation but often combined with economic and political tools in comprehensive foreign policy packages (Woodward, 2025).

2.3. Nation Branding and Image Projection

Sports diplomacy overlaps significantly with nation branding, where states attempt to construct and disseminate a favorable image to global audiences. Hosting the Olympics, investing in foreign sports clubs, or cultivating elite athletes can all serve to project an image of modernity, openness, and competence (Almahraj, 2023).

Examples abound: South Korea's successful hosting of the 1988 Olympics symbolized its transformation into a modern democracy, while Qatar's investments in football clubs and hosting of the 2022 World Cup represent efforts to diversify its economy and reposition itself internationally (Grix & Brannagan, 2024). Such cases illustrate how sports can simultaneously serve domestic identity formation and international legitimation.

2.4. The Sportswashing Debate

A more critical perspective emphasizes the risks of sportswashing, where states use sport to obscure negative aspects of their regimes, particularly human rights abuses (Almeida & Ozdemir, 2024). For instance, petro-monarchies in the Gulf have been accused of using high-profile sports investments to distract from democratic deficits and labor rights violations (Costa & Moriconi, 2024).

Yet, scholars caution against reducing sports diplomacy to mere sportswashing. As Grix and Brannagan (2024) argue, soft power gains are incremental, contested, and subject to long-term narrative battles. While initial investments may attract criticism, they can gradually normalize a state's international image over time. The key analytical challenge is therefore to distinguish between genuine cultural exchange and strategic image management while recognizing that both often coexist in practice.

2.5. Institutional and Governance Perspectives

Beyond soft power and branding, sports diplomacy is shaped by the governance structures of international sports organizations such as the IOC and FIFA. These bodies mediate state influence through complex systems of bidding, hosting, and rule-making (Konjer et al., 2022; Schreiner et al., 2022). They propagate global models of elite sport, diffusing norms of professionalism, commercialization, and integrity (Chappelet, 2021). At the same time, their autonomy limits direct political control, forcing states to negotiate influence through incentives and compliance rather than commands.

3. HISTORICAL EVOLUTION OF SPORTS DIPLOMACY

3.1. Antiquity: The Olympic Truce and Early Diplomatic Functions

The roots of sports diplomacy stretch deep into antiquity. In Ancient Greece, athletic contests were not only cultural spectacles but also political instruments. The Olympic Truce (Ekecheiria) symbolized the recognition that athletic competition could transcend political rivalries and provide neutral ground for exchange. The truce ensured safe passage for athletes and spectators, temporarily suspending hostilities among warring city-states. This practice was far more than ceremonial: it represented an early institutionalization of sport as a diplomatic mechanism, embedding values of fairness, honor, and dialogue into inter-polis relations.

Beyond Greece, other civilizations also used athletic spectacles to signal cultural superiority and political stability. Roman gladiatorial games, although brutal, conveyed imperial strength and cohesion, while Mayan and Aztec ball games often carried religious and political significance. These historical examples illustrate the symbolic power of sport to communicate legitimacy and provide an arena for identity negotiation long before the modern nation-state emerged.

3.2. Early Modern Era: Nationalism and Symbolic Representation

With the rise of nation-states in the 18th and 19th centuries, sport began to be intertwined with national identity formation. The codification of modern sports such as football, rugby, and cricket coincided with industrialization and imperial expansion, providing states with tools to cultivate discipline, cohesion, and pride. Colonial powers used sport both to assert dominance and to integrate colonies into imperial culture.

In this period, international sporting contests, such as early cricket tours between Britain and its colonies, were not framed explicitly as diplomacy but functioned as soft mechanisms of empire. They offered colonized populations a paradoxical mixture of cultural subordination and empowerment, as local teams gradually competed on equal terms with their colonizers. By the late 19th century, the revival of the Olympic Games under Pierre de Coubertin institutionalized sport as a global platform with explicit peacebuilding ambitions, foreshadowing the modern nexus of sport and diplomacy.

3.3. The Cold War: Sports as Proxy Battleground and Bridge

The Cold War (1947–1991) marked the high point of sport's politicization in international relations. Superpowers, the United States and the Soviet Union, invested heavily in Olympic success as a proxy for ideological supremacy. Every medal table was interpreted as evidence of systemic superiority, transforming athletes into symbolic soldiers of the ideological struggle.

Yet beyond rivalry, sport also offered unexpected bridges of cooperation. The most famous case is Ping-Pong Diplomacy in 1971, when table tennis matches between American and Chinese players paved the way for President Nixon's historic visit to Beijing (Myhre, 2023; Abramczyk, 2024). This episode highlighted the low-political-cost, high-symbolic-value nature of sports diplomacy: by using a seemingly apolitical platform, states could initiate dialogue without losing face.

Similarly, the 1988 Seoul Olympics represented South Korea's diplomatic coming of age. By successfully staging the Games and preventing a Soviet/Eastern bloc boycott, South Korea signaled its modernization and democratic transition, while simultaneously opening channels of communication with former adversaries (Grix et al., 2021). The Games provided not only a stage for athletic performance but also a theatrical space of national transformation, where political legitimacy was re-scripted before a global audience.

3.4. Post-Cold War Globalization: Mega-Events as Nation Branding

Following the Cold War, sport became a central tool of global cultural diplomacy. The expansion of television broadcasting and later digital media transformed mega-events into global spectacles watched by billions. Hosting the Olympics or the FIFA World Cup became a coveted prize, signaling a nation's capacity for organization, security, and innovation.

Countries like South Korea, Japan, and China strategically used these opportunities to assert themselves as modern powers. The 2002 FIFA World Cup, co-hosted by Japan and South Korea, was particularly significant: despite deep historical animosities, the event facilitated bilateral cooperation and allowed both nations to rebrand themselves as advanced democracies integrated into global networks (Grix et al., 2021). Likewise, the Beijing Olympics in 2008 symbolized China's arrival as a global power, while also raising questions about human rights and authoritarianism.

The United Kingdom provides another instructive case. A "serial host" of international sporting events, Britain has leveraged mega-events to reinforce its global cultural leadership. Following the success of the 2012 London Olympics, the UK secured over 120 international events in the following decade, employing what scholars term a strategy of "defensive marketing", reinforcing an already strong global brand rather than merely seeking to improve it (Woodward, 2025; Grix & Brannagan, 2024).

3.5. The Rise of Sports Diplomacy in the Middle East

The early 21st century has witnessed a remarkable surge of sports diplomacy in the Middle East, particularly in the Gulf. Countries such as Qatar, Saudi Arabia, and the United Arab Emirates have invested billions in hosting mega-events, acquiring football clubs, and sponsoring global leagues.

Qatar's hosting of the 2022 FIFA World Cup epitomized this strategy. While criticized as an instance of "sportswashing," the event undeniably positioned Qatar on the global map, diversified its economy beyond hydrocarbons, and allowed it to project itself as a modern, globally integrated state (Almeida & Ozdemir, 2024; Costa & Moriconi, 2024). Saudi Arabia has followed a similar path, investing heavily in Formula 1, boxing, and football, aiming to use sport as a vector of Vision 2030 modernization and as a soft-power shield against criticism of its domestic politics (Grix & Brannagan, 2024).

These cases illustrate both the opportunities and risks of sports diplomacy: while such investments generate visibility and influence, they also attract intense scrutiny around labor practices, human rights, and political freedoms. Nevertheless, the Gulf states demonstrate how even small or medium-sized powers can leverage sport to punch above their weight in international affairs.

3.6. Contemporary Trends: Regional Powers and Emerging Economies

Beyond the Middle East, emerging economies such as Brazil, India, and South Africa have increasingly turned to sports diplomacy to amplify their regional influence. Brazil's hosting of the 2014 World Cup and 2016 Olympics showcased its global ambitions, though the events also underscored governance and economic challenges. India is expanding its influence through the global success of cricket and the Indian Premier League, while South Africa continues to leverage sport as a post-apartheid unifier and as a means of continental leadership.

Meanwhile, South Korea and Japan remain archetypes of how sustained sports diplomacy, built on both event hosting and cultural exports like Taekwondo or Judo, can produce long-term soft power dividends. These strategies show how regional powers use sport not only to cultivate external visibility but also to reinforce internal cohesion and identity (Grix et al., 2021).

3.7. Summary of Historical Trajectories

From antiquity to globalization, the role of sport in diplomacy has evolved dramatically. What began as symbolic rituals of peace in Ancient Greece has transformed into complex, multi-level practices involving states, international organizations, non-state actors, and transnational corporations. Sport now functions simultaneously as a tool of peace, a weapon of propaganda, and a commodity of global capitalism.

The historical trajectory highlights three enduring lessons:

- *Continuity of symbolism:* From the Olympic truce to mega-event opening ceremonies, sport communicates legitimacy and identity.
- *Dual potential:* Sport can both unite (Ping-Pong Diplomacy) and divide (boycotts, propaganda).
- *Growing complexity:* The rise of non-state actors, transnational corporations, and digital platforms ensures that sports diplomacy is no longer monopolized by governments but operates within a pluralistic governance environment.

4. KEY ACTORS IN SPORTS DIPLOMACY

States and governments are among the primary actors in the field of sports diplomacy, as they possess both the resources and the political will to integrate sport into their foreign policy frameworks. Governmental agencies often design sport diplomacy strategies to enhance national prestige, strengthen bilateral and multilateral relations, and improve the visibility of their countries in the global arena. These strategies may involve hosting international mega-events, supporting bilateral exchanges of athletes and coaches, or funding sport-for-development programs abroad. The use of sport as an official tool of diplomacy underscores the recognition that athletic achievements and cultural events can be as effective as traditional diplomatic negotiations in shaping international perceptions. For example, countries such as the United Kingdom, South Korea, and Qatar have developed long-term national plans that explicitly position sport as a core element of soft power. Such policies illustrate a shift away from sport as mere entertainment and toward sport as a deliberate instrument of cultural diplomacy (Grix & Brannagan, 2024).

In addition to states, international organizations play a pivotal role. The International Olympic Committee (IOC), the Fédération Internationale de Football Association (FIFA), and other sport federations mediate between governments, set rules and standards, and oversee the organization of major international competitions. These bodies often frame themselves as politically neutral, but their decisions frequently have significant political consequences. By awarding the right to host Olympic Games or World Cups, they influence international relations, urban development, and national branding strategies. The International Olympic Committee, for instance, has historically presented the Olympic Games as a universal celebration of peace and cooperation, while simultaneously navigating boycotts, human rights debates, and political controversies (Woodward, 2025). FIFA similarly operates as a gatekeeper for global football, shaping not only sporting rules but also the distribution of diplomatic opportunities tied to the sport's immense popularity. UNESCO and other United Nations-affiliated organizations also incorporate sport into development and peacebuilding programs, reflecting a broader acknowledgment that sport is a cost-effective and highly visible means of fostering international understanding (Ozsari, 2018).

Non-state actors also exert considerable influence. Athletes, in particular, often function as unofficial ambassadors. Their performances and public personas transcend national borders, enabling them to foster connections with foreign audiences in ways that are often more accessible and authentic than government communication. Athletes such as Muhammad Ali, Pele, or more recently Serena Williams and Lionel Messi have been symbolic figures whose global visibility extended beyond their sport, representing values such as resilience, equality, or cultural pride. Governments frequently capitalize on this influence by designating athletes as cultural ambassadors or by supporting their roles in campaigns aligned with foreign policy objectives (Abdi et al., 2018). At the same time, the independence of athletes can also create challenges for states, since personal statements or actions sometimes contradict official diplomatic stances. This dual potential highlights both the power and the risks of relying on individual figures within sports diplomacy.

Media institutions are another critical actor in the ecosystem of sports diplomacy. Broadcasting networks, social media platforms, and international press agencies mediate the narratives of sports events and thus shape how they are perceived globally. The media has the capacity to amplify the diplomatic messages embedded in mega-events, while also exposing controversies such as corruption, labor conditions, or human rights violations. Through selective coverage, media can legitimize or delegitimize the image a state seeks to project through sport. As a result, sports diplomacy increasingly relies on managing media narratives, not only by states but also by international organizations and sponsors (Almeida & Ozdemir, 2024). Non-governmental organizations also leverage sport for development and peace, often working at the grassroots level to address issues such as gender inequality, education, and health. These NGOs operate in contexts where formal diplomacy may be absent or limited, using sport as a practical entry point for dialogue and cooperation (Rodríguez et al., 2024).

5. MECHANISMS AND PRACTICES OF SPORTS DIPLOMACY

The most visible mechanisms of sports diplomacy are mega-events such as the Olympic Games and the FIFA World Cup. These events provide host states with global platforms to demonstrate organizational competence, cultural vibrancy, and political stability. They also facilitate opportunities for cultural exchange between athletes and spectators from diverse backgrounds. However, hosting such events requires massive financial investment and carries risks, including potential accusations of sportswashing when regimes use them to distract from internal problems or human rights concerns (Grix & Brannagan, 2024). Despite these challenges, the allure of hosting remains strong, as the potential soft power benefits and economic gains are perceived as outweighing the risks. Mega-events also allow states to build infrastructure, boost tourism, and present a vision of national modernity, all of which contribute to long-term image-building (Kobierecki, 2023).

Beyond mega-events, bilateral and multilateral exchanges constitute another important practice of sports diplomacy. Friendly matches, shared training programs, and intercultural festivals involving sport provide channels for informal dialogue and the development of mutual trust. Such initiatives are often more modest in scale than mega-events but can yield long-lasting interpersonal ties. For example, the historic Ping-Pong diplomacy between the United States and China demonstrated how even small-scale exchanges can open pathways for high-level political dialogue (Myhre, 2023). Similarly, cultural institutes such as the Goethe-Institut in Germany or the British Council have incorporated sports into their programming, thereby reinforcing broader strategies of cultural diplomacy (Almahraj, 2023).

Athlete ambassadors represent another significant mechanism. By design, these programs rely on the personal influence of high-profile athletes to communicate national values or to support humanitarian initiatives. Such ambassadors participate in international campaigns, public speaking engagements, or symbolic matches that aim to bridge divides between communities. Their effectiveness lies in their perceived authenticity, as audiences are often more receptive to athletes than to politicians. However, the growing commercialization of sport raises concerns about whether such representations are always authentic or whether they risk being subsumed by corporate or political interests (Rookwood, 2021).

Sports for Development and Peace (SDP) programs constitute a further important dimension. Unlike mega-events, SDP initiatives are typically long-term, community-based projects that aim to leverage sport for reconciliation, education, gender equality, or public health. These initiatives illustrate how sport can serve diplomatic functions not only at the level of international prestige but also within local communities, creating grassroots pathways to peace and cooperation (Rodríguez et al., 2024). By engaging youth, marginalized groups, and conflict-affected populations, SDP programs demonstrate how the universal language of sport can be used to promote human rights and development. International organizations, states, and NGOs increasingly cooperate in these efforts, highlighting the multi-actor and multi-level character of sports diplomacy in the twenty-first century (Corvino et al., 2023).

Taken together, the diverse actors and mechanisms of sports diplomacy illustrate that this field cannot be understood solely as a matter of statecraft. Rather, it represents a complex network of interactions among states, organizations, athletes, NGOs, and media. Each actor contributes differently to the practice of sports diplomacy, whether through symbolic representation, organizational capacity, or grassroots engagement. Similarly, the mechanisms range from spectacular mega-events to local peacebuilding initiatives, encompassing both the projection of national identity and the pursuit of humanitarian goals. The interplay between these actors and practices underscores the multifaceted and evolving nature of sports diplomacy, positioning it as a field that is simultaneously political, cultural, and social in its scope.

6. REGIONAL PERSPECTIVES IN SPORTS DIPLOMACY

The practice of sports diplomacy varies significantly across regions, shaped by different historical legacies, political systems, and cultural priorities. While the universal appeal of sport makes it a common diplomatic tool, the way states and regions deploy it reflects their unique foreign policy objectives and societal contexts. A comparative analysis of regional perspectives illustrates both the diversity and the convergence of sports diplomacy strategies worldwide.

6.1. Europe and the EU's Sports Diplomacy Strategy

In Europe, sports diplomacy is strongly institutionalized, particularly through the policies of the European Union. The EU has recognized sport as a valuable instrument for strengthening both internal cohesion and external relations. The European Commission and the European Parliament have developed strategic frameworks that link sport with public diplomacy, international cooperation, and the promotion of European values. These initiatives aim to foster peace, inclusivity, and dialogue while also addressing social issues such as discrimination, health, and integration of minorities (Kobayashi et al., 2023).

Sport in the EU context is framed as both an economic and cultural resource. Member states are encouraged to integrate sport into broader strategies of cultural diplomacy, emphasizing its capacity to promote dialogue with neighboring countries, candidate states, and global partners. This approach highlights sport as a tool not only for nation-branding but also for representing the EU's collective identity as a global actor committed to democratic norms and multilateral cooperation. Programs supported by EU funding often focus on youth mobility, joint training programs, and exchanges between European athletes and their counterparts in other regions. Moreover, the EU has emphasized the role of sport in its neighborhood policies, using athletic cooperation as a channel to build trust in regions experiencing political instability. This institutional approach demonstrates the EU's ambition to embed sport within a broader normative framework, positioning it as part of its external relations strategy (Grix & Brannagan, 2024).

Yet, despite this institutionalization, challenges remain. Different member states vary widely in their approaches to sport, with some prioritizing elite performance while others focus more on grassroots development. This diversity sometimes complicates the creation of unified strategies. Nonetheless, the EU's sports diplomacy demonstrates how regional organizations can leverage sport as a means of representing collective identity, transcending national boundaries, and promoting shared values.

6.2. United States: Sports as a Foreign Policy Tool

The United States employs sports diplomacy as an extension of its broader public diplomacy and soft power strategies. American sporting culture, particularly the global reach of basketball, baseball, and American football, has long been a medium for promoting national values abroad. The U.S. government has actively integrated sport into its foreign policy through cultural exchange programs, international tours, and the designation of athletes as goodwill ambassadors (Jensen, 2015).

One of the most prominent aspects of U.S. sports diplomacy has been its focus on youth and community engagement. Programs sponsored by the State Department send American athletes and coaches abroad to conduct clinics and workshops, particularly in developing countries. These initiatives aim to promote leadership, teamwork, and democratic values while fostering goodwill toward the United States. At the same time, American athletes frequently serve as role models and symbols of cultural dynamism. Through the visibility of figures such as Michael Jordan, Serena Williams, or LeBron James, the United States projects an image of innovation, diversity, and opportunity (Athayde & Figueiredo, 2023).

Mega-events have also played a role in U.S. sports diplomacy, though less consistently than in other regions. The Olympics hosted in Los Angeles in 1984 and in Atlanta in 1996 were used to highlight the country's economic power and organizational capabilities. Additionally, the broadcasting of events such as the Super Bowl has extended American cultural influence abroad, reinforcing the global visibility of U.S. sports industries. This intersection of sports, media, and commerce positions American sports diplomacy not only as a cultural tool but also as an economic instrument that supports trade, branding, and investment opportunities (Dubinsky, 2022a).

6.3. Asia: Rising Powers and Sports Investments

Asia has become one of the most dynamic regions in the global practice of sports diplomacy, with states such as China, Japan, South Korea, India, and Qatar investing heavily in mega-events and athletic infrastructure. The common thread across these countries is the use of sport as a platform for asserting modernity, national pride, and international relevance (Grix et al., 2021).

China exemplifies the ambitious use of sport as a national strategy. The 2008 Beijing Olympics projected an image of China as a modern, confident power, while the 2022 Winter Olympics reinforced its global leadership in sport and technology. These events were carefully orchestrated to showcase national achievements, consolidate domestic support, and signal China's rise in the international order. Similarly, South Korea has leveraged major events such as the 1988 Seoul Olympics, the 2002 FIFA World Cup, and the 2018 PyeongChang Winter Olympics to reinforce its democratic transformation, technological prowess, and cultural exports, particularly through the global spread of the Korean Wave (Hallyu). Japan has also strategically hosted events, such as the 1964 Tokyo Olympics and the 2020 Games, to present itself as a modern, peaceful nation integrated into the global system, while simultaneously redefining its international role (Grix et al., 2021).

Smaller states in Asia, particularly in the Gulf region, have also embraced sports diplomacy as a central element of nation-building. Qatar's investments in global football, including ownership of Paris Saint-Germain and hosting the 2022 FIFA World Cup, illustrate how small states can amplify their visibility and mitigate security concerns through sport. This strategy, often labeled as sportswashing, has sparked debates regarding the ethical dimensions of such investments (Almeida & Ozdemir, 2024). Nonetheless, Qatar and other Gulf states have successfully used sport to project modernity, diversify their economies, and assert influence within international organizations.

6.4. Middle East and Africa: Nation-Building Through Sports

In the Middle East and Africa, sports diplomacy is often closely tied to nation-building and the pursuit of stability. Gulf states such as Qatar, Saudi Arabia, and the United Arab Emirates view sport as a key sector for economic diversification and global image-building. Their strategies involve hosting mega-events, sponsoring prominent international teams, and constructing state-of-the-art facilities. These initiatives seek not only to project a modern and progressive image but also to unify domestic populations around national projects. While critics highlight human rights concerns, supporters argue that these investments facilitate modernization and integration into global networks (Costa & Moriconi, 2024).

In Africa, sports diplomacy plays a somewhat different role. Many states utilize sport, particularly football, as a means of fostering national identity and international solidarity. For example, South Africa's hosting of the 2010 FIFA World Cup was framed as a symbol of continental pride and post-apartheid reconciliation, offering a narrative of unity and progress. Across the continent, sports are increasingly linked with development goals, as international organizations and NGOs partner with local communities to use sport as a tool for education, gender equality, and peacebuilding (Rodríguez et al., 2024). These efforts highlight sport's role as both a diplomatic tool and a grassroots instrument of social change.

6.5. Comparative Insights

Across these regional contexts, certain commonalities emerge. Sport is consistently used to project national identity, foster international visibility, and cultivate goodwill. However, differences arise in terms of emphasis and approach. Europe highlights institutionalization and collective identity, the United States emphasizes cultural outreach and youth programs, Asian powers focus on mega-events and technological leadership, and Middle Eastern and African states employ sport as part of modernization and nation-building strategies. This diversity demonstrates the adaptability of sports diplomacy, while also underscoring its limitations when confronted with ethical controversies or accusations of political manipulation.

7. CHALLENGES AND CRITIQUES IN SPORTS DIPLOMACY

While sports diplomacy has been praised for its capacity to foster international understanding, project soft power, and create moments of symbolic reconciliation, it is far from an unproblematic or universally effective practice. The strategic use of sport for diplomatic purposes often encounters significant challenges that complicate its outcomes and invite critical reflection. These challenges stem from political exploitation, ethical controversies, financial inequalities, and questions of long-term efficacy. A nuanced analysis of these dimensions is essential to appreciate both the potential and the limitations of sports diplomacy.

One of the most persistent critiques concerns the politicization of sport. Although sporting institutions frequently claim neutrality, the reality is that international competitions and mega-events are deeply entangled with political agendas. Hosting rights are often awarded through processes that reflect geopolitical influence rather than purely sporting considerations. For instance, the Olympic Games and FIFA World Cup have repeatedly been associated with allegations of corruption, vote-buying, and political favoritism (Woodward, 2025). This undermines the narrative of sport as a neutral ground for cultural exchange, revealing the ways in which it becomes a tool for states to advance their political ambitions. Furthermore, the staging of such events often serves to legitimize ruling regimes, even when those regimes face international criticism for human rights abuses or authoritarian practices (Grix & Brannagan, 2024).

A related critique is the phenomenon widely described as sportswashing. This term refers to the use of sporting events, investments, or sponsorships by states to distract global attention from domestic controversies, particularly regarding governance, human rights, or corruption. The Gulf states have been at the center of such debates, especially Qatar and Saudi Arabia, whose significant investments in football and other global sports have been framed as attempts to sanitize their international image (Almeida & Ozdemir, 2024). Critics argue that while these efforts may succeed in projecting modernity and cultural vibrancy, they simultaneously risk masking systemic issues such as labor exploitation or restrictions on civil liberties. Yet, sportswashing is not exclusive to authoritarian regimes. Democratic states have also been accused of using mega-events to obscure domestic inequalities, suppress dissent, or overstate the benefits of hosting. This indicates that the critique of sportswashing must be applied broadly, recognizing the political instrumentalization of sport across different regimes.

Financial inequality presents another major challenge. Hosting mega-events requires immense financial resources, often diverting funds away from pressing social needs. Critics argue that investments in stadiums and infrastructure frequently fail to deliver long-term economic benefits, instead leaving behind debts and underutilized facilities. The concept of "white elephants" has become a recurring theme in evaluations of Olympic Games and World Cups, with stadiums constructed at great cost only to be abandoned after the events conclude (Byrne & Ludvigsen, 2023). This raises ethical questions about whether the symbolic diplomatic gains of hosting justify the economic sacrifices, particularly in developing countries where resources are scarce. While proponents emphasize the potential for tourism, urban regeneration, and global visibility, empirical evidence often shows that these benefits are overstated or unevenly distributed (Wise & Ludvigsen, 2023).

The uneven distribution of soft power gains also deserves attention. Not all states benefit equally from sports diplomacy. Large, resource-rich countries or those with strong political connections to international sporting organizations are more likely to secure hosting rights and dominate global sports governance. Smaller or less wealthy states often remain excluded from these opportunities, reinforcing global inequalities. Even when smaller states succeed in leveraging sport, as in the case of Qatar, their actions are met with heightened scrutiny and skepticism, often framed as illegitimate attempts to "buy" influence (Grix et al., 2023). This double standard reveals the political asymmetries inherent in global sport and highlights the difficulty of creating a truly level playing field in international relations.

Another critique relates to the ethical governance of sports organizations themselves. Bodies such as FIFA and the International Olympic Committee wield enormous influence, yet they are frequently criticized for lacking transparency, accountability, and ethical standards. Scandals involving bribery, vote manipulation, and abuse of power have tarnished their reputations and raised doubts about their legitimacy as custodians of global sport (Chatziefstathiou & Rofe, 2024). These governance issues directly affect the credibility of sports diplomacy, since the legitimacy of the diplomatic outcomes is tied to the integrity of the institutions that manage international competitions. As long as these institutions remain vulnerable to corruption, the use of sport as a diplomatic tool will continue to face skepticism.

The relationship between sports diplomacy and human rights represents another critical area of concern. Mega-events frequently attract scrutiny for labor practices, displacement of local populations, and restrictions on freedom of expression. In some cases, preparations for events have involved forced evictions, exploitative working conditions, or the silencing of dissent. These realities contrast sharply with the rhetoric of peace, inclusion, and universal values that often accompanies sports diplomacy narratives (Almahraj, 2023). Critics argue that the failure to align practice with principle undermines the credibility of sport as a force for good in international relations. While recent reforms have sought to integrate human rights commitments into bidding processes, the effectiveness of these measures remains limited and contested (Maleske, 2024).

Questions of long-term efficacy also complicate the evaluation of sports diplomacy. While high-profile events and symbolic moments can generate temporary goodwill or media attention, their ability to produce sustained diplomatic change is less certain. For example, Ping-Pong Diplomacy is often celebrated as a breakthrough in U.S.-China relations, yet subsequent decades demonstrated that sport alone cannot resolve deep political tensions. Similarly, while the PyeongChang Olympics facilitated temporary dialogue between North and South Korea, the long-term political relationship remains fragile (Grix et al., 2021). This suggests that sports diplomacy should not be viewed as a substitute for traditional diplomacy, but rather as a complementary tool whose success depends on broader political contexts.

Cultural misinterpretation and overemphasis on sport's universal appeal also pose challenges. While sport is often described as a universal language, its meanings vary across cultures and contexts. The assumption that athletic exchanges inherently promote understanding can be overly simplistic, ignoring the potential for sport to reinforce stereotypes, exacerbate rivalries, or provoke nationalistic tensions. International competitions sometimes fuel animosity rather than reconciliation, as seen in instances where sporting matches have triggered riots or heightened diplomatic disputes. Thus, the outcomes of sports diplomacy are not always positive, and careful attention must be paid to the risks of unintended consequences.

Finally, there is the critique that sports diplomacy may contribute to a spectacle-driven diplomacy that privileges symbolism over substance. Governments may prioritize image-building through sport while neglecting deeper structural reforms or substantive engagement with international partners. The reliance on symbolic gestures risks creating a form of shallow diplomacy that generates media attention but little enduring impact on international relations. This critique aligns with broader concerns in international politics about the rise of performative diplomacy, where appearances and narratives are valued over meaningful policy outcomes (Syvertsen et al., 2023).

In sum, while sports diplomacy provides significant opportunities for states and non-state actors to pursue foreign policy objectives, its limitations and risks are equally evident. Political instrumentalization, sportswashing, financial burdens, governance failures, human rights controversies, cultural misinterpretations, and questions of long-term efficacy all complicate the optimistic narrative of sport as a universal force for peace and cooperation. These challenges underscore the need for a more critical and context-sensitive understanding of sports diplomacy, one that recognizes its potential but remains vigilant about its limitations and ethical implications.

8. THE FUTURE OF SPORTS DIPLOMACY

The evolution of sports diplomacy reflects both enduring traditions and emerging global dynamics. While its historical role as a cultural bridge and soft power instrument remains central, the future of sports diplomacy will increasingly be shaped by digital technologies, sustainability imperatives, human rights considerations, and its integration into conflict resolution and peacebuilding frameworks. These transformations signal that sports diplomacy will not remain static but will adapt to new challenges and opportunities in global politics.

8.1. Digital Diplomacy and the Role of Media

The rise of digital communication has fundamentally transformed the conduct and perception of sports diplomacy. Social media platforms, streaming services, and interactive technologies now allow states, athletes, and organizations to directly engage with global audiences in real time. Digital diplomacy through sport enables governments to bypass traditional channels, crafting narratives that resonate with younger, digitally connected populations. Events like the Olympics or World Cup no longer unfold solely on the field; they are simultaneously played out across millions of online conversations, hashtags, and multimedia campaigns (Dubinsky, 2022b).

This immediacy enhances the visibility of sports diplomacy but also amplifies risks. Positive narratives of cooperation and cultural celebration can spread rapidly, but so can criticism of human rights violations, corruption, or organizational failures. Governments and sporting bodies are increasingly aware that controlling digital narratives is as important as organizing the events themselves. The role of athletes as digital influencers further complicates this landscape, since their personal statements on social media can shape diplomatic perceptions in ways that are not fully controlled by states (Almahraj, 2023). The future of sports diplomacy will therefore depend on a more sophisticated engagement with digital media, balancing opportunities for outreach with strategies to mitigate reputational risks.

8.2. Sustainability and Human Rights in Mega-Events

Another defining issue for the future of sports diplomacy will be the integration of sustainability and human rights considerations into the hosting and management of mega-events. In recent years, global awareness of climate change, labor exploitation, and social inequality has placed unprecedented pressure on both governments and sporting organizations to align events with ethical standards. Future Olympic Games, FIFA World Cups, and other mega-events will increasingly be judged not only by their athletic success but also by their environmental impact, inclusivity, and legacy planning (Kobayashi et al., 2023).

The adoption of human rights pledges in bidding processes represents a step toward greater accountability (Maleske, 2024). Civil society organizations and advocacy groups have pushed for greater transparency in how host countries treat workers, protect local communities, and ensure freedom of expression during events. Sustainability is also becoming a non-negotiable priority, with expectations for green infrastructure, carbon neutrality, and environmentally conscious legacy planning. States that fail to meet these expectations risk reputational damage, undermining the soft power gains they seek. Conversely, those that successfully integrate sustainability and human rights into their strategies will likely strengthen their credibility as global leaders, reinforcing the legitimacy of sports diplomacy as a constructive practice.

8.3. Sports Diplomacy in Conflict Resolution and Peacebuilding

The potential of sport to contribute to conflict resolution and peacebuilding has long been acknowledged, but its role is expected to expand in the future as governments, NGOs, and international organizations increasingly integrate sports into peacebuilding programs. Sport provides a neutral and accessible platform for fostering trust, empathy, and cooperation among groups divided by conflict. Initiatives that engage youth through community sports can help to transform perceptions, reduce prejudices, and establish habits of cooperation that extend beyond the playing field (Rodríguez et al., 2024).

The structured environment of team sports encourages skills such as conflict resolution, fairness, and mutual respect, which are crucial in societies emerging from conflict. The United Nations has recognized sport as a cost-effective peacebuilding tool, and international donors increasingly fund sport-based projects in post-conflict regions. In the future, sports diplomacy is likely to become more closely intertwined with humanitarian strategies, serving as a bridge between local communities and international actors. For instance, programs in conflict-affected regions of Africa and the Middle East that utilize football or basketball as peacebuilding instruments illustrate how sports can contribute to reconciliation and development simultaneously (Pukallus & Brouwers, 2023).

Moreover, the symbolic power of joint participation in international events will remain important. Instances where adversarial states march together under a unified flag or participate in joint teams demonstrate the potential of sport to de-escalate tensions and create opportunities for dialogue. These symbolic gestures, while not sufficient to resolve deep political conflicts, can open doors to more substantive diplomatic negotiations, highlighting sport's unique role as both a symbolic and practical peacebuilding instrument.

8.4. Integration with Broader Foreign Policy and Development Goals

Sports diplomacy will also increasingly intersect with broader development agendas, including the United Nations Sustainable Development Goals (SDGs). Initiatives that use sport to promote education, health, gender equality, and environmental protection highlight its alignment with global development priorities (Gadais et al., 2021). Governments and international organizations will likely expand investments in such programs, recognizing sport not merely as entertainment but as a cross-sectoral tool that supports both domestic welfare and international cooperation.

In this sense, the future of sports diplomacy will involve a dual focus: the pursuit of prestige through mega-events and the implementation of grassroots initiatives that address social challenges. The balance between these two levels will shape perceptions of authenticity and effectiveness. States that emphasize both grand spectacle and genuine social engagement are more likely to achieve sustainable soft power gains, while those that focus narrowly on image-building may face criticism and diminishing returns.

8.5. Global Governance and the Future of Sporting Institutions

The governance of international sport will also shape the trajectory of sports diplomacy. Organizations such as FIFA, the International Olympic Committee, and continental federations wield immense power, but their legitimacy depends on transparency and ethical conduct. Reforms that enhance accountability and responsiveness will be critical for sustaining the credibility of sports diplomacy. If governance scandals persist, the diplomatic potential of sport risks being undermined, as states and publics lose trust in the institutions responsible for managing global competitions (Chatziefstathiou & Rofe, 2024).

Future governance will need to reconcile the competing demands of commercialization, inclusivity, and political neutrality. The increasing involvement of corporate sponsors, media conglomerates, and private investors complicates the picture, raising questions about whether sports diplomacy is truly driven by cultural and diplomatic objectives or by profit motives. Addressing this tension will be central to ensuring that sports diplomacy retains its relevance and legitimacy in international relations.

8.6. Concluding Reflections on Future Directions

Looking forward, sports diplomacy will remain an essential dimension of global engagement, but its effectiveness will hinge on its ability to adapt to changing contexts. The digital age, sustainability imperatives, human rights accountability, and the integration of sport into peacebuilding frameworks represent both opportunities and challenges. The future will likely see greater emphasis on collaborative, multi-actor approaches, involving not only states but also international organizations, NGOs, athletes, and media networks. The interplay of these actors will determine whether sports diplomacy continues to expand as a credible tool of soft power and global cooperation or whether it becomes increasingly discredited as a vehicle for spectacle-driven politics.

Ultimately, the evolution of sports diplomacy reflects broader transformations in international relations. Just as traditional diplomacy has had to adapt to the forces of globalization, digitalization, and civil society engagement, sports diplomacy must also evolve to remain relevant. By embracing transparency, inclusivity, and genuine social responsibility, sports diplomacy can contribute meaningfully to international cooperation and peace. If, however, it remains tied to narrow political agendas or exploitative practices, its promise may remain unfulfilled. The challenge for the future lies in reconciling the symbolic appeal of sport with the substantive demands of ethical governance, social justice, and sustainable global development.

REFERENCES

Abdi, K., Talebpour, M., Fullerton, J. A., Ranjkesh, M. J., & Nooghabi, H. J. (2018). Converting sports diplomacy to diplomatic outcomes: Introducing a sports diplomacy model. *International Area Studies Review, 21*(4), 365–382. DOI: 10.1177/2233865918808058

Abramczyk, E. (2024). Growth of political relations or sportswashing? The nuances of sports as soft diplomacy. DOI: 10.33774/apsa-2024-gf408

Almahraj, Y. A. (2023). British press coverage of international sports events hosted by Saudi Arabia: Content analysis study in light of country concept model. *Humanities & Social Sciences Communications, 10*(1), 46. Advance online publication. DOI: 10.1057/s41599-023-02266-w

Athayde, P. F. A., & Figueiredo, A. J. (2023). Public management of sport: A description and comparative analysis of the organizational structure in Brazil and Portugal. *Retos, 51*, 979–988. DOI: 10.47197/retos.v51.101356

Byrne, S., & Ludvigsen, J. A. L. (2023). An Olympic embrace? A critical evaluation of the IOC's commitment to human rights. *International Journal of Sport Policy, 16*(2), 217–233. DOI: 10.1080/19406940.2023.2271487

Chappelet, J.-L. (2021). The governance of the Olympic system: From one to many stakeholders. *Journal of Global Sport Management, 8*(4), 783–800. DOI: 10.1080/24704067.2021.1899767

Chatziefstathiou, D., & Rofe, J. S. (2024). Human rights and the Olympics: From an ideological paradox to a new anti-corruption legacy. *Frontiers in Sports and Active Living, 6*, 1365150. Advance online publication. DOI: 10.3389/fspor.2024.1365150 PMID: 39359486

Corvino, C., Moriconi, M., Costa, C. M., & D'Angelo, C. (2023). Sport as a tool for social inclusion, employment, and improved health. *Frontiers in Sports and Active Living, 5*, 1273858. Advance online publication. DOI: 10.3389/fspor.2023.1273858 PMID: 37691643

Costa, R., & Moriconi, M. (2024). Current political uses of sport revised: Beyond public diplomacy and sportswashing. *Frontiers in Sports and Active Living, 6*, 1316732. Advance online publication. DOI: 10.3389/fspor.2024.1316732 PMID: 39229250 de Almeida, M. A. B., & Ozdemir, M. B. (2024). The men's World Cup in Qatar 2022 through the lens of the Western media: Soft power, sports diplomacy and sportswashing. *Sociology International Journal*, *8*(4), 190–198. DOI: 10.15406/sij.2024.08.00394

Dubinsky, Y. (2022a). Country image, cultural diplomacy, and sports during the COVID-19 pandemic: Brand America and Super Bowl LV. *Place Branding and Public Diplomacy*, *19*(3), 249–262. DOI: 10.1057/s41254-021-00257-9

Dubinsky, Y. (2022b). The Olympic Games, nation branding, and public diplomacy in a post-pandemic world: Reflections on Tokyo 2020 and beyond. *Place Branding and Public Diplomacy*, *19*(3), 386–400. DOI: 10.1057/s41254-021-00255-x

Gadais, T., Décarpentrie, L., Webb, A., Ayoub, M., Bardocz-Bencsik, M., & Bélanger, C. (2021). A method for conducting preliminary analysis of the nature and context of sport for development and peace projects in fieldwork research: An illustration with a Malagasy non-governmental organization. *Frontiers in Sports and Active Living*, *3*, 658496. Advance online publication. DOI: 10.3389/fspor.2021.658496 PMID: 34805977

Garsten, C., & Sörbom, A. (2023). Discreet Diplomacy. *Cambridge Anthropology*, *41*(1), 98–117. DOI: 10.3167/cja.2023.410108

Grix, J., & Brannagan, P. M. (2024). Sports mega-events as foreign policy: Sport diplomacy, soft power, and sportswashing. *The American Behavioral Scientist*, 00027642241262042. Advance online publication. DOI: 10.1177/00027642241262042

Grix, J., Dinsmore, A., & Brannagan, P. M. (2023). Unpacking the politics of sportswashing: It takes two to tango. *Politics*. Advance online publication. DOI: 10.1177/02633957231207387

Grix, J., Jeong, J., & Kim, H.-M. (2021). Understanding South Korea's use of sports mega-events for domestic, regional and international soft power. *Societies (Basel, Switzerland)*, *11*(4), 144. DOI: 10.3390/soc11040144

Kobayashi, K., Hörne, J., Cho, Y., & Lee, J. W. (2023). Mediating the East Asian era of the Olympic Games (2018–2022). *Communication & Sport*, *12*(1), 3–15. DOI: 10.1177/21674795231208363

Kobierecki, M. M. (2023). Sport at the World Expo: Analysis of sports diplomacy at the non-sporting event. *Place Branding and Public Diplomacy*, *19*(4), 413–427. DOI: 10.1057/s41254-023-00294-6

Konjer, M., Meier, H. E., & Krieger, J. (2022). International sport governing bodies as agents of diffusion: The case of World Athletics. *Frontiers in Sports and Active Living*, *4*, 1025023. Advance online publication. DOI: 10.3389/fspor.2022.1025023 PMID: 36439621

Maleske, C. (2024). Developing human rights strategies for large-scale sport events: An examination of the United Bid and planning phase of the 2026 FIFA World Cup. *Deep Blue (University of Michigan)*. DOI: 10.7302/23781

Myhre, M. H. (2023). Russia's cultural statecraft. *Nordisk Øst-Forum*, *37*, 1–17. DOI: 10.23865/noros.v37.6034

Na, D., & Dallaire, C. (2022). The diplomatic roles of Korean state-run sport for development programs. *International Review for the Sociology of Sport*, *57*(8), 1177–1193. DOI: 10.1177/10126902211065337

Ozsari, A. (2018). Sport diplomacy as public diplomacy element. *International Journal of Sport Culture and Science*, *6*(28), 339–348. DOI: 10.14486/IntJSCS765

Pigman, G. A. (2014). International Sport and Diplomacy's Public Dimension: Governments, Sporting Federations and the Global Audience. *Diplomacy and Statecraft*, *25*(1), 94–114. DOI: 10.1080/09592296.2014.873613

Pukallus, S., & Brouwers, L. A. C. M. (2023). Peacebuilding and social change through soap opera: The two elements of moral authority of Team Kenya. *Journal of Peacebuilding & Development*, *19*(1), 32–47. DOI: 10.1177/15423166231220706

Rodríguez, S., León-Prieto, C., Rodríguez-Jaime, M. F., & Lugo, L. S. (2024). Spielen für den Frieden: Ein Scoping-Review über Sportprogramme als Botschafter des Friedensvermittler. *German Journal of Exercise and Sport Research*. Advance online publication. DOI: 10.1007/s12662-024-00967-1

Rookwood, J. (2021). From sport-for-development to sports mega-events: Conflict, authoritarian modernisation and statecraft in Azerbaijan. *Sport in Society*, *25*(4), 847–865. DOI: 10.1080/17430437.2021.2019710

Schreiner, L., Kastrup, V., & Mayer, J. (2022). Coordination processes in partnerships between German governmental organizations and German sports federations in jointly implemented SDP projects. *Frontiers in Sports and Active Living*, *4*, 989284. Advance online publication. DOI: 10.3389/fspor.2022.989284 PMID: 36406771

Syvertsen, A., Erevik, E. K., Fodstad, E. C., Girard, L., Kaur, P., Kristensen, J. H., Kolberg, E., Mentzoni, R. A., Morken, A. M., Sagoe, D., & Pallesen, S. (2023). An empirical study on attitudes toward gambling when sportswashing is involved. *Frontiers in Psychology*, *14*, 1147332. Advance online publication. DOI: 10.3389/fpsyg.2023.1147332 PMID: 37915529

Wise, N., & Ludvigsen, J. A. L. (2023). New notions of soft power: Impact rhetoric in mega-event bid documents. *Local Economy*, *38*(4), 306–322. DOI: 10.1177/02690942231213590

Woodward, R. (2025). Sport, soft disempowerment and the 1966 FIFA World Cup. *British Politics*, *20*(4), 707–724. Advance online publication. DOI: 10.1057/s41293-025-00281-w

Chapter 10
The Techno-Geopolitical Turn: AI, Big Data, and the New Diplomacy

Munir Ahmad
https://orcid.org/0000-0003-4836-6151
Survey of Pakistan, Pakistan

Anorgul Ashirova
Mamun University, Uzbekistan

Temur Eshchanov
Urgench State University, Uzbekistan

ABSTRACT

This chapter explores the "techno-geopolitical turn" in diplomacy, where artificial intelligence, big data, and digital platforms are reshaping the tools and arenas of international relations. It examines how AI enhances intelligence gathering and scenario planning, how big data enables predictive and proactive foreign policy, and how digital platforms transform public diplomacy through narrative contestation. While these technologies expand opportunities for cooperation and strategic foresight, they also introduce risks of bias, disinformation, and widening digital divides. The chapter highlights emerging debates on digital sovereignty, multilateral governance, and cyber diplomacy, arguing for balanced policy frameworks that promote innovation, accountability, and inclusivity while affirming the enduring role of human judgment in global diplomacy.

DOI: 10.4018/979-8-3373-4937-4.ch010

1. INTRODUCTION

All diplomacy has been the product of the prevalent forces of the era. From the initial use of emissaries and written letters to telegraphs, telephones, and eventually digital communication, the conduct of statecraft has always evolved alongside the development of technology. Today, diplomacy is experiencing yet another fundamental shift, a so-called "techno-geopolitical turn." This is a moment marked by the increasing centrality of artificial intelligence (AI), big data, and digital platforms in defining the conduct of international relations, reconfiguring international diplomacy both in terms of the tools and the arenas of international diplomacy (Ghose & Das, 2025; Kalantzakos, 2023; Li et al., 2024; Liu & Miao, 2024).

The classical model of diplomacy as an exclusive procedure conducted behind closed doors between representatives of the state no longer properly reflects the dynamics of the twenty-first century. Instead, foreign policy and geopolitical contestation are now embedded in technological infrastructures, algorithms, and massive data ecosystems. Computational models, predictive analytics, and digital platforms are becoming increasingly popular not only for informing decision-making but also for public opinion, narrative building, and projection of power across borders, by and among states, multilateral organizations, and non-state actors. This new paradigm is a departure from human-centric, deliberative statecraft towards technology-mediated forms of interaction that redefine agency and influence in international politics.

Within this new context, AI, big data, and digital platforms emerge as important diplomatic tools. AI allows for improved intelligence gathering, scenario planning, and real-time risk assessment, providing decision-makers with unrivalled insight into complex global dynamics (Khedr et al., 2022). Predictive potential nature of big data enables states to foresee the direction of migration, economic shocks, or security crises, thus shifting diplomacy from reactive to proactive measures. Digital platforms, in turn, are venues for both collaboration and competition, places where states, corporate and civil society actors compete to produce narratives, wield soft power and capture global audiences. Collectively, these technologies are altering the operational underpinnings of diplomacy while simultaneously posing critical inquiries regarding issues of sovereignty, transparency, and equity in an increasingly digitally stratified world.

This chapter surveys these developments by looking at the role of the techno-geopolitical turn in reconfiguring international relations. How do AI and big data change the way diplomatic decisions are made? How are digital platforms changing public diplomacy and narrative warfare? What are the challenges of these technologies for multilateralism, global governance, and the balance of power? By exploring these questions, the chapter offers a critical account of how new technologies are empowering and destabilizing diplomatic practices. It contends that with the techno-geopolitical turn, opportunities for new forms of strategic advantage and collaboration are available, but asymmetries are intensified, new vulnerabilities created, and the nature of diplomacy itself needs to be reconceptualized in a world mediated algorithmically.

2. AI AND THE TRANSFORMATION OF DIPLOMATIC DECISION-MAKING

2.1. Traditional Decision Making and Emerging Pressures

The expanding application of artificial intelligence to diplomatic practice is one of the deeper and more disruptive shifts in the conduct of international relations in the twenty-first century. Traditionally, diplomatic decision-making has depended on a mix of human judgment, on classified intelligence, and on the use of negotiation tactics based on a cultural understanding of the other side built on historical precedent and on political intuition. Many experienced diplomats used personal networks, experience, and intuition to cope with crises and opportunities. While these things are still essential, the scale, complexity, and speed of contemporary global challenges have increasingly highlighted the limitations of traditional approaches. Military conflicts break out with unprecedented speed; cyber operations take place in milliseconds across borders; pandemics travel globally within weeks, and climate-induced disasters upend entire regions with little or no notice. Even supply chain glitches, once considered manageable trade problems, currently have knock-on effects on energy security, inflation worldwide, and domestic stability.

In this new environment, the human faculties are no longer enough. Diplomats need tools that will not only crunch large amounts of heterogeneous information but also discover hidden interconnections, strongly predict risks, and produce structured foresight. More than ever, AI-based systems are being used to bridge this gap, not as substitutes for human agency but as much-needed tools that help intelligence gathering, planning scenarios, and negotiation tactics. By combining the computational power of computers with human reasoning, states are starting to develop hybrid decision-making systems that go beyond traditional statecraft. These advances are bringing about a transformation of diplomacy that fundamentally changes both the practice and philosophy of international relations and raises questions about where authority, expertise, and legitimacy lie in an age of algorithmic augmentation.

2.2. AI-Enhanced Intelligence Gathering and Situational Awareness

AI-based analytics now allow governments, multilaterals, and even non-state actors to digest unheard-of amounts of data extracted from not only varied but also non-military sources. These include satellite imagery, financial transactions, mobile phone metadata, social media discourse, and environmental sensor networks around the globe. Machine learning algorithms can search through these firehoses for subtle patterns that human analysts may miss, like irregular troop movements, unusual changes in trading patterns, or sudden spikes in online dissent that may indicate political unrest or regime vulnerability (Apostolakis et al., 2022; Cui & Yasseri, 2024; Rashida Farsath et al., 2024).

In particular, natural language processing (NLP) systems have become essential tools for the monitoring of global information environments. For example, natural language processing can analyse millions of documents, news articles, and online posts across dozens of languages in real-time to identify changes in sentiment, discourse, or rhetorical frames, which give insight into public opinion during an unfolding crisis. For example, in the context of humanitarian emergencies, NLP can be used to understand how narratives are circulating within communities, which can help governments and aid agencies to better target their responses. By augmenting these sorts of real-time assessments with classified information and traditional reporting, AI improves situational awareness, enabling decision-makers to respond faster, more completely, and often in more proactive ways. In doing so, AI mitigates the danger of blind spots and slow reactions that have historically plagued diplomacy and reinforces states' ability to take action before crises spiral out of control.

2.3. Scenario Planning, Predictive Modeling, and Negotiation Support

Beyond intelligence gathering, AI is also instrumental in scenario planning by modelling the potential outcome of diplomatic decisions across a range of variables. Reinforcement learning, predictive modelling, and agent-based simulations can help policymakers assess the effects of alternative strategies while taking into consideration historical data, adversarial behaviour, and complex feedback loops. Such tools are turning scenario planning into a data-driven discipline that is constantly improving as circumstances evolve (Mell et al., 2021; Spaniol & Rowland, 2023; Vaithilingam et al., 2024; Zeleznikow, 2021).

These simulations are particularly useful in high-uncertainty settings, such as peace negotiations, sanctions regimes, or environmental agreements, where there are many opportunities for unintended consequences and miscalculations can be expensive. AI models can be used to predict whether sanctions will erode an adversary's power, drive him to seek new alliances, or whether a water-sharing agreement will mitigate tensions or intensify competition in parched lands. In the negotiation process itself, AI can analyse previous agreements, identify likely "red lines" of negotiating parties, and even come up with compromise offers that are maximally beneficial to the parties involved with minimal losses. Some prototypes even simulate opponent bargaining tactics so that diplomats can practice responses before interacting with the other party in the real world. In the end, human diplomats always have the final say, but the inclusion of AI adds a new dimension of strategic foresight to negotiations, making them more informed, less susceptible to miscalculation, and more resilient to uncertainty.

2.4. Practical Applications in Global Diplomacy

There is nothing speculative about AI applications to diplomacy; they are already increasingly embedded in practice throughout institutions and issue areas. United Nations and other organizations are using AI-based image recognition technologies to monitor ceasefire violations, analyze satellite images of troop movements, and identify patterns of displacement that indicate ethnic cleansing or humanitarian crises (Fournier-Tombs, 2021; ITU, 2023). These tools enable faster and verifiable reporting to the international community. Algorithms analyze inspection reports, open-source intelligence, and environmental data to detect potential non-compliance with nuclear, chemical, or climate treaties. AI enhances verification by triangulating multiple data streams, decreasing opportunities for fraud. AI models combine climate data, economic indicators, and demographic changes to forecast refugee movements, food shortages, or disease outbreaks. These predictions allow states to plan diplomatic responses to humanitarian emergencies before they become sources of regional instability. AI tools can be used to map vulnerable populations, identify potential logistical bottlenecks, and optimize the delivery of resources, making humanitarian diplomacy more effective. Not only does this save lives, but it also strengthens diplomatic credibility by showing effective and unbiased aid.

Taken together, these examples teach us that AI is not something that is confined to the research laboratory or the policy forum, but is already a practical tool shaping foreign policy and redefining the operational environment of international diplomacy. It has an uneven take-up across countries, but even small-scale deployments reveal how fundamentally AI is changing the toolkit and rhythm of inter-state interaction.

2.5. Risks, Biases, and the Problem of Opacity

The increasing use of AI by high-stakes diplomats is not without great risk and difficulty. Perhaps the most troubling is algorithmic bias, in which models trained on incomplete, skewed, or politically motivated datasets produce flawed or discriminatory results. In diplomatic terms, such biases might lead to misinterpretation of events, for example, misinterpreting a peaceful protest as a revolt, or systematically under-representing marginalized voices in conflict mediation processes. The risk is not simply technical: outputs can be biased, affecting diplomatic narratives, diverting interventions, or inflaming tensions between states (Chesterman, 2021; Fernández, 2023; Hutson, 2021).

Equally disconcerting, AI decision-making is typically opaque, what's known as the "black box" problem (von Eschenbach, 2021). Many state-of-the-art models, particularly deep learning systems, make recommendations or predictions without giving clear explanations of how they got to that conclusion. In diplomacy, where legitimacy, accountability, and justification to domestic and international audiences are of paramount importance, such opacity presents serious challenges. Diplomatic actors have to be able to explain these decisions in front of parliaments, publics, and international partners; a reliance on opaque algorithms threatens to damage credibility, create suspicion, and erode trust. Without mechanisms like explainability and accountability, the advantages of AI can be overshadowed by the perception of undemocratic manipulation or the absence of democratic oversight.

2.6. Ethics, Governance, and Trust Issues

These issues raise larger ethical and governance issues about the proper use of AI for foreign policy. If critical elements of international decision-making are left to opaque computational systems, then we run the risk of eroding the very claims to transparency, trust, and accountability that are vital to diplomatic legitimacy (Camilleri, 2024; Reinhardt, 2023; Ryan, 2020). Who is to blame if an AI-based prediction ultimately results in miscalculation, failed negotiations, or even conflict escalation? Is it the programmers' fault, the intelligence agencies' fault, or the diplomats' fault?

Furthermore, the proliferation of AI also threatens to further exacerbate mistrust among states. Potential adversaries can suspect algorithmic or model manipulation, implicit biases in models, or hidden influence operations in computational tools. Such doubts could undermine trust in multilateral institutions or international agreements, especially over sensitive issues such as arms control, crisis mediation, or humanitarian intervention. The absence of agreed-upon international norms around the use of AI in diplomacy compounds these issues, leaving states to operate in a fragmented and competitive landscape where suspicion often trumps cooperation.

In view of these risks, the integration of AI into diplomacy requires strong governance frameworks and safeguards. Diplomatic institutions need to ensure human oversight of all AI-assisted processes, insist on explainability for algorithmic outputs, and have mechanisms for accountability for decisions made with the aid of AI. Standard requirements for auditing datasets, validating models, and documenting decision pathways will be important to avoid misuse or unintended consequences (Kilburg, 2025; Konovalova, 2023; Varela, 2024).

There will be a need for open data sources with open training datasets and international standards for ethical data use. Just as agreements have been made for nuclear weapons or climate change, new treaties are needed to govern the responsible use of AI for international affairs. Cooperative arrangements could help set up verification protocols, independent monitoring bodies, and dispute resolution mechanisms to foster trust among states.

AI presents incredible opportunities to amplify foresight, efficiency, and inclusivity in diplomacy, but its integration should occur carefully within an ethical framework that respects the supremacy of human judgment. The challenge for the coming decades can be to strike this balance, harnessing the transformative power of AI while ensuring fairness, accountability, and legitimacy. If it is applied correctly, AI could not become a destabilizing force, but a basis for more effective and cooperative diplomacy in an increasingly complex world. Table 1 provides a comprehensive overview of how AI is reshaping diplomatic decision-making, highlighting traditional challenges, transformative applications, risks, and emerging governance pathways.

Table 1. AI and the Transformation of Diplomatic Decision-Making

Dimension	Traditional Approach	AI-Enabled Transformation	Risks and Limitations	Governance& Ethical Needs
Decision-Making Context	Reliance on human judgment, intuition, cultural knowledge, historical precedent, and personal networks.	AI augments decision-making by processing vast datasets, detecting hidden patterns, and providing foresight in crises.	Risk of over-reliance on automation; erosion of diplomatic expertise if human judgment is sidelined.	Hybrid frameworks that balance computational insights with human agency.
Intelligence & Situational Awareness	Classified reports, field intelligence, and traditional media monitoring.	AI processes satellite imagery, financial data, mobile metadata, and NLP-driven sentiment analysis in real time.	Potential for biased interpretations of data; surveillance concerns.	Ensure diverse, representative datasets; maintain transparency in NLP and monitoring.
Scenario Planning & Negotiation Support	Speculative, experience-driven forecasts and bilateral negotiations.	Predictive modeling, reinforcement learning, and simulations test multiple strategies; AI identifies negotiation red lines and compromise options.	Models may misrepresent adversarial intentions; simulations risk oversimplification.	Validation protocols, adversarial testing, and retaining final authority with human diplomats.
Practical Applications	Manual monitoring and reporting (UN observers, field missions, inspections).	Conflict monitoring (AI image recognition), arms control verification, crisis forecasting, and humanitarian aid optimization.	Uneven adoption across states; resource gaps limit global access.	Promote equitable access, open-source tools, and shared best practices.
Risks & Opacity	Transparent but slower human-led processes.	AI accelerates analysis but introduces "black box" opacity and embedded biases.	Bias in training data, lack of explainability, and risk of misinterpretation fuel conflict.	Mandate explainable AI, dataset auditing, and accountable reporting mechanisms.
Ethical & Trust Challenges	Diplomacy relies on transparency, accountability, and negotiated trust.	AI integration raises suspicions of manipulation, covert influence, or hidden biases in computational tools.	Risk of eroding confidence in multilateral institutions and agreements.	Develop international norms and ethical standards for AI in diplomacy.
Responsible AI Diplomacy	Limited oversight structures for emerging technologies.	Emerging proposals for explainability, accountability, transparency, and international AI governance.	Lack of global consensus; risk of fragmented governance.	Establish treaties, independent monitoring bodies, and trust-building mechanisms.

3. BIG DATA AND PREDICTIVE FOREIGN POLICY

The advent of big data has changed the pace and logic of international relations, moving diplomacy away from a reactive practice and instead towards one that is increasingly anticipating, modelling, and pre-empting what can happen in the future.

3.1. Reactive to Predictive Diplomacy

For most of modern history, diplomacy has been largely characterized by its reactive nature. Often, foreign ministries, embassies, and international organizations reacted after the crises had already taken place-whether wars, humanitarian disasters, or sudden political revolutions. The technologies at hand were limited: cumbersome intelligence cables, random reports from diplomats in the field, and red tape that clogged information flow. This responsive posture often meant that policymakers were falling one or two steps behind the course of events. Time and time again, early prevention was neglected, with devastating results that led to all-out war, humanitarian disasters, or long-term instability. For example, during the Rwandan genocide in 1994, international actors received no timely and usable information, and their response was triggered only after catastrophic violence had already reached genocidal levels.

The interconnection of big data with diplomatic practice is a fundamental part of this new paradigm. By tapping into massive and varied data streams-satellite imagery tracking environmental and military shifts, financial transactions flagging illicit activity, mobility data charting mass movements of people, social media sentiment analysis uncovering political undercurrents, and environmental sensors tracking climate anomalies-foreign ministries can now pick up weak signals of disruption long before they turn into crises. These cues can include movements of troops, increases in the price of food, or a sudden spike in online hate speech that predicts ethnic violence.

This turn from the past to the future gives diplomats a strategic advantage. In other words, instead of being limited to reactive firefighting, they are enabled to take anticipatory action, from quiet diplomatic engagement and prophylactic mediation to ensuring the early deployment of humanitarian assistance or security guarantees. This is predictive analytics applied to diplomacy, and it has the effect of lengthening the time horizon of diplomacy from its traditional role as an art in post-crisis negotiation to a pre-crisis intervention. This anticipatory diplomacy not only makes it more effective but also has the potential to save lives, reduce costs, and stabilize regions before instability spreads across borders. The contrast between traditional reactive diplomacy and AI-enabled predictive diplomacy can be systematically captured in Table 2, which highlights their defining features, tools, and implications for global stability.

Table 2. From Reactive to Predictive Diplomacy

Dimension	Traditional Reactive Diplomacy	Predictive Big Data-Driven Diplomacy
Orientation	Responds after crises erupt	Anticipates crises before escalation
Primary Tools	Diplomatic cables, reports from embassies, intelligence summaries, crisis negotiations.	Satellite imagery, financial data analysis, mobility records, social media sentiment mining, predictive analytics
Information Flow	Fragmented, slow, and limited to official/ state channels	Continuous, real-time, and multi-source (state + open-source + private)
Diplomatic Action	Reactive firefighting through mediation, sanctions, or humanitarian aid after the onset	Preventive diplomacy, early mediation, pre-positioned humanitarian resources, strategic signaling
Examples	Delayed international response during the Rwandan genocide (1994) due to insufficient intelligence	Anticipating refugee flows in the Syrian conflict through mobility and social data analysis
Implications	Higher costs, late interventions, missed opportunities, prolonged instability	Reduced human and economic costs, proactive stabilization, and extended diplomatic foresight

3.2. Monitoring Global Dynamics at Scale

The potential of big data is to be able to record and analyze global systems at scales thought unimaginable in previous times. Diplomacy, policymaking, and analysts can now observe multiple aspects of life on the planet at the same time, creating insights that link local dynamics to global patterns. States can identify concealed supply chain vulnerabilities through real-time analysis of international trade flows, port operations, and sanctions compliance. For instance, during the COVID-19 pandemic, disruptions in shipping data exposed bottlenecks in supplies of vital medical goods, which have informed diplomatic negotiations around vaccine allocation. Similarly, transaction data can reveal efforts to bypass economic sanctions, as illustrated in the tracking of maritime oil transfers from the North Korean government.

Integrated platforms that merge information like rainfall, crop yields, and commodity prices provide early alerts of food insecurity. The 2010 Arab Spring, for example, was preceded by global spikes in wheat prices, showing how economic and environmental data can precede political unrest. Such indicators are now routinely being used by agencies such as the World Food Programme to mobilise aid and engage governments diplomatically before famine causes instability.

Whereas mass migration of refugees was only understood after they crossed borders, it can now be predicted. By examining geospatial mobility profiles, displaced community cell phone data, and social media communications, international organizations can be able to predict refugee movement many days before they overwhelm host states. This was seen during the Syrian conflict, where data-driven project predictions were integral to EU humanitarian planning, as well as refugee resettlement policies.

By merging satellite imagery, cyber threat intelligence, and open-source analysis, early warnings about military build-ups or extremist mobilization online can be detected. For instance, commercial satellite images of Russian military troop movements in early 2022 provided governments with a predictive image of the invasion of Ukraine and informed pre-emptive diplomatic actions, sanctions, and military assistance.

By combining these different datasets, governments and international organisations can create a multidimensional map of risk environments. This makes diplomacy a practice not only of dialogue but also of constant data-driven monitoring intelligence built into all elements of foreign policy. The diverse applications of big data in monitoring global systems are summarized in Table 3, which compares the domains, data sources, and diplomatic implications of large-scale monitoring.

Table 3. Applications of Big Data in Monitoring Global Dynamics

Domain	Key Data Sources	Example Applications	Diplomatic Implications
Economic Systems	Trade flows, port/shipping activity, transaction records, sanctions compliance data	Detection of supply chain disruptions during COVID-19; monitoring sanctions evasion via illicit maritime oil transfers	Shapes trade negotiations, strengthens sanctions enforcement, and improves crisis supply management.
Food & Resource Security	Rainfall and climate data, crop yield reports, commodity prices, satellite imagery	Wheat price spikes before the Arab Spring (2010) as early signals of unrest; WFP uses food security indicators for early aid mobilization	Enables early humanitarian diplomacy, preventive food aid, and negotiation of agricultural agreements
Human Mobility	Geospatial mobility records, cell phone metadata, and social media communications	Forecasting refugee flows during the Syrian conflict: EU humanitarian planning based on displacement data.	Supports refugee resettlement planning, humanitarian diplomacy, and early engagement with host states
Security & Conflict	Satellite surveillance, cyber threat intelligence, open-source analysis	Observation of Russian troop movements before the Ukraine invasion (2022); tracking extremist mobilization online	Informs preemptive sanctions, deterrence strategies, and coordinated security responses

3.3. Predictive Modeling and Diplomatic Foresight

While the aggregation of large volumes of data is a fundamental step, the real game-changer with big data is predictive modelling (Mostafaei et al., 2025). Advanced algorithms, machine learning systems, and computational models can generate variables from economics, demographics, politics, and ecology to create (virtual) scenarios for the future and stress test policy alternatives.

Predictive models can be used to pinpoint geographic areas at high risk of famine, disease outbreaks, or displacement. By anticipating these risks months in advance, it then becomes possible for humanitarian actors to pre-position resources, negotiate humanitarian corridors, and engage in preventive diplomacy with host or neighbouring states. For instance, predictive famine models that were applied in the Horn of Africa have made it possible to intervene earlier, resulting in lower death counts during crises caused by droughts. International organizations can use a combination of social media analysis, electoral data, and ethnic demographics to identify areas where political tensions may escalate into violence. The UN has increasingly turned to such tools to start preventive dialogues, send in peacekeepers ahead of time, or support electoral commissions to defuse a volatile situation.

Predictive models for climate change can simulate water shortages, sea level rise, or extreme weather events, enabling states to negotiate water-sharing agreements, disaster relief structures, and prepare for climate-driven migration. The South Asian monsoon forecasting system, for example, supports regional collaboration between India, Pakistan, and Bangladesh, minimizing the risks of water-related conflict.

This use of predictive technologies in diplomacy is what academics have called "diplomatic foresight." Diplomacy is no longer limited to dealing with the present but has been expanded into dealing with possible futures. Decision-makers can run policies through different scenarios, for example, how sanctions can impact food markets or how migration flows can change under climate stress. This leads to agility and readiness, to diplomacy being an active instrument rather than a reactive one. The key applications of predictive modelling in diplomacy are outlined in Table 4, showing how data-driven foresight tools support humanitarian response, conflict prevention, and climate preparedness.

Table 4. Predictive Modeling Applications in Diplomacy

Application Area	Key Data/Models Used	Example Applications	Diplomatic Implications
Humanitarian Response	Predictive famine and disease models, geospatial and epidemiological data	Forecasting drought-induced famine in the Horn of Africa: Pre-positioning humanitarian aid	Enables preventive diplomacy, early aid negotiation, and reduced mortality
Conflict Prevention	Social media analysis, electoral data, demographic and ethnic mapping, early-warning algorithms	UN use of models to anticipate election violence and deploy peacekeepers	Supports preventive dialogue, electoral stability, and reduced likelihood of armed conflict
Climate Preparedness	Climate simulations, hydrological and weather models, migration forecasts	South Asian monsoon forecasting for water-sharing agreements (India, Pakistan, Bangladesh)	Promotes regional cooperation, anticipatory disaster diplomacy, and reduced resource conflicts

3.4. Big Data as a Multilateral Cooperation Tool

While big data is empowering to nations, it also offers unprecedented opportunities for multilateral collaboration. Shared datasets serve as a sort of public global good and facilitate collective actions to tackle transnational challenges.

Health security has been a key lesson from the COVID-19 pandemic, which highlighted the need for the sharing of health-related data in real-time across borders. Tools combining epidemiological data, mobility patterns, and genomic sequencing enabled states to monitor variants and plan state responses. The World Health Organization's pandemic Early Warning and Preparedness System is one example of how interoperability of data can increase readiness and build trust among countries.

Regional climate observatories use atmospheric, hydrological, and oceanographic data to build joint models of future risk. These platforms inform joint agreements for emissions reduction, adaptation, and disaster management. For example, the European Copernicus Climate Data Store has been used by states in the EU to plan coordinated responses to climate.

Big data can help to build confidence among even adversaries. For example, seismic data is often shared to monitor nuclear tests in an agreement under the Comprehensive Test Ban Treaty, or satellite images are shared in anti-piracy efforts in the Gulf of Aden. Such selective cooperation is symptomatic of how data, in spite of geopolitical rivalry, creates platforms for limited trust and collaboration.

Through these mechanisms, big data becomes not merely a technological tool but a diplomatic enabler, deepening transparency, increasing interdependence, and bolstering global governance structures. Table 5 summarizes how shared big data platforms facilitate multilateral cooperation across health, climate, and security domains, transforming information into a diplomatic public good

Table 5. Multilateral Cooperation through Big Data

Domain	Shared Data Platforms	Example Applications	Diplomatic Implications
Health Security	Epidemiological, genomic, and mobility datasets	WHO pandemic monitoring systems for variant tracking and vaccine distribution	Enhances transparency, fosters cross-border trust, and strengthens collective crisis response
Climate Action	Regional climate observatories, atmospheric and hydrological datasets	EU Copernicus Climate Data Store for emissions reduction and adaptation strategies	Supports coordinated mitigation, informs adaptation frameworks, and enables joint agreements
Security Cooperation	Seismic monitoring, satellite imagery, joint intelligence databases	Shared seismic data for nuclear test monitoring (CTBT); anti-piracy satellite cooperation in the Gulf of Aden	Builds confidence among rivals, enables limited trust and security collaboration

3.5. Issues of Sovereignty, Reliability, and Inequality

Yet big data's promise also brings with it the big challenges that make its incorporation into foreign policy so difficult. Many states are adamant about retaining exclusive control over data generated within their borders. While this is in the national interest, it also limits the cross-border flows of data required to address common challenges like pandemics, climate change, and transnational crime. Claims to data sovereignty are fast emerging as a diplomatic flashpoint, with echoes of past territorial and resource wars.

The myth that more data will result in better intelligence is a false assumption. Data may not be complete, biased, or purposefully manipulated. For instance, social media creates vast quantities of data, but a lot of it may be disinformation, fake accounts, or noise. Relying on such faulty data can lead to miscalculated decision-making, diplomatic embarrassment, or ill-informed interventions.

Perhaps the most serious problem is the uneven distribution of big data capabilities. Computational infrastructure, highly trained staff, and high-speed networks for data analysis are dominated by a few states and companies, as well as by elite research institutes. By contrast, many developing states are not resourced to play a meaningful role and are instead reliant on external actors. As a result of this, it creates a data divide that further entrenches existing geopolitical asymmetries; data-rich states can have disproportionate influence over global governance norms while data-poor states risk being excluded from their development.

These issues highlight the dual nature of big data, both as an empowering and marginalising technology that opens up opportunities for improvement but also reinforces established structural biases.

3.6. The Double-Edged Sword of Big Data Diplomacy

Big data is by definition a two-edged sword. On the one hand, it offers an opportunity for preventive, anticipatory, and collaborative diplomacy that can save lives, mitigate conflict, and make the world more resilient. On the other hand, open challenges on sovereignty, accountability, and inequality threaten to weaponize data as an instrument of domination. States might use data-driven surveillance for authoritarian purposes, politicize predictive models, or monopolize flows of data to consolidate power.

The challenge for diplomacy in the big data age is therefore to find a delicate balance. The predictive power must be channelled without jeopardising fairness; transparency must be fostered without undermining sovereignty; and inclusivity must be pursued to ensure that big data closes rather than opens up gaps between nations. The future of diplomacy will hinge on whether or not big data becomes a truly global commons, a shared resource for cooperation, or a conflicted battleground that will intensify competition and mistrust.

4. DIGITAL PLATFORMS AND THE CONTESTATION OF NARRATIVES

4.1. From Closed Chambers to Open Platforms

Diplomacy, once relegated to the secretive world of backstage negotiations at embassies, in summits, and at multi-lateral forums, is more and more transitioning to the public, fast-paced arena of digital platforms. Social media (Twitter/X, TikTok, Facebook, Instagram, YouTube, and emerging apps) have become central arenas for crafting, challenging, and disseminating global narratives. While traditional diplomacy's pace was measured in communiques, carefully considered speeches, and months-long cultural programs, digital diplomacy is characterized by immediacy, interactivity, and global reach.

A tweet from a head of state, a viral hashtag, or a livestreamed protest can echo around the world within minutes, changing perceptions and impacting diplomatic atmospheres. For example, leaders such as Ukraine's Volodymyr Zelenskyy have used Twitter/X to mobilize international support to circumvent traditional gatekeepers, including newspapers or television broadcasters. This acceleration has not just changed the pace of international relations but also the texture, leading to a realm where responsiveness and adaptability are integral to successful statecraft.

4.2. Platforms as Arenas of Influence and Disinformation

Digital platforms are at once powerful tools of domination and vulnerable arenas of manipulation. On the positive side, they have enhanced the soft power (persuasion through attraction, culture, and values rather than coercion) of states. Increasingly, governments create digital public diplomacy campaigns to reach audiences around the world. From the global expansion of K-pop and Korean dramas to fans sharing Korean content on TikTok and YouTube, South Korea's leveraging of cultural exports into potent diplomatic resources is par excellence exemplified. Similarly, the European Union has used social media to publicize humanitarian aid, climate, and peacebuilding missions, presenting itself as a responsible actor, grounded in values, in world politics.

However, these same properties of speed, virality, and amplification also make platforms open to a form of exploitation. Deepfakes, orchestrated troll farms, fake accounts, and disinformation campaigns have been used to destabilize societies and warp truth. From Russian disinformation during the 2016 U.S. elections to disinformation around Brexit and European parliamentary elections to competing narratives around the origins and response to COVID-19, information warfare is no longer marginal to global competition but central to it. On this basis, the platform transforms into information-neutral carriers and turns into the battlefield where narratives are fought out as fiercely as territories.

One of the most striking characteristics of this digital environment is the pluralisation of diplomatic actors. Where state and international organizations once dominated diplomatic practice, private technology companies, advocacy groups, and individual influencers today play a key role at the center of global narratives. The corporations that run the information infrastructures are Meta, Google, ByteDance, and X Corp. Their algorithms, moderation policies, and advertising guidelines have significant geopolitical implications. For example, TikTok's data practices have caused tensions between the United States, China, and Europe, underscoring the intersection between corporate governance and national security.

At the same time, voices from outside the state-from grass roots to high-profile actors-have asserted themselves as informal but influential diplomats. Pro-democracy bloggers or digital rights activists in authoritarian regimes, or young climate activists like Greta Thunberg, can organise transnational communities and help shape agendas globally. They often have a larger reach and credibility with young audiences than official government channels do. This erosion of state and non-state power creates difficulties in international relations as governments must compete with competing states as well as civil society actors and voices of individuals who wield digital legitimacy.

4.3. Strategic Communication, Propaganda, and Narrative Warfare

The challenge to narratives has become sophisticated information warfare. Digital age strategic communication is no longer limited to the projection of a positive national image; it is about coordinated activities involving social media, targeted advertising, and information manipulation to influence both domestic and foreign perceptions. Governments are now using microtargeting technologies, bots, and algorithmic amplification in unprecedentedly precise ways to deliver tailored messages. Propaganda, which once depended on broadcast television or print, is now dispersed in real time, amplified by those with influence, and curated by algorithms to maximize audiences. The emergence of synthetic media and deepfakes brings an additional layer of complexity, as fake videos can erode public trust in genuine communications.

Far more threatening is the combination of such tactics with cyber operations. In recent months and years, hack-and-leak tactics, in which sensitive data is stolen and then selectively released in a manner that destabilizes the electoral process, have been deployed to disrupt everything from the 2016 U.S. elections to contemporary European political campaigns. This confluence of hacking and narrative warfare is a testament to the way in which the control of information has become as strategically important as control of territory in geopolitics today.

The Internet has certainly made it easier for everyone to get in on the global discussion. The great powers no longer have a monopoly on the international debate; smaller states, civil society organizations, and even individuals have access to the new media, giving them the means to project messages to international audiences. This democratization provides for pluralism, allowing for the marginalized to have a voice in discussions around climate change, human rights, and development.

However, with this inclusivity comes new vulnerabilities. Filter bubbles and echo chambers compound polarization and make finding agreement across societies more difficult. State-sponsored disinformation does the same, exploiting these divides and eroding trust between societies and between allies and multilateral institutions. Furthermore, the heavy dependence on privately owned platforms brings up difficult questions of sovereignty and accountability. Should corporations be entrusted to protect the integrity of world diplomacy? Or should governments have a stronger regulatory role, at the expense of politicising and splintering digital governance?

What remains unclear is a paradox: while platforms broaden participation and global visibility, they also create avenues for manipulation and coercion for which diplomacy as traditionally understood was not designed. The multidimensional role of digital platforms in diplomacy can be summarized across five interconnected domains. Table 6 highlights their transformative impact, key opportunities, and associated risks, illustrating how digital ecosystems have reshaped the tempo, tools, and actors of global statecraft.

Table 6. Dimensions of Digital Platforms in Modern Diplomacy

Dimension	Key Characteristics	Positive Implications	Risks & Challenges	Illustrative Examples
From Closed Chambers to Open Platforms	Diplomacy shifts from embassies & summits to fast-moving digital arenas	Greater immediacy, global reach, direct leader-to-public engagement	Volatility of narratives, pressure for instant responses	Zelenskyy is using Twitter/X to rally support during the Ukraine war
Arenas of Influence & Disinformation	Platforms amplify soft power and cultural exports, but are vulnerable to manipulation.	States project values, culture, and humanitarian roles	Disinformation campaigns, deepfakes, coordinated troll farms	K-pop diplomacy; Russian interference in the 2016 U.S. elections
New Diplomatic Actors	Tech companies, NGOs, and influencers join states as key players	Expanded participation, grassroots mobilization, and youth engagement	Tech governance clashes, blurred accountability, and influence rivalries	TikTok data tensions; Greta Thunberg's climate activism
Strategic Communication & Narrative Warfare	Narrative battles use algorithms, bots, targeted ads, and synthetic media	Precision messaging, wider reach, innovative engagement	Hack-and-leak ops, propaganda, erosion of trust in authentic content	Deepfake propaganda; 2016 U.S. election hacks
Democratization & Regulatory Dilemmas	Platforms empower smaller states & individuals, democratizing global voice.	Inclusion of marginalized voices, enhanced pluralism	Echo chambers, polarization, sovereignty conflicts over platform control	Climate justice campaigns; EU debates on platform regulation

Digital platforms are simultaneously tools and battlegrounds in this new world. They enable states to circumvent traditional media gatekeepers and engage publics directly, but they also open governments up to complex dangers of information manipulation, disinformation, and loss of narrative control. The capacity to tell compelling digital stories is no longer a choice; it's a fundamental expectation of today's diplomacy.

For 21st-century diplomats, success will now hinge not only on an understanding of international law and negotiation processes but also on digital literacy, narrative strategy, and information resilience. The challenge to narratives on social media brings to light a fundamental change: diplomacy is no longer merely about negotiations behind closed doors; it's about competing in the open market of stories, perceptions, and identities. In the end, it will be the balance between persuasion and credibility, openness and security that will determine whether digital platforms reinforce international cooperation or accelerate fragmentation and conflict in global politics.

5. SOVEREIGNTY, MULTILATERALISM, AND POWER ASYMMETRIES

5.1. The Emergence of Digital Sovereignty

The spread of digitalization in the international political arena has challenged some of the core concepts upon which international relations are constructed. And amongst them, sovereignty has acquired a new digital dimension. Digital sovereignty is the power of states to control digital infrastructures, control the flow of data across borders and within borders, and to protect cyberspaces from foreign interference. Much like territorial boundaries or natural resources, digital infrastructures, such as data centres, undersea cables, social media platforms, or national cloud systems, are increasingly seen as strategic assets.

Countries have been adopting alternative models of digital sovereignty. Russia and China have made strides in implementing "sovereign internet" architectures that impose tight controls over cyberspace: They create domestic platforms and track information flows across borders. These models enact a securitized conception of digital ecosystems. By contrast, the European Union has adopted a regulatory regime based on the principles of transparency, accountability, and the protection of rights, including through the GDPR and Digital Services Act. Together, these different approaches show the rather messy reality that digital sovereignty is not monolithic, but a spectrum of practices that are determined by political culture, capacity, and ideology.As states assert sovereignty in cyberspace, cyber diplomacy has become a key tool in managing tensions among actors in the digital space. Bilateral relations have increasingly shifted to preventing cyber incidents, exchanging best practices, and developing mechanisms for crisis communication to prevent escalation, especially in the wake of cyberattacks against critical infrastructure. At the multilateral level, the United Nations and the OSCE are taking the lead on establishing norms for responsible state behaviour in cyberspace and designing confidence-building mechanisms.

This represents a fundamental reconfiguration of the very idea of diplomacy. Classic talks are now complemented with new topics specific to the digital world, such as data governance, algorithmic transparency, and the regulation of international platforms. While sovereignty was once relegated to territory and resources, it has now spanned into the digital realm, where there is an inherent need for cooperation and negotiation in order to reduce the risk posed by connected infrastructures.

5.2. Technological Asymmetries and the Global Digital Divide

The quest for digital sovereignty has uncovered deep technological asymmetries between the Global North and the Global South. Some countries, including those in North America, Europe, and East Asia, are backed by large tech companies with the expertise, resources, and infrastructure to control AI, big data, and cybersecurity. In contrast, many developing countries experience deficient capacity, weak regulatory institutions, and dependence on foreign providers of digital services.

This imbalance causes structural weaknesses. Outsourcing services, such as cloud services, cybersecurity, and artificial intelligence systems, to external actors creates a kind of digital dependency that weakens sovereignty and limits policy independence. If not addressed, these disparities stand to create a digital two-tier system, where technologically advanced states can determine the rules of the digital game and the Global South can be relegated to mere end-users, with little input into international standards or rules.

The increasing inequalities have generated a push for international negotiations on AI ethics, cybersecurity, and digital governance. The United Nations, G20, OECD, ITU, and UNESCO have made steps to develop common principles and standards. The UNESCO Recommendation on the Ethics of Artificial Intelligence and the UN's Open-Ended Working Group on ICTs are recent milestones in the process.

However, these negotiations are still informed by ideological and strategic polarities. Liberal democracies prioritize openness, human rights, and the free flow of data, while authoritarian regimes prioritize sovereignty, national security, and information control. The digital world is often stuck in this state of tension, which threatens to splinter the digital order into regional blocs of incompatible standards. Consequently, as part of an evolving "great power competition," establishing the "rules of the road" of AI and data governance has become another arena for geopolitical competition.

Despite the centrality of multilateral engagement, multilateral efforts continue to be stymied by trust deficits. The lack of transparency around AI systems, the difficulties around cyberattack attribution, and the absence of robust verification mechanisms generate high levels of distrust among states. The challenges of attribution also make plausible deniability and false flag operations possible, making accountability difficult. Additionally, differences in privacy systems and digital rights norms make it difficult to reach a consensus on international mechanisms.

This persistent lack of transparency and trust has the potential to further entrench a fragmented digital order of suspicion and asymmetry. One of the main dilemmas of diplomacy is to balance states' sovereign rights with the need for global cooperation. The future of international relations will be shaped by whether states are able to create inclusive governance mechanisms or whether we will continue down a path of rivalry and fragmentation in the digital domain. To illustrate the diverse dynamics shaping digital sovereignty and its intersections with multilateralism, power asymmetries, and trust, Table 7 summarizes the main themes discussed in this section. It highlights the key features, examples, and challenges associated with each sub-dimension, providing a concise comparative overview of how sovereignty and diplomacy are evolving in the digital domain.

Table 7. Dynamics of Sovereignty, Multilateralism, and Power Asymmetries in the Digital Era

Theme	Key Features	Illustrative Examples	Challenges / Implications
The Rise of Digital Sovereignty	States seek control over digital infrastructures, data flows, and cyberspace.	China's "Great Firewall" and sovereign internet laws, Russia's domestic internet routing, the EU's GDPR and Digital Services Act.	Balancing national control with global interoperability, risk of internet fragmentation.
Cyber Diplomacy and Negotiating Digital Interdependence	Cyber-specific dialogues, norms, and crisis mechanisms emerge alongside traditional diplomacy.	UN GGE and OEWG initiatives; OSCE confidence-building measures.	Managing escalation risks; bridging divergent state interests in data governance and algorithmic transparency.
Technological Asymmetries and Global Digital Divide	Advanced economies dominate AI, cybersecurity, and cloud infrastructure; developing states remain dependent.	U.S. and Chinese tech giants shaping global standards; reliance of African states on foreign cloud services.	Risk of digital dependency; limited agency for the Global South in rule-setting; potential two-tier digital order.
Multilateral Negotiations and Competing Visions	International forums attempt to set shared rules, but ideological divides persist.	UNESCO's AI Ethics Recommendation; UN's ICT working group; G20 discussions on digital economy.	Fragmentation into regional blocs; stalemates over sovereignty vs. openness; politicization of standards.
Transparency, Trust, and Limits of Cooperation	Trust deficits and opaque digital systems hinder collective governance.	Attribution problems in cyberattacks (e.g., false flag operations); disputes over data privacy regimes.	Weak verification mechanisms; entrenched suspicion; difficulty achieving global consensus.

6. CONCLUSION

The rise of artificial intelligence, big data, and digital platforms has ushered in a deep techno-geopolitical shift in diplomacy, thereby transforming the way states, institutions, and non-state actors interact with each other in the global setting. As seen throughout the preceding sections, these technologies are not simply adjunct tools, but transformative forces. AI complements decision-making through greater intelligence gathering and scenario planning, big data facilitates predictive foreign policy that shifts diplomacy from reactive to proactive, and digital platforms open up new arenas of narrative competition and public diplomacy. Together, they are changing the pace, scale, and content of world diplomacy, and redefining both the possibilities for cooperation and the dangers of conflict.

As we look to the future, the future of diplomacy in an algorithmic world holds both potential and threat. On the one hand, the use of predictive analytics, real-time monitoring, and AI-driven decision support systems holds promise for more anticipatory and responsive diplomacy, able to react to crises before they become an issue. On the other hand, technological asymmetries, algorithmic black boxes, and digital disinformation campaigns might lead to destabilizing international relations, further widening the digital gap between "haves" and "have-nots," and eroding confidence in multilateral institutions. The techno-geopolitical turn is therefore not a linear track toward the future but a contested terrain of interlinking innovation and instability.

It is clear that, to move through this new landscape, policy pathways require an emphasis on balance. Digital diplomacy needs to be encouraged, but it needs to be supported by robust mechanisms for accountability, transparency, and ethical governance. International AI ethics, cybersecurity, and data governance norms will be key to avoiding the weaponization and monopolization of technology tools by a few key players. Supporting multilateral data sharing efforts and developing inclusive digital infrastructures is one means of narrowing North-South polarities and creating a more equitable digital multilateral order. Most importantly, diplomacy in the digital age needs to acknowledge that the legitimacy of international cooperation lies not just in the efficiency of technology but in democratic values, human rights, and mutual trust.

Finally, it is important to note that, despite the central role of technology, human judgment remains crucial in the field of diplomacy. Algorithms can make predictions, models can simulate results, and platforms can help amplify messages, but the interpretation of inputs and ethical responsibility for decisions is still essentially human work. Diplomacy has always been about negotiation, trust, and judgment under uncertainty, qualities that no machine will ever completely replicate. As such, the techno-geopolitical turn should be seen not as the displacement of conventional diplomacy but rather as its transformation, where human agency and technological systems necessarily interact. The challenge for the next decades will be to channel the power of new technologies while ensuring the preservation of the values and practices that make diplomacy an indispensable tool to promote peace, cooperation, and world order.

REFERENCES

Apostolakis, K. C., Dimitriou, N., Margetis, G., Ntoa, S., Tzovaras, D., & Stephanidis, C. (2022). DARLENE – Improving situational awareness of European law enforcement agents through a combination of augmented reality and artificial intelligence solutions. *Open Research Europe*, *1*, 87. Advance online publication. DOI: 10.12688/openreseurope.13715.2 PMID: 37645167

Camilleri, M. A. (2024). Artificial intelligence governance: Ethical considerations and implications for social responsibility. *Expert Systems: International Journal of Knowledge Engineering and Neural Networks*, *41*(7), e13406. DOI: 10.1111/exsy.13406

Chesterman, S. (2021). Through a glass, darkly: Artificial intelligence and the problem of opacity. *The American Journal of Comparative Law*, *69*(2), 271–294. Advance online publication. DOI: 10.1093/ajcl/avab012

Cui, H., & Yasseri, T. (2024). AI-enhanced collective intelligence. *Patterns, 5*(11). https://doi.org/, A. (2023). Opacity, Machine Learning and Explainable AI. In *International Library of Ethics, Law and Technology* (Vol. 41). https://doi.org/DOI: 10.1016/J.PATTER.2024.101074/Fernández

Fournier-Tombs, E. (2021). Towards a United Nations Internal Regulation for Artificial Intelligence. *Big Data & Society*, *8*(2), 20539517211039493. Advance online publication. DOI: 10.1177/20539517211039493

Ghose, A., & Das, M. (2025). Techno-nationalism and Techno-globalism in Asia: Geopolitical Dynamics and Intellectual Property Implications of Semiconductor Innovations. *Decoding the Chessboard of Asian Geopolitics*, 323–342. DOI: 10.1007/978-981-96-3073-8_16

Hutson, M. (2021). The opacity of artificial intelligence makes it hard to tell when decision-making is biased. *IEEE Spectrum*, *58*(2), 40–45. Advance online publication. DOI: 10.1109/MSPEC.2021.9340114

ITU. (2023). *United Nations activities on artificial intelligence (AI)*. https://www.itu.int/hub/publication/s-gen-unact-2023/

Kalantzakos, S. (2023). Between Rocks and Hard Places: Geopolitics of Net Zero Futures and the Tech Imperium. In *Archimedes* (Vol. 65). DOI: 10.1007/978-3-031-25577-9_1

Khedr, A. ; M. ;, Salim, A. ;, Alali, A. I. ;, El-Sawy, A. A., Alimenti, F., Kobayashi, H., Osamy, W., Khedr, A. M., Salim, A., Alali, A. I., & El-Sawy, A. A. (2022). Recent Studies Utilizing Artificial Intelligence Techniques for Solving Data Collection, Aggregation and Dissemination Challenges in Wireless Sensor Networks: A Review. *Electronics 2022, Vol. 11, Page 313, 11*(3), 313. DOI: 10.3390/electronics11030313

Kilburg, D. (2025). *AI Use Cases for Diplomats: Applying Artificial Intelligence to Diplomacy*. CRC Press. DOI: 10.1201/9781003612308

Konovalova, M. (2023). AI AND DIPLOMACY: CHALLENGES AND OPPORTUNITIES. *Journal of Liberty and International Affairs*, *9*(2), 520–530. DOI: 10.47305/JLIA2392520k

Li, J., Shapiro, D. M., Ufimtseva, A., & Zhang, P. (2024). Techno-nationalism and cross-border acquisitions in an age of geopolitical rivalry. *Journal of International Business Studies*, *55*(9), 1190–1203. DOI: 10.1057/s41267-024-00721-7

Liu, H., & Miao, C. (2024). Digital geopolitics in a VUCA world: China encounters a new global order. *Global Policy*, *15*(S6), 67–83. DOI: 10.1111/1758-5899.13435

Mell, J., Beissinger, M., & Gratch, J. (2021). An expert-model and machine learning hybrid approach to predicting human-agent negotiation outcomes in varied data. *Journal on Multimodal User Interfaces*, *15*(2), 215–227. Advance online publication. DOI: 10.1007/s12193-021-00368-w

Mostafaei, H., Kordnoori, S., Ostadrahimi, M., & Banihashemi, S. S. A. (2025). Applications of artificial intelligence in global diplomacy: A review of research and practical models. *Sustainable Futures : An Applied Journal of Technology, Environment and Society*, *9*, 100486. DOI: 10.1016/j.sftr.2025.100486

Rashida Farsath, K., Jitha, K., Mohammed Marwan, V. K., Muhammed Ali Jouhar, A., Muhammed Farseen, K. P., & Musrifa, K. A. (2024). AI-Enhanced Unmanned Aerial Vehicles for Search and Rescue Operations. *2024 5th International Conference on Innovative Trends in Information Technology, ICITIIT 2024*. DOI: 10.1109/ICITIIT61487.2024.10580372

Reinhardt, K. (2023). Trust and trustworthiness in AI ethics. *AI and Ethics*, *3*(3), 735–744. Advance online publication. DOI: 10.1007/s43681-022-00200-5

Ryan, M. (2020). In AI We Trust: Ethics, Artificial Intelligence, and Reliability. *Science and Engineering Ethics*, *26*(5), 2749–2767. Advance online publication. DOI: 10.1007/s11948-020-00228-y PMID: 32524425

Spaniol, M. J., & Rowland, N. J. (2023). AI-assisted scenario generation for strategic planning. *Futures & Foresight Science*, *5*(2), e148. Advance online publication. DOI: 10.1002/ffo2.148

Vaithilingam, P., Arawjo, I., & Glassman, E. L. (2024). Imagining a Future of Designing with AI: Dynamic Grounding, Constructive Negotiation, and Sustainable Motivation. *Proceedings of the 2024 ACM Designing Interactive Systems Conference, DIS 2024*, 289–300. DOI: 10.1145/3643834.3661525

Varela, D. T. (2024). Diplomacy in the Age of AI: Challenges and Opportunities. *Journal of Artificial Intelligence General Science (JAIGS) ISSN:3006-4023, 2*(1), 101–128. DOI: 10.60087/jaigs.v2i1.101

von Eschenbach, W. J. (2021). Transparency and the Black Box Problem: Why We Do Not Trust AI. *Philosophy & Technology*, *34*(4), 1607–1622. Advance online publication. DOI: 10.1007/s13347-021-00477-0

Zeleznikow, J. (2021). Using Artificial Intelligence to provide Intelligent Dispute Resolution Support. *Group Decision and Negotiation*, *30*(4), 789–812. Advance online publication. DOI: 10.1007/s10726-021-09734-1 PMID: 33867681

Chapter 11 Security Diplomacy and Artificial Intelligence in the Middle East: Case Study the Arab League and the Gulf Cooperation Council

Nora Mamoud Jamal
https://orcid.org/0009-0005-3286-0384
Alneelin University, Sudan

ABSTRACT

This research analyzes the concept and role of security diplomacy in the Middle East, tracing its development through the various historical eras the region has experienced. The main research problem lies in whether the mechanisms currently used contribute to strengthening security diplomacy in the Middle East. Based on this problem, the study proposed several hypotheses, including that the lack of collective political will among the member states of the Arab League and the Gulf Cooperation Council (GCC) limits the effectiveness of security diplomacy.And the weak implementation of artificial intelligence applications to develop traditional diplomatic performance and move towards modern digital diplomacy.

1. INTRODUCTION

This research analyses the concept and role of security diplomacy in the Middle East, tracing its development through the various historical eras the region has experienced. The main research problem lies in whether the mechanisms currently used contribute to strengthening security diplomacy in the Middle East. Based on

DOI: 10.4018/979-8-3373-4937-4.ch011

this problem, the study proposed several hypotheses, including that the lack of collective political will among the member states of the Arab League and the Gulf Cooperation Council (GCC) limits the effectiveness of security diplomacy and the weak implementation of artificial intelligence applications to develop traditional diplomatic performance and move towards modern digital diplomacy.

The significance of the study lies in its analysis of the role of regional institutions, namely, the Arab League and the GCC in managing security crises in the region, offering an objective, scholarly evaluation of their historical roles and development.

The research aims to analyse the role of both the Arab League and the Gulf Cooperation Council in managing and resolving crises in the Middle East through traditional security diplomacy, and how to develop the operational diplomatic mechanisms of these institutions through artificial intelligence applications and assess their effectiveness and impact on the security and stability of the Middle East region. Among the key findings of the study is the weakness of the Arab League in utilizing executive mechanisms in the field of security diplomacy. One of the most important recommendations made is to present a strategic vision for enhancing the efficiency of Arab security cooperation tools in light of geopolitical changes, and to contribute to building a future-oriented framework for restructuring security diplomacy instruments in the Middle East to ensure collective Arab security. This is achieved through the use of artificial intelligence applications.

Throughout history, the Middle East has consistently attracted the interest of major global powers. The concept and naming of the "Middle East" are generally attributed to U.S. naval officer Captain Alfred Thayer Mahan, known for his influential writings on naval strategy. In an article in The National Review in 1902, Mahan argued that Britain should assume responsibility for safeguarding security in the (Persian) Gulf and along its shores (referred to as the "Middle East") in order to protect the route to India and curb Russian expansion. From that point on, the term "Middle East" began to gain widespread usage (Bilgin, 2004). It is no accident that all major powers throughout history have attempted to pursue their interests in this region. Beyond its exceptional geographic and strategic position, the Middle East is also the birthplace and sacred homeland of the three leading monotheistic faiths,Islam, Christianity, and Judaism (Stivachtis, 2018).

The Middle East is one of the most turbulent regions in the world, and an arena for protracted conflicts, whether internal or regional. It is characterised by an important geographical and strategic location located at the junction of the three major continents (Asia, Africa and Europe) and overlooks the largest bodies of water (Indian Ocean, Jordan Sea, Arabian Gulf, Mediterranean Sea, Black Sea) in addition to rivers (Nile River, Euphrates River, Tigris River, Tigris River, Jordan). These countries include Central Asia, the Arabian Gulf, Egypt, the Levant region, Türkiye, Iran, Cyprus and Sudan. Economically, the Middle East is of vital importance to most countries of the world due to the availability of natural resources, mineral wealth and energy sources. The region is characterised by cultural, national, religious and linguistic diversity, which is sometimes a source of strength and homogeneity and sometimes a source of conflict and division. This has been one of the most prominent factors driving the differences and political conflicts between the countries of the region. (Hisham Mahmoud Al-Aqdahi, 2009). Any conflict, whether between states or within a state in the Middle East, has the capacity not only to destabilize the entire region and disrupt the regional balance of power, but also to impact global stability. Consequently, the Middle East has long stood at the heart of international affairs, representing an area of significant economic, political, and cultural sensitivity (Stivachtis, 2018). Among the most important political conflicts in the Middle East region are the Arab-Israeli conflict 1948, the Iranian crisis 1946, the Iran-Iraq war 1980-1988, the Lebanese civil war 1975-1990, the Gulf Wars 1990-1991, the Iraq war 2003-2011, the Arab Spring 2011.

As a result of these political and ethnic conflicts within the Middle East, the idea of national security, the ability of a nation to protect its internal values from external threats (Al-Aqdahi, 2009). Diplomacy was used as a means of achieving security and the term security diplomacy emerged in the Middle East to maintain security and eliminate internal regional conflicts through diplomatic institutions within the Middle East, namely the Arab League in 1945 and the Gulf Cooperation Council in 1981.

This study will examine the role of these regional diplomatic institutions in managing and resolving internal and regional crises in the Middle East, and how Artificial Intelligence has enabled the development of traditional diplomatic mechanisms into modern mechanisms in accordance with Artificial Intelligence applications and comparisons between mechanisms through historical tracking and the functional performance of these institutions in resolving regional issues.

1.1. Research Question

The objective of this research is guided by the following research questions: What is the concept of diplomacy and its tools? What is the concept of national security and security diplomacy, and what is its importance in the Arab regional context? What are the most prominent successes and failures experienced by regional organizations, particularly the Arab League and the Gulf Cooperation Council, in managing security crises? How can artificial intelligence contribute to enhancing the diplomatic efficiency of these institutions? Finally, what are the potential advantages and disadvantages of applying artificial intelligence in the domain of security diplomacy?

1.2. The Historical Development of the Concept of Diplomacy

The term diplomacy originates from the ancient Greek word derived from diplo, meaning "document." In Ancient Greece, diplomacy was conducted through ambassadors, who functioned similarly to consular officials (proxenos). The information gathered through such diplomatic activities often influenced the destiny of states. Diplomats in this period were generally regarded as messengers. In Ancient Rome, diplomacy toward foreigners was governed by the ius gentium (law of nations), which applied to merchants, travellers, and visitors. In contrast, diplomatic rules concerning Roman citizens were regulated under civitas gentium. One of the earliest known examples of diplomacy is the Treaty of Kadesh, concluded between the Egyptians and the Hittites in 1278 BC, which brought peace between the two sides (Abdurahmanli, 2021)

The era of modern diplomacy began to take shape mainly during the 17th and 18th centuries. A key turning point in this period was the French Revolution of 1789. Following this, the Congress of Vienna in 1815 played a crucial role in redefining the borders of Europe and establishing the groundwork for future international organizations. Modern diplomacy, in essence, rests on maintaining a balance of power between forces that promote war and those that promote peace (Abdurahmanli, 2021). And it was mentioned When the diplomat Harold Nicholson defined diplomacy in the Oxford English Dictionary as the management of international relations through negotiations through ambassadors and envoys, in 1982 the British diplomat Adam Watson described it as dialogue between states. And the agreed definition is that diplomacy is the science and art of managing and organizing relations between countries through negotiations and possessing intelligence, experience and competence (Jeffrey Begman, 2012). In this regard, the historical transformation of diplomacy from classical balance-of-power models into a more proactive, interest-driven, and, when necessary, institution-challenging framework is clearly reflected in contemporary international relations shaped by competitive dynamics (Turan, 2024).

The Explanatory Dictionary of the Romanian Language defines diplomacy as the set of methods, instruments, and activities employed by a state in its international relations to pursue its goals and implement its foreign policy (Bălcescu, 2017). Foreign policy is the plan drawn up to guide foreign relations, while diplomacy is the process of implementing that plan (Zaki, 1992). The importance of diplomacy lies in establishing friendly relations between countries to ensure their common interests. And easing tensions and turning them into peaceful negotiations.

2. DEFINITION OF SECURITY DIPLOMACY

Security diplomacy emerged in the post–Cold War era following the collapse of the Soviet Union. Although traditional state-to-state conflicts continued, such as the war between Serbia and Bosnia-Herzegovina, new asymmetric threats increasingly arose from regions like the Middle East and Southeast Asia. These threats targeted the legitimacy of governments and challenged established political orders, with instability frequently leading to violence aimed at influencing both domestic and foreign policy (Kron, 2015).

Security diplomacy involves employing the full range of a nation-state's security capabilities to strengthen the security institutions of a partner country. This may include, but is not limited to, military cooperation and exchanges, defence equipment sales, joint training exercises, rule-of-law and human rights training, as well as capacity-building for humanitarian disaster response. In practice, security diplomacy integrates defence, legal, human rights, and humanitarian support initiatives tailored to the specific needs of partner states. It extends beyond traditional defence diplomacy by requiring coordinated efforts among security institutions to complement diplomatic agencies and provide policymakers with broader strategic options (Kron, 2015).

2.1. Security diplomacy and the Middle East

In the 1940s, after the end of World War II in 1945, the concept of security diplomacy emerged in the Middle East. During that period several Arab countries had obtained an independence of sorts from Britain or France-Egypt, Iraq, Syria, Lebanon, and Jordan (Ibrahim,1996).

The region has witnessed historical regional conflicts such as the Palestinian issue, the Arab-Israeli conflict, the Gulf Wars, and civil wars in Lebanon and Yemen, which led to the establishment of diplomatic mechanisms to mitigate the intensity of conflicts and ensure and preserve Arab nationalism. Yet, a series of setbacks in the late 1960s, most notably the crushing Arab defeat in the 1967 war against Israel, severely weakened the pan-Arab project, leaving it almost irreparably damaged. The 1980s did, however, offer brief signs of revival. During this period, three Arab subregional organizations were created to promote closer socio-economic cooperation: the Gulf Cooperation Council (GCC) in 1981, the Arab Cooperation Council (ACC) in 1989, and the Arab Maghreb Union (AMU) in the same year. This momentum was short-lived, as a major turning point soon followed. The Second Gulf War, coupled with the end of the Cold War, profoundly reshaped the Arab world and is widely viewed as a decisive watershed that helped produce the region's contemporary geopolitical landscape (Ibrahim, 1996). Moreover, concerns surrounding

Arab national security had already intensified during the 1970s as the Arab-Israeli conflict reached a critical stage (Al-Aqdahi, 2009).

Under these circumstances, security diplomacy in the Middle East emerged as one of the most important tools for ensuring internal and regional stability in a complex political and security environment, avoiding conflicts, building alliances, and containing security threats such as wars, terrorism, and armed militias. This security diplomacy was represented by the Arab League and the Gulf Cooperation Council.

2.2. The League of Arab States (LAS) 1945

The call for Arab unity has been around for ages, but the idea of establishing an Arab organization that would include all Arab countries only became clear during World War II. Britain sought to win over the Arabs and ease Arab hostility toward it, so it announced its welcome of the idea of independence for some Arab countries. This announcement was made by British Foreign Minister Eden in May 1941. (Moneim, 1986). The Arab League is a regional political organization that exercises collective diplomacy on behalf of Arab states within a regional framework. It is a tool for cooperation among Arab member states. It is a tool for supporting the mixed historical ties that bind these states together and for respecting the sovereignty of its member states. (Zaki, 2015)

The first phase in the formation of the League of Arab States began with Egypt inviting Iraq, Lebanon, Syria, Jordan, Saudi Arabia, Yemen, and Palestine to exchange views on Arab unity. This phase was known as the Arab Unity Consultations and took place in Alexandria in August 1942. This resulted in the signing of the Alexandria Protocol in 1944, which laid down the basic principles for the formation of the League of Arab States (Key Events in the History of the League of Arab States, 1945-1995). There are twenty-two Arab countries, and the following are the member states of the League of Arab States, listed in order of seniority of membership in the League of Arab States (Jordan, Saudi Arabia, Syria, Lebanon, Iraq, Egypt, Yemen, Libya, Sudan, Morocco, Tunisia, Kuwait, Algeria, Oman, Qatar, Bahrain, United Arab Emirates, Mauritania, Somalia, Palestine, Djibouti, Comoros (Samir et al, 2023).

2.3. The Arab League and the conflicts in the Middle East

It is difficult to clearly define the true role played by the Arab League in the Palestinian cause, as many of the decisions and actions undertaken by the organization were conducted in secrecy and remain inaccessible. However, based on available records and public statements, the League's involvement can be summarized in two main dimensions. Economically, the Arab League Council resolved to boycott Israeli goods and products, both within Palestine and across the markets of member states, as a means of applying economic pressure. Additionally, it approved the establishment of an office in Palestine to promote and support local Arab industries. Politically, the League sought to unify Palestinian leadership by fostering cooperation among various national parties and forces, aiming to lay the groundwork for the creation of an independent Palestinian government capable of representing the collective will of its people (Nafaa, 1983). The League demanded an end to Jewish immigration to Palestine. No member state was permitted to conclude a political, economic or military agreement with Israel (Moneim, 1986).

2.4. The effectiveness of the League of Arab States in resolving conflicts Arab

The strength and effectiveness of the League of Arab States in resolving conflicts between Arab countries through mediation, a diplomatic and security tool. It succeeded in resolving, the Syrian-Egyptian conflict in 1961, Yemeni civil war in 1963, the Yemen War in 1972, the Egyptian-Libyan war in 1977, and the Lebanese civil war 1975 (Selim, 1983).

The Arab League failed to resolve conflicts such as the 1990 Gulf War, the 1948 Yemeni Civil War, the 1958 Egyptian-Sudanese conflict, and the 1958 Moroccan-Algerian conflict (Asraa et al, 2023).

2.5. The Arab League's position on the Arab Spring revolutions of 2011

During the Tunisian Revolution, the Arab League adopted a position of relative neutrality, declaring that the events in Tunisia were an internal matter and refraining from direct interference. In contrast, during the Egyptian Revolution, the League expressed support for the revolutionary spirit of the Egyptian youth, commending their determination and capacity for transformation and reform. However, the Syrian Revolution marked a significant shift in the League's approach. It took a more active stance by seeking to protect civilians, urging Arab countries to withdraw their ambassadors from Damascus, and calling on both regional and international organizations to recognize the National Coalition for Syrian Revolutionary and Opposition Forces (Asraa et al, 2023).

From these examples, it becomes evident that the historical evolution of the Arab League's diplomatic role has been hindered by a persistent lack of genuine cooperation and collective will among its member states. This fragmentation has frequently resulted in internal disputes and weakened the organization's ability to act decisively. Furthermore, the absence of an effective mechanism for enforcing decisions has undermined its credibility. The League's reliance on traditional diplomatic tools, such as mediation, has often proven insufficient in addressing complex modern crises that demand more dynamic, coordinated, and innovative diplomatic strategies (Al-Sadiq Shaaban, 1989).

2.6. Gulf Cooperation Council (GCC)

Several regional and international circumstances contributed to paving the way for the establishment of the Gulf Cooperation Council (GCC). Among the most significant factors was the sharp rise in oil prices, which enhanced the geopolitical and economic importance of the Gulf region and underscored the need for coordinated policies to manage oil revenues and protect shared interests. Additionally, the Iranian-Iraqi conflict of 1947 and the emergence of Arab Islamic movements opposed to both American and Soviet influence created an atmosphere of regional instability that demanded a unified Gulf response. The competition between the United States and the Soviet Union over control of oil resources and investments in the region further intensified the sense of urgency for collective security.

The polarisation of the Arab and Islamic world following the 1978 Camp David Accords between Egypt and Israel also contributed to divisions within the Arab sphere, prompting Gulf leaders to seek stronger regional cohesion. Moreover, the limited military capabilities and small geographical size of several Gulf states made independent defense difficult, reinforcing the necessity for cooperation (Al-Astal, 1999).

One of the crises faced by the Gulf Cooperation Council was the border crisis between the Gulf states (Saudi Arabia, the United Arab Emirates, Qatar, Bahrain, Oman, and Bahrain). The Council was able to resolve this crisis through negotiation and the demarcation of borders without military intervention. In addition, there were the wars in Iraq in 2003 and Yemen. Among the most important achievements of the Council is the formation of the Joint Peninsula Shield Force to serve as the unified military command of the Gulf Cooperation Council. It also established a joint defense agreement, the Islamic Military Alliance to fight terrorism, and a strategic partnership between NATO and the Arab Gulf states. However, the most important dilemma facing the Council is Iraq and Yemen, because Gulf security integration comes through their integration and the improvement of their political and security situations (Karim, 2022).

The role of artificial intelligence (AI) in managing diplomatic and security negotiations within the Arab League and the Gulf Cooperation Council (GCC) has become increasingly significant in recent years. One of the primary drivers of this transformation is the information and communication technology revolution, which has fundamentally altered how states, institutions, and individuals interact, share information, and make decisions. This digital shift has reshaped the global political, social, economic, and diplomatic landscape, introducing new methods for conducting diplomacy and influencing international affairs.

This emerging form of diplomacy, often referred to as digital or cyber diplomacy, relies heavily on communication technologies, public relations, cultural engagement, and media outreach. It utilizes soft power tools rather than military means to achieve foreign policy objectives, promoting dialogue, cooperation, and influence through non-coercive strategies. Within this framework, artificial intelligence technologies have proven particularly valuable.

AI applications enhance diplomatic effectiveness by processing and analysing vast quantities of data rapidly and accurately, allowing policymakers to make informed decisions based on real-time insights. These technologies also enable the prediction and simulation of potential negotiation outcomes, offering diplomats a strategic advantage in understanding counterparts' positions and forecasting the implications of different policy options. Consequently, the integration of AI into diplomatic and security processes helps institutions like the Arab League and the GCC to respond more efficiently to crises, improve communication channels, and support evidence-based decision-making in a complex and rapidly evolving international environment (Al-Safi, 2024).

3. DEFINITION OF ARTIFICIAL INTELLIGENCE

The concept of artificial intelligence was formulated as the science of engineering intelligent machines in 1956 by scientists Marvin Minsky and John McCarthy at Stanford University. Research then developed, leading to the fifth generation of computers and technologies, which became fundamental to national and international strategic planning. (Ali bin Khalfan, 2024)

Artificial intelligence refers to the ability of machines, particularly computer systems, to imitate human intelligence, which includes functions such as language processing, as well as speech and image recognition. The generation of artificial intelligence requires generating artificial intelligence requires specialised hardware and software to write and train "self-learning algorithms," which are the core of artificial intelligence. In general, various artificial intelligence systems work by feeding them large amounts of diverse data, which, through processing and analysis by algorithms, trains the artificial intelligence program to recognise patterns and connections and make predictions. (Aqeel, 2023). Such capabilities equip diplomats with enhanced instruments for scenario analysis, enable the development of more advanced communication materials, and deliver richer insights into public opinion offering the potential to transform conventional methods of diplomacy and negotiation (Mostafaei, 2025)

3.1. The Impact of AI on Traditional Diplomacy in the Middle East

Through historical tracking of crises in the Middle East and the varying roles of the Arab League and the Gulf Cooperation Council between success and failure in resolving these crises, With the escalation of security threats, there is a need to employ artificial intelligence in the service of security diplomacy in the Middle East and for these regional institutions to seek modern tools to deal with crises. It can be said that artificial intelligence in the security and diplomatic context has transformed from a mere technology into a strategic tool to support decision-making, as it provides enormous possibilities for data analysis, early prediction, and risk management.

AI has the capacity to transform public diplomacy by providing sophisticated tools for crafting tailored and influential messaging, monitoring real-time public sentiment, and adapting engagement strategies to diverse cultural settings. These developments can greatly strengthen both the impact and outreach of diplomatic initiatives (Mostafaei, 2025)

3.2. Artificial intelligence and diplomacy

Artificial intelligence can significantly enhance the role of regional diplomatic institutions in the Middle East, such as the League of Arab States and the Gulf Cooperation Council, by providing strategic tools that support decision-making and diplomatic practice. Game theory assists in analysing strategic interactions and predicting negotiation outcomes, while agent-based modelling simulates the behaviour of states and diplomats to better understand complex diplomatic dynamics. Multi-Criteria Decision Analysis (MCDA) enables policymakers to assess options across political, economic, and strategic dimensions, leading to more balanced decisions. AI-driven prediction tools also help identify emerging crises early through big data analysis, offering guidance on potential solutions. Additionally, AI-based simulations create virtual negotiation environments for training and testing diplomatic strategies, and big data enhances core diplomatic functions such as reporting, information gathering, and crisis response, ultimately improving overall diplomatic effectiveness (qatar.georgetown.edu). Train diplomats to deal with complex negotiation scenarios to enhance their readiness for effective negotiation performance. Big data has found its place as a tool for diplomacy in collecting, analysing and integrating large amounts of data into reports and summaries and protecting consular and other diplomatic activities. Big data has an impact on important diplomatic functions, particularly core diplomatic functions, such as collecting data and diplomatic reports and negotiating to provide a modern diplomatic tool that facilitates global and regional relations.

The above highlights the importance of artificial intelligence and its impact on diplomacy and international relations. Consequently, artificial intelligence applications will play an effective role in the Middle East, a region dominated by tension and political conflict, through regional institutions. The League of Arab States has called for the use of artificial intelligence applications to address traditional and modern challenges in the region and for the need to build Arab capabilities in the field of smart technologies, protect Arab interests, and strengthen joint Arab cooperation (Obeid, 2025).

The Gulf Cooperation Council is keen to actively develop artificial intelligence technologies. Saudi Arabia, the United Arab Emirates and Qatar in particular have shown a strong commitment to developing artificial intelligence infrastructure and utilising it in all areas, including security and diplomacy. For example, the United Arab Emirates has established a special office and government for artificial intelligence and founded the Mohammed bin Zayed University for Artificial Intelligence. Similarly, Saudi Arabia held an international summit on artificial intelligence in October 2020 to lay the foundation for empowering young people to innovate solutions to all crises (Khalfan, 2024) Qatar has been keen to conduct simulation training for international negotiations in cooperation with the Institute of Diplomatic Studies and the College of International Affairs in Qatar, where students are trained in decision-making and crisis management (qatar.georgetown.edu).

The rest of the Gulf Cooperation Council countries are also showing the same level of interest and development in order to achieve regional and international security stability. From the above, a comparison can be drawn between the Arab League and the Gulf Cooperation Council in the use of artificial intelligence in the fields of diplomatic security:

The Arab League: A theoretical coordination framework that proposes general strategies but is weak in scientific implementation. This is due to the weak will of member states, weak funding and research capabilities, and the absence of joint projects or regional platforms for artificial intelligence in security. An applied and practical framework that translates artificial intelligence into concrete projects in security, diplomacy, and development. This is due to the advanced economic and technological capabilities of the Gulf states and their determination to stabilise internal security in the region to reduce political tensions.

4. CONCLUSION

This paper addressed the role of the League of Arab States and the Gulf Cooperation Council in security diplomacy in the Middle East region through the historical development of the role of these institutions in resolving regional crises and demonstrated their role in promoting collective security.

However, the Gulf Cooperation Council is more oriented towards the use of artificial intelligence than the Arab League. The use of artificial intelligence provides new opportunities to enhance decision-making and crisis prediction in the region.

Thus, the adoption of artificial intelligence applications enhances the ability of the League of Arab States and the Gulf Cooperation Council to develop their traditional security diplomacy, which has clearly emerged in the historical crises faced by these institutions, and to provide modern mechanisms to address current and future complex security challenges and crises in the Middle East region.

REFERENCES

Abdel Moneim, A. F. (1986). *The Arab League 1945–1985: A historical and political study* (pp. 12–13, 44–50).

Abdurahmanli, E. (2021). *Definition of diplomacy and types of diplomacy used between states. Anadolu Akademi Sosyal Bilimler Dergisi*, 583.

Al-Aqdahi, H. M. (2009). *Political stability in the contemporary world.*

Al-Astal, K. M. (1999). *Towards formulating a theory of security for the Arab Gulf Cooperation Council.* Emirates Centre for Strategic Studies and Research.

Al-Safi, Y.. (2024). *Digital diplomacy and artificial intelligence: Qualification rules for the diplomatic and consular service.* Democratic Arabic Center for Strategic, Political and Economic Studies.

Aqeel, A. (2023). International relations in the age of artificial intelligence. Hammurabi Centre for Research and Strategic Studies, 3.

Bălcescu, N. (2017). Diplomacy and security. *International Conference Knowledge-Based Organization*, 23, 251–252. https://doi.org/DOI: 10.1515

Begman, J. (2012). *Contemporary diplomacy.*

Bilgin, P. (2004). *Whose "Middle East"? Geopolitical inventions and practices of security. International Relations*, 18(1), 18–19. Sage Publications. DOI: 10.1177/0047117804041739

Bin Khalfan, A. (2024). *Applications of artificial intelligence in the security field (Applied to the Gulf Cooperation Council countries)* (pp. 2561–2601).

Ibrahim, S. E. (1996). Future visions of the Arab Middle East. Sage Publications, 27, 426–427.

Karim, A. (2022). *The security challenges of the Cooperation Council for the Arab States of the Gulf in light of international changes. Political Issues*, (70).

Kron, N. D. (2015). *Security diplomacy: Beyond defense* (pp. 6–7).

League of Arab States. (1995). *Key events in the history of the League of Arab States, 1945–1995* (pp. 5–6). Publications of the League of Arab States.

Mostafaei, H. (2025). Applications of artificial intelligence in global diplomacy. *Sustainable Futures : An Applied Journal of Technology, Environment and Society, 12*, 16–17.

Nafaa, H., ... (1983). *The Arab League: Reality and ambition* (pp. 142–143).

Obeid, Z. (2025). *The Arab League's interest in technology and artificial intelligence. Arab Affairs Online.* https://arabaffairsonline.com

Samir, I., ... (2023). *Developing a strategy to activate the role of the League of Arab States during the period (2022–2027).* Democratic Arabic Center. https://democraticac.de/?p=91023

Selim, M. E. S., ... (1983). *The Arab League: Reality and ambition* (p. 176).

Shaaban, A.-S. (1989). Journal of Social Sciences. *Kuwait University*, *7*(4), 19–20.

Stivachtis, Y. (2018, October 4). *Conflict and diplomacy in the Middle East*. E-International Relations. https://www.e-ir.info/2018/10/04/conflict-and-diplomacy-in-the-middle-east

Turan, A. (2024). External Factors Affecting Türkiye-Russia Rivalry in the Second Karabakh War. *European Journal of Transformation Studies*, *12*(2), 172–195.

Zaki, A. (2015). *The role of functional theory in analysing the policies of the Arab League 1954–2014* (pp. 1–2).

Zaki, F. (1992). *Diplomacy in a changing world.*

Chapter 12
ASEAN Summits at the Digital Frontier:
Forging Networked Diplomacy, Cybersecurity Resilience, and AI Cooperation

Budi Riyanto
https://orcid.org/0000-0001-6330-0308
LSPR Institute of Communication and Business, Indonesia

Noprita Herari
https://orcid.org/0009-0009-2497-5340
Universitas Negeri Jakarta, Indonesia

Past Novel Larasaty
https://orcid.org/0000-0002-3734-1760
LSPR Institute of Communication and Business, Indonesia

ABSTRACT

This chapter critically interrogates ASEAN's digital turn, arguing that while successive Summits have rhetorically placed digital diplomacy, cybersecurity, and AI governance at the strategic frontier, the gap between ambition and implementation remains stark. Despite headline initiatives such as DEFA, the ASEAN Digital Masterplans, and emerging AI governance frameworks, national fragmentation, weak enforcement, and the gravitational pull of US–China techno-strategic rivalry constrain ASEAN's agency. The chapter contends that achieving the digital dimension of the ASEAN Community Vision 2045 demands not continuity of the "ASEAN Way," but its recalibration toward regulatory convergence, agile governance, and a more networked posture in the contested global digital order.

DOI: 10.4018/979-8-3373-4937-4.ch012

1. INTRODUCTION

To comprehend ASEAN's intricate and evolving engagement with digital diplomacy, cybersecurity, and AI governance, a multi-faceted theoretical framework is essential. While mainstream International Relations (IR) theories offer valuable lenses, a more nuanced understanding requires incorporating critical perspectives that interrogate the underlying power structures and societal impacts of digital transformation.

1.1. Theoretical Framework

Neoliberal institutionalism, as articulated by scholars like Keohane and Martin (1995), provides a compelling explanation for ASEAN's propensity for cooperation and regime-building in new domains such as the digital economy (Keohane & Martin, 1995). This perspective emphasizes how international institutions, like ASEAN, can facilitate cooperation by reducing transaction costs, providing information, establishing focal points for policy coordination, and fostering iterated interactions that build trust and predictability.[7] The creation of various ASEAN frameworks and strategies related to the digital sphere, often endorsed or initiated at Summits, can be seen as attempts to build regional regimes that enable member states to collectively address shared challenges and harness common opportunities.

The ASEAN Digital Economy Framework Agreement (DEFA) stands as a prime example of such an endeavor. With negotiations targeted for conclusion by the end of 2025, DEFA aims to become the world's first region-wide, binding agreement focused exclusively on digital economy governance (Hourn, 2025). Its overarching goal is to harmonize digital trade rules, facilitate seamless cross-border data flows, and establish a coherent regulatory framework for key digital sectors, thereby unlocking a projected $1 to $2 trillion in regional digital economic value by 2030 (Lee et al., 2025; Hourn, 2025). From a neoliberal institutionalist viewpoint, DEFA represents a rational attempt by ASEAN member states to create an institutional structure that lowers barriers to digital trade. Divergent national regulations currently cost ASEAN businesses an estimated $15–20 billion annually in compliance overhead, a burden that disproportionately affects the 70% of small and medium-sized enterprises (SMEs) that lack the resources to navigate these conflicting rules (Wilson, 2025). By establishing common standards, DEFA allows member states to capture significant collective economic gains that would be unattainable through unilateral action alone.

1.2. Constructivism

Constructivist approaches provide complementary insights, particularly in understanding how ASEAN Summits and related initiatives contribute to norm-setting and the development of a shared regional identity around digital issues. As argued by Acharya (2011), ASEAN has a history of internalizing and adapting global norms while also generating its own (Acharya, 2011). In the digital context, ASEAN Summits serve as platforms where shared meanings and expectations regarding appropriate behavior in cyberspace or the ethical development of AI can be negotiated and propagated. ASEAN's engagement with AI governance, exemplified by the ASEAN Guide on AI Governance and Ethics (ASEAN Secretariat, 2024b) and its crucial 2025 expansion covering Generative AI (ASEAN Secretariat, 2025a), can be interpreted as an endeavor to construct a regional "digital norm". These guides emphasize principles such as human-centricity, fairness, transparency, and accountability, but are explicitly tailored to the ASEAN context, adopting a voluntary, risk-based approach that is technology and sector agnostic (ASEAN Secretariat, 2024b; Carnicelli et al., 2025). This deliberate framing distinguishes ASEAN's approach from more prescriptive and legally binding models like the European Union's AI Act (Hamzah, 2024). By developing its own AI governance principles, ASEAN is not merely adopting external models but is actively seeking to define its own path, reflecting its specific political, economic, and socio-cultural realities. This aligns with constructivist arguments that states' identities and interests are socially constructed and that international organizations play a role in shaping these identities and the norms that guide behavior (Di Riscio, 2025). The consistent emphasis on "ASEAN centrality" in regional affairs, including in the digital realm, is a core component of this identity construction.

2. CRITICAL LENSES ON ASEAN'S DIGITAL FRONTIER

While valuable, mainstream IR theories do not fully capture the asymmetries of power and the deeper societal implications of digitalization. Broadening the analytical toolkit with critical perspectives provides a more complete picture of the challenges confronting ASEAN.

2.1. Digital Colonialism and Sovereignty

The concept of digital colonialism posits that contemporary digital infrastructures, dominated by foreign multinational corporations and states, replicate and extend traditional colonial hierarchies (Kwet, 2019; Chagnon et al., 2022). It operates not through territorial conquest but through control over digital ecosystems, data flows, and algorithmic governance, enabling a new form of extractive capitalism (Couldry & Mejias, 2022). This lens is crucial for analyzing ASEAN's digital transformation, as the region's digital economy is built largely upon infrastructure and platforms controlled by US and Chinese tech giants (Couldry & Mejias, 2022; Rana & Azeez, 2025). This creates structural dependencies that challenge regional autonomy, a phenomenon some scholars term "technological neo-colonialism" (Rana & Azeez, 2025). The immense data generated by Southeast Asia's 402 million internet users is often mined, stored, and capitalized upon by foreign entities, with value flowing out of the region (Yale Review of International Studies, 2025). In response, many ASEAN states are pursuing "digital sovereignty", the capacity for self-determination in the digital realm, through policies like data localization and the promotion of domestic infrastructure, framing it as a cornerstone of national security and economic independence (Rana & Azeez, 2025; Gunther, 2024).

2.2. Critical Security Studies and Digital Ethics

Traditional security studies focus on the state as the primary referent object to be secured from external military threats. Critical security studies broadens and deepens this agenda, questioning who or what is being secured, from what threats, and by what means (Peoples & Vaughan-Williams, 2021; Krause & Williams, 1997). Applying this to the digital realm shifts the focus from merely protecting state-controlled critical infrastructure to ensuring the human security of individuals and communities (DCAF, 2024). This includes protection from threats like mass surveillance, the erosion of digital rights, online harassment, and the societal disruption caused by disinformation and large-scale cybercrime (DCAF, 2024). This perspective aligns with the work of Joseph Nye, who argues that "cyber power" is diffused, empowering smaller state and non-state actors and creating a volatile new context for international politics where vulnerabilities are asymmetric (Nye, 2010). Furthermore, the framework of digital ethics, as developed by scholars like Luciano Floridi, urges a holistic approach that evaluates the moral problems arising from the entire digital ecosystem, data, algorithms, and practices, rather than focusing narrowly on high-level principles (Floridi & Taddeo, 2025; Floridi et al., 2019). This provides a robust methodology for assessing whether ASEAN's governance initiatives genuinely promote fairness, accountability, and human-centric values in practice.

2.3. Global South Perspectives

Situating ASEAN's experience within the broader context of the Global South reveals shared challenges and aspirations. Countries across the Global South often face a structural digital divide, limited capacity to shape global digital governance agendas, and the risk of becoming passive recipients of technology and norms designed elsewhere (Haidar et al., 2025; Internet Governance Project, 2018). They are frequently the primary targets for data extraction with weak governance guardrails in place, while being underrepresented in forums that set the global digital agenda (Haidar et al, 2025). ASEAN's efforts to chart a "middle path" in digital governance can be seen as part of a wider movement among middle-power countries to assert agency and avoid the binary choices presented by great power competition, striving for a more inclusive and equitable global digital order (Tech for Good Institute, 2023).

3. THE "ASEAN WAY" IN THE DIGITAL AGE

Any theoretical analysis of ASEAN must critically examine the "ASEAN Way," the organization's traditional mode of interaction characterized by consensus-based decision-making, non-interference in internal affairs, and extensive consultation (Jones & Smith, 2007). These principles have been crucial for maintaining regional cohesion and accommodating the diversity of its member states. However, they also present significant constraints when addressing fast-moving digital challenges that demand agility, decisiveness, and sometimes binding commitments. The "ASEAN Way" may inadvertently contribute to a "lowest common denominator" effect in cybersecurity and AI governance, where agreements reflect the comfort level of the most cautious states, potentially limiting the effectiveness of regional responses. Scholarly critiques suggest that the "ASEAN Way" can weaken policy effectiveness, lead to reactive rather than proactive stances, and hinder the development of stronger institutional structures (Pratiwi et al., 2024). The digital era, therefore, places the "ASEAN Way" under considerable strain. The ASEAN Community Vision 2045 itself calls for strengthening ASEAN's institutions to be more "resilient, innovative, agile, adaptive, responsive, and decisive," implicitly acknowledging the need for an evolution in how ASEAN operates to meet future challenges (ASEAN Secretariat, 2025d). The push for DEFA to be a legally binding agreement might be interpreted as an attempt at such adaptation.

3.1. The Evolution and Intensification of Networked Diplomacy

The evolution of ASEAN's approach to digital issues has seen its Summits and related mechanisms increasingly function as arenas for "networked diplomacy." This signifies a gradual shift from purely traditional intergovernmental communication towards more digitally-enabled and multi-layered interactions, although the core tenets of state-led diplomacy remain firmly entrenched. This section traces this evolution, examining how ASEAN has utilized its high-level platforms to engage with the complexities of the digital age, with a particular focus on developments leading up to and including 2025. Initially, digital topics within ASEAN were addressed in a more siloed manner, often confined to specialized ministerial meetings such as the ASEAN Telecommunications and IT Ministers Meeting (TELMIN), which was later upgraded to the ASEAN Digital Ministers' Meeting (ADGMIN). However, the growing strategic importance of the digital economy, cybersecurity, and emerging technologies like AI has propelled these issues onto the agenda of the ASEAN Summits themselves. The 5th ADGMIN in Bangkok in January 2025, and the subsequent First ASEAN Digital Senior Officials' Meeting (ADGSOM) Leaders' Retreat in Jakarta in April 2025, serve as prominent examples of high-level sectoral engagement instrumental in operationalizing Summit directives (ASEAN Secretariat, 2025c). The theme of the 5th ADGMIN, "Secure, Innovative, Inclusive: Shaping ASEAN's Digital Future," clearly encapsulates the strategic and comprehensive focus that digital issues now command, underscoring a collective recognition that the digital future must be actively shaped through collaborative regional efforts (ASEAN Secretariat, 2025b).

The COVID-19 pandemic served as an unexpected yet powerful catalyst, significantly accelerating ASEAN's adoption of digital tools for diplomacy. Prior to 2020, ASEAN's diplomatic practices heavily relied on in-person meetings. The pandemic-induced travel restrictions forced a rapid pivot to virtual platforms for conducting Summits, ministerial meetings, and working-level consultations (Pratiwi et al., 2024). While in-person Summits have largely resumed, the experience has lowered the barriers to using digital platforms for ongoing inter-sessional work, expert consultations, and preparatory meetings, expanding the scope and continuity of networked diplomacy.

ASEAN-led forums that emanate from or report to the Summits, such as ADGMIN, play a critical role in operationalizing Summit mandates. These sectoral bodies translate the strategic visions articulated by leaders into concrete action plans and initiatives. The outcomes of the 5th ADGMIN in January 2025 provide a compelling illustration of this dynamic (ASEAN Secretariat, 2025b). Key outcomes included:

a) Progress on DEFA: Ministers made significant progress on DEFA, with a continued commitment to conclude negotiations by the end of 2025 (ASEAN Secretariat, 2025b).
b) ASEAN Digital Masterplan (ADM) Planning: The meeting reviewed the implementation of ADM2025 and entrusted Vietnam with leading the development of the successor plan, ADM2030, in 2025 (ASEAN Secretariat, 2025b; ASEAN Secretariat, 2025c).
c) Strengthened Cybersecurity Cooperation: Commitments were made to enhance cybersecurity cooperation, including support for the operationalization of the ASEAN Regional CERT (Computer Emergency Response Team) and welcoming the ASEAN Recommendations on Anti-Online Scams (ASEAN Secretariat, 2025b).
d) Advancements in AI Governance: A significant development was the unveiling of the Expanded ASEAN Guide on AI Governance and Ethics - Generative AI. The meeting also welcomed the establishment of the Working Group on AI Governance (WG-AI), led by Singapore, and approved the Declaration on the Establishment of an ASEAN AI Safety Network (AI SAFE) (ASEAN Secretariat, 2025b).
e) New Digital Initiatives: Ministers endorsed the creation of an ASEAN digital innovation sandbox and agreed to launch an ASEAN digital scholarship program. A Working Group on Submarine Cables (WG-SC) was also established to facilitate the protection of this critical infrastructure (ASEAN Secretariat, 2025b).

ASEAN's engagement with its Dialogue Partners, including Australia, China, the European Union, India, Japan, the Republic of Korea (ROK), and the United States, is a crucial dimension of its networked diplomacy. These partners are often global leaders in digital technology and governance, making their engagement vital for ASEAN's digital aspirations. The 5th ADGMIN highlighted the depth of these engagements through various Digital Work Plans (ASEAN Secretariat, 2025b). While these partnerships offer substantial benefits, they also introduce complexities. Dialogue Partners often have competing economic interests and may promote divergent technological standards or governance models. ASEAN's consensus-based approach and its strategic imperative to maintain positive relations with all major powers often lead to a "hedging" strategy, where the region adopts elements from various external models or avoids making strong commitments to any single one (Faizal & Teo, 2024).

However, this state-centric view of networked diplomacy is incomplete. A parallel, and often adversarial, "counter-network" of civil society organizations (CSOs) operates across the region, utilizing the same digital tools to monitor state actions, advocate for policy changes, and build transnational coalitions (Regus et al., 2024). Groups such as Access Now, which campaigns against internet shutdowns and provides digital security support to activists, and the Southeast Asia Freedom of Expression Network (SAFEnet), which focuses on defending freedom of expression online, play a crucial role (Access Now, n.d.; SAFEnet, n.d.). Regional platforms like EngageMedia foster collaboration among digital rights advocates, holding both governments and corporations accountable (EngageMedia, n.d.). Coalitions like the ASEAN Coalition to #StopDigitalDictatorship exemplify this networked CSO diplomacy, serving as an informal accountability mechanism that challenges official narratives and highlights the gap between Summit rhetoric and the on-the-ground reality of digital rights in the region (Manushya Foundation, n.d.). This dynamic creates a more contested and realistic picture of regional governance, where official channels are constantly being observed, critiqued, and influenced by this vibrant civil society network.

4. ASEAN'S SUMMIT-DRIVEN RESPONSES ON CYBERSECURITY

The escalating global landscape of cyber threats has positioned cybersecurity as a paramount concern for ASEAN, with its Summits serving as the primary platforms for articulating regional anxieties and forging collective responses. The period leading up to 2025 has seen an intensification of these threats, demanding more robust and coordinated regional action.

Recent intelligence from cybersecurity firms underscores the evolving and increasingly severe threat landscape in Southeast Asia. The Mandiant M-Trends 2025 report, covering incidents from 2024, highlights a marked increase in financially motivated cyber threat activity globally. For the Asia-Pacific region, including Southeast Asia, the use of exploits as an initial infection vector was nearly double the global average, indicating a strong focus by attackers on exploiting vulnerabilities at scale (Mandiant, 2025). Advanced persistent threat (APT) groups, particularly those with ties to China, were observed deploying custom malware and targeting edge devices. Kaspersky reports from 2024 and early 2025 paint a similarly concerning picture. Over 53 million bruteforce attacks targeting Remote Desktop Protocol (RDP) were detected and blocked in the region throughout 2024, averaging more than 145,000 attempts daily (Williams, 2025). Indonesia and Malaysia saw significant increases in these attacks, with rises of 25% and 14% respectively compared to 2023 (Williams, 2025). Additionally, nearly 50 million on-device malware attacks, often spread via compromised USB drives, were detected in SEA businesses in 2024, a 15% increase from 2023 (Shahrizal, 2025).

The pervasive issue of online scam operations has also reached crisis levels. These operations, often run by transnational criminal networks from centers in countries including Cambodia, Myanmar, Laos, and the Philippines, involve the trafficking of hundreds of thousands of individuals forced to carry out online fraud (UN News, 2025). The financial and human costs are immense, prompting high-level ASEAN attention, as evidenced by the Vientiane Declaration on Enhancing Law Enforcement Cooperation in Combating Transnational Crime, adopted at the 43rd ASEAN Summit (ASEAN Secretariat, 2024a). This evolving threat landscape underscores the urgency for ASEAN to move beyond technical fixes towards addressing cybersecurity as a systemic economic and social threat.

Table 1. Key ASEAN Summit and Ministerial Outcomes on Cybersecurity (2017-2025)

Year	Summit Name/ Location or Ministerial Meeting	Declaration/Initiative Reference	Cybersecurity Focus Area	Key Outcomes/Commitments
2017	31st ASEAN Summit, Manila	ASEAN Declaration to Prevent and Combat Cybercrime	Cybercrime, regional cooperation	Commitment to enhance cooperation in preventing and combating cybercrime, including information sharing and capacity building; Endorsement of ASEAN Cybersecurity Cooperation Strategy.
2018	33rd ASEAN Summit, Singapore	Chairman's Statement	Cybersecurity as a key security challenge, CBMs	Reaffirmed commitment to implement the ASEAN Cybersecurity Cooperation Strategy; Called for strengthening ARF CBMs.
2021	38th/39th ASEAN Summits (Virtual, Brunei Darussalam)	Chairman's Statement	Endorsement of new strategies, critical infrastructure protection	Endorsed the ASEAN Cybersecurity Cooperation Strategy 2021-2025; Stressed importance of protecting critical information infrastructure.

continued on following page

Table 1. Continued

Year	Summit Name/ Location or Ministerial Meeting	Declaration/Initiative Reference	Cybersecurity Focus Area	Key Outcomes/Commitments
2023	43rd ASEAN Summit, Jakarta	Vientiane Declaration on Enhancing Law Enforcement Cooperation in Combating Transnational Crime	Combating online job scams and related transnational crime	Commitment to strengthen cooperation against online job scams and other cyber-enabled transnational crimes.
2025	5th ASEAN Digital Ministers' Meeting (ADGMIN), Bangkok	Joint Media Statement	Regional CERT operationalization, anti-online scam measures, submarine cable security, implementation of cyber norms	Lauded progress of ASEAN Regional CERT; Welcomed ASEAN Recommendations on Anti-Online Scams; Established Working Group on Submarine Cables (WG-SC); Acknowledged endorsement of ASEAN Checklist for Implementation of Norms of Responsible State Behaviour in Cyberspace. (ASEAN Secretariat, 2025b)

Note: This table is illustrative and populated with specific details from cited Summit and Ministerial documents.

A cornerstone of ASEAN's regional approach is the ASEAN Cybersecurity Co-operation Strategy (ACCS) 2021-2025, which outlines key pillars for cooperation: policy coordination, capacity building, research and development, norm promotion, and engagement with Dialogue Partners (ASEAN Secretariat, 2021b). Progress under the ACCS includes efforts to enhance regional cyber readiness through initiatives like the ASEAN Regional CERT. The 5th ADGMIN in January 2025 lauded the progress of the Regional CERT, launched in 2024 and coordinated by Malaysia, towards becoming fully operational (Crowell Global Advisors, 2025). Its mandate is to strengthen region-wide cyber resilience by providing a platform for information sharing, cyber exercises, and capacity building. However, its ultimate effectiveness will heavily depend on overcoming persistent challenges related to trust, reluctance in information sharing due to sovereignty concerns, and the significant disparities in national CERT capacities (Mahusin & Prilliadi, 2024).

From a critical security perspective, ASEAN's state-centric approach reveals significant gaps. The focus on protecting state systems and critical infrastructure, while important, often underemphasizes the human security dimension of cyber-security (DCAF, 2024). The explosion of online scams, for example, is not just a form of cybercrime but a "human rights crisis" that inflicts devastating financial and psychological harm on millions of citizens (UN News, 2025). Similarly, while ASEAN has made efforts to adopt norms of responsible state behavior in cyberspace, these high-level declarations often prioritize inter-state stability with less emphasis on protecting citizens' digital rights, such as freedom of expression and privacy, from state surveillance or censorship enacted in the name of security (DCAF, 2024; Media Defence, 2025).

This conceptual framing helps explain the "implementation deficit" often observed between aspirational Summit declarations and on-the-ground realities. The gap is not merely a function of limited resources or political will; it stems from a strategic misalignment. By defining security too narrowly, regional frameworks may fail to address the most pervasive threats to ASEAN's populace and can even be used to justify measures that undermine human security. This deficit is exacerbated by the non-binding nature of many agreements and the principle of non-interference, which limit the ability of regional bodies to enforce or monitor implementation (Mahusin & Prilliadi, 2024).4

4.1. The Dual Role of the Private Sector and Civil Society

The cybersecurity landscape is further complicated by the dual role of non-state actors. Private technology companies are indispensable partners, providing the infrastructure, services, and expertise necessary for a functioning digital economy. However, they are also potential sources of vulnerability, and their platforms can be vectors for cyber threats. Simultaneously, civil society organizations are crucial for monitoring how cybersecurity laws and policies impact digital rights. They advocate for a rights-respecting approach to security, often highlighting instances where vague legal language is used to suppress dissent or conduct surveillance, thereby acting as a watchdog against the potential for state overreach in the name of cybersecurity (Manushya Foundation, n.d.; Media Defence, 2025). A multi-pronged approach that engages both state and non-state actors is therefore imperative for developing efficient and transparent cybersecurity strategies that respect human rights (DCAF, 2024).

Table 2. Comparative Snapshot of Cyber Incidents and Reported Readiness in Selected ASEAN Member States (2024-2025)

ASEAN Member State	Major Reported Cyber Incidents/Threats (2024-2025)	Key National Cybersecurity Focus/ Initiatives (2024-2025)
Indonesia	Significant increase (25%) in RDP bruteforce attacks in 2024 (Williams, 2025); High volume of online scam operations.	Focus on implementing PDP Law; Combating online scams; National cybersecurity strategy implementation.
Malaysia	Notable increase (14%) in RDP bruteforce attacks in 2024 (Williams, 2025); 47% surge in offline malware attacks in 2024 (Shahrizal, 2025); High volume of online scam operations.	Strengthening national CERT; Active role in regional cybersecurity initiatives (e.g., ASEAN Regional CERT coordination); Combating online scams.
Philippines	Over 80% of organizations faced avg. 3 breaches in 2024; 315,000+ credentials compromised H1 2024 (PhilSec Summit, 2024).	Implementation of National Cybersecurity Plan (NCSP) 2023-2028; Addressing data breaches and phishing; Combating online scams. (PhilSec Summit, 2024)
Singapore	Highest surge (88%) in offline malware attacks in SEA in 2024 (Shahrizal, 2025).	Advanced cybersecurity measures; Focus on critical infrastructure protection; International cooperation; Leading ASEAN WG-AI which has safety implications.
Thailand	20% increase in offline malware attacks in 2024 (Shahrizal, 2025); Target of international scam rings (e.g., $60M medical equipment scam bust May 2025) (Khaosod English, 2025).	Law enforcement actions against cybercrime and scam operations; Implementation of PDPA.
Vietnam	25% increase in offline malware attacks in 2024 (Shahrizal, 2025); Targeted by international scam rings (Khaosod English, 2025).	Strengthening cybersecurity frameworks as part of national digital transformation; Combating online fraud.

Note: This table synthesizes information from various reports. "Online scam operations" refers to reports of scam centers operating in or transiting through these countries.

4.2. ASEAN's AI Landscape and Governance Debates

Artificial Intelligence stands as a transformative technology with profound implications for economic development, societal structures, and international relations. ASEAN, recognizing both the immense potential and the inherent complexities of AI, has begun to chart its regional approach, with Summits serving as crucial platforms for shaping cooperation and guiding policy development. The year 2025 is particularly significant, witnessing the launch of expanded regional AI governance guidelines and a flurry of national AI strategy advancements.

A landmark development in ASEAN's approach to AI governance was the release of the ASEAN Guide on AI Governance and Ethics in February 2024 (ASEAN Secretariat, 2024b) [10], followed swiftly by the Expanded ASEAN Guide on AI Governance and Ethics - Generative AI in January 2025 (ASEAN Secretariat, 2025a). This rapid expansion to address Generative AI (GenAI) indicates that the disruptive potential of these new models is compelling ASEAN to be more responsive in its governance efforts. The discussions at ADGMIN 2025 reportedly shifted from *whether* to adopt AI to *how* to adopt it responsibly, with a particular focus on establishing safety measures for GenAI (Crowell Global Advisors, 2025).

The ASEAN AI Guides are founded on seven key principles: Transparency and Explainability; Fairness and Equity; Security and Safety; Human-centricity; Privacy and Data Governance; Accountability and Integrity; and Robustness and Reliability (ASEAN Secretariat, 2024b; Rajah & Tann Asia, 2025). The 2025 GenAI expansion specifically addresses risks such as hallucinations, disinformation, deepfakes, infringement of intellectual property rights, privacy concerns, and the propagation of embedded biases (ASEAN Secretariat, 2025a). It provides policy recommendations across nine ecosystem dimensions, including accountability, data, trusted development, incident reporting, testing, and security (ASEAN Secretariat, 2025a).

Crucially, the ASEAN AI Guides adopt a voluntary, risk-based, and technology- and sector-agnostic approach (ASEAN Secretariat, 2024b; Carnicelli et al., 2025). They are intended as practical resources for member states and organizations, seeking to foster innovation while managing risks, rather than imposing stringent regulations akin to the EU AI Act (Hamzah, 2024; ASEAN Secretariat, 2025d).[14] This pragmatic "middle path" reflects ASEAN's desire to accommodate the diverse levels of AI readiness across its member states and to avoid stifling nascent AI industries (Hamzah, 2024). While this flexibility could enable faster AI adoption, its voluntary nature raises questions about ensuring consistent ethical safeguards and accountability mechanisms across the region (Saleem, 2025).

While ASEAN develops regional guidelines, individual member states are concurrently formulating and implementing their own national AI strategies. By 2025, nearly all member states have either launched formal strategies or are in advanced stages of developing them. However, these national approaches exhibit significant diversity in terms of focus, maturity, and governance mechanisms, making true regional harmonization a considerable challenge (Prilliadi, 2025; Nettel et al., 2024; Prastyo, 2024). This "multi-speed ASEAN" in AI could exacerbate the existing digital divide and hinder the creation of a seamless regional AI market (Isono & Prilliadi, 2023).

4.3. The 'Super App' Ecosystem: Private Sector as Driver and Governance Challenge

A critical analysis reveals a significant disconnect between ASEAN's top-down, state-led AI governance approach and the bottom-up, market-driven reality of AI deployment. The primary vectors for AI adoption in the daily lives of millions of ASEAN citizens are not government programs but the region's powerful "super apps" like Grab and Gojek (Rahmat et al., 2024). These platforms, which began as ride-hailing services, have evolved into comprehensive ecosystems offering transportation, food delivery, logistics, and financial services, effectively becoming a form of de facto digital public infrastructure (Khan, 2024). They deploy AI at a massive scale for logistics optimization, demand prediction, and personalized marketing. This presents a profound governance challenge: the data collection practices, algorithmic fairness, and labor market impacts of these privately-owned ecosystems are often moving far faster than national or regional regulations can address. The voluntary, principles-based regional AI guides are largely insufficient to govern these powerful, data-intensive platforms, creating a significant gap where market forces, rather than public policy, dictate the rules of AI engagement for a vast portion of the population.

Table 3. Updated Overview of ASEAN Member States' National AI Strategies/ Policies (Status as of mid-2025)

ASEAN Member State	Official National AI Strategy/Policy Document Name	Year of Publication/ Adoption (Latest Update)	Key Stated Priorities	Key Governance Approach
Brunei Darussalam	Guide on AI Governance and Ethics for Brunei Darussalam; National AI Strategy (planned)	AI Guide: April 2024; National Strategy: Announced May 2025, in development	Ethical & responsible AI, transparency, security, fairness, data protection, human-centricity, accountability.	Voluntary AI guidelines referencing ASEAN Guide; Risk-based, tech/ sector agnostic.
Cambodia	Digital Economy and Society Policy Framework 2021-2035; National AI Strategy (in development)	Framework: 2021; National Strategy: Development ongoing as of March 2025	Productivity, research, human capital, digital infra, int'l cooperation, public sector AI, ethics.	Policy framework approach; Unified approach to guide AI development towards national objectives.
Indonesia	National Strategy for Artificial Intelligence (Stranas KI) 2020-2045; National AI Roadmap	Stranas KI: 2020; AI Roadmap: August 2025	Health, bureaucracy reform, education & research, food security, mobility & smart cities, ethics & data privacy.	Sector-specific focus; Multi-stakeholder consultation; Flexible, incentive-based regulations planned.
Malaysia	National AI Roadmap 2021-2025 (Phase 1); AI Technology Action Plan 2026-2030 (in development)	Roadmap: 2021; Action Plan: In development	AI talent, AI adoption in key sectors (SMEs, traffic, finance, agriculture), ethical AI, innovation, public sector AI adoption.	National AI Office (NAIO) coordinating; Public-private partnerships; AI Code of Ethics; AI Adoption Regulatory Framework.

continued on following page

Table 3. Continued

ASEAN Member State	Official National AI Strategy/Policy Document Name	Year of Publication/ Adoption (Latest Update)	Key Stated Priorities	Key Governance Approach
Philippines	National AI Strategy for the Philippines (NAIS-PH) (approved May 2025); National AI Strategy Roadmap 2.0 (NAISR 2.0)	NAIS-PH: May 2025, NAISR 2.0: July 2024	Inclusive AI innovation, governance, competitive industries (agri, edu, smart cities, creative, nat'l security).	DOST-led NAIS-PH; DTI's NAISR 2.0; AI Factory & Refinery; HPC expansion; AI Hub (i-Hub).
Singapore	National AI Strategy (NAIS)	2019 (updated periodically, e.g., NAIS 2.0)	Economic transformation, talent development, industry adoption (finance, healthcare), ethics & governance, global AI hub.	Innovation-focused, ethics-embedded, sector-specific strategies; Strong government support and investment; Leads ASEAN WG-AI.
Vietnam	National Strategy on R&D and Application of AI to 2030; "AI for All" program	Strategy: 2021; "Al for All": April 2025	Make Viet Nam an AI innovation hub, develop AI applications, build AI workforce, ethical AI.	State-led investment, legal framework development; "Al for All" program; Focus on AI literacy.

Source: Synthesized from multiple reports. Note: The level of detail and formalization of AI strategies varies significantly across member states.

5. ANALYZING SPECIFIC SUMMIT OUTCOMES AND REGIONAL DYNAMICS IN 2025

ASEAN's engagement with networked diplomacy, cybersecurity, and AI is not a series of isolated endeavors but rather a complex interplay of interconnected issues. These intersections are often brought into sharp focus through specific Summit-endorsed initiatives and the prevailing regional dynamics. This section delves into particular case studies and cross-cutting themes that illustrate these interdependencies, particularly in the 2025 context.

5.1. The ASEAN Digital Economy Framework Agreement (DEFA)

DEFA is arguably the most significant and ambitious digital initiative undertaken by ASEAN. Negotiations were officially launched in September 2023 and are targeted for conclusion by the end of 2025, a key deliverable reiterated at the 5th ADGMIN (ASEAN Secretariat, 2025b; The ASEAN Magazine, 2024). It aims to be the world's first region-wide, legally binding agreement focused exclusively on digital economy governance, distinguishing it from digital trade chapters embedded in broader free trade agreements (Hourn, 2025; Lee et al., 2025). The core objective of DEFA is to create a seamless and integrated ASEAN digital economy, projected to double in value to $2 trillion by 2030 (Hourn, 2025). It covers nine core elements: digital trade, cybersecurity, digital ID, digital payments, cross-border data flows, emerging technologies, talent mobility, and competition policy (Said & Nabilah, 2024).

Despite its transformative potential, DEFA negotiations face substantial challenges. These include harmonizing diverse national regulations, bridging significant gaps in digital development, ensuring inclusive benefits, and navigating sensitivities around data sovereignty and national security (Prilliadi 2025; Honey, 2025).[29] The "ASEAN Way" of consensus-based decision-making could also lead to compromises that dilute the agreement's ambitious scope.[7] Robust implementation mechanisms, including monitoring and effective dispute settlement procedures, will be critical to ensure DEFA delivers on its promises (Elsig & Polanco Lazo., 2025).

Table 4. Key Provisions and Negotiating Status of the ASEAN Digital Economy Framework Agreement (DEFA) (as of mid-2025)

Core DEFA Pillar/Chapter	Key Provisions & Objectives	Negotiating Status (General Outlook for late 2025)	Anticipated Impact Areas
Digital Trade & E-commerce	Facilitate cross-border e-commerce, paperless trading, streamlined customs procedures, consumer protection. Objective: Boost intra-ASEAN digital trade.	Negotiations ongoing; focus on harmonizing rules and reducing non-tariff barriers. Targeted for conclusion by end of 2025.	Increased e-commerce volume, easier market access for MSMEs, reduced trade friction, enhanced consumer trust.
Cross-Border Data Flows & Data Governance	Establish rules for trusted and secure cross-border data flows, promote data protection standards, address data localization issues. Objective: Balance data-driven innovation with privacy and security.	Highly sensitive area; negotiations aim for common principles while respecting national regulations. Progress on ASEAN MCCs is a positive step.	Facilitate regional data-driven services (cloud, AI), potential for harmonized data privacy standards, challenges with diverse national laws.
Cybersecurity	Enhance regional cybersecurity cooperation, establish common baseline security standards for digital platforms, incident response coordination. Objective: Build a secure and resilient regional digital environment.	Active discussions, linking to ACCS and Regional CERT efforts. Focus on trust and security for digital transactions.	Improved collective defense against cyber threats, increased trust in digital services, protection of critical digital infrastructure.

Core DEFA Pillar/Chapter	Key Provisions & Objectives	Negotiating Status (General Outlook for late 2025)	Anticipated Impact Areas
Digital Payments & Financial Services	Promote interoperable cross-border digital payment systems, facilitate digital financial inclusion. Objective: Create a seamless regional digital payment landscape.	Building on existing bilateral QR code linkages. Strong momentum for integration.	Easier and cheaper cross-border transactions, increased financial inclusion, growth of fintech sector.
Emerging Technologies (e.g., AI, IoT)	Foster cooperation in the development and deployment of emerging technologies, promote ethical guidelines (linking to ASEAN AI Guides). Objective: Position ASEAN to leverage new tech for growth.	Discussions on principles and cooperation mechanisms. AI governance guides provide a foundation.	Accelerated adoption of AI and IoT, potential for regional innovation hubs, need for aligned ethical frameworks.

Note: This table is based on publicly available information and analyses regarding DEFA's scope and objectives as of mid-2025.

5.2. Cross-Border Data Flows, Data Sovereignty, and Data Governance

The burgeoning regional digital economy inherently relies on the seamless flow of data across borders. However, this imperative often clashes with national concerns regarding data security, privacy, and data sovereignty, the principle that data is subject to the laws of the nation where it is collected (Gunther, 2024). DEFA is central to this balancing act, aiming to establish common rules for trusted cross-border data flows (Hourn, 2025). Achieving this is complicated by the diverse national approaches to data protection and the growing trend of data localization, which is a key tenet of the broader push for digital sovereignty across the region (Rana & Azeez, 2025). As of early 2025, the landscape remains a patchwork. For instance, Indonesia's Personal Data Protection (PDP) Law officially came into full effect in October 2024, but the crucial PDP Body responsible for enforcement had not yet been established as of May 2025, hindering full implementation (TMT Law Practice, 2025). This regulatory divergence creates uncertainty and compliance burdens, and without greater harmonization, data localization pressures could fragment the envisioned regional digital market (Wilson, 2025).

5.3. The US-China Technological Competition

The pervasive influence of the US-China technological competition casts a long shadow over ASEAN's digital ambitions. This rivalry manifests in domains critical to the digital economy, including the rollout of 5G infrastructure, the setting of standards for AI, the security of subsea cables, and the promotion of competing norms for internet governance (Faizal & Teo, 2024; Lee, 2022; Rühlig & Seaman, 2019). ASEAN member states find themselves in a delicate geostrategic position, seeking to benefit from the technological advancements offered by both Washington and Beijing while striving to avoid being forced to choose sides (Faizal & Teo, 2024). This has led to a strategic balancing or hedging strategy.

Summit statements typically emphasize inclusivity, openness, and "ASEAN Centrality," welcoming cooperation with all partners while avoiding definitive public stances on contentious issues, such as the exclusion of particular vendors from national 5G networks (Faizal & Teo, 2024). While this hedging strategy can be seen as astute diplomacy, it also carries the risk of policy incoherence if member states adopt divergent national approaches to critical technology choices, potentially fragmenting the regional digital market and undermining the objectives of DEFA (Higgins et al., 2024).

5.4. ASEAN in the World: A Comparative View on Digital Governance

ASEAN's "middle path" is not just a reaction to US-China rivalry but also a deliberate positioning relative to other global governance models. A comparative analysis highlights the distinctiveness of its approach.

The European Union (EU): The EU represents a rights-based, regulatory-heavy model. Its landmark Digital Services Act (DSA) and Digital Markets Act (DMA) aim to create a safer digital space and a fairer, more contestable market (European Commission, n.d.; European Parliament, 2021). The DSA imposes strict content moderation and transparency obligations on platforms to protect users from illegal content, while the DMA targets large "gatekeeper" platforms with a list of "do's and don'ts" to prevent anti-competitive behavior (AlgorithmWatch, 2023). This approach prioritizes regulation and fundamental rights, standing in stark contrast to ASEAN's voluntary, innovation-first orientation.

The African Union (AU): As another Global South bloc, the AU's Digital Transformation Strategy for Africa (2020-2030) offers a useful comparison. It shares many of ASEAN's goals, such as creating a Digital Single Market, bridging the digital divide, and fostering inclusive growth (African Union, 2020). However, a key emphasis of the AU's strategy is on ensuring "African ownership" of digital tools and management, reflecting a strong post-colonial desire for digital self-determination (African Union, 2020). This positions ASEAN's efforts within a broader Global South movement, though ASEAN's approach has been more focused on economic integration and less explicit in its rhetoric of digital sovereignty compared to some of its African counterparts. This comparative context reveals that ASEAN's soft governance is a strategic choice to prioritize rapid economic growth and accommodate internal diversity, even at the potential cost of regulatory coherence and robust rights protections.

6. NAVIGATING CHALLENGES AND OPPORTUNITIES IN ASEAN'S DIGITAL FUTURE

As ASEAN strides further into the digital age, particularly beyond the critical juncture of 2025, its pursuit of a digitally integrated future is characterized by a complex interplay of significant challenges and substantial opportunities. The effectiveness with which the region navigates these complexities will largely determine its trajectory in the global digital landscape.

6.1. The Persistent Digital Divide

A primary and fundamental challenge is the persistent digital divide, which exists not only among ASEAN member states but also significantly within them. Disparities in internet access, digital literacy, affordability, and the quality of digital infrastructure are stark. While some ASEAN nations boast high connectivity rates, others lag considerably, particularly in rural and underserved communities (Sefrina, 2024). This divide is more than a technical gap; it is a structural issue of digital justice that reflects and reinforces deeper socio-economic inequalities (Haidar et al, 2025).

Crucially, access alone is insufficient. Digital literacy, encompassing the skills to effectively use, critically evaluate, and safely navigate the digital environment, is a vital and often overlooked component of digital readiness (Fong, 2025). Research shows that even among tech-savvy youth, there are significant gaps in the ability to discern misinformation and protect against cyber threats (Fong, 2025). The failure to address this literacy gap is not merely a social issue but a fundamental threat to ASEAN's entire digital economy ambition. A region with a large, digitally under-skilled population cannot sustain a $2 trillion digital economy, becomes more vulnerable to cyber threats like scams and disinformation, and risks exacerbating inequalities that could lead to social and political instability. Therefore, digital literacy is not a "soft" issue but a core component of both economic and human security.

Table 5. Key Digital Development Indicators for ASEAN Member States (Latest available 2023-2025 data)

ASEAN Member State	Internet Penetration (% of pop., Jan 2024)	Mobile Connections (per 100 inhab., Jan 2024)	AI Readiness Index (Oxford Insights, 2024 Rank)	Cybersecurity Index (ITU GCI, Latest Score)
Brunei Darussalam	119.7% (DataReportal, 2024a) [35]	~130-140 (Est.)	Not Specified	High (Est.)
Cambodia	76.9% (DataReportal, 2024c)	~120 (Est.)	Not Specified	37.1/100 (2024) (World Bank, n.d.-c)
Indonesia	66.5% (DataReportal, 2024b)	126.8 (DataReportal, 2024b)	Not Specified	94.88/100 (2020, improvement noted by 2024) (Matondang, 2025)
Lao PDR	~50-60% (Est.)	~70-80 (Est.)	Not Specified	Low-Moderate (Est.)
Malaysia	97.4% (DataReportal, 2024d)	~140-150 (Est.)	Not Specified	Moderate-High (Est.)
Myanmar	~40-50% (Est.)	~90-100 (Est.)	Not Specified	Low (Est.)
Philippines	73.6% (DataReportal, 2024e)	99.3 (DataReportal, 2024e)	56th (up from 65th) (OpenGovAsia, 2025b; Nettel, 2024)	Moderate (Est.)
Singapore	97.6% (DataReportal, 2024f)	~150-160 (Est.)	Top Global Performer	Very High (Consistently top ranks)
Thailand	88.0% (DataReportal, 2024g)	~130-140 (Est.)	Not Specified	Moderate-High (Est.)
Vietnam	79.1% (DataReportal, 2024h)	169.8 (DataReportal, 2024h)	Not Specified	Moderate (Est.)

Note: This table compiles data from various sources. "Est." indicates estimates based on regional/income group averages or general knowledge when specific 2024-2025 data is not available. DataReportal figures often source from ITU, GSMA Intelligence, and other platforms.

Harmonization of Legal and Regulatory Frameworks

Further complicating the regional landscape are the significant disparities in legal and regulatory frameworks for cyber and AI across member states. While ASEAN has made strides in developing regional guidelines, the harmonization of national laws remains a slow and arduous process. The development of the ASEAN Digital Masterplan 2030 (ADM2030), led by Vietnam in 2025, presents a critical opportunity to chart a more cohesive and effectively resourced digital future (ASEAN Secretariat, 2025c). A key challenge for ADM2030 will be securing sustainable funding and establishing robust capacity-building mechanisms. Many ASEAN member states face competing development priorities and may lack the financial capacity to fully invest in cutting-edge digital infrastructure or ambitious AI research programs.

6.2. The "ASEAN Way" Revisited and Strategic Opportunities

The foundational principle of national sovereignty and the "ASEAN Way" of consensus-based decision-making continue to present challenges for achieving timely and effective governance in the fast-evolving digital domain. The ASEAN Community Vision 2045 explicitly calls for strengthening ASEAN's institutions to be more "resilient, innovative, agile, adaptive, responsive, and decisive" in addressing cross-cutting issues, implicitly acknowledging the need for an evolution in how ASEAN operates (ASEAN Secretariat, 2025d).

Despite these hurdles, ASEAN possesses significant opportunities. The region boasts a large, youthful, and increasingly digitally savvy population, representing a substantial potential digital consumer base and a dynamic workforce. The digital economy in Southeast Asia is already experiencing rapid expansion, offering vast avenues for inclusive growth and job creation (World Bank, n.d.-a; Beirne & Fernandez, 2021). A crucial opportunity lies in ASEAN's potential to develop common positions on global digital governance issues, thereby increasing the region's collective influence. The principle of "ASEAN Centrality," consistently reaffirmed at Summits, faces a significant test in the digital domain. The region's ability to act as a cohesive and influential player will depend critically on its capacity to overcome internal fragmentation and develop unified positions on key issues.

7. CONCLUSION

ASEAN's journey into the digital age, significantly steered and articulated through its Summits and ministerial bodies like ADGMIN, reflects a region grappling with transformative technologies amidst a complex geopolitical landscape and diverse internal capacities. This analysis has shown a clear and growing recognition at the highest political levels of the centrality of digital issues to ASEAN's future prosperity, security, and regional identity, as enshrined in the aspirations of the ASEAN

Community Vision 2045: a "resilient, innovative, dynamic and people-centred ASEAN" (ASEAN Secretariat, 2025d).

ASEAN has made notable progress in establishing a foundational architecture for regional digital cooperation. Key achievements include the formulation of comprehensive strategies such as the ASEAN Digital Masterplan 2025, the ASEAN Cybersecurity Cooperation Strategy 2021-2025, and the forward-looking ASEAN AI Governance Guides. The negotiation of the ambitious ASEAN Digital Economy Framework Agreement (DEFA) stands as a testament to the region's aspiration for deeper digital integration.

However, the path is fraught with persistent challenges that go beyond mere technical or capacity gaps. The "implementation deficit" between high-level commitments and tangible progress is not just a matter of will but often reflects a conceptual misalignment in state-centric security approaches that overlook human security (Mahusin & Prilliadi, 2024). The deep-seated digital divide, if not addressed through a concerted focus on digital literacy and inclusion, threatens to undermine the very foundations of the digital economy (Sefrina, 2024). The traditional "ASEAN Way," while a cornerstone of regional stability, can constrain the agility required to govern the rapid pace of digital change. Furthermore, the region's digital transformation is unfolding within a global structure that raises legitimate concerns about digital colonialism, forcing ASEAN to navigate a difficult path toward digital sovereignty while managing its dependence on foreign technology ecosystems (Faizal & Teo, 2024; Li et al., 2025).

ASEAN Summits will undoubtedly remain the apex for political endorsement and strategic direction-setting in the digital domain. They provide the indispensable political will required to advance major regional initiatives. However, the analysis also underscores the increasing criticality of empowered and agile sub-Summit mechanisms. Sectoral bodies like ADGMIN, along with their associated working groups (such as the WG-AI and WG-SC), have emerged as the engine rooms for developing technical standards and operationalizing strategies. The effectiveness of ASEAN's digital agenda will increasingly depend on the capacity of these bodies to translate broad political commitments into concrete and rapidly adaptable policy actions.

The year 2025, with major initiatives like DEFA and ADM2030 development coming to the fore, represents a critical juncture where ASEAN's ability to address these structural gaps will be severely tested. ASEAN Summits will undoubtedly remain the apex for political endorsement, but the analysis underscores the increasing criticality of empowered and agile sub-Summit mechanisms. Sectoral bodies like ADGMIN and their associated working groups have emerged as the engine rooms for operationalizing strategies. Their effectiveness will depend on their capacity to translate broad political commitments into adaptable policy actions that account for the complex interplay of state interests, powerful private sector actors, and the rights of citizens. To secure its digital future, ASEAN must evolve its governance model beyond adopting frameworks toward building a more adaptive, multi-stakeholder ecosystem.

To strengthen its digital future and bridge the gap between vision and implementation, ASEAN should adopt a more inclusive and adaptive approach to regional digital governance. First, by establishing a Multi-Stakeholder Digital Advisory Group, ASEAN can institutionalize collaboration among the private sector, academia, and civil society, ensuring that ADGMIN and DEFA processes are informed by real-world technical, market, and human rights expertise. Second, digital literacy must be elevated as a core economic and security priority, with ADM2030 dedicating ring-fenced funding to accessible, region-wide programs that empower all social groups, especially vulnerable and rural communities. Third, ASEAN should embrace flexible cooperation mechanisms, such as the ASEAN Minus X formula, to enable willing members to advance on critical issues like cross-border cybersecurity, data protection, and transnational online crime. Finally, to uphold its "people-centered" principle, ASEAN should develop a Regional Human Rights Impact Assessment Framework that ensures all major digital initiatives, such as DEFA and AI-driven public services, are transparently evaluated for privacy, freedom of expression, and algorithmic fairness, with clear mitigation strategies guiding implementation.

Looking forward, ASEAN has the potential to carve out a distinctive regional approach to digital governance. However, its ability to do so, and to truly realize the principle of "ASEAN Centrality" in the digital age, will depend on its capacity to overcome the implementation deficit, bridge the digital divide, and adapt its traditional decision-making processes. If it can effectively assert its collective voice and advance common regional interests in global digital governance forums, ASEAN will not only determine its own future in the digital age but also contribute significantly to shaping a more balanced, inclusive, and stable global digital order in the 21st century.

REFERENCES

Access Now. (n.d.). About Us. Retrieved September 26, 2025, from https://www.accessnow.org/about-us/

Acharya, A. (2011). *Whose ideas matter? Agency and power in Asian regionalism.* Cornell University Press.

African Union. (2020). *The Digital Transformation Strategy for Africa.* African Union.

AlgorithmWatch. (2023). The Digital Services Act (DSA) explained. https://algorithmwatch.org/en/dsa-explained/

Beirne, J., & Fernandez, D. (Eds.). (2021). *Harnessing digitalization for sustainable economic development: Insights for Asia* (ADB Institute Book No. 23). Asian Development Bank Institute. https://www.adb.org/publications/harnessing-digitalization-sustainable-economic-development

Carnicelli, L., Valentina, M., & Zoromski, C. (2025, April 30). *Brunei releases voluntary AI guidelines to enhance responsibility and trust. US-ASEAN Business Council.* https://www.usasean.org/article/brunei-releases-voluntary-ai-guidelines-enhance-responsibility-and-trust

Chagnon, C. W., Durante, F., Gills, B. K., Hagolani-Albov, S. E., Hokkanen, S., Kangasluoma, S. M. J., Konttinen, H., Kröger, M., LaFleur, W., Ollinaho, O., & Vuola, M. P. S. (2022). From extractivism to global extractivism: The evolution of an organizing concept. *The Journal of Peasant Studies*, *49*(4), 760–792. DOI: 10.1080/03066150.2022.2069015

Couldry, N., & Mejias, U. A. (2022). *The cost of connection: How data is colonizing human life and appropriating it for capitalism.* Stanford University Press.

Crowell Global Advisors. (2025, January 28). *5th ASEAN Digital Ministers' Meeting: Supercharging ASEAN's growth story with AI [Client alert].* Crowell & Moring LLP. Retrieved from https://www.crowell.com/en/insights/client-alerts/5th-asean-digital-ministers-meeting-supercharging-aseans-growth-story-with-ai

DataReportal. (2024a). *Digital 2024: Brunei Darussalam.* https://datareportal.com/reports/digital-2024-brunei-darussalam

DataReportal. (2024b). *Digital 2024: Indonesia.* https://datareportal.com/reports/digital-2024-indonesia

DataReportal. (2024c). *Digital 2024: Cambodia.* https://datareportal.com/reports/digital-2024-cambodia

DataReportal. (2024d). *Digital 2024: Malaysia.* https://datareportal.com/reports/digital-2024-malaysia

DataReportal. (2024e). *Digital 2024: Philippines.* https://datareportal.com/reports/digital-2024-philippines

DataReportal. (2024f). *Digital 2024: Singapore.* https://datareportal.com/reports/digital-2024-singapore

DataReportal. (2024g). *Digital 2024: Thailand.* https://datareportal.com/reports/digital-2024-thailand

DataReportal. (2024h). *Digital 2024: Vietnam.* https://datareportal.com/reports/digital-2024-vietnam

DCAF. (2024). *Cybersecurity governance in Southeast Asia.* https://www.dcaf.ch/sites/default/files/publications/documents/Cybersecurity_Governance_in_Southeast_Asia_Thematic_Brief.pdf

Di Riscio, R. A. (2025). *Digital Detente: The Weaponization of AI and LLMs in US-China Geopolitics, 2022-2025.* ResearchGate. https://www.researchgate.net/publication/389944211_Digital_Detente_The_Weaponization_of_AI_and_LLMs_in_US-China_Geopolitics_2022-2025

Elsig, M., & Polanco Lazo, R. (2025, April 23). *Implementation options for ASEAN's Digital Economy Framework Agreement. World Economic Forum.* Retrieved from https://www.weforum.org/stories/2025/04/implementation-lessons-for-asean-s-digital-economy-framework/

EngageMedia. (n.d.). *Digital Rights.* Retrieved September 26, 2025, from https://engagemedia.org/digitalrights/

European Commission. (n.d.). *The Digital Markets Act.* Retrieved September 26, 2025, from https://commission.europa.eu/strategy-and-policy/priorities-2019-2024/europe-fit-digital-age/digital-markets-act-ensuring-fair-and-open-digital-markets_en

European Parliament. (2021, December 9). *EU Digital Markets Act and Digital Services Act explained.* https://www.europarl.europa.eu/pdfs/news/expert/2021/12/story/20211209STO19124/20211209STO19124_en.pdf

Faizal, M., & Teo, S. (2024). ASEAN Digital Transformation and the US–China Technological Competition. In *Strategic Currents* (pp. 67–90). China and US Competition for Influence., DOI: 10.1142/9789811288081_0004

Floridi, L., Cath, C., & Taddeo, M. (2019). Digital ethics: Its nature and scope. In C. Öhman & D. Watson (Eds.), *The 2018 Yearbook of the Digital Ethics Lab* (pp. 9-17). Springer. DOI: 10.1007/978-3-030-17152-0_2

Floridi, L., & Taddeo, M. (Eds.). (2025). *A Companion to Digital Ethics*. Wiley-Blackwell. DOI: 10.1002/9781394240821

Fong, K. S. L. (2025, September 26). *Digital literacy vital for enhancing ASEAN's digital integration agenda.* Fulcrum. https://fulcrum.sg/digital-literacy-vital-for-enhancing-aseans-digital-integration-agenda/

Gunther, M. (2024, March 5). Digital sovereignty in ASEAN. PublicAffairsAsia. https://ps-engage.com/digital-sovereignty-in-asea/

Haidar, A., Pigatto, J., Karczeski, L., & Wanjiru, M. B. (2025, July 17). *How do we build for the Global South?* Paradigm Initiative. Retrieved from https://paradigmhq.org/how-do-we-build-for-the-global-south/

Hamzah, H. (2024). *A comparative review of the EU AI Act and the ASEAN AI Guide*. KPMG. Retrieved from https://kpmg.com/xx/en/our-insights/ai-and-technology/eu-ai-act-and-the-asean-ai-guide.html

Higgins, S., Dai, C., Woo, T., Dickerson, D., & Maisto, D. (2024*). Navigating the geopolitical cloud: ASEAN's diverse approach to digital sovereignty. Forrester.* https://www.forrester.com/blogs/navigating-the-geopolitical-cloud-aseans-diverse-approach-to-digital-sovereignty/

Honey, S. (2025, February 11). *Navigating digital trade fragmentation in the age of geo-economics*. The Hinrich Foundation. Retrieved from https://www.hinrichfoundation.com/research/article/digital/navigating-digital-trade-fragmentation-in-the-age-of-geoeconomics/

Hourn, K. K. (2025, May 26). *Why ASEAN's new Digital Economy Framework Agreement is a game-changer. World Economic Forum.* Retrieved from https://www.weforum.org/stories/2025/05/asean-digital-economy-framework-agreement-a-gamechanger/

Internet Governance Project. (2018). *Internet governance in the Global South.* https://nupri.prp.usp.br/internet-governance-in-the-global-south/

Isono, I., & Prilliadi, H. (2023, November). *Accelerating artificial intelligence discussions in ASEAN: Addressing disparities, challenges, and regional policy imperatives* (ERIA Discussion Paper Series No. 488). Economic Research Institute for ASEAN and East Asia (ERIA). https://www.eria.org/uploads/Accelerating-AI-Discussions-in-ASEAN.pdf

Jones, D. M., & Smith, M. L. R. (2007). Making process, not progress: ASEAN and the evolving East Asian regional order. *International Security*, *32*(1), 148–184. DOI: 10.1162/isec.2007.32.1.148

Keohane, R. O., & Martin, L. L. (1995). The promise of institutionalist theory. *International Security*, *20*(1), 39–51. DOI: 10.2307/2539214

Khan, A. (2024, Oktober 3). Battle of the Super Apps: Gojek vs Grab - Who Comes Out On Top? Miracuves. Retrieved from https://miracuves.com/battle-of-the-super-apps-gojek-vs-grab/

Khaosod English. (2025, May 29). *Thai Police Crack Down on International Scam Ring After 5-Year Probe.* https://www.khaosodenglish.com/news/2025/05/29/thai-police-crack-down-on-international-scam-ring-after-5-year-probe/

Krause, K., & Williams, M. C. (Eds.). (1997). *Critical security studies: Concepts and cases.* University of Minnesota Press.

Kwet, M. (2019). Digital colonialism: US empire and the new imperialism in the Global South. *Race & Class*, *60*(4), 3–26. DOI: 10.1177/0306396818823172

Lee, B. T. F., Dinh, L. D., Sims, J. P., & Bettani, S. A. (2025). ASEAN Digital Economy Framework Agreement (DEFA): Implications for digital trade and regional economic integration. *Journal of Strategic and Global Studies*, *8*(1), 5. Advance online publication. DOI: 10.7454/jsgs.v8i1.1166

Lee, H. (2022, September 2). *The US–China 'standard-off' over technology.* East Asia Forum. Retrieved from https://eastasiaforum.org/2022/09/02/the-us-china-standard-off-over-technology/

Li, L., Abbas, S. T., Khan, G. R., & Ali, S. (2025). Competing narratives of technological sovereignty: A constructivist analysis of US-China AI diplomacy. *Contemporary Journal of Social Science Review*, *3*(2), 538–554. DOI: 10.12345/hwdr9b75

Mahusin, M., & Prilliadi, H. (2024). *Strengthening ASEAN's Cybersecurity: Collaborative Strategies for Enhanced Resilience and Regional Cooperation.* Economic Research Institute for ASEAN and East Asia (ERIA). https://www.eria.org/research/strengthening-asean-s-cybersecurity--collaborative-strategies-for-enhanced-resilience-and-regional-cooperation

Mandiant. (2025, April 24). *M-Trends 2025 Report (16th ed.).* Google Cloud. https://cloud.google.com/security/resources/m-trends

Manushya Foundation. (n.d.). *Digital Rights.* Retrieved September 26, 2025, from https://www.manushyafoundation.org/digital-rights

Matondang, N. R. A. (2025, February). *Analyzing the implication of ASEAN Cybersecurity Cooperation Strategy (ACCS) 2021–2025 in Indonesia's cyber regulations* [Conference paper, IMPACT 1.0: Innovative Models for Public Administration and Collaborative Digital Transformation]. Airlangga University. https://www.researchgate.net/publication/389039193_ANALYZING_THE_IMPLICATION_OF_ASEAN_CYBERSECURITY_COOPERATION_STRATEGY_ACCS_2021-2025_IN_INDONESIA'S_CYBER_REGULATIONS

Media Defence. (2025, January). Introduction to Digital Rights – South and Southeast Asia. https://www.mediadefence.org/resource-hub/introduction-to-digital-rights-south-and-southeast-asia/

Nettel, P. F., Hankins, E., Stirling, R., Cirri, G., Grau, G., Rahim, S., & Crampton, E. (2024, December 20). *Government AI Readiness Index 2024 (7th ed.).* Oxford Insights. https://oxfordinsights.com/wp-content/uploads/2024/12/2024-Government-AI-Readiness-Index-2.pdf

News, U. N. (2025, May 21). *Scam centres are a 'human rights crisis', independent experts warn.* https://news.un.org/en/story/2025/05/1163521

Nye, J. S.Jr. (2010). *Cyber Power.* Belfer Center for Science and International Affairs, Harvard Kennedy School.

OpenGovAsia. (2025b, May 22). *The Philippines President approves comprehensive AI roadmap.* https://opengovasia.com/2025/05/22/the-philippines-president-approves-comprehensive-ai-roadmap/

Peoples, C., & Vaughan-Williams, N. (2021). *Critical security studies: An introduction* (3rd ed.). Routledge.

PhilSec Summit. (2024). *The alarming state of cybersecurity in the Philippines: Trends and insights from 2024.* Retrieved from https://www.philsecsummit.com/the-alarming-state-of-cybersecurity-in-the-philippines-trends-and-insights-from-2024/

Prastyo, A. B. (2024). *Indonesia's Approach on Cyberattack Attribution through its Foreign Policy.* ResearchGate. https://www.researchgate.net/publication/376656684_Indonesia's_Approach_on_Cyberattack_Attribution_through_its_Foreign_Policy

Pratiwi, A. D., Hennida, C., Susanto, J., Mikhael, T., Totokusumo, R. A., & Viona, A. (2024). COVID-19 infodemic in Southeast Asia: Regionalism approach and responses. *Asian Security, 20*(3), 158–176. DOI: 10.1080/14799855.2025.2500091

Prilliadi, H. (2025, May). *Harnessing AI for ASEAN's future: Governance, adoption, and sustainability under the DEFA* (Policy Brief No. 2025-1). Economic Research Institute for ASEAN and East Asia (ERIA). https://www.eria.org/uploads/Harnessing-AI-for-ASEAN%E2%80%99s-Future.pdf

Rahmat, A., Wahdaniah, W., Bahasoan, A. N., Hayadin, M. R., & Fausiah, F. (2024, August 11). *Digital Giants Duel: How Go-Jek and Grab Are Transforming Indonesia's Economic Landscape.* ProBisnis: Jurnal Manajemen, 15(4), 533–542. Retrieved from https://ejournal.joninstitute.org/index.php/ProBisnis/article/view/529

Rajah & Tann Asia. (2025, February 12). *Expanded ASEAN Guide on AI governance and ethics.* AI Toolkit. Retrieved from https://aitoolkit.rajahtannasia.com/2025/02/12/expanded-asean-guide-on-ai-governance-and-ethics/

Rana, V., & Azeez, G. K. (2025, March 19). *Southeast Asia's quest for digital sovereignty.* The Diplomat. Retrieved from https://thediplomat.com/2025/03/southeast-asias-quest-for-digital-sovereignty/

Regus, M., Epafras, L. C., & Madung, O. G. (2024). Security governance, non-governmental actors, and the limited statehood legitimacy in the Southeast Asia landscape: A conceptual analysis. *The Journal of Politics*, *10*(2). Advance online publication. DOI: 10.7454/jp.v10i2.1235

Rühlig, T., & Seaman, J. (2019, June 28). *5G and the US–China tech rivalry – a test for Europe's future in the digital age* [SWP Comment No. 2019/C 29]. Stiftung Wissenschaft und Politik (SWP). DOI: 10.18449/2019C29

SAFEnet. (n.d.). Southeast Asia Freedom of Expression Network. Retrieved September 26, 2025, from https://safenet.or.id/

Said, F., & Nabilah, F. (2024, July 4). *Advancing ASEAN's digital economy: Challenges in cybersecurity and IP protection.* Fulcrum. Institute of Strategic and International Studies (ISIS) Malaysia. Retrieved from https://fulcrum.sg/aseanfocus/advancing-aseans-digital-economy-challenges-in-cybersecurity-and-ip-protection/

Saleem, F. (2025, September 23). *Which way for ASEAN's AI governance approach?* The Interpreter, Lowy Institute. https://www.lowyinstitute.org/the-interpreter/which-way-asean-s-ai-governance-approach

Secretariat, A. S. E. A. N. (2007). *The ASEAN Charter.* ASEAN Secretariat. https://asean.org/wp-content/uploads/images/archive/publications/ASEAN-Charter.pdf

Secretariat, A. S. E. A. N. (2018). *ASEAN Framework on Digital Data Governance.* ASEAN Secretariat. https://asean.org/wp-content/uploads/2021/08/ASEAN-Data-Management-Framework.pdf

Secretariat, A. S. E. A. N. (2021a). *ASEAN Digital Masterplan 2025*. ASEAN Secretariat. https://asean.org/book/asean-digital-masterplan-2025/

Secretariat, A. S. E. A. N. (2021b). *ASEAN Cybersecurity Cooperation Strategy 2021-2025*. ASEAN Secretariat. https://asean.org/wp-content/uploads/2022/02/01-ASEAN-Cybersecurity-Cooperation-Paper-2021-2025_final-23-0122.pdf

Secretariat, A. S. E. A. N. (2024a). *ASEAN Annual Report 2024*. https://asean.org/wp-content/uploads/2024/12/ASEAN-AR-2024_e-pub_web.pdf

Secretariat, A. S. E. A. N. (2024b). *ASEAN Guide on AI Governance and Ethics*. https://asean.org/book/asean-guide-on-ai-governance-and-ethics/

Secretariat, A. S. E. A. N. (2025a). *Expanded ASEAN Guide on AI Governance and Ethics - Generative AI*. https://asean.org/book/expanded-asean-guide-on-ai-governance-and-ethics-generative-ai/

Secretariat, A. S. E. A. N. (2025b, January 17). *Joint Media Statement of the 5th ASEAN Digital Ministers' Meeting and Related Meetings*. https://asean.org/joint-media-statement-of-the-5th-asean-digital-ministers-meeting-and-related-meetings/

Secretariat, A. S. E. A. N. (2025c, April 23). *ASEAN digital senior officials call for the development of a secure, innovative, and inclusive digital ecosystem to shape ASEAN's digital future*. https://asean.org/asean-digital-senior-officials-call-for-the-development-of-a-secure-innovative-and-inclusive-digital-ecosystem-to-shape-aseans-digital-future/

Secretariat, A. S. E. A. N. (2025d). *ASEAN Community Vision 2045*. https://asean.org/wp-content/uploads/2025/05/ASEAN-2045-Our-Shared-Future.pdf

Sefrina, M. (2024, March). *An inclusive digital economy in the ASEAN region* (ERIA Discussion Paper Series No. 505). Economic Research Institute for ASEAN and East Asia (ERIA). https://www.eria.org/uploads/An-Inclusive-Digital-Economy-in-the-ASEAN-Region.pdf

Shahrizal. (2025, May 2). *SEA businesses face 50 million offline cyber threats in 2024: Kaspersky*. Business Today (Malaysia). Retrieved from https://www.businesstoday.com.my/2025/05/02/sea-businesses-face-50-million-offline-cyber-threats-in-2024-kaspersky/

Tech for Good Institute. (2023). *Towards an ASEAN Digital Community 2045*. https://techforgoodinstitute.org/blog/perspectives/towards-an-asean-digital-community-2045/

The ASEAN Magazine. (2024, February 1). *The ASEAN Digital Economy Framework Agreement.* https://theaseanmagazine.asean.org/article/the-asean-digital-economy-framework-agreement/

TMT Law Practice (AP Law Solution). (2025, May 27). *Preparing for Enforcement: The Role of Indonesia's Upcoming PDP Body in Shaping Personal Data Protection.* https://www.ap-lawsolution.com/actio/preparing-for-enforcement-the-role-of-indonesias-upcoming-pdp-body-in-shaping-personal-data-protection

Williams, S. (2025, May 13). *Bruteforce cyber attacks surge in SEA, over 53 million blocked.* SecurityBrief Asia. Retrieved from https://securitybrief.asia/story/bruteforce-cyber-attacks-surge-in-sea-over-53-million-blocked

Wilson, N. (2025, July 17). *The Digital Economy Framework Agreement: ASEAN's anchor in a turbulent digital economy.* TechWonk Blog. Information Technology Industry Council. Retrieved from https://www.itic.org/news-events/techwonk-blog/the-digital-economy-framework-agreement-aseans-anchor-in-a-turbulent-digital-economy

World Bank. (n.d.-a). *Digital.* World Bank. Retrieved June 7, 2025, from https://www.worldbank.org/en/topic/digital

World Bank. (n.d.-c). *Economy profile: Cambodia.* Data360. Retrieved August 25, 2025, from https://data360.worldbank.org/en/economy/KHM

Yale Review of International Studies. (2025, July 26). *Data colonialism in the Global South: Who owns Asia's digital future?* https://yris.yira.org/column/data-colonialism-in-the-global-south-who-owns-asias-digital-future/

Chapter 13
Digital Diplomacy in Cambodia:
Embracing Artificial Intelligence for Strategic Engagement and National Development

Sovanna Huot
https://orcid.org/0009-0006-8335-442X
Department of Political Science, University of Delhi, New Delhi, India

ABSTRACT

This chapter examines how Cambodia has changed from a historically passive position in international relations to a proactive and adaptable role in digital diplomacy throughout the artificial intelligence (AI) era. Cambodia has modernized consular operations, incorporated AI-enabled tools into its foreign service, and closely matched ASEAN's digital governance initiatives in recent years. Its digital underpinnings have been reinforced, and socio-economic goals have been advanced through bilateral and multilateral partnerships that have facilitated technology transfer, capacity building, and infrastructure expansion. According to the study, Cambodia's digital diplomacy serves as a strategic platform for influence projection in addition to increasing service efficiency. This case serves as an example of how small and underdeveloped nations can use digital transformation to improve governance, accomplish development objectives, and become more relevant in the AI-driven global order.

DOI: 10.4018/979-8-3373-4937-4.ch013

1. INTRODUCTION

1.1 Context and Background

A historic and unparalleled wave of digital revolution has reshaped almost every aspect of political, economic, and social life in the first few decades of the twenty-first century. The swift development of artificial intelligence (AI), bolstered by associated technology advancements like big data analytics, machine learning, natural language processing, blockchain, and next-generation communication infrastructures like 5G networks, is at the front of this shift. When taken as a whole, these advancements have given governments the ability to gather, analyse, and act upon information more quickly than they could have twenty years before (Nye, 2020; West & Allen, 2020). These innovations have had significant ramifications in the field of diplomacy. The ability of digital technologies to enable instantaneous, data-driven, and highly targeted forms of engagement has complemented, and in some cases redefined, traditional forms of statecraft, which were centred on in-person negotiations, tightly planned summits, and controlled press briefings. According to Nye (2020), these technologies are catalysts that change the strategic context in which diplomacy functions rather than merely being "tools" to be added to current diplomatic practice. States can now anticipate problems and take advantage of opportunities with never-before-seen agility thanks to AI's contributions to predictive policy modelling, sentiment analysis of public opinion around the world, automated multilingual communication, and real-time crisis monitoring (West & Allen, 2020).

Smaller and developing nations are also emerging as important players in this new digital order, even though the academic and policy literature on digital diplomacy has traditionally concentrated on major powers like the US, China, and EU members (Bjola & Zaiotti, 2021). These governments have several strategic advantages, including as institutional agility, the capacity to quickly absorb specialized technologies, and a strong incentive to use digital platforms to magnify their global voice, even though they frequently lack the financial and technical resources to do so. According to Brady and Thorhallsson (2021), tiny states can compensate for structural limitations in traditional power politics by using digital diplomacy as a cost-effective and influence-multiplying tool for multilateral governance.

This new trend of tiny states embracing technology is best represented by Cambodia. Cambodia has always pursued a foreign policy that balances regional integration, multilateral engagement, and development-oriented alliances due to its strategic location in mainland Southeast Asia (Vann & Heng, 2020; Vichana, 2023). The Cambodian government has significantly increased its involvement in digital transformation during the last five years, both in its diplomatic apparatus and in domestic governance. The understanding that artificial intelligence (AI) and associated technologies are not optional upgrades but rather necessary tools for preserving relevance and competitiveness in a world that is becoming more interconnected and digitally mediated is at the heart of this change. The modernization of the Ministry of Foreign Affairs and International Cooperation (MFAIC) has been one of the most obvious areas of advancement. Online consular appointment systems, automated document authentication procedures, and increased e-services for Cambodian nationals residing overseas are among the digital and AI-enabled services that the MFAIC has been offering since 2019 (RGC, 2022). These programs enhance openness, cut down on bureaucratic red tape, and conform to global e-governance best practices. By simplifying service delivery, the MFAIC not only boosts productivity but also improves Cambodia's standing as a nation that can use technology to benefit its people and interact positively with other countries.

Cambodia's active involvement in ASEAN's regional digital governance framework supports this domestic change. According to Association of Southeast Asian Nations (2021), the nation has consistently contributed to the ASEAN Digital Masterplan 2025, which delineates regional goals in cybersecurity, infrastructure, and AI ethics. Cambodia enhances its diplomatic capital in Southeast Asia by presenting itself as a cooperative and forward-thinking member state by coordinating national policy with ASEAN's collective agenda. Its participation in ASEAN discussions on AI also shows a proactive approach to establishing the rules and guidelines that would control developing technology in the area. These efforts are supported by a larger strategic vision that is outlined in the Cambodia Digital Economy and Society Policy Framework 2021–2035. Digital transformation is specifically framed in this long-term plan as a catalyst for innovation, inclusive socioeconomic growth, and increased global competitiveness. It ensures that Cambodia's worldwide engagement in AI and digital diplomacy is directly tied to national priorities like poverty reduction, education reform, and industrial upgrading by integrating foreign policy objectives with domestic development goals. Furthermore, Cambodia's adoption of AI and digital diplomacy aligns with its long-standing foreign policy tenets of constructive engagement, multilateral cooperation, and regional stability. This is in line with Acharya's (2017) finding that small states can actively participate in multilateral processes and exert influence that is out of proportion to their material size when they strategically adapt. By incorporating AI into its diplomatic operations, Cambodia not only broadens the scope and speed of its engagement but also strengthens its standing as a reliable and creative collaborator in forming ASEAN's digital governance agenda and participating in international debates on the responsible and equitable application of AI.

When combined, these changes show Cambodia as neither diplomatically marginal nor technologically inactive. Rather, the nation is becoming an example of how small governments may use AI and digital technology to improve regional integration, fortify governance, and simultaneously achieve their diplomatic and developmental goals. According to Cambodia's experience, small-state agency in international affairs can be greatly increased in the digital age through institutional innovation, strategic adaptation, and regional cooperation.

1.2. Problem Statement

Cambodia's contribution to the global discourse on AI-driven diplomacy is still underrepresented in scholarly literature and policy analysis, despite the obvious advancements the nation has made recently. From introducing online visa systems to taking part in regional discussions on AI ethics and digital economy integration, Cambodia has made remarkable progress in modernizing its diplomatic infrastructure over the past five years, especially since 2019 (US-ASEAN Business Council, 2023) prepared by Masaya and Nguyen. But little scholarly attention has been paid to these trends, with the majority of studies that have been done so far concentrating only on Cambodia's digital infrastructure, broadband expansion, or private-sector tech adoption (United Nations Economic and Social Commission for Asia and the Pacific, 2022). The diplomatic, developmental, and geopolitical relevance of Cambodia's digital diplomacy trajectory is obscured by this gap in the literature. Analysts run the risk of maintaining antiquated ideas of Cambodia as a passive beneficiary of outside initiatives rather than as an active and adaptable agent in the AI era if they ignore the country's expanding role. Furthermore, little research has been done on how AI adoption in governance and its effects on foreign policy interact, especially when it comes to small-state agency in ASEAN and larger global governance frameworks. It is imperative that this omission be addressed because Cambodia's experience demonstrates both domestic change and a reinterpretation of the role emerging nations may play in establishing inclusive and equitable digital orders.

1.3. Research Objectives

The present chapter seeks to examine Cambodia's constructive and proactive incorporation of AI and digital platforms into its diplomatic and governance frameworks is the goal of this chapter. In particular, it aims to: (1) analyse Cambodia's diplomatic institutions' early adoption of AI and digital technology, paying particular attention to the last five years, (2) investigate how Cambodia's socioeconomic development plans, such as the Digital Economy and Society Policy Framework 2021–2035, are being matched with digital diplomacy, and (3) access how Cambodia's place in the larger worldwide AI governance discussion as well as ASEAN's digital governance agenda.

1.4. Research Questions

The following research questions serve as a guide for the study: (1) how is Cambodia modernizing its diplomatic services and improving engagement with audiences at home and abroad using artificial intelligence (AI) and digital platforms? (2) What are the primary advantages and disadvantages Cambodia has encountered in the past five years while implementing AI for development and diplomacy? And (3) What aspects of small-state digital diplomacy in Southeast Asia and elsewhere are reflected in and influenced by Cambodia's experience?

1.5. Significance of the Study

This chapter adds to a more modern and sophisticated understanding of small-state diplomacy in the digital era by concentrating on Cambodia's recent trajectory. It emphasizes how, even for governments with little funding, AI can be a strategic facilitator for public service delivery, governance change, and global influence. This upbeat narrative dispels antiquated notions about Cambodia's inaction in international affairs and instead portrays it as a proactive, flexible actor that can use technology to further its foreign policy objectives as well as its own domestic development. The results are useful to a variety of audiences. By providing empirical findings from a poor country setting, they fill a significant gap in the literature on small-state digital diplomacy for academics. They offer useful guidance to policymakers on how developing nations might incorporate AI into diplomatic strategy in ways that support their goals for national development. In a broader sense, the Cambodian case shows that digital diplomacy is not just for technologically powerful nations; it is a tool that can be used by any state that is prepared to make investments in innovation, strategic collaboration, and capacity-building.

2. LITERATURE REVIEW

2.1. Outlining AI and Digital Diplomacy in International Relations

Digital diplomacy, according to Bjola and Holmes (2015), involves much more than just digitizing current diplomatic processes or implementing new media platforms superficially. According to their conceptualization, it is a structural and revolutionary reconfiguration of the diplomatic arena that reinterprets how nations interact, negotiate, and influence one another on the global scene. They contend that the spread of ICTs has changed the temporal and spatial aspects of diplomacy, enabling governments to respond to crises in real time, broaden the scope of international discourse, and develop strategic narratives that appeal to a wide range of culturally and geographically diverse audiences. The increasing importance of digital tools as tools of statecraft in the twenty-first century is highlighted by this rethinking.

Based on this fundamental knowledge, West and Allen (2020) argue that integrating artificial intelligence (AI) into diplomatic practice enhances foreign ministries' operational and analytical capacities by orders of magnitude. To find latent patterns, predict political flashpoints, and avert future humanitarian crises, he shows how AI-powered predictive analytics enable diplomatic actors to sort through large, multifaceted datasets, from open-source social media content to satellite imagery, in almost real time. They go on to say that as decision-makers can now rely on an endless supply of evidence-based insights, AI's capacity to provide context-specific policy suggestions signifies a significant improvement in diplomatic readiness. AI-enabled translation systems in multilingual settings eliminate enduring language barriers, enabling smaller and linguistically weaker states to engage in intricate multilateral talks on an equal footing. According to USC Center on Public Diplomacy (2023, June 8), sentiment analysis powered by AI is becoming an increasingly important tool in 21st-century diplomacy. Foreign ministries may ensure that their narratives are compelling and relevant by monitoring changes in public opinion throughout the world and adjusting their communication tactics almost instantly. They also show how natural language processing (NLP) algorithms can quickly combine diplomatic cables, policy briefs, and multilateral agreements into comprehensible, useful intelligence that guides daily operations and strategic planning after being trained on a variety of corpora. These findings collectively imply that AI is serving as both a "strategic equalizer" for countries historically underrepresented in international political hierarchies and a "force multiplier" for governments with current capacity. This indicates that the use of AI in foreign policy in Cambodia presents a chance to advance bureaucratic modernization rather than just copying the strategies of more powerful nations. Therefore, Cambodia's use of AI-enabled diplomatic instruments demonstrates both the generality of these technology developments and their unique suitability for emerging economies' requirements.

2.2. Small States and Adaptation to Technology

Small states face a number of persistent structural limitations, such as lower financial resources, fewer overseas diplomatic posts, and diminished influence when it comes to defining the agenda at the top echelons of global administration, as acknowledged by Brady and Thorhallsson (2021). Cooper and Shaw (2009) contend, however, that these limitations do not imply irrelevance. Rather, they contend that small governments may exert influence by combining strategic alliance-building, agility, and specialized knowledge. This implies that small governments might use unique qualities that enable them to "punch above their weight" in particular fields rather than trying to compete with major ones on a scale. According to Manor (2019), small states now have an unparalleled opportunity to interact directly with international publics, transnational networks, and diasporic groups by circumventing conventional diplomatic gatekeepers thanks to the growth of digital platforms. He claims that in addition to expanding tiny states' diplomatic sphere of influence, this direct interaction gives them the ability to influence policy debate in ways that are contextually relevant, culturally aware, and responsive. Eliminating communication middlemen gives small governments more authority over their stories and the ability to build long-lasting, reciprocal connections with stakeholders around the world. According to Bjola and Manor (2022), tiny states may be able to take the lead in specific policy areas using digital diplomacy. They point to Singapore's leadership in smart city diplomacy and Estonia's standing as a global leader in cybersecurity governance as examples of how technology innovation can be easily incorporated into national diplomatic branding. These states have shown that influence in the digital age can be gained by knowledge, trustworthiness, and consistency in policy advocacy rather than being solely dependent on material power by fusing technical innovation with national identity. Cambodia can immediately benefit from this analytical framework. By investing in AI-powered public service delivery systems, growing its e-government platforms, and taking part in ASEAN-led digital governance projects, Cambodia has recently shown similar aspirations. In addition to increasing its administrative effectiveness, these actions fortify its capacity to establish itself as an active and beneficial participant in the regional technology policy environment.

2.3. The Technological and Diplomatic Development of Cambodia

According to Vann and Heng (2020), Cambodia's diplomatic reorientation since the early 1990s has been marked by an openness to multilateral development partnerships, a balanced foreign policy stance, and a strong emphasis on regional stability. Over the past five years, this approach has come into more contact with a purposeful digital transformation plan in both foreign policy and governance. The Royal Government of Cambodia (RGC, 2022) articulates a comprehensive long-term strategy in its *Digital Economy and Society Policy Framework 2021–2035*, which links digital innovation directly to economic diversification, enhanced human capital, and improved competitiveness in the global economy. The necessity of incorporating technology into all facets of statecraft, from foreign involvement to domestic service delivery, is emphasized in this document, which also highlights AI as a major innovation facilitator.

The Ministry of Foreign Affairs and International Cooperation (MFAIC) has launched a number of modernization projects, according to (RGC, 2022). These include enhanced e-consular services for Cambodian nationals overseas, AI-assisted document verification, and online appointment scheduling systems. Also, these actions do not only boost administrative effectiveness but also present Cambodia as a technologically advanced and responsive nation. According to US-ASEAN Business Council (2023), strengthening ties with ASEAN members and bilateral partners including China, Japan, South Korea, and India has supported Cambodia's diplomatic modernization. These partnerships have made it possible to train Cambodian diplomats in AI applications, expand the nation's digital infrastructure, and assist the nation's involvement in cooperative projects including regional digital economy integration plans and smart city efforts. When taken as a whole, these developments show that Cambodia is establishing itself as an active co-creator in establishing the diplomatic and digital standards of the ASEAN area rather than merely a passive recipient of foreign technical advancements.

2.4. The Literature's Gaps

The academic literature on AI and diplomacy is still strongly biased in favour of superpowers like the US, China, and the EU, as noted by USC Center on Public Diplomacy (2023, June 8). They contend that this disparity restricts our comprehension of how developing nations, especially those with limited financial resources, incorporate cutting-edge technologies into their diplomatic approaches.

The few scholarly works that do discuss Cambodia's digital transformation typically ignore the strategic, normative, and diplomatic ramifications of integrating AI in favour of concentrating on specific infrastructure indicators, such internet adoption rates or e-commerce growth figures. In-depth, empirically supported case studies that relate Cambodia's AI adoption to its foreign policy aims, its function in regional governance, and its pursuit of national development objectives are conspicuously lacking. Furthermore, not many studies examine Cambodia's significant contributions to ASEAN's agenda for digital governance or its participation in important discussions about inclusive innovation, digital equity, and ethical AI. This lacuna in the literature highlights the need for additional in-depth, situation-specific studies that acknowledge Cambodia's proactive adoption of new technologies and its potential to act as a template for other states in a similar situation. In addition to adding to the body of knowledge on small-state digital diplomacy, addressing these gaps will help policymakers better understand how AI might be used to promote constructive socioeconomic change. The linkages between digital diplomacy, AI, small-state advantages, technological adaptation, and Cambodia's successful development results through ASEAN and international cooperation are depicted in Figure 1.

Figure 1. Digital Diplomacy & Small-State Innovation (Cambodia)

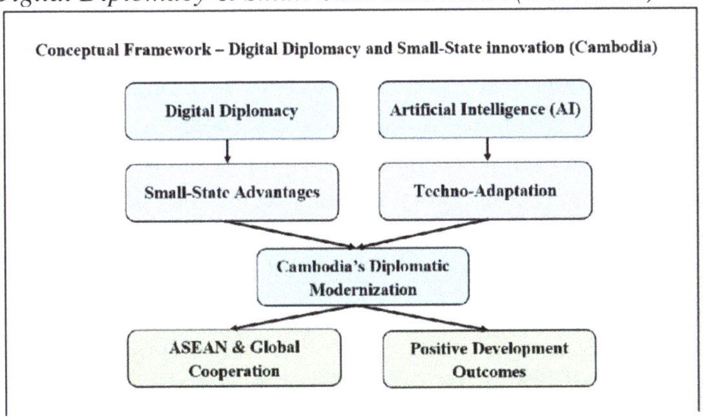

3. METHODOLOGY

3.1. Analytical Framework

The depth, breadth, and dynamics of Cambodia's incorporation of AI into its diplomatic practice were examined in this study using a qualitative, interpretive case study methodology. Because it allows for a comprehensive, context-rich analysis of intricate political and technological processes that are impossible to completely comprehend by merely quantitative measures, the case study technique was selected (Yin, 2009). By taking this approach, the study aimed to analyse the institutional logics, adaptive strategies, and governance innovations that support Cambodia's digital diplomacy trajectory rather than just listing efforts or cataloguing improvements.

The analytical framework was grounded in three intersecting theoretical domains. First, the conceptual underpinnings for comprehending how nations use digital technologies as strategic tools to engage publics, shape narratives, and affect policy results were established by Bjola and Holmes (2015), who developed the idea of digital diplomacy. This viewpoint guided the investigation to look at how diplomatic practices are changing qualitatively, including how AI is changing agenda-setting, negotiation, and cross-border interaction.

Second, Cambodia was positioned within the larger framework of international relations using Thorhallsson's (2019) small-state agency theory, which holds that states with limited material resources can still exert influence through the development of strategic alliances, niche specialization, and flexibility in responding to global change. The identification of trends in Cambodia's use of AI to get beyond structural disadvantages usually connected to its size and economic status was guided by this theoretical thread.

Third, as Vichana (2023) discusses, adaptive governance theory provided a framework for examining how state institutions in developing nations modify organizational structures and policy procedures in response to new technology. The study evaluated whether Cambodia's digital diplomacy reforms were reactive, incremental, or proactively anticipatory of future technology and geopolitical trends by including adaptive governance into the framework.

Cambodia was chosen as the case with a purpose rather than at random. While increasing its involvement in ASEAN's digital integration frameworks, the nation has shown a notable acceleration in the adoption of AI-enabled governance technologies during the last five years. The intersection of regional diplomacy and domestic transformation offered a rich empirical setting for investigating the mutual relationship between international posture and technology uptake. Thus, the framework made it possible for the study to examine both the strategic alignment between regional multilateral activities and national development goals, as well as the operational improvements inside Cambodia's diplomatic apparatus.

3.2. Sources and Scopes

In order to assure validity and lower the possibility of source bias, the study's empirical foundation was based on a thorough documentary analysis that drew from primary and secondary sources. The Cambodia Digital Economy and Society Policy Framework 2022–2035 (RGC, 2022), the Ministry of Foreign Affairs and International Cooperation's (MFAIC) annual reports, and official press releases outlining AI-related policy measures and diplomatic initiatives were among the official Cambodian government publications from which primary data was gathered. To track the official institutionalization of AI technologies inside governance and diplomatic activities, legislative texts, strategic plans, and ministerial instructions were also analysed.

To put Cambodia's involvement in group efforts at digital governance in perspective, ASEAN frameworks were examined at the regional level, particularly the ASEAN Digital Masterplan 2025, the ASEAN Declaration on Digital Governance, and related ministerial communiqués. Official records, summaries, and transcripts from ASEAN Digital Ministers' Meetings (2019–2024) as well as a few United Nations meetings on digital cooperation were added to these publications. In international settings, this gave a clear picture of Cambodia's declared stances, pledges, and policy contributions. The study included publicly available speeches, interviews, and declarations made by Cambodian foreign ministry representatives both domestically and abroad to increase the empirical depth. Regarding the nation's AI-driven digital diplomacy, these sources provide qualitative insights into institutional narratives, political framing, and policy intent.

Peer-reviewed scholarly journals, articles from policy think tanks, and regional analytical studies were the sources of secondary data. Cooper and Shaw (2009) provided information for the study of small-state adaptive strategies, whereas Hossain et al. (2024), Manor (2019) and West and Allen (2020) were significant in defining AI's operational relevance in diplomacy. In addition to providing theoretical depth, this secondary literature made it possible to compare Cambodia's experience with more general trends seen in other settings. The study's temporal scope was restricted to the years 2019 through 2024. This period was chosen because it coincided with increased participation in regional and international digital diplomacy platforms and includes Cambodia's most recent wave of digital governance reforms, such as the institutionalization of AI in foreign affairs. Geographically, the study concentrated on Cambodia, but it also extended the analytical lens to its regional multilateral interactions within ASEAN and its bilateral partnerships, especially with China, Japan, South Korea, and India. A nuanced evaluation of the interactions between national initiatives and regional and international systems was made possible by this dual focus.

3.3. Analytical Criteria

To guarantee consistency and comparability across data sources, the study used four interconnected evaluative criteria, each of which was divided into operational indicators. The first criterion looked at how institutions were using digital tools and artificial intelligence in diplomatic roles. This included mapping particular projects including the implementation of automated translation in multilateral negotiations, e-authentication services for official documents, and the MFAIC's AI-assisted online consular appointment system. The technical capability, operational scope, adoption rate, and effects on efficiency and transparency of each program were examined.

The second criterion evaluated Cambodia's involvement in discussions about digital governance on a regional and international level. The frequency, topical scope, and substantive depth of Cambodia's interventions were assessed using content analysis of ASEAN and UN meeting records. The consistency of Cambodia's policy stances, their alignment with ASEAN digital agendas, and their support for inclusive technological growth were all given special consideration in the study. The final criterion assessed diplomatic applications of domestic digital infrastructure. This included assessing secure embassy communication networks, data-sharing protocols with regional partners, and participation in joint cyber-resilience projects. Infrastructure was examined not only for its technical specifications but also for its strategic utility in supporting diplomatic outreach and foreign policy execution.

The socioeconomic effects and connections to national development strategies were examined in the fourth criterion. Here, Cambodia's development priorities in innovation, education, and economic diversification were compared to digital diplomacy projects. This step assessed the potential benefits of AI-enabled diplomatic reforms for domestic policy objectives, such as better access to citizen services, increased development of human capital, or enhanced national branding internationally. Throughout the investigation, these standards were used in an iterative and reflective manner. Thematic coding was used to find patterns, and emerging themes were contrasted with the theoretical predictions made in the analytical framework. The conclusions were theoretically sound and empirically supported thanks to the triangulation of policy documents, official declarations, and multilateral records, which produced a solid account of Cambodia's changing approach to digital diplomacy, as summarized in Table 1.

Figure 2. Overview of the Methodology

Section	Description	Crucial Components
Analytical Framework	Cambodia is the main case in this qualitative interpretive case study technique that examines AI-driven digital diplomacy.	• The notion of digital diplomacy. • The theory of small-state agencies. • The notion of adaptive government. • Cambodia was chosen with a purpose. • Institutional improvements and strategic alignments were examined.
Sources and Scopes	Methodical examination of primary and secondary sources from 2019 to 2024 with an emphasis on the regional, bilateral, and local settings of Cambodia.	• Press releases, ASEAN frameworks, UN forum records, government publications, MFAIC reports, and official speeches are examples of primary sources. • Academic journals, think-tank studies, and policy analyses are examples of secondary sources. • Scope: ASEAN and bilateral interactions in addition to Cambodia's domestic projects.
Analytical Criteria	To evaluate Cambodia's AI-enabled diplomatic reform, four evaluative areas were operationalized into quantifiable indicators.	1. Using AI technologies in diplomacy institutionally. 2. Taking part in regional and international discussions on digital governance. 3. Digital infrastructure at home with diplomatic uses. 4. Socioeconomic effects associated with development plans.

4. CAMBODIA'S DIGITAL DIPLOMACY IN ACTION

4.1. E-Governance and Foreign Services Modernization

Through the integration of e-governance tools and AI-enabled administrative systems, Cambodia has made a concerted effort in recent years to modernize its foreign service architecture. A key institutional player in this change is the Ministry of Foreign Affairs and International Cooperation (MFAIC), which is leading projects that reorganize the state's ability to provide diplomatic and consular services effectively, safely, and in accordance with 21st-century governance norms (RGC, 2022). The advent of internet platforms for consular services is a fundamental element of this transformation. Without physically visiting embassies or consulates, these portals enable Cambodian citizens, especially those residing overseas, to apply for visas, renew their passports, validate their civil status documents, and access emergency assistance services. These methods greatly improve service accessibility for both foreign nationals wishing to interact with Cambodia's diplomatic missions and members of the Cambodian diaspora by eliminating logistical and geographic constraints (RGC, 2022).

Equally important is the deployment of digital appointment scheduling systems that allow real-time booking and rescheduling through web or mobile applications. These new technologies replace paper-based queue management with automated systems that make embassy operations more efficient, cut down on wait times for citizens, and make it easier to plan how to use consular staff resources. The MFAIC's dedication to reducing bureaucracy is part of a larger government goal to show that it is good at managing things, which will increase trust at home and abroad (Thorhallsson, 2019). The AI-assisted document authentication system may be the most technologically advanced overhaul. The MFAIC can currently execute cross-database checks in seconds, find errors in supplied documents, and identify possible forgeries with high accuracy (US-ASEAN Business Council, 2023) thanks to optical character recognition (OCR) and machine learning-based verification models. This not only lowers the chance of fraud, but it also makes Cambodia's diplomatic and legal documents more trustworthy when they are used across borders. This is becoming more important in international trade, migration, and security cooperation.

These measures are more than just improvements to the administration; they are part of a planned digital signalling strategy. By using advanced governance tools, Cambodia is sending a message to foreign partners that it is a reliable, forward-thinking, and technologically advanced player in international affairs. This digital modernization has both a practical purpose in improving service delivery and a symbolic purpose in boosting Cambodia's soft power by making people think of it as modern and efficient.

4.2. Cambodia in ASEAN's Digital and AI Agenda

Cambodia's strong role in ASEAN's digital and AI policy environment is the second main aspect of its digital diplomacy in action. The country has intentionally matched its national policies with the ASEAN Digital Masterplan 2025, a regional framework that delineates priority domains including e-commerce integration, cross-border data flow oversight, and AI ethics (ASEAN Secretariat, 2022). This alignment is not just talk; it is put into action by Cambodia's participation in working groups, policy debates, and ministerial forums that shape the region's digital governance path. Cambodia's participation in discussions around AI ethics and governance in ASEAN is one area of involvement that stands out. Cambodian officials have supported ideas that stress AI governance that considers the technology realities and capacity limits of developing member states. This position shows that Cambodia is working for digital equity, making sure that less-developed economies can still benefit from new technologies even if their governance systems are too strict or need too many resources (Hossain et al., 2024).

Cybersecurity has become another important part of Cambodia's ASEAN policy. Cambodia helps make the area more cyber-resilient, fight transnational cybercrime, and create standard incident response protocols by taking part in programs like the ASEAN Cyber Capacity Programme. This promise is not just about national security; it also makes Cambodia look like a reliable partner for cross-border digital infrastructure projects (RGC, 2022). Being a part of ASEAN's digital economy integration programs has also helped in real ways. Cambodia may take advantage of economies of scale that would be impossible to accomplish on its own by using regional data sharing platforms, harmonized e-trade facilitation systems, and joint AI research programs. This strategically places Cambodia as a positive contributor to the region, which can lead to diplomatic benefits in other areas of policy, such as trade talks and working together to protect the environment.

4.3. Bilateral and Multilateral Cooperations

Cambodia's digital diplomacy is gaining a lot of ground outside of ASEAN because to bilateral and multilateral collaborations that directly assist the transfer of technology, the construction of digital competence, and the development of infrastructure. Working with China has been notably helpful in building up Cambodia's digital backbone infrastructure. This includes building Fiber-optic networks across the country, rolling out 5G connectivity, and setting up AI research and innovation centres in Phnom Penh. These projects frequently come with training programs for Cambodian engineers and policy leaders to make sure that technology transfer goes hand in hand with the development of human capital (Te Velde et al., 2020,

July). When working with South Korea, the focus has been on building up AI and e-governance skills. The Korea International Cooperation Agency (KOICA) has paid for programs that have taught Cambodian government workers how to use machine learning, data analytics, and AI to help make policy (Kim & Kim, 2022). These talents are directly useful for making Cambodia's foreign service and public administration work better.

Partnerships with Japan have mostly been about smart city pilot projects. For example, in Sihanoukville, AI-driven urban planning, and smart traffic systems are all being tested. These projects serve as both infrastructure improvements and diplomatic demonstrations of Cambodia's readiness to use technology for sustainable development (JICA, 2025). India and Cambodia have mostly worked together on cybersecurity and digital diplomacy training, with India giving both technical help and seminars for Cambodian diplomats to learn from each other. Through such partnerships, Cambodia strengthens its technological resilience while diversifying its diplomatic alliances, thereby reducing overdependence on any single technology partner (Cooper & Shaw, 2009). These bilateral and multilateral arrangements are more than transactional; they form part of a strategic capacity-building ecosystem in which Cambodia positions itself as both a beneficiary and a contributor in the global digital transformation.

4.4. Emerging AI Applications and National Development

One characteristic that sets Cambodia's digital diplomacy apart is that it is integrated into a whole-of-government strategy for integrating AI that covers several areas of domestic growth, rather than being limited to foreign policy in the strictest sense. In urban planning, AI-enabled traffic optimization systems are being piloted in Phnom Penh to analyse congestion patterns and adjust signal timings dynamically, improving mobility and reducing environmental impact (RGC, 2022). In order to extend access to government services outside of regular business hours, AI-powered chatbots have been implemented on government websites to answer common questions in both Khmer and English.

AI-powered adaptive learning platforms are being tested in rural schools to offer individualized instruction in foreign languages and STEM subjects, among other essential areas. This tackles the government's goal of creating a workforce that is digitally savvy as well as disparities in educational quality (West & Allen, 2020). In order to support the dual objectives of food security and export competitiveness, machine learning models are being applied in agriculture to predict insect outbreaks, manage irrigation schedules, and track crop health using satellite images (US-ASEAN Business Council, 2023).

The Cambodia Digital Economy and Society Policy Framework 2022–2035, which recognizes AI as a key technology for attaining economic diversification, innovation-led growth, and inclusive development, is closely related to these domestic applications (RGC, 2022). These domestic AI achievements strengthen Cambodia's diplomatic narrative from a foreign policy standpoint, allowing the nation to legitimately portray itself as a state that is not only embracing digital technologies but also incorporating them into development plans that yield quantifiable socioeconomic advantages, as viewed in Table 2.

Figure 3. The Practice of Digital Diplomacy in Cambodia

Section	Important Tasks and Initiatives	Strategic Impacts
Modernization of Foreign Services and E-Government	• Digital appointment scheduling tools; online consular service platforms; and AI-assisted document authentication.	• Improved administrative; credibility and soft power; shorter waiting times and more efficiency; and more accessibility for diaspora.
ASEAN's Digital and AI Agenda: Cambodia	Participation in the ASEAN Cyber Capacity Program; contributions to discussions on AI ethics; and alignment with the ASEAN Digital Masterplan 2025	Raising awareness in the region, promoting digital equity, and bolstering confidence in international initiatives
Collaboration on a bilateral and multilateral level	Japan: Smart city pilots; South Korea: AI and e-governance training; China: research centers for digital infrastructure and AI; India: collaboration in cybersecurity	Enhanced AI human capital; diversified technological alliances; expanded digital infrastructure
New Applications for AI and National Progress	AI-powered public service chatbots; AI-enabled traffic optimization; AI-powered educational adaptive learning systems; AI in agriculture forecasting and monitoring	Increased food security and export competitiveness; better urban mobility; longer service delivery; higher-quality education

5. THE DIGITAL FUTURE OF CAMBODIA: OBSTACLES AND PROSPECTS

5.1. Structural and Institutional Barriers

The full potential of Cambodia's digital transformation is still limited by institutional and systemic obstacles, even in spite of notable advancements in digital diplomacy and the incorporation of artificial intelligence (AI) into governance. The digital divide between urban and rural areas is one of the most enduring problems. Many rural regions still lack dependable internet connection and enough capacity to implement AI-enabled apps, despite significant investments in broadband and mobile network infrastructure in major cities like Phnom Penh (International Telecommunication Union, 2023). This discrepancy restricts Cambodians' ability to participate inclusively in digital governance projects as well as their access to digital public services.

Digital literacy is another difficulty. In the context of small-state capacity, Thorhallsson (2019) points out that technological adaptation necessitates both infrastructure and human capital that can use cutting-edge instruments efficiently. The effectiveness and reach of digital initiatives are diminished in Cambodia due to low levels of computer literacy among specific population groups, including rural populations, senior residents, and some public sector workers. The adoption of AI-powered services may stay low in the absence of focused training and ongoing public education initiatives, so obliterating much of their intended usefulness. The governance of cybersecurity is still in its infancy from an institutional standpoint. A thorough regulatory framework that systematically covers data protection, cybercrime, and hazards unique to artificial intelligence has not yet been put into place in Cambodia (ASEAN Secretariat, 2022). According to Hossain et al. (2024), the lack of robust cybersecurity regulations and enforcement tools not only exposes vital infrastructure to intrusions but also erodes confidence among global partners involved in digital collaboration and cross-border data sharing. Budgetary restrictions make these difficulties worse. According to Cooper and Shaw (2009), small governments like Cambodia frequently have resource constraints that limit their capacity to hire staff, acquire state-of-the-art technologies, and sustain long-term research and development initiatives. Implementations that are fragmented or at the pilot stage and do not expand across ministries and sectors may result from this funding deficit.

5.2. Strategic Possibilities for Empowering Small States

Notwithstanding these systemic constraints, Cambodia has significant strategic potential to use digital transformation to strengthen small-state agency in the global order. By forming narratives, establishing specialized agendas, and enlisting coalitions, Bjola and Holmes (2015) contend that digital diplomacy gives smaller actors a platform to project influence out of proportion to their size. Cambodia can strengthen its diplomatic voice on topics like inclusive technological development, ethical AI governance, and digital equity by actively participating in ASEAN's digital governance initiatives. In addition to gaining access to common infrastructure and group capacity-building initiatives, Cambodia can help shape regional policy standards by aligning with the ASEAN Digital Masterplan 2025 (ASEAN Secretariat, 2022). By supporting context-sensitive governance frameworks that consider the realities of developing nations, Cambodia can ensure that regional regulations are not unduly influenced by the technological and regulatory preferences of larger economies. This alignment is especially crucial in discussions surrounding AI ethics.

By participating in digital diplomacy, Cambodia can also establish itself as a leader in policy innovation in specialized fields like artificial intelligence (AI) for sustainable development, digital inclusion tactics, or cyber-resilience frameworks designed for low-resource environments. Because Cambodia is seen as a positive and progressive regional actor, this approach may have diplomatic spillover benefits in trade, investment, and security issues.

5.3. Bridging Domestic Development and Global Diplomacy

Using digital diplomacy as a link between international involvement and local development goals is one of Cambodia's most alluring options. Adopting AI tools can improve governments' operational and analytical capabilities, allowing them to provide more effective, focused, and citizen-centered services, as noted by West and Allen (2020). AI-powered chatbots, e-consular portals, and automated document verification in Cambodia not only boost the quality of public services but also generate a positive feedback loop whereby the success of domestic administration raises the nation's standing abroad. This connection is especially evident in digital skills programs aimed at young people. Cambodia's demographically youthful population, with a median age of about 26, can provide the groundwork for a workforce that is proficient in digital technology and able to support both the country's domestic economy and its diplomatic efforts abroad (World Bank, 2023). In addition to preparing young Cambodians for engagement in the global digital economy, programs focused on AI literacy, coding, and data analytics training increase the talent pool for positions in technical innovation, international negotiation, and policy analysis.

Additionally, digital diplomacy can be used to further inclusive development objectives, such expanding telemedicine services to disadvantaged areas or enhancing rural education access using AI-enabled e-learning platforms. These programs have the potential to improve Cambodia's standing as a nation dedicated to sustainable and fair technological advancement when they are in line with its foreign policy narrative.

5.4. Future Readiness and Ethical Considerations

The ethical regulation of AI and digital technologies is becoming increasingly important as Cambodia continues its digital transition. Adoption of AI entails concerns of algorithmic discrimination, data privacy violations, and surveillance abuse in the absence of suitable controls; these problems have surfaced in numerous jurisdictions worldwide (Hossain et al., 2024). Failing to address these vulnerabilities might erode both international legitimacy and local trust, especially given Cambodia's ambitions to portray itself as a responsible and rights-respecting digital actor.

Cambodia must embrace a rights-based digital governance paradigm based on accountability, openness, and inclusivity to protect against these threats. This could entail setting up impartial oversight organizations, embracing globally accepted data protection guidelines like the General Data Protection Regulation (GDPR) principles of the EU, and instituting frequent consultations on AI policy with the private sector and civil society (ICNL, 2025). Resilience in the face of geopolitical unpredictability and technological volatility is another requirement for future readiness. To prevent becoming overly reliant on one supplier or geopolitical group, which could restrict policy autonomy, Cambodia must diversify its technology alliances (Cooper & Shaw, 2009). To keep up with the quick developments in AI and digital governance, public officials will also need to invest in ongoing professional development. Effective implementation of these moral and calculated steps would enable Cambodia to establish itself as both a recipient of the global digital revolution and a player in the creation of a just and sustainable digital order.

6. CONCLUSION

An examination of Cambodia's changing digital diplomacy reveals a revolutionary era where AI and other cutting-edge technologies are essential to the implementation of foreign policy and the country's development plan, rather than being merely supplemental instruments. The implementation of AI-enabled document authentication systems, the development of online consular service platforms, and the introduction of digital appointment scheduling for both citizens and foreign nationals are just a few of the reforms that Cambodia has successfully started over the past five years to modernize its foreign service architecture. These actions have simplified the provision of services, decreased inefficiencies in the bureaucracy, and enhanced the state's reputation as a technologically capable and progressive one. In addition to modernizing its own country, Cambodia has been actively involved in regional digital governance frameworks, especially by contributing to ASEAN's Digital Masterplan 2025 and taking part in talks on cybersecurity, AI ethics, and facilitating cross-border digital trade. In addition to improving Cambodia's policy alignment with regional interests, this engagement has given the nation the chance to shape emergent digital standards in Southeast Asia. Cambodia has established strategic alliances with nations including China, Japan, South Korea, and India on both a bilateral and international level. Large-scale investments in digital infrastructure, the creation of technical skills, and the testing of cutting-edge technologies in fields like smart city development and AI-based governance tools have all been made possible by these partnerships. Crucially, these collaborations have been used to advance skills and transfer technology, making Cambodia's human capital base more equipped to meet the needs of the AI era.

When taken as a whole, these projects show a distinct trend: Cambodia is shifting from gradual modernization to a more intentional, integrated approach that views AI as a cross-cutting facilitator of socioeconomic development, governance reform, and diplomatic impact. The research's conclusions encourage a reevaluation of Cambodia's position within the global order. Cambodia has historically been viewed as a relatively tiny and resource-constrained entity that is reactive to political and technological advancements outside of its control. Its recent history of integrating AI and digital diplomacy, however, points to a more dynamic and forward-thinking character.

Cambodia has shown that to increase their capabilities at home and their influence abroad, tiny governments can proactively coordinate technology change with diplomatic policy. Its strategic bilateral partnerships and participation in ASEAN's AI and digital governance agenda demonstrate an awareness that, in the twenty-first century, diplomatic power is becoming increasingly dependent on technological prowess. Cambodia has started to present a more assertive and creative image by integrating AI into the day-to-day operations of its foreign service and expanding its use in domestic economic areas. This change implies that Cambodia is actively defining its own path, selectively embracing technology, forming regional alliances, and crafting narratives that emphasize its significance in the AI-driven world rather than merely adjusting to the digital order imposed by more powerful nations. The passive roles that have always been assigned to tiny developing states are significantly altered by this repositioning. Other small and developing nations attempting to negotiate the quickly evolving global digital landscape can learn a lot from Cambodia's experience. One important takeaway is that, despite their difficulties, resource constraints do not always mean that meaningful engagement in the development and use of developing technologies is impossible. Even states with little resources can influence digital norms and reap the benefits of technological integration through strategic focus, targeted collaborations, and alignment between domestic and foreign policy priorities.

The significance of connecting digital diplomacy to tangible domestic development results is another important implication. Adoption of AI in Cambodia has been linked to advancements in urban administration, agricultural productivity, education quality, and public service delivery. This linkage strengthens public support and political legitimacy for such projects by ensuring that digital diplomacy is a tangible driver of socio-economic change rather than an abstract exercise. The situation in Cambodia further emphasizes how important it is to have a whole-of-government strategy. Coordination between government agencies, the corporate sector, civil society, and international partners is necessary for the digital transformation of foreign policy; it cannot be isolated within foreign affairs departments. In addition to optimizing the effects of technology adoption, this integrated approach increases resilience against possible hazards including cybersecurity threats, data misuse, or reliance on outside technology suppliers. Going forward, Cambodia's capacity to keep up its pace will rely on preserving policy consistency, making investments in human capital and digital literacy, and incorporating ethical considerations into the application of AI. If these prerequisites are satisfied, Cambodia may be able to serve as a model for how small developing nations might use digital diplomacy and artificial intelligence (AI) to improve their standing in international affairs and their capacity for domestic governance.

In conclusion, Cambodia's experience with digital diplomacy shows that in the AI era, influence is no longer just determined by size and resource base. Even smaller states can establish themselves as innovative and credible players on the international scene by demonstrating strategic vision, flexibility, and a dedication to integrating technology with development and foreign policy agendas.

REFERENCES

Acharya, A. (2017). After liberal hegemony: The advent of a multiplex world order. *Ethics & International Affairs, 31*(3), 271–285. DOI: 10.1017/S089267941700020X

Association of Southeast Asian Nations. (2021). *ASEAN digital masterplan 2025*. ASEAN Secretariat. https://asean.org/wp-content/uploads/2021/09/ASEAN-Digital-Masterplan-EDITED.pdf

Bjola, C., & Holmes, M. (2015). *Digital diplomacy: Theory and practice*. Routledge. DOI: 10.4324/9781315730844

Bjola, C., & Manor, I. (2022). The rise of hybrid diplomacy: From digital adaptation to digital adoption. *International Affairs, 98*(2), 471–491. DOI: 10.1093/ia/iiac005

Bjola, C., & Zaiotti, R. (2021). *Digital diplomacy and international organisations: Autonomy, legitimacy and contestation*. Routledge.

Brady, A.-M., & Thorhallsson, B. (2021). *Small states and the new security environment*. Springer., DOI: 10.1007/978-3-030-51529-4

Cooper, A. F., & Shaw, T. M. (2009). The diplomacies of small states at the start of the twenty-first century: How vulnerable? How resilient? In Cooper, A. F., & Shaw, T. M. (Eds.), *The diplomacies of small states: Between vulnerability and resilience* (pp. 1–18). Springer., DOI: 10.1057/9780230246911_1

Hossain, M. A., Azim, K. S., Jafor, A. H. M., Shayed, A. U., Nikita, N. A., & Khan, O. U. (2024). AI and machine learning in international diplomacy and conflict resolution. *Advanced International Journal of Multidisciplinary Research, 3*(5), 1–17. DOI: 10.62127/aijmr.2024.v02i05.1095

ICNL. (2025). *Summary analysis of Cambodia's draft law on personal data protection*. International Center for Not-for-Profit Law Open. https://data.opendevelopmentcambodia.net/en/dataset/087a5b1e-bc04-4da1-8870-c375b87e01f2/resource/fd8b0cb3-afc4-44d0-a9c8-1e482a9f7e2c/download/icnl-comments-on-cambodia-draft-law-on-personal-data-protection_july2025.pdf

International Telecommunication Union. (2023). *Measuring digital development: Facts and figures 2023*. I. T. D. Sector. https://www.itu.int/itu-d/reports/statistics/wp-content/uploads/sites/5/2023/11/Measuring-digital-development-Facts-and-figures-2023-E.pdf

JICA. (2025). *Cambodia newsletter: November 2024–January 2025 (Vol. 2)*. Japan International Cooperation Agency (JICA) Cambodia Office. https://www.jica.go.jp/english/overseas/cambodia/others/__icsFiles/afieldfile/2025/06/02/newsletter202501_en.pdf

Kim, B. K., & Kim, T. (2022). *Scaling-up dynamics in KOICA's peace-development nexus projects in the Mekong region: Cases of Lao PDR and Cambodia*. UNRISD Working Paper. https://hdl.handle.net/10419/273861

Manor, I. (2019). *The digitalization of public diplomacy* (Vol. 15). Springer. DOI: 10.1007/978-3-030-04405-3

Nye, J. S. (2020). *Do morals matter?: Presidents and foreign policy from FDR to Trump*. Oxford University Press.

RGC. (2022). *Cambodia digital government policy 2022–2035*. Royal Government of Cambodia, Phnom Penh: Ministry of Post and Telecommunications. https://asset.cambodia.gov.kh/mptc/media/Cambodia_Digital_Government_Policy_2022_2035_English.pdf

Secretariat, A. S. E. A. N. (2022). *Digital policy action areas for a connected ASEAN: ASEAN best practice benchmarking and an action plan for regional harmonization*. ITU Publications Asia-Pacific Region. https://asean.org/wp-content/uploads/2024/03/Digital-Policy-Action-Areas-for-a-Connected-ASEAN.pdf

Te Velde, D. W., Chandarany, O., Hokkheang, H., Monyoudom, Y., Kelsall, T., Lemma, A., Krishnan, A., Banga, K., Broden, A., Nourrice, M., & Evans, J. (2020, July). *Fostering an inclusive digital transformation in Cambodia*. Supporting Economic Transformation. https://set.odi.org/wp-content/uploads/2020/06/Fostering-an-Inclusive-Digitalisation-Transformation-in-Cambodia-Final.pdf

Thorhallsson, B. (2019). Small states and the changing global order: What small state theory can offer New Zealand foreign policymaking. In Brady, A.-M. (Ed.), *Small states and the changing global order: New Zealand faces the future* (pp. 379–395). Springer., DOI: 10.1007/978-3-030-18803-0_22

United Nations Economic and Social Commission for Asia and the Pacific. (2022). *Asia-Pacific digital transformation report 2022*. United Nations. https://www.unescap.org/sites/default/d8files/knowledge-products/ESCAP-2022-Flagship-Asia-Pacific-Digital-Transformation-Report.pdf

US-ASEAN Business Council. (2023). *AI governance in Southeast Asia*. US-ASEAN Business Council. https://www.usasean.org/sites/default/files/2023-10/%5BUS-ASEAN%5D%20AI%20Governance%20in%20Southeast%20Asia.pdf

USC Center on Public Diplomacy. (2023, June 8). *AI and the future of public diplomacy*. USC Annenberg Center on Communication Leadership & Policy. https://uscpublicdiplomacy.org/blog/ai-and-future-public-diplomacy

Vann, B., & Heng, K. (2020). Youth's role in advancing Cambodia's digital diplomacy. *Asia Times*. https://asiatimes.com/2020/08/youths-role-in-advancing

Vichana, S. (2023). *Digital government in Cambodia: Challenges and solutions* [Master Of Public Management, KDI School of Public Policy and Management]. https://www.researchgate.net/publication/376686542

West, D. M., & Allen, J. R. (2020). *Turning point: Policymaking in the era of artificial intelligence*. Brookings Institution Press.

World Bank. (2023). *Cambodia economic update: From recovery to reform (Cambodia Economic Update)*. World Bank. https://documents1.worldbank.org/curated/en/099112023082512660/pdf/P1773400acb58a0260905e06ed54ad7edf5.pdf

Yin, R. K. (2009). *Case study research: Design and methods* (Vol. 5). SAGE.

Compilation of References

Abdel Moneim, A. F. (1986). *The Arab League 1945–1985: A historical and political study* (pp. 12–13, 44–50).

Abdi, K., Talebpour, M., Fullerton, J. A., Ranjkesh, M. J., & Nooghabi, H. J. (2018). Converting sports diplomacy to diplomatic outcomes: Introducing a sports diplomacy model. *International Area Studies Review*, *21*(4), 365–382. DOI: 10.1177/2233865918808058

Abdurahmanli, E. (2021). *Definition of diplomacy and types of diplomacy used between states. Anadolu Akademi Sosyal Bilimler Dergisi*, 583.

Abramczyk, E. (2024). Growth of political relations or sportswashing? The nuances of sports as soft diplomacy. DOI: 10.33774/apsa-2024-gf408

AbuGhanem, M., & Eleuch, H. (2024). Full quantum tomography study of Google's Sycamore gate on IBM's quantum computers. *EPJ Quantum Technology*, *11*(1), 36. Advance online publication. DOI: 10.1140/epjqt/s40507-024-00248-8

Access Now. (n.d.). About Us. Retrieved September 26, 2025, from https://www.accessnow.org/about-us/

Acemoğlu, D. (2022). Yapay zekayı yeniden tasarlamak (H. Dölkeleş, Çev.). In Cohen, J., & Chasman, D. (Eds.), *Yapay zekayı yeniden tasarlamak: Otomasyon çağında iş, demokrasi, adalet* (pp. 7–31). Elif Yayınevi.

Acharya, A. (2011). *Whose ideas matter? Agency and power in Asian regionalism*. Cornell University Press.

Acharya, A. (2017). After liberal hegemony: The advent of a multiplex world order. *Ethics & International Affairs*, *31*(3), 271–285. DOI: 10.1017/S089267941700020X

Addeo, F., D'Auria, V., Delli Paoli, A., Punziano, G., Ragnedda, M., & Ruiu, M. L. (2023). Measuring digital capital in Italy. *Frontiers in Sociology*, *8*, 1–12. DOI: 10.3389/fsoc.2023.1144657 PMID: 37274604

Adler-Nissen, R. (2011). On a field trip with Bourdieu. *International Political Sociology*, *5*(3), 327–330. DOI: 10.1111/j.1749-5687.2011.00137_1.x

African Union. (2020). *The Digital Transformation Strategy for Africa*. African Union.

Airoldi, M. (2022). *Machine habitus: Toward a sociology of algorithms*. Polity Press.

Ajaj, R., Buheji, M., & Hassoun, A. (2024). Optimizing the readiness for industry 4.0 in fulfilling the Sustainable Development Goal 1: Focus on poverty elimination in Africa. *Frontiers in Sustainable Food Systems*, *8*, 1393935. Advance online publication. DOI: 10.3389/fsufs.2024.1393935

Akıllı, E. (2025, Nisan). Rewiring diplomacy in the technopolar world | opinion. *Daily Sabah*. https://www.dailysabah.com/opinion/op-ed/rewiring-diplomacy-in-the-technopolar-world

Akman, M. K. (2024). Secret Diplomacy and Information Rights: interdisciplinary analyses through strategic intelligence, public relations and international security.

Al Mokdad, A. (2025, July). *AI diplomacy in the Global South — strategy or afterthought?* Medium. Retrieved from: https://medium.com/@almokdadali1/ai-diplomacy-in-the-global-south-strategy-or-afterthought-fb63218bf109

Al-Aqdahi, H. M. (2009). *Political stability in the contemporary world*.

Al-Astal, K. M. (1999). *Towards formulating a theory of security for the Arab Gulf Cooperation Council*. Emirates Centre for Strategic Studies and Research.

Alex, K. (2024). *Agriculture and Aquaculture Applications of Biosensors and Bioelectronics*. IGI Global.

AlgorithmWatch. (2023). The Digital Services Act (DSA) explained. https://algorithmwatch.org/en/dsa-explained/

Allison, R. (2017). Russia and the post-2014 international legal order: Revisionism and realpolitik. *International Affairs*, *93*(3), 519–543. DOI: 10.1093/ia/iix061

Almahraj, Y. A. (2023). British press coverage of international sports events hosted by Saudi Arabia: Content analysis study in light of country concept model. *Humanities & Social Sciences Communications*, *10*(1), 46. Advance online publication. DOI: 10.1057/s41599-023-02266-w

Al-Muwil, A., Weerakkody, V., El-Haddadeh, R., & Dwivedi, Y. K. (2019). Balancing digital-by-default with inclusion: A study of the factors influencing e-inclusion in the UK. *Information Systems Frontiers*, *21*(3), 635–659. DOI: 10.1007/s10796-019-09914-0

Al-Safi, Y.. (2024). *Digital diplomacy and artificial intelligence: Qualification rules for the diplomatic and consular service*. Democratic Arabic Center for Strategic, Political and Economic Studies.

Alvarado-Valiente, J., Romero-Álvarez, J., Moguel, E., García-Alonso, J., & Murillo, J. (2024). Orchestration for quantum services: The power of load balancing across multiple service providers. *Science of Computer Programming, 237*, 103139. DOI: 10.1016/j.scico.2024.103139

Aoi, C. (2024). The Indo-Pacific, Geopolitics, and Strategic Communications: Construction of 'the Indo-Pacific'. *Defence Strategic Communications, 14*(14), 26–67.

Apostolakis, K. C., Dimitriou, N., Margetis, G., Ntoa, S., Tzovaras, D., & Stephanidis, C. (2022). DARLENE – Improving situational awareness of European law enforcement agents through a combination of augmented reality and artificial intelligence solutions. *Open Research Europe, 1*, 87. Advance online publication. DOI: 10.12688/openreseurope.13715.2 PMID: 37645167

Aqeel, A. (2023). International relations in the age of artificial intelligence. Hammurabi Centre for Research and Strategic Studies, 3.

Arapov, S., Dadabaev, T., & Laumulin, C. (2017). The use of digital diplomacy as a tool for symbolic violence: Framing analysis of Russian–Turkish relations on Twitter. *Cambridge Journal of Eurasian Studies, 1*(41), 124–128. DOI: 10.22261/UZV32B

Arceneaux, P. (2024). Value creation through organizational storytelling: Strategic narratives in foreign government public relations. *Public Relations Review, 50*(2), 102433. DOI: 10.1016/j.pubrev.2024.102433

Ashok, M., Madan, R., Joha, A., & Sivarajah, U. (2022). Ethical framework for Artificial Intelligence and Digital technologies. *International Journal of Information Management, 62*, 102433. DOI: 10.1016/j.ijinfomgt.2021.102433

Association of Southeast Asian Nations. (2021). *ASEAN digital masterplan 2025*. ASEAN Secretariat. https://asean.org/wp-content/uploads/2021/09/ASEAN-Digital-Masterplan-EDITED.pdf

Atad, E., Lev-On, A., & Yavetz, G. (2023). Diplomacy under fire: Engagement with governmental versus non-governmental messages on social media during armed conflicts. *Government Information Quarterly, 40*(3), 101835. DOI: 10.1016/j.giq.2023.101835

Athayde, P. F. A., & Figueiredo, A. J. (2023). Public management of sport: A description and comparative analysis of the organizational structure in Brazil and Portugal. *Retos, 51*, 979–988. DOI: 10.47197/retos.v51.101356

Awate, P. L., & Nagne, A. D. (2025). Satellite Imagery and GIS Applications in Precision Agriculture. In Rani, S., Dutta, S., Rocha, Á., & Cengiz, K. (Eds.), *AI and Data Analytics in Precision Agriculture for Sustainable Development* (pp. 185–206). Springer Nature Switzerland., DOI: 10.1007/978-3-031-93087-4_11

Ayodele, O. (2021). The digital transformation of diplomacy: Implications for the African Union and continental diplomacy. *The South African Journal of International Affairs*, *28*(3), 379–401. DOI: 10.1080/10220461.2021.1968944

Bal, R., & Gill, I. S. (2020). *Policy Approaches to Artificial Intelligence Based Technologies in China, European Union and the United States* (SSRN Scholarly Paper No. 3699640). Social Science Research Network. DOI: 10.2139/ssrn.3699640

Bălcescu, N. (2017). Diplomacy and security. *International Conference Knowledge-Based Organization*, 23, 251–252. https://doi.org/DOI: 10.1515

Balestrini, M., Kotsev, A., Ponti, M., & Schade, S. (2021). Collaboration matters: Capacity building, up-scaling, spreading, and sustainability in citizen-generated data projects. *Humanities & Social Sciences Communications*, *8*(1), 169. DOI: 10.1057/s41599-021-00851-5

Bannykh, G. (2020, March). Digital capital and the labor market: Factors of mutual influence. In *International Scientific Conference" Far East Con"(ISCFEC 2020)* (pp. 2946-2953). Atlantis Press. DOI: 10.2991/aebmr.k.200312.420

Bano, M., Chaudhri, Z., & Zowghi, D. (2023). The role of generative AI in global diplomatic practices: A strategic framework. *arXiv preprint,* arXiv:2401.05415.

Bansal, R., Khanna, M., & Rajput, N. K. (2024). A Qualitative Evaluation of Multiple Quantum Computing Frameworks. *2024 2nd International Conference on Advances in Computation, Communication and Information Technology (ICAICCIT), 1*, 1296-1302. DOI: 10.1109/ICAICCIT64383.2024.10912413

Barichella, A. (2022). *Cyberattacks in Russia's hybrid war against Ukraine and its ramifications for Europe*. Jacques Delors Institute.

Basu, A., & Nachiappan, K. (2023). Will India Negotiate?. Hybridity, Conflict, and the Global Politics of Cybersecurity, 189.

Batan, A. (2025). Assessing the Role of Public-Private Partnerships in Advancing Sustainable Development Goals Through Agri-Tech and Renewable Energy Solutions. *Transactions on Social Innovation, Digital Inclusion, and Ethical AI, 15*(2), 1–11.

Bean, E., Burleigh, C., Haskell, C., Burris-Melville, T., Payne, J., & Pathak, B. (2025). Eavesdropping on UNESCO AI Policy, Leadership, and Ethics. *Journal of Leadership Studies*, *18*(4), 98–110. DOI: 10.1002/jls.70007

Begman, J. (2012). *Contemporary diplomacy.*

Beirne, J., & Fernandez, D. (Eds.). (2021). *Harnessing digitalization for sustainable economic development: Insights for Asia* (ADB Institute Book No. 23). Asian Development Bank Institute. https://www.adb.org/publications/harnessing-digitalization-sustainable-economic-development

Bendett, S. (2024). The Role of AI in Russia's Confrontation with the West. *Center for a New American Security.* Pp. 1-31.

Bernstein, D., & Lange, T. (2008). Post-quantum cryptography. *Nature*, *549*(7671), 188–194. DOI: 10.1038/nature23461 PMID: 28905891

Bhutani, V., Bahadur, P. S., & Sansaniwal, S. K. (2025). Leveraging Technology for Ethical and Sustainable Global Development. In *Bridging Technology and Development for Sustainable Innovation and Geopolitical Dynamics* (pp. 279–302). IGI Global Scientific Publishing., DOI: 10.4018/979-8-3693-9072-6.ch011

Bi, S., Yuan, X., & Ni, W. (2025). *Building Sustainable and Trustworthy Indigenous Knowledge Preservation Ecosystem* (No. arXiv:2504.17281). arXiv. https://doi.org//arXiv.2504.17281DOI: 10.48550

Bilgin, P. (2004). *Whose "Middle East"? Geopolitical inventions and practices of security. International Relations*, 18(1), 18–19. Sage Publications. DOI: 10.1177/0047117804041739

Bin Khalfan, A. (2024). *Applications of artificial intelligence in the security field (Applied to the Gulf Cooperation Council countries)* (pp. 2561–2601).

Bjola, C., Cassidy, J., & Manor, I. (2019). Public diplomacy in the digital age. *Lahey Diplomasi Dergisi*, *14*(1-2), 83–101. DOI: 10.1163/1871191X-14011032

Bjola, C., & Holmes, M. (2015). *Digital diplomacy: Theory and practice*. Routledge. DOI: 10.4324/9781315730844

Bjola, C., & Kornprobst, M. (2025). Studying tech diplomacy—Introduction to the special issue on tech diplomacy. *Global Policy*, *0*, 1–8. DOI: 10.1111/1758-5899.70035

Bjola, C., & Manor, I. (2022). The rise of hybrid diplomacy: From digital adaptation to digital adoption. *International Affairs*, *98*(2), 471–491. DOI: 10.1093/ia/iiac005

Bjola, C., & Zaiotti, R. (2021). *Digital diplomacy and international organisations: Autonomy, legitimacy and contestation*. Routledge.

Bohlen, A. (1966). Changes in Russian diplomacy under Peter the Great. *Cahiers du Monde Russe et Sovietique*, *7*(3), 341–358. DOI: 10.3406/cmr.1966.1672

Boretti, A. (2024). Technical, economic, and societal risks in the progress of artificial intelligence driven quantum technologies. *Discover Artificial Intelligence*, *4*(1), 67. DOI: 10.1007/s44163-024-00171-y

Bourdieu, P. (2014). *On the StateLectures at the College de France, 1989-1992* (D. Fernbach, Çev.). Polity Press.

Bourdieu, P. (2016). *Sosyoloji meseleleri* (F. Öztürk, B. Uçar, M. Gültekin, & A. Sümer, Çev.). Heretik Yayıncılık.

Bourdieu, P. (2018). *Bir pratik teorisi için taslak: Kabiliye üzerine üç etnoloji çalışması* (N. Ötken, Çev.). Bilgi Üniversitesi.

Bourdieu, P. (2022). *Genel sosyoloji: College de France dersleri (1981-1983)* (E. Emirosmanoğlu, Çev.). İletişim Yayınları.

Bourdieu, P. (1989). Social space and symbolic power. *Sociological Theory*, *7*(1), 14–25. DOI: 10.2307/202060

Bourdieu, P. (2011). The Forms of capital. In Szeman, I., & Kaposy, T. (Eds.), *Cultural Theory: An Anthology* (pp. 81–98). Wiley-Blackwell.

Bradshaw, S., & Howard, P. N. (2018). The global organization of social media disinformation campaigns. *Journal of International Affairs, 71*(1.5), 23-32.

Brady, A.-M., & Thorhallsson, B. (2021). *Small states and the new security environment.* Springer., DOI: 10.1007/978-3-030-51529-4

Brovina, N., Gashi, B., & Kabashi, D. (2024). The Impact of Digital Diplomacy On National Security: Navigating The Positive and Negative Aspects.

Byrne, S., & Ludvigsen, J. A. L. (2023). An Olympic embrace? A critical evaluation of the IOC's commitment to human rights. *International Journal of Sport Policy*, *16*(2), 217–233. DOI: 10.1080/19406940.2023.2271487

Byrnjolfsson, E. (2022). Sorun işler değil, ücretlerdir (H. Dölkeleş, Çev.). In Acemoğlu, D. (Ed.), *Yapay Zekayı Yeniden Tasarlamak: Otomasyon Çağında İş, Demokrasi Ve Adalet* (pp. 55–60). Elif Yayınevi.

Calderón Gómez, D. (2021). The third digital divide and Bourdieu: Bidirectional conversion of economic, cultural, and social capital to (and from) digital capital among young people in Madrid. *New Media & Society*, *23*(9), 2534–2553. DOI: 10.1177/1461444820933252

Calhoun, C. (2016). Bourdieu sosyolojisinin ana hatları (G. Çeğin, Çev.). In Çeğin, G., Göker, E., Arlı, A., & Tatlıcan, Ü. (Eds.), *Ocak ve Zanaat Pierre Bourdieu Derlemesi* (pp. 77–131). İletişim Yayınları.

Camilleri, M. A. (2024). Artificial intelligence governance: Ethical considerations and implications for social responsibility. *Expert Systems: International Journal of Knowledge Engineering and Neural Networks*, *41*(7), e13406. DOI: 10.1111/exsy.13406

Can, M., & Vieira, A. (2022). The Chinese Military-Civil Fusion Strategy: A State Action Theory Perspective. *The International Spectator*, *57*(3), 85–102. DOI: 10.1080/03932729.2022.2080262

Carnicelli, L., Valentina, M., & Zoromski, C. (2025, April 30). *Brunei releases voluntary AI guidelines to enhance responsibility and trust. US-ASEAN Business Council.* https://www.usasean.org/article/brunei-releases-voluntary-ai-guidelines-enhance-responsibility-and-trust

Castells, M. (2007). Communication, power and counter-power in the network society. *International Journal of Communication*, *1*, 238–266.

Chagnon, C. W., Durante, F., Gills, B. K., Hagolani-Albov, S. E., Hokkanen, S., Kangasluoma, S. M. J., Konttinen, H., Kröger, M., LaFleur, W., Ollinaho, O., & Vuola, M. P. S. (2022). From extractivism to global extractivism: The evolution of an organizing concept. *The Journal of Peasant Studies*, *49*(4), 760–792. DOI: 10.1080/03066150.2022.2069015

Chahri, S. (2021). Artificial intelligence act.

Chakraborty, C., Bhattacharya, M., Pal, S., & Agoramoorthy, G. (2023). India's Quantum Move: From Budget Allocation, Action and Future Challenges. *Molecular Biotechnology*, •••, 1–13. DOI: 10.1007/s12033-023-00975-w PMID: 38095823

Chamberlain, W., & Anseeuw, W. (2019). Inclusive businesses in agriculture: Defining the concept and its complex and evolving partnership structures in the field. *Land Use Policy*, *83*, 308–322. DOI: 10.1016/j.landusepol.2019.02.008

Chappelet, J.-L. (2021). The governance of the Olympic system: From one to many stakeholders. *Journal of Global Sport Management*, *8*(4), 783–800. DOI: 10.1080/24704067.2021.1899767

Charles, J. (2024). Rethinking diplomacy: how small states can leverage new media for the conduct of diplomacy in the digital age (Master's thesis, University of Malta).

Chatziefstathiou, D., & Rofe, J. S. (2024). Human rights and the Olympics: From an ideological paradox to a new anti-corruption legacy. *Frontiers in Sports and Active Living*, *6*, 1365150. Advance online publication. DOI: 10.3389/fspor.2024.1365150 PMID: 39359486

Chernobrov, D. (2022). Strategic humour: Public diplomacy and comic framing of foreign policy issues. *British Journal of Politics and International Relations*, *24*(2), 277–296. DOI: 10.1177/13691481211023958

Chesterman, S. (2021). Through a glass, darkly: Artificial intelligence and the problem of opacity. *The American Journal of Comparative Law*, *69*(2), 271–294. Advance online publication. DOI: 10.1093/ajcl/avab012

Chib, S., Mehta, A. K., Selvakumar, P., Saravanan, A., Mishra, B. R., & Manjunath, T. C. (2025). Mental Health Challenges and Solutions in High-Pressure Work Environments. In Harriott, S. (Ed.), *Innovative Approaches to Managing Conflict and Change in Diverse Work Environments* (pp. 247–272). IGI Global Scientific Publishing. DOI: 10.4018/979-8-3693-9556-1.ch011

Choi, J. R., Straubhaar, J., Skouras, M., Park, S., Santillana, M., & Strover, S. (2020). Techno-Capital: Theorizing media and information literacy through information technology capabilities. *New Media & Society*, •••, 1–23. DOI: 10.1177/1461444820925800

Chong, D., & Druckman, J. (2007). A theory of framing and opinion formation in competitive elite environments. *Journal of Communication*, *57*(1), 99–118. DOI: 10.1111/j.1460-2466.2006.00331.x

Christou, G., Meyer, T., & Fanni, R. (2025). The European union: Assessing global leadership through actorness in artificial intelligence. *Journal of European Integration*, *47*(3), 383–401. DOI: 10.1080/07036337.2024.2377200

Clementson, D. E. (2020). Narrative persuasion, identification, attitudes, and trustworthiness in crisis communication. *Public Relations Review*, *46*(2), 101889. DOI: 10.1016/j.pubrev.2020.101889

Çokgüçlü, Y. (2022). Asya Pasifik ve Hint Pasifik'te ABD Öncülüğünde Geliştirilen İttifakların (Aukus- The Quad) ABD-Çin İlişkilerine Etkisi. *The International Journal of Social Sciences (Islamabad)*, *6*(25), 326–347. Advance online publication. DOI: 10.52096/usbd.6.25.21

Collective, T. (2025, June 12). The role of artificial ıntelligence in shaping public diplomacy. *Tech Collective.* https://techcollectivesea.com/2025/06/12/artificial-intelligence-public-diplomacy/

Cook, F. (2007). It's a small world after all: Multiculturalism, authenticity, connectedness among trends to watch in next 50 years. *The Public Relations Strategist, 13*(1), 30–33.

Cooper, A. F., & Shaw, T. M. (2009). The diplomacies of small states at the start of the twenty-first century: How vulnerable? How resilient? In Cooper, A. F., & Shaw, T. M. (Eds.), *The diplomacies of small states: Between vulnerability and resilience* (pp. 1–18). Springer., DOI: 10.1057/9780230246911_1

Corvino, C., Moriconi, M., Costa, C. M., & D'Angelo, C. (2023). Sport as a tool for social inclusion, employment, and improved health. *Frontiers in Sports and Active Living, 5*, 1273858. Advance online publication. DOI: 10.3389/fspor.2023.1273858 PMID: 37691643

Costa, F., & Rodrigues, M. (2020). Industry. *Technological Progress and Development: The Case of Southeast Asia., 9*(6), 1–7. DOI: 10.31270/IJAME/v09/i06/2020/1

Costa, R., & Moriconi, M. (2024). Current political uses of sport revised: Beyond public diplomacy and sportswashing. *Frontiers in Sports and Active Living, 6*, 1316732. Advance online publication. DOI: 10.3389/fspor.2024.1316732 PMID: 39229250

Couldry, N., & Mejias, U. A. (2022). *The cost of connection: How data is colonizing human life and appropriating it for capitalism.* Stanford University Press.

Couldry, N., & Mejias, U. A. (2023). The decolonial turn in data and technology research: What is at stake and where is it heading? *Information Communication and Society, 26*(4), 786–802. DOI: 10.1080/1369118X.2021.1986102

Crowell Global Advisors. (2025, January 28). *5th ASEAN Digital Ministers' Meeting: Supercharging ASEAN's growth story with AI [Client alert].* Crowell & Moring LLP. Retrieved from https://www.crowell.com/en/insights/client-alerts/5th-asean-digital-ministers-meeting-supercharging-aseans-growth-story-with-ai

Cui, H., & Yasseri, T. (2024). AI-enhanced collective intelligence. *Patterns, 5*(11). https://doi.org/, A. (2023). Opacity, Machine Learning and Explainable AI. In *International Library of Ethics, Law and Technology* (Vol. 41). https://doi.org/DOI: 10.1016/J.PATTER.2024.101074/Fernández

Cull, N. J. (2013). The long road to public diplomacy 2.0: The internet in US public diplomacy. *International Studies Review, 15*(1), 123–139. DOI: 10.1111/misr.12026

Cummings, S., Dhewa, C., Kemboi, G., & Young, S. (2023). Doing epistemic justice in sustainable development: Applying the philosophical concept of epistemic injustice to the real world. *Sustainable Development (Bradford), 31*(3), 1965–1977. DOI: 10.1002/sd.2497

Cyriac, R., Eswaran, S., & Selvarajan, S. (2024). Quantum Computing in Cryptographic Systems. *International Journal of Advanced IT Research and Development*. DOI: 10.69942/1920184/20240101/03

da Silva, J. B.Jr, Valdez, M. L., Sealey-Thomas, R., Galiano, S. G., Garcia-Saisó, S., Huerta, P., & D'Agostino, M. (2024). Digital health diplomacy and universal health coverage. *Bulletin of the World Health Organization, 103*(2), 174. PMID: 39882492

Dahiya, R., & Selvakumar, P. Vidyadhara, & Manjunath, T. C. (2025). Design and aerodynamics: Principles and advances. In M. Mellal (Ed.), *Innovations and Developments in Unmanned Aerial Vehicles* (pp. 145-170). IGI Global Scientific Publishing.

Dahiya, R., & Selvakumar, P. Vidyadhara, & Manjunath, T. C. (2025). Design and Aerodynamics: Principles and Advances. In M. Mellal (Ed.), Innovations and Developments in Unmanned Aerial Vehicles (pp. 145-170). IGI Global Scientific Publishing.

DataReportal. (2024a). *Digital 2024: Brunei Darussalam*. https://datareportal.com/reports/digital-2024-brunei-darussalam

DataReportal. (2024b). *Digital 2024: Indonesia*. https://datareportal.com/reports/digital-2024-indonesia

DataReportal. (2024c). *Digital 2024: Cambodia*. https://datareportal.com/reports/digital-2024-cambodia

DataReportal. (2024d). *Digital 2024: Malaysia*. https://datareportal.com/reports/digital-2024-malaysia

DataReportal. (2024e). *Digital 2024: Philippines*. https://datareportal.com/reports/digital-2024-philippines

DataReportal. (2024f). *Digital 2024: Singapore*. https://datareportal.com/reports/digital-2024-singapore

DataReportal. (2024g). *Digital 2024: Thailand*. https://datareportal.com/reports/digital-2024-thailand

DataReportal. (2024h). *Digital 2024: Vietnam*. https://datareportal.com/reports/digital-2024-vietnam

DCAF. (2024). *Cybersecurity governance in Southeast Asia.* https://www.dcaf.ch/sites/default/files/publications/documents/Cybersecurity_Governance_in_Southeast_Asia_Thematic_Brief.pdf

de Almeida, M. A. B., & Ozdemir, M. B. (2024). The men's World Cup in Qatar 2022 through the lens of the Western media: Soft power, sports diplomacy and sportswashing. *Sociology International Journal, 8*(4), 190–198. DOI: 10.15406/sij.2024.08.00394

de la Puente Pacheco, M. A., Torres, J., Blanco Troncoso, A. L., Guzmán Murillo, H. J., & Carrascal, J. X. M. (2025). Enhancing Critical Thinking and Argumentation Skills in Colombian Undergraduate Diplomacy Students: ChatGPT-Assisted and Traditional Debate Methods. *Journal of Political Science Education, 21*(4), 1–11. DOI: 10.1080/15512169.2025.2449936

Demaidi, M. N. (2025). Artificial intelligence national strategy in a developing country. *AI & Society, 40*(2), 423–435. DOI: 10.1007/s00146-023-01779-x

Derian, J. D., & Wendt, A. (2020). 'Quantizing international relations': The case for quantum approaches to international theory and security practice. *Security Dialogue, 51*(5), 399–413. DOI: 10.1177/0967010620901905

Devanny, J. (2024). Artificial Intelligence and Cyber Power.

Devitt, S. (2016). Performing Quantum Computing Experiments in the Cloud. *Physical Review. A, 94*(3), 32329. DOI: 10.1103/PhysRevA.94.032329

Dhiman, J. S. (2025). *CHIPS and Science Act: A Catalyst for US Semiconductor Industry.* INTERANTIONAL JOURNAL OF SCIENTIFIC RESEARCH IN ENGINEERING AND MANAGEMENT., DOI: 10.55041/IJSREM38266

Di Martino, L. (2020). Conceptualising public diplomacy listening on social media. *Place Branding and Public Diplomacy, 16*(2), 131–142. DOI: 10.1057/s41254-019-00135-5

Di Riscio, R. A. (2025). *Digital Detente: The Weaponization of AI and LLMs in US-China Geopolitics, 2022-2025.* ResearchGate. https://www.researchgate.net/publication/389944211_Digital_Detente_The_Weaponization_of_AI_and_LLMs_in_US-China_Geopolitics_2022-2025

Dubinsky, Y. (2022a). Country image, cultural diplomacy, and sports during the COVID-19 pandemic: Brand America and Super Bowl LV. *Place Branding and Public Diplomacy, 19*(3), 249–262. DOI: 10.1057/s41254-021-00257-9

Dubinsky, Y. (2022b). The Olympic Games, nation branding, and public diplomacy in a post-pandemic world: Reflections on Tokyo 2020 and beyond. *Place Branding and Public Diplomacy*, *19*(3), 386–400. DOI: 10.1057/s41254-021-00255-x

Dunjko, V., & Briegel, H. (2018). Machine learning & artificial intelligence in the quantum domain: A review of recent progress. *Reports on Progress in Physics*, *81*(7), 074001. Advance online publication. DOI: 10.1088/1361-6633/aab406 PMID: 29504942

Dyer-Witheford, N., Kjosen, A. M., & Steinhoff, J. (2022). *Yapay zeka ve kapitalizmin geleceği: İnsandışı bir güç* (B. Cezar, Çev.). İletişim Yayınları.

Edinger, H. (2022). Offensive ideas: Structural realism, classical realism and Putin's war on Ukraine. *International Affairs*, *98*(6), 1873–1893. DOI: 10.1093/ia/iiac217

Edwards, L. (2009). Symbolic power and public relations practice: Locating ındividual practitioners in their social context. *Journal of Public Relations Research*, *21*(3), 251–272. DOI: 10.1080/10627260802640674

Elliott, C., Colvin, A., Pearson, D., Pikalo, O., Schlafer, J., & Yeh, H. (2005). *Current status of the DARPA Quantum Network*. Storage and Retrieval for Image and Video Databases.

Elsig, M., & Polanco Lazo, R. (2025, April 23). *Implementation options for ASEAN's Digital Economy Framework Agreement. World Economic Forum.* Retrieved from https://www.weforum.org/stories/2025/04/implementation-lessons-for-asean-s-digital-economy-framework/

EngageMedia. (n.d.). *Digital Rights.* Retrieved September 26, 2025, from https://engagemedia.org/digitalrights/

Entman, R. M. (2008). Theorizing mediated public diplomacy: The U.S. case. *The International Journal of Press/Politics*, *13*(2), 87–102. DOI: 10.1177/1940161208314657

Ericson, P., Dobbe, R., & Lindgren, S. (2024). Tracing class and capitalism in critical AI research. *TripleC*, *22*(1), 307–328. DOI: 10.31269/triplec.v22i1.1464

Eriksen, M. (2016). Assessing Russia's Doctrine of Realpolitik as Strategic Re-Contouring of Regional Power-Balance in The Post-Soviet Periphery. *Politeja* 41: 305–328. https://www.jstor.org/stable/24920236

Ertem-Eray, T. (2023). Extending the cultural-economic model of public relations through Bourdieu's theoretical lens to inform public diplomacy efforts. *Public Relations Inquiry*, *12*(3), 271–291. DOI: 10.1177/2046147X231180862

European Commission. (n.d.). *The Digital Markets Act.* Retrieved September 26, 2025, from https://commission.europa.eu/strategy-and-policy/priorities-2019-2024/europe-fit-digital-age/digital-markets-act-ensuring-fair-and-open-digital-markets_en

European Parliament. (2021, December 9). *EU Digital Markets Act and Digital Services Act explained.* https://www.europarl.europa.eu/pdfs/news/expert/2021/12/story/20211209STO19124/20211209STO19124_en.pdf

Evsikov, K. (2022). Information Security of the Digital State in the Quantum Era. *Courier of Kutafin Moscow State Law University (MSAL)).* DOI: 10.17803/2311-5998.2022.92.4.046-058

Faizal, M., & Teo, S. (2024). ASEAN Digital Transformation and the US–China Technological Competition. In *Strategic Currents* (pp. 67–90). China and US Competition for Influence., DOI: 10.1142/9789811288081_0004

Farahani, M., & Ghasemi, G. (2024). *Artificial intelligence and inequality: Challenges and opportunities.* Qeios., DOI: 10.32388/7HWUZ2

Farhad, S. (2025). Passengers in Flight: AI Governance Capacity in the Global South. *Digital Society : Ethics, Socio-Legal and Governance of Digital Technology, 4*(2), 39. DOI: 10.1007/s44206-025-00195-6

Fasinu, E. S., Olaniyan, B. J. T., & Afolaranmi, A. O. (2024). Digital Diplomacy in the Age of Social Media: Challenges and Opportunities for Crisis Communication. *African Journal of Social Sciences and Humanities Research, 7*(3), 24–38. DOI: 10.52589/AJSSHR-0TOOED5F

Fedorov, A., Akimov, A., Biamonte, J., Kavokin, A., Khalili, Y., Kiktenko, E., Kolachevsky, N. N., Kurochkin, Y. V., Lvovsky, A. I., Rubtsov, A. N., Shlyapnikov, G. V., Straupe, S. S., Ustinov, A. V., & Zheltikov, A. (2019). Quantum technologies in Russia. *Quantum Science and Technology, 4*(4), 040501. Advance online publication. DOI: 10.1088/2058-9565/ab4472

Feijóo, C., Kwon, Y., Bauer, J. M., Bohlin, E., Howell, B., Jain, R., Potgieter, P., Vu, K., Whalley, J., & Xia, J. (2020). Harnessing artificial intelligence (AI) to increase wellbeing for all: The case for a new technology diplomacy. *Telecommunications Policy, 44*(6), 1–14. DOI: 10.1016/j.telpol.2020.101988 PMID: 32377031

Fetzer, J. H. (1990). What is artificial intelligence? J. H. Fetzer (Ed.), In *Artificial Intelligence: Its Scope and Limits* (pp. 3-27). Springer Netherlands. DOI: 10.1007/978-94-009-1900-6_1

Fitsilis, F., & de Almeida, P. G. R. (2024). Artificial intelligence and its regulation in representative institutions. In *Research Handbook on Public Management and Artificial Intelligence* (pp. 151–166). Edward Elgar Publishing. DOI: 10.4337/9781802207347.00019

Fitzpatrick, K. (2017). Public Diplomacy in the Public Interest. *The Journal of Public Interest Communications*, *1*(1), 78. DOI: 10.32473/jpic.v1.i1.p78

Floridi, L., Cath, C., & Taddeo, M. (2019). Digital ethics: Its nature and scope. In C. Öhman & D. Watson (Eds.), *The 2018 Yearbook of the Digital Ethics Lab* (pp. 9-17). Springer. DOI: 10.1007/978-3-030-17152-0_2

Floridi, L., & Taddeo, M. (Eds.). (2025). *A Companion to Digital Ethics*. Wiley-Blackwell. DOI: 10.1002/9781394240821

Fong, K. S. L. (2025, September 26). *Digital literacy vital for enhancing ASEAN's digital integration agenda.* Fulcrum. https://fulcrum.sg/digital-literacy-vital-for-enhancing-aseans-digital-integration-agenda/

Fournier-Tombs, E. (2021). Towards a United Nations Internal Regulation for Artificial Intelligence. *Big Data & Society*, *8*(2), 20539517211039493. Advance online publication. DOI: 10.1177/20539517211039493

Fox, N. J. (2024). Artificial ıntelligence and the black hole of capitalism: A more-than-human political ethology. *Social Sciences (Basel, Switzerland)*, *13*(10), 507. DOI: 10.3390/socsci13100507

Freud, S. (2023). *Kitle psikolojisi ve ego analizi* (E. Yıldırım, Çev.). Oda Yayınları.

Gadais, T., Décarpentrie, L., Webb, A., Ayoub, M., Bardocz-Bencsik, M., & Bélanger, C. (2021). A method for conducting preliminary analysis of the nature and context of sport for development and peace projects in fieldwork research: An illustration with a Malagasy non-governmental organization. *Frontiers in Sports and Active Living*, *3*, 658496. Advance online publication. DOI: 10.3389/fspor.2021.658496 PMID: 34805977

Garakhanova, N. (2023). Yapay zekâ çağında kültürel diplomasi. In Çakmak, F. (Ed.), *Sosyal & beşerî bilimler alanında akademik çalışmalar* (pp. 77–114). Gece Kitaplığı.

Garsten, C., & Sörbom, A. (2023). Discreet Diplomacy. *Cambridge Anthropology*, *41*(1), 98–117. DOI: 10.3167/cja.2023.410108

Gehl Sampath, P. (2021). Governing artificial intelligence in an age of inequality. *Global Policy*, *12*(S6), 21–31. DOI: 10.1111/1758-5899.12940

Gercek, A., & Seskir, Z. (2024). Navigating the Quantum Divide(s). *IEEE Engineering Management Review*. Advance online publication. DOI: 10.1109/EMR.2025.3547927

Ghasemaghaei, M., & Kordzadeh, N. (2024). Understanding how algorithmic injustice leads to making discriminatory decisions: An obedience to authority perspective. *Information & Management*, *61*(2), 103921. DOI: 10.1016/j.im.2024.103921

Ghose, A., & Das, M. (2025). Techno-nationalism and Techno-globalism in Asia: Geopolitical Dynamics and Intellectual Property Implications of Semiconductor Innovations. *Decoding the Chessboard of Asian Geopolitics*, 323–342. DOI: 10.1007/978-981-96-3073-8_16

Gilboa, E. (1998). Media diplomacy: Conceptual divergence and applications. *The Harvard International Journal of Press/Politics*, *3*(3), 56–75. DOI: 10.1177/1081180X98003003005

Gilboa, E. (2000). Mass communication and diplomacy: A theoretical framework. *Communication Theory*, *10*(3), 275–309. DOI: 10.1111/j.1468-2885.2000.tb00193.x

Gilboa, E. (2002). Global Communication and Foreign Policy. *Journal of Communication*, *52*(4), 731–748. DOI: 10.1111/j.1460-2466.2002.tb02571.x

Gilboa, E. (2008). Searching for a theory of public diplomacy. *The Annals of the American Academy of Political and Social Science*, *616*(1), 55–77. DOI: 10.1177/0002716207312142

Gitonga, C. (2025). The Impact of Quantum Computing on Cryptographic Systems: Urgency of Quantum-Resistant Algorithms and Practical Applications in Cryptography. *European Journal of Information Technologies and Computer Science*. DOI: 10.24018/compute.2025.5.1.146

Gombar, M. (2025). Algorithmic Manipulation and Information Science: Media Theories and Cognitive Warfare in Strategic Communication. *European Journal of Communication and Media Studies*, *4*(2), 1–11. DOI: 10.24018/ejmedia.2025.4.2.41

Gomez, C., Guardia, A., Mantari, J. L., Coronado, A. M., & Reddy, J. N. (2022). A contemporary approach to the MSE paradigm powered by artificial intelligence from a review focused on polymer matrix composites. *Mechanics of Advanced Materials and Structures*, *29*(21), 3076–3096. DOI: 10.1080/15376494.2021.1886379

Götz, E. (2017). Putin, the State, and War: The Causes of Russia's Near Abroad Assertion Revisited. *International Studies Review*, *19*(2), 228–253. DOI: 10.1093/isr/viw009

Graham, T. (2024). Realpolitik vs. Messianism in Russian Foreign Policy. *Orbis, 68*(3), 462–469. DOI: 10.1016/j.orbis.2024.05.007

Gramsci, A. (2014). *Hapishane Defterleri* (A. Cemgil, Çev.). Belge Yayınları.

Gray, J., & Baturo, A. (2021). Delegating diplomacy: Rhetoric across agents in the United Nations General Assembly. *International Review of Administrative Sciences, 87*(4), 718–736. DOI: 10.1177/0020852321997560

Grix, J., & Brannagan, P. M. (2024). Sports mega-events as foreign policy: Sport diplomacy, soft power, and sportswashing. *The American Behavioral Scientist*, 00027642241262042. Advance online publication. DOI: 10.1177/00027642241262042

Grix, J., Dinsmore, A., & Brannagan, P. M. (2023). Unpacking the politics of sportswashing: It takes two to tango. *Politics*. Advance online publication. DOI: 10.1177/02633957231207387

Grix, J., Jeong, J., & Kim, H.-M. (2021). Understanding South Korea's use of sports mega-events for domestic, regional and international soft power. *Societies (Basel, Switzerland), 11*(4), 144. DOI: 10.3390/soc11040144

Guillou, M., & Matheron, G. (2012). *The World's Challenge: Feeding 9 Billion People*. Editions Quae.

Gunther, M. (2024, March 5). Digital sovereignty in ASEAN. PublicAffairsAsia. https://ps-engage.com/digital-sovereignty-in-asea/

Guo, L., & McCombs, M. (2011, May). Network agenda setting: A third level of media effects. In *annual conference of the International Communication Association, Boston, MA*.

Hachkevych, A., & Nykolyshyn, M. (2023). AI Toolkit for Diplomats. *International Science Journal of Jurisprudence & Philosophy*, *2*(3), 45–54. DOI: 10.46299/j.isjjp.20230203.03

Haidar, A., Pigatto, J., Karczeski, L., & Wanjiru, M. B. (2025, July 17). *How do we build for the Global South?* Paradigm Initiative. Retrieved from https://paradigmhq.org/how-do-we-build-for-the-global-south/

Haileslassie, A., Craufurd, P. Q., Blummel, M., Gumma, M. K., Palanisami, K., & Nageswara Rao, V. (2013). *Drivers and major changes in agricultural production systems in drylands of South Asia: Assessing implications for key environmental indicators and research needs.* 11th International Conference on Dryland Development : "Global Climate Change and its Impact on Food & Energy Security in the Dry lands," Beijing, China. https://oar.icrisat.org/7145/

Hakala, J., & Melnychuk, J. (2021). *Russia's Strategy in Cyberspace*. NATO Strategic Communications Centre of Excellence.

Hamzah, H. (2024). *A comparative review of the EU AI Act and the ASEAN AI Guide*. KPMG. Retrieved from https://kpmg.com/xx/en/our-insights/ai-and-technology/eu-ai-act-and-the-asean-ai-guide.html

Hanita, M., & Daryanto, E. (2025). Digital Diplomacy Strategy to Win Indonesian Papuan Opinion for National Resilience. Journal of Law. *Politic and Humanities*, *5*(3), 1486–1496. DOI: 10.38035/jlph.v5i3.1226

Hansson, S., Madisson, M. L., & Ventsel, A. (2023). Discourses of blame in strategic narratives: The case of Russia's 5G stories. *European Security*, *32*(1), 62–84. DOI: 10.1080/09662839.2022.2057188

Hart, C. (2018). Event-frames affect blame assignment and perception of aggression in discourse on political protests: An experimental case study in critical discourse analysis. *Applied Linguistics*, *39*(3), 400–421.

He, Govoni, M., & Galli, G. (2020). Quantum simulations of materials on near-term quantum computers. *npj Computational Materials, 6*, 1-8. DOI: 10.1038/s41524-020-00353-z

Hennessey, E. (2019, February 1). *What is science diplomacy? | EBSCOhost*. https://openurl.ebsco.com/contentitem/gcd:135719927?sid=ebsco:plink:crawler&id=ebsco:gcd:135719927

Higgins, S., Dai, C., Woo, T., Dickerson, D., & Maisto, D. (2024*). Navigating the geopolitical cloud: ASEAN's diverse approach to digital sovereignty. Forrester.* https://www.forrester.com/blogs/navigating-the-geopolitical-cloud-aseans-diverse-approach-to-digital-sovereignty/

Hildebrandt, M. (2020). The Artificial Intelligence of European Union Law. *German Law Journal*, *21*(1), 74–79. DOI: 10.1017/glj.2019.99

Hirunyatrakul, P. (2025). Intersection Thesis and Pathways for AI-Prosperity Alignment in the Global South: An Examination of AI for Good in Thailand [Doctoral, UCL (University College London)]. In *Doctoral thesis, UCL (University College London)*. (pp. 1–275). https://discovery.ucl.ac.uk/id/eprint/10207371/

Hlihor, E. (2024). Public diplomacy in the era of artificial intelligence – opportunities and challenges in promoting security in international politics –. *Romanian Military Thinking*, *4*(4), 656–671. DOI: 10.55535/RMT.2024.4.42

Hobbs, M., Li, M., Huang, Z. A., & Desmoulins, L. (2025). Storytelling and grand strategy in public diplomacy: A case study of the speeches of president Xi Jinping. *Public Relations Review, 51*(4), 102594. DOI: 10.1016/j.pubrev.2025.102594

Hodge, B. (2012). Ideology, identity, interaction: Contradictions and challenges for critical discourse analysis. Critical Approaches to Discourse Analysis across Disciplines, 5(2).

Holmes, M., & Wheeler, N. J. (2024). The role of artificial intelligence in nuclear crisis decision making: A complement, not a substitute. *Australian Journal of International Affairs, 78*(2), 164–174. DOI: 10.1080/10357718.2024.2333814

Honey, S. (2025, February 11). *Navigating digital trade fragmentation in the age of geoeconomics.* The Hinrich Foundation. Retrieved from https://www.hinrichfoundation.com/research/article/digital/navigating-digital-trade-fragmentation-in-the-age-of-geoeconomics/

Horowitz, M. (2019). When speed kills: Lethal autonomous weapon systems, deterrence and stability. *The Journal of Strategic Studies, 42*(6), 764–788. DOI: 10.1080/01402390.2019.1621174

Hossain, M. A., Azim, K. S., Jafor, A. H. M., Shayed, A. U., Nikita, N. A., & Khan, O. U. (2024). AI and Machine Learning in International Diplomacy and Conflict Resolution. AIJMR-Advanced International Journal of Multidisciplinary Research, 2(5).

Hossain, M. A., Azim, K. S., Jafor, A. H. M., Shayed, A. U., Nikita, N. A., & Khan, O. U.Mir Abrar HossainKazi Sanwarul AzimA H M JaforAzher Uddin ShayedNabila Ahmed NikitaObyed Ullah Khan. (2024). AI and machine learning in ınternational diplomacy and conflict resolution. *AIJMR - Advanced International. Journal of Multidisciplinary Research, 2*(5), 1–17. DOI: 10.62127/aijmr.2024.v02i05.1095

Hourn, K. K. (2025, May 26). *Why ASEAN's new Digital Economy Framework Agreement is a game-changer. World Economic Forum.* Retrieved from https://www.weforum.org/stories/2025/05/asean-digital-economy-framework-agreement-a-gamechanger/

House, R. J. (1998). A brief history of GLOBE. *Journal of Managerial Psychology, 13*(3–4), 230–240. DOI: 10.1108/02683949810215048

Huckin, T., Andrus, J., & Clary-Lemon, J. (2012). Critical discourse analysis and rhetoric and composition. College Composition & Communication, 64(Special Issue: Research Methodologies), 107-129.

Hughes, C., Finke, D., German, D.-A., Merzbacher, C., Vora, P. M., & Lewandowski, H. J. (2021). Assessing the Needs of the Quantum Industry. *IEEE Transactions on Education, 65*(4), 592–601. DOI: 10.1109/TE.2022.3153841

Hutson, M. (2021). The opacity of artificial intelligence makes it hard to tell when decision-making is biased. *IEEE Spectrum, 58*(2), 40–45. Advance online publication. DOI: 10.1109/MSPEC.2021.9340114

Ibrahim, S. E. (1996). Future visions of the Arab Middle East. Sage Publications, 27, 426–427.

ICNL. (2025). *Summary analysis of Cambodia's draft law on personal data protection*. International Center for Not-for-Profit Law Open. https://data.opendevelopmentcambodia.net/en/dataset/087a5b1e-bc04-4da1-8870-c375b87e01f2/resource/fd8b0cb3-afc4-44d0-a9c8-1e482a9f7e2c/download/icnl-comments-on-cambodia-draft-law-on-personal-data-protection_july2025.pdf

International Telecommunication Union. (2023). *Measuring digital development: Facts and figures 2023*. I. T. D. Sector. https://www.itu.int/itu-d/reports/statistics/wp-content/uploads/sites/5/2023/11/Measuring-digital-development-Facts-and-figures-2023-E.pdf

Internet Governance Project. (2018). *Internet governance in the Global South.* https://nupri.prp.usp.br/internet-governance-in-the-global-south/

Inuwa-Dutse, I. (2023). *FATE in AI: Towards algorithmic inclusivity and accessibility*. In *Proceedings of the 3rd ACM Conference on Equity and Access in Algorithms, Mechanisms, and Optimization (EAAMO '23)* (Article 13, pp. 1–14). Association for Computing Machinery. DOI: 10.1145/3617694.3623233

Iqbal, B. A., & Rahman, M. N. (2025). Digital Diplomacy Among BRICS Countries. In Innovations and Tactics for 21st Century Diplomacy (pp. 383-396). IGI Global.

Irimiea, S. B. (2017). Professional discourse as social practice. *European Journal of Interdisciplinary Studies, 3*(4), 108–119. DOI: 10.26417/ejis.v9i1.p108-119

Isono, I., & Prilliadi, H. (2023, November). *Accelerating artificial intelligence discussions in ASEAN: Addressing disparities, challenges, and regional policy imperatives* (ERIA Discussion Paper Series No. 488). Economic Research Institute for ASEAN and East Asia (ERIA). https://www.eria.org/uploads/Accelerating-AI-Discussions-in-ASEAN.pdf

ITU. (2023). *United Nations activities on artificial intelligence (AI)*. https://www.itu.int/hub/publication/s-gen-unact-2023/

Jang, B., Choung, J., & Kang, I. (2022). Knowledge production patterns of China and the US: Quantum technology. *Scientometrics, 127*(10), 5691–5719. DOI: 10.1007/s11192-022-04478-4

Jha, A., & Kumar, S. (2023). Linguistic strategies in media discourse analysis of global politics. *ijpmonline, 2(2),* 8-12.

Jiang, Y., Li, X., Luo, H., Yin, S., & Kaynak, O. (2022). Quo vadis artificial intelligence? *Discover Artificial Intelligence, 2*(1), 1–19. DOI: 10.1007/s44163-022-00022-8

JICA. (2025). *Cambodia newsletter: November 2024–January 2025 (Vol. 2).* Japan International Cooperation Agency (JICA) Cambodia Office. https://www.jica.go.jp/english/overseas/cambodia/others/__icsFiles/afieldfile/2025/06/02/newsletter202501_en.pdf

Johnson, J. (2023). *AI and the bomb: Nuclear strategy and risk in the digital age.* Oxford University Press. DOI: 10.1093/oso/9780192858184.001.0001

Jones, D. M., & Smith, M. L. R. (2007). Making process, not progress: ASEAN and the evolving East Asian regional order. *International Security, 32*(1), 148–184. DOI: 10.1162/isec.2007.32.1.148

Jones, P. E., & Collins, C. (2006). Political analysis versus critical discourse analysis in the treatment of ideology: Some implications for the study of communication. *Atlantic Journal of Communication, 14*(1-2), 28–50. DOI: 10.1080/15456870.2006.9644768

Jönsson, C. (2016). Diplomacy, communication and signalling. In Constantinou, C. M., Kerr, P., & Sharp, P. (Eds.), *SAGE Handbook of Diplomacy* (p. 79). SAGE Publications. DOI: 10.4135/9781473957930.n7

Joseph, D., Misoczki, R., Manzano, M., Tricot, J., Pinuaga, F. D., Lacombe, O., Leichenauer, S., Hidary, J., Venables, P., & Hansen, R. (2022). Transitioning organizations to post-quantum cryptography. *Nature, 605*(7909), 237–243. DOI: 10.1038/s41586-022-04623-2 PMID: 35546191

Jourdaın, A.,& Naulın, S. (2020). *Pierre Bourdieu'nün kuramı ve sosyolojik kullanımları* (Ö. Elitez, Çev.). İletişim Yayınları.

Ju, W., Sannusi, S. N., & Mohamad, E. (2023). "Public goods" or "diplomatic tools": Framing research on Chinese and American media reports regarding Chinese COVID-19 vaccine. *Media Asia, 50*(1), 43–81. DOI: 10.1080/01296612.2022.2081651

Kadyan, P., & Singh, R. (2025). Smart HRM: Unleashing the Power of Business Intelligence for Workforce Excellence. In Harnessing Business Intelligence for Modern Talent Management (pp. 275-308). IGI Global Scientific Publishing.

Kalantzakos, S. (2023). Between Rocks and Hard Places: Geopolitics of Net Zero Futures and the Tech Imperium. In *Archimedes* (Vol. 65). DOI: 10.1007/978-3-031-25577-9_1

Kalın, İ. (2011). Soft power and public diplomacy in Türkiye. *Perceptions: Journal of International Affairs*, *16*(3), 5–23.

Kaljurand, M. (2019). Diplomacy in the digital age. *The Fletcher Forum of World Affairs*, *43*(1), 53–62.

Kantsepolsky, B., Aviv, I., Weitzfeld, R., & Bordo, E. (2023). Exploring Quantum Sensing Potential for Systems Applications. *IEEE Access : Practical Innovations, Open Solutions*, *11*, 31569–31582. DOI: 10.1109/ACCESS.2023.3262506

Karim, A. (2022). *The security challenges of the Cooperation Council for the Arab States of the Gulf in light of international changes. Political Issues*, (70).

Karl, P. A. (1982). Media diplomacy. *Proceedings of the Academy of Political Science*, *34*(4), 143–152. DOI: 10.2307/3700976

Kathala, K. C. R., & Palakurthi, S. (2024). AI Literacy Framework and Strategies for Implementation in Developing Nations. *Proceedings of the 2024 the 16th International Conference on Education Technology and Computers*. DOI: 10.1145/3702163.3702449

Kaur, M., Selvakumar, P., & Dinesh, N. Mohit, Chandel, P. S., & Manjunath, T. C. (2025). Reconstruction and preservation strategies for cultural heritage. In S. Oflazoğlu & M. Dora (Eds.), *Preserving Cultural Heritage in Post-Disaster Urban Renewal* (pp. 385-412). IGI Global Scientific Publishing.

Kaur, M., Selvakumar, P., & Dinesh, N. Mohit, Chandel, P. S., & Manjunath, T. C. (2025). Reconstruction and Preservation Strategies for Cultural Heritage. In S. Oflazoğlu & M. Dora (Eds.), Preserving Cultural Heritage in Post-Disaster Urban Renewal (pp. 385-412). IGI Global Scientific Publishing.

Kazemian, B., & Hashemi, S. (2014). Critical discourse analysis of Barack Obama's 2012 speeches: Views from systemic functional linguistics and rhetoric. [TPLS]. *Theory and Practice in Language Studies*, *4*(6), 1178–1187. DOI: 10.4304/tpls.4.6.1178-1187

Keohane, R. O., & Martin, L. L. (1995). The promise of institutionalist theory. *International Security*, *20*(1), 39–51. DOI: 10.2307/2539214

Kgoale, T., & Odeku, K. (2023). *An analysis of the international and European Union legal instruments for holding artificial intelligence accountable*. Juridical Tribune., DOI: 10.24818/TBJ/2023/13/3.06

Khalidi, R. I. (2014). From the editor: Israel: A carceral state. Journal of Palestine Studies, 43(4), 5-10.

Khan, A. (2024, Oktober 3). Battle of the Super Apps: Gojek vs Grab - Who Comes Out On Top? Miracuves. Retrieved from https://miracuves.com/battle-of-the-super-apps-gojek-vs-grab/

Khanal, S., Zhang, H., & Taeihagh, A. (2025). Why and how is the power of Big Tech increasing in the policy process? The case of generative AI. *Policy and Society*, *44*(1), 52–69. DOI: 10.1093/polsoc/puae012

Khaosod English. (2025, May 29). *Thai Police Crack Down on International Scam Ring After 5-Year Probe*. https://www.khaosodenglish.com/news/2025/05/29/thai-police-crack-down-on-international-scam-ring-after-5-year-probe/

Khedr, A. ; M. ;, Salim, A. ;, Alali, A. I. ;, El-Sawy, A. A., Alimenti, F., Kobayashi, H., Osamy, W., Khedr, A. M., Salim, A., Alali, A. I., & El-Sawy, A. A. (2022). Recent Studies Utilizing Artificial Intelligence Techniques for Solving Data Collection, Aggregation and Dissemination Challenges in Wireless Sensor Networks: A Review. *Electronics 2022, Vol. 11, Page 313, 11*(3), 313. DOI: 10.3390/electronics11030313

Kilburg, D. (2025). *AI Use Cases for Diplomats: Applying Artificial Intelligence to Diplomacy*. CRC Press. DOI: 10.1201/9781003612308

Kim, B. K., & Kim, T. (2022). *Scaling-up dynamics in KOICA's peace-development nexus projects in the Mekong region: Cases of Lao PDR and Cambodia*. UNRISD Working Paper. https://hdl.handle.net/10419/273861

Kirilkina, I., & Karochkin, S. (2025). The impact of the expansion of artificial intelligence on modern diplomacy in countries worldwide. *Journal of Countries Studies*, 2(4), 535–557.

Kishan Thussu, D. (2000). Media wars and public diplomacy. *Javnost - The Public*, *7*(3), 5-17. DOI: 10.1080/13183222.2000.11008747

Knoblock, N. (Ed.). (2020). *Language of conflict: Discourses of the Ukrainian crisis*. Bloomsbury Publishing. DOI: 10.5040/9781350098633

Kobayashi, K., Hörne, J., Cho, Y., & Lee, J. W. (2023). Mediating the East Asian era of the Olympic Games (2018–2022). *Communication & Sport*, *12*(1), 3–15. DOI: 10.1177/21674795231208363

Kobierecki, M. M. (2023). Sport at the World Expo: Analysis of sports diplomacy at the non-sporting event. *Place Branding and Public Diplomacy*, *19*(4), 413–427. DOI: 10.1057/s41254-023-00294-6

Köhler, I. (2019). *Framing the threat: How politicians justify their policies*. Walter de Gruyter GmbH & Co KG. DOI: 10.1515/9783110626056

Kommineni, M., Chundru, S., Maroju, P. K., & Selvakumar, P. (2025). Ethical Implications of AI in Sustainable Development Pedagogy. In Chinedu, C., Mafarja, N., Hussein, M., & Saleem, A. (Eds.), *Rethinking the Pedagogy of Sustainable Development in the AI Era* (pp. 17–36). IGI Global Scientific Publishing. DOI: 10.4018/979-8-3693-9062-7.ch002

Konjer, M., Meier, H. E., & Krieger, J. (2022). International sport governing bodies as agents of diffusion: The case of World Athletics. *Frontiers in Sports and Active Living*, *4*, 1025023. Advance online publication. DOI: 10.3389/fspor.2022.1025023 PMID: 36439621

Konovalova, M. (2023). AI AND DIPLOMACY: CHALLENGES AND OPPORTUNITIES. *Journal of Liberty and International Affairs*, *9*(2), 520–530. DOI: 10.47305/JLIA2392520k

Korkmaz, S. C. (2024). Emerging Technologies and Power Asymmetry in International System: An Analysis over Artificial Intelligence. In *Artificial Intelligence*. CRC Press. DOI: 10.1201/9781003483571-7

Krause, K., & Williams, M. C. (Eds.). (1997). *Critical security studies: Concepts and cases*. University of Minnesota Press.

Krelina, M. (2021). Quantum technology for military applications. *EPJ Quantum Technology*, *8*(1), 1–53. DOI: 10.1140/epjqt/s40507-021-00113-y

Kron, N. D. (2015). *Security diplomacy: Beyond defense* (pp. 6–7).

Kukkola, J., Ristolainen, M., & Nikkarila, J.-P. (2017). *Game Changer: Structural transformation of cyberspace*. Finnish Defence Research Agency.

Kumar, N., & George, J. (2019). Regional Cooperation for Sustainable Food Security in South Asia: An overview and policy lessons. In *Regional Cooperation for Sustainable Food Security in South Asia*. Routledge India.

Kuus, M. (2015). Symbolic power in diplomatic practice: Matters of style in Brussels. *Cooperation and Conflict, 50*(3), 368–384. DOI: 10.1177/0010836715574914

Kwet, M. (2019). Digital colonialism: US empire and the new imperialism in the Global South. *Race & Class, 60*(4), 3–26. DOI: 10.1177/0306396818823172

Lakoff, R. T. (2004). *Language and woman's place: Text and commentaries* (Vol. 3). Oxford University Press.

Langer, A. (2023). Geopolitical role construction through language: A critical discourse analysis of EU and US policy statements towards Venezuela (2017-2019).

Latif, M. A., Rooh, S., Malik, M. F., & Samad, A. (2025). Digital Diplomacy and Disinformation: Reshaping Global Public Opinion. [DSSR]. *Dialogue Social Science Review, 3*(5), 150–169.

Lawal, Y. (2025). AI and IoT-Based Smart Irrigation: A Review of Challenges and Future Trends. *International Congresses of Turkish Science and Technology Publishing*, 770–776.

Lazarus, A., & Fatehi, F. (2025). The Diplomat Within: Leading with Unity in a Multipolar World. *Leader to Leader, 2025*(115), 32–38. DOI: 10.1002/ltl.20861

League of Arab States. (1995). *Key events in the history of the League of Arab States, 1945–1995* (pp. 5–6). Publications of the League of Arab States.

Lee, H. (2022, September 2). *The US–China 'standard-off' over technology*. East Asia Forum. Retrieved from https://eastasiaforum.org/2022/09/02/the-us-china-standard-off-over-technology/

Lee, B. T. F., Dinh, L. D., Sims, J. P., & Bettani, S. A. (2025). ASEAN Digital Economy Framework Agreement (DEFA): Implications for digital trade and regional economic integration. *Journal of Strategic and Global Studies, 8*(1), 5. Advance online publication. DOI: 10.7454/jsgs.v8i1.1166

Li, J., Shapiro, D. M., Ufimtseva, A., & Zhang, P. (2024). Techno-nationalism and cross-border acquisitions in an age of geopolitical rivalry. *Journal of International Business Studies, 55*(9), 1190–1203. DOI: 10.1057/s41267-024-00721-7

Li, L., Abbas, S. T., Khan, G. R., & Ali, S. (2025). Competing narratives of technological sovereignty: A constructivist analysis of US-China AI diplomacy. *Contemporary Journal of Social Science Review, 3*(2), 538–554. DOI: 10.12345/hwdr9b75

Linders, D. (2013). Towards open development: Leveraging open data to improve the planning and coordination of international aid. *Government Information Quarterly, 30*(4), 426–434. DOI: 10.1016/j.giq.2013.04.001

Lindsay, J. (2020). Demystifying the Quantum Threat: Infrastructure, Institutions, and Intelligence Advantage. *Security Studies*, *29*(2), 335–361. DOI: 10.1080/09636412.2020.1722853

Lin, Z. (2024). A virtual battlefield for embassies: Longitudinal network analysis of competing mediated public diplomacy on social media. *Political Communication*, *41*(5), 808–836. DOI: 10.1080/10584609.2024.2312865

Lippert, B., & Perthes, V. (2020). Strategic rivalry between United States and China: causes, tragectories, and implications for Europe. 53. DOI: 10.18449/2020RP04

Lips, K. R., & Gore, M. L. (2025). Science diplomacy: Using global environmental change as an opportunity for public diplomacy. In *Handbook on Public Diplomacy* (pp. 310–322). Edward Elgar Publishing. DOI: 10.4337/9781803926568.00035

Lisenco, V. (2025). Digital diplomacy for peace: A new frontier in international relations. Revista Moldovenească de Drept Internaţional şi Relaţii Internaţionale, (1), 39-52.

Liu, H., & Miao, C. (2024). Digital geopolitics in a VUCA world: China encounters a new global order. *Global Policy*, *15*(S6), 67–83. DOI: 10.1111/1758-5899.13435

Liu, J. (2024). Artificial Intelligence and International Law: The Impact of Emerging Technologies on the Global Legal System. *Economics. Law & Policy*, *7*(2), p73. Advance online publication. DOI: 10.22158/elp.v7n2p73

Li, X., & Wake, A. (2024). Diplomacy, propaganda, and journalism in the digital landscape. In *Transnational Broadcasting in the Indo Pacific: The Battle for Trusted News and Information* (pp. 115–133). Springer International Publishing. DOI: 10.1007/978-3-031-47571-9_6

Longhini, A., & Zimmerman, E. (2021). Regional security dialogues in Europe and in Asia: The role of Track 1.5 forums in the practice of international security. *European Journal of International Security*, *6*(4), 481–502. DOI: 10.1017/eis.2021.14

Lu, C., Cao, Y., Peng, C.-Z., & Pan, J. (2022). Micius quantum experiments in space.

Luoma-aho, V., & Badham, M. (2025). Future roles for communicators in digital media-arenas: Boxturners and global diplomats. *Corporate Communication Review*, *1*(1), 31–39. DOI: 10.63904/ccr.v1i1.9

Luo, Y., & Yu, L. (2022). Capital or technology? Which is better at promoting the value of AI companies—Theoretical analysis and empirical test. *Systems*, *10*(5), 152–174. DOI: 10.3390/systems10050152

Maathuis, C., & Cools, K. (2025). Risks and Control Measures for Building Trustworthy Autonomous Weapon Systems. *International Conference on Cyber Warfare and Security*. DOI: 10.34190/iccws.20.1.3191

Mahrenbach, L. (2024). *Whose AI is it anyway? Moving global debates from 'mine' to 'ours'*. Observer Research Foundation. https://www.orfonline.org/expert-speak/whose-ai-is-it-anyway-moving-global-debates-from-mine-to-ours

Mahusin, M., & Prilliadi, H. (2024). *Strengthening ASEAN's Cybersecurity: Collaborative Strategies for Enhanced Resilience and Regional Cooperation*. Economic Research Institute for ASEAN and East Asia (ERIA). https://www.eria.org/research/strengthening-asean-s-cybersecurity--collaborative-strategies-for-enhanced-resilience-and-regional-cooperation

Maleske, C. (2024). Developing human rights strategies for large-scale sport events: An examination of the United Bid and planning phase of the 2026 FIFA World Cup. *Deep Blue (University of Michigan)*. DOI: 10.7302/23781

Mandiant. (2025, April 24). *M-Trends 2025 Report (16th ed.)*. Google Cloud. https://cloud.google.com/security/resources/m-trends

Manfredi-Sánchez, J. L., & Smith, N. R. (2023). Public diplomacy in an age of perpetual crisis: Assessing the EU's strategic narratives through six crises. *Journal of Communication Management (London)*, *27*(2), 241–258. DOI: 10.1108/JCOM-04-2022-0037

Manor, I. (2019). *The digitalization of public diplomacy* (Vol. 15). Springer. DOI: 10.1007/978-3-030-04405-3

Manor, I., & Huang, Z. A. (2022). Digitalization of public diplomacy: Concepts, trends, and challenges. *Communication and the Public*, *7*(4), 167–175. DOI: 10.1177/20570473221138401

Manushya Foundation. (n.d.). *Digital Rights*. Retrieved September 26, 2025, from https://www.manushyafoundation.org/digital-rights

Mao, R., Zhang, T., Liu, Q., Hussain, A., & Cambria, E. (2024). Unveiling diplomatic narratives: Analyzing United Nations Security Council debates through metaphorical cognition. In *Proceedings of the Annual Meeting of the Cognitive Science Society* (Vol. 46).

Marschlich, S. (2022). *Corporate diplomacy: How multinational corporations gain organizational legitimacy: A neo-institutional public relations perspective*. Springer Nature. DOI: 10.1007/978-3-658-36818-0

Marschlich, S., & Storie, L. (2022). The past, the present, and the future of public diplomacy research. In *Research Handbook on Strategic Communication* (pp. 301–318). Edward Elgar Publishing. DOI: 10.4337/9781800379893.00028

Martynova, E., & Shcherbovich, A. (2024). Digital transformation in Russia: Turning from a service model to ensuring technological sovereignty. *Computer Law & Security Review*, *55*, 106075. Advance online publication. DOI: 10.1016/j.clsr.2024.106075

Massa, A., & Anzera, G. (2024). “Outrageous” diplomacy: Investigating the Russian Ministry of Foreign Affairs on Twitter. *Global Society*, *38*(4), 444–466. DOI: 10.1080/13600826.2024.2350999

Matondang, N. R. A. (2025, February). *Analyzing the implication of ASEAN Cybersecurity Cooperation Strategy (ACCS) 2021–2025 in Indonesia's cyber regulations* [Conference paper, IMPACT 1.0: Innovative Models for Public Administration and Collaborative Digital Transformation]. Airlangga University. https://www.researchgate.net/publication/389039193_ANALYZING_THE_IMPLICATION_OF_ASEAN_CYBERSECURITY_COOPERATION_STRATEGY_ACCS_2021-2025_IN_INDONESIA'S_CYBER_REGULATIONS

Mazumdar, B. T. (2024). Digital diplomacy: Internet-based public diplomacy activities or novel forms of public engagement? *Place Branding and Public Diplomacy*, *20*(1), 24–43. DOI: 10.1057/s41254-021-00208-4

McCombs, M. E., & Shaw, D. L. (1972). The Agenda-Setting Function of Mass Media. *Public Opinion Quarterly*, *36*(2), 176–187. DOI: 10.1086/267990

Mearsheimer, J. J. (2014). Why the Ukraine Crisis Is the West's Fault: The Liberal Delusions That Provoked Putin. *Foreign Affairs*, *93*(5), 77–89.

Media Defence. (2025, January). Introduction to Digital Rights – South and Southeast Asia. https://www.mediadefence.org/resource-hub/introduction-to-digital-rights-south-and-southeast-asia/

Mell, J., Beissinger, M., & Gratch, J. (2021). An expert-model and machine learning hybrid approach to predicting human-agent negotiation outcomes in varied data. *Journal on Multimodal User Interfaces*, *15*(2), 215–227. Advance online publication. DOI: 10.1007/s12193-021-00368-w

Menon, V., & Adhikari, M. (2023). Quantum computing in India: Recent developments and future. *IET Quantum Communication*, *4*(2), 93–95. DOI: 10.1049/qtc2.12056

Mirahmadi, S., & Omidi, A. (2024). Applications of Artificial Intelligence in Foreign Policy Decision-Making: Capacities and Challenges. *Political Strategic Studies*, *13*(50), 259–300.

Mirza, S. J., Shah, E. A., Tamour, F. A., Hussain, H., & Khan, M. B. (2025). The Role of Social Media Analytic in Crafting International Political Narrative. *The Critical Review of Social Sciences Studies*, *3*(2), 2456–2468. DOI: 10.59075/gft9jn19

Mishra, R., Devi, M. P., Gupta, S., & Kumar, D. (2024). Smart Farming Beyond Boundaries: Global Collaboration and Innovation. In *Agriculture 4.0*. CRC Press. DOI: 10.1201/9781003570219-20

Miskimmon, A., & O'Loughlin, B. (2025). Strategic narrative and public diplomacy: What artificial intelligence means for the endless problem of plural meanings of plural things. In Handbook on Public Diplomacy (pp. 34-46). Edward Elgar Publishing.

Mitić, A. (2024). Global Strategic Narrative Wars: The Battle for Serbia.

Monteh, R. N. (2025). The Origin and Evolution of Military Drone (UAVs) Technology in Warfare Equipment in Africa. *Political Science and Security Studies Journal*, *6*(2), 20–36. DOI: 10.33445/psssj.2025.6.2.3

Moral, P. (2023). Restoring reputation through digital diplomacy: the European Union's strategic narratives on Twitter during the COVID-19 pandemic.

Mostafaei, H. (2025). Applications of artificial intelligence in global diplomacy. *Sustainable Futures : An Applied Journal of Technology, Environment and Society*, *12*, 16–17.

Mostafaei, H., Kordnoori, S., Ostadrahimi, M., & Banihashemi, S. S. A. (2025). Applications of artificial intelligence in global diplomacy: A review of research and practical models. *Sustainable Futures : An Applied Journal of Technology, Environment and Society*, *9*, 1–15. DOI: 10.1016/j.sftr.2025.100486

Mrisho, L., Mbilinyi, N., Ndalahwa, M., Ramcharan, A., Kehs, A., McCloskey, P., Murithi, H., Hughes, D., & Legg, J. (2020). Evaluation of the accuracy of a smartphone-based artificial intelligence system, PlantVillage Nuru, in diagnosing of the viral diseases of cassava (p. 2020.01.26.919449). *bioRxiv*. DOI: 10.1101/2020.01.26.919449

Myhre, M. H. (2023). Russia's cultural statecraft. *Nordisk Øst-Forum*, *37*, 1–17. DOI: 10.23865/noros.v37.6034

Na, D., & Dallaire, C. (2022). The diplomatic roles of Korean state-run sport for development programs. *International Review for the Sociology of Sport*, *57*(8), 1177–1193. DOI: 10.1177/10126902211065337

Nafaa, H., ... (1983). *The Arab League: Reality and ambition* (pp. 142–143).

Naghiyev, N. I. (2025). *The EU's Response to China's Growing Influence in Central and Eastern Europe* [Thesis]. http://dspace.khazar.org/handle/20.500.12323/7987

Nakanishi, Y. J., & Auza, P. M. (2023). Connected Vehicles and Driving Automation Systems. In Nof, S. Y. (Ed.), *Springer Handbook of Automation* (pp. 1079–1113). Springer International Publishing., DOI: 10.1007/978-3-030-96729-1_50

Nesadurai, H. (2008). The Association of Southeast Asian Nations (ASEAN). *New Political Economy, 13*(2), 225–239. DOI: 10.1080/13563460802018588

Nettel, P. F., Hankins, E., Stirling, R., Cirri, G., Grau, G., Rahim, S., & Crampton, E. (2024, December 20). *Government AI Readiness Index 2024 (7th ed.).* Oxford Insights. https://oxfordinsights.com/wp-content/uploads/2024/12/2024-Government-AI-Readiness-Index-2.pdf

News, U. N. (2025, May 21). *Scam centres are a 'human rights crisis', independent experts warn.* https://news.un.org/en/story/2025/05/1163521

Nocetti, J. (2011). Digital Kremlin": power and the internet in Russia. Russie. Nei. Visions, 59(5).

Nocetti, J. (2020, December). *The Outsider: Russia in the Race for Artificial Intelligence* (Russie Nei Reports No. 34). Institut Français Des Relations Internationales (IFRI).

Nye, J. S. (2023b). *Yumuşak Güç: Dünya Siyasetinde Başarının Araçları* (R. İnan-Aydın, Çev.). Serbest Akademi.

Nye, J. S. (1991). *Bound to Lead: The Changing Nature of American Power.* Basic Books.

Nye, J. S. (2005). Soft Power: The Means To Success. In *World Politics.* Public Affairs.

Nye, J. S. (2020). *Do morals matter?: Presidents and foreign policy from FDR to Trump.* Oxford University Press.

Nye, J. S. (2021). Soft power: The evolution of a concept. *Journal of Political Power, 14*(1), 196–208. DOI: 10.1080/2158379X.2021.1879572

Nye, J. S. (2023a). *Soft power and great-power competition: Shifting sands in the balance of power between the United States and China.* Springer. DOI: 10.1007/978-981-99-0714-4

Nye, J. S.Jr. (2010). *Cyber Power.* Belfer Center for Science and International Affairs, Harvard Kennedy School.

Obeid, Z. (2025). *The Arab League's interest in technology and artificial intelligence. Arab Affairs Online.* https://arabaffairsonline.com

Obioha Val, O., Olaniyi, O. O., Gbadebo, M. O., Balogun, A. Y., & Olisa, A. O. (2025). Cyber Espionage in the Age of Artificial Intelligence: A Comparative Study of State-Sponsored Campaign. Oluwaseun Oladeji and Gbadebo, Michael Olayinka and Balogun, Adebayo Yusuf and Olisa, Anthony Obulor, Cyber Espionage in the Age of Artificial Intelligence: A Comparative Study of State-Sponsored Campaign (January 22, 2025).

Ociepka, B. (2012). Impact of new technologies on international communication: The case of public diplomacy. *Informacijos Mokslai*, *59*, 24–36.

OpenGovAsia. (2025b, May 22). *The Philippines President approves comprehensive AI roadmap*. https://opengovasia.com/2025/05/22/the-philippines-president-approves-comprehensive-ai-roadmap/

Orszag, M., Retamal, J., Saavedra, C., & Wallentowitz, S. (2007). Quantum Optics III. *Journal of Physics: Conference Series*, *84*, 11001. DOI: 10.1088/1742-6596/84/1/011001

Ozor, N., Nwakaire, J., Nyambane, A., Muhatiah, W., & Nwobodo, C. (2025). Enhancing Africa's agriculture and food systems through responsible and gender inclusive AI innovation: Insights from AI4AFS network. *Frontiers in Artificial Intelligence*, *7*, 1472236. Advance online publication. DOI: 10.3389/frai.2024.1472236 PMID: 39917548

Ozsari, A. (2018). Sport diplomacy as public diplomacy element. *International Journal of Sport Culture and Science*, *6*(28), 339–348. DOI: 10.14486/IntJSCS765

Pagen, J. (2020). A New Russian Realpolitik: Putin's Operationalization of Psychology and Propaganda. *Global Security and Intelligence Studies*, *5*(1), 55–79. DOI: 10.18278/gsis.5.1.5

Pagliaro, H., Michel, R., & Rafael, S. (2021). The problem of automated facial recognition technologies in Brazil: Social countermovements and the new frontiers of fundamental rights. *Latin American Human Rights Studies*, *1*(1), 1. Advance online publication. DOI: 10.31261/LAHRS.2021.01.01

Parker, E. (2021). Commercial and Military Applications and Timelines for Quantum Technology. DOI: 10.7249/RRA1482-4

Park, J. H., & Park, H. W. (2025). An innovative study of the role of public diplomacy in examining the 'Anti-Korean Wave' on YouTube. *Asia Pacific Viewpoint*, *66*(1), 115–129. DOI: 10.1111/apv.12443

Pasupuleti, M. K. (2025). AI's role in global stability, diplomacy, and peacebuilding. *International Journal of Academic and Industrial Research Innovations*, *5*(2), 1–11. DOI: 10.62311/nesx/32268

Pavón-Guinea, A., & Codina, M. (2024). Public diplomacy: A framework-based literature review and decentering research agenda. *Place Branding and Public Diplomacy*, *20*(3), 255–274. DOI: 10.1057/s41254-023-00319-0

Peoples, C., & Vaughan-Williams, N. (2021). *Critical security studies: An introduction* (3rd ed.). Routledge.

Perdani, M. K., Afandi, R., Lusa, S., Sensuse, D. I., Putro, P. A. W., & Indriasari, S. (2024). Social media as an instrument of public diplomacy in the digital era: A systematic literature review. *Policy & Governance Review*, *8*(3), 284–302. DOI: 10.30589/pgr.v8i3.976

Pfister, R., Schubert, G., & Kröll, M. (2023). Transfer of Logistics Optimizations to Material Flow Resource Optimizations using Quantum Computing. 32-42. DOI: 10.1016/j.procs.2024.01.004

PhilSec Summit. (2024). *The alarming state of cybersecurity in the Philippines: Trends and insights from 2024.* Retrieved from https://www.philsecsummit.com/the-alarming-state-of-cybersecurity-in-the-philippines-trends-and-insights-from-2024/

Pigman, G. A. (2014). International Sport and Diplomacy's Public Dimension: Governments, Sporting Federations and the Global Audience. *Diplomacy and Statecraft*, *25*(1), 94–114. DOI: 10.1080/09592296.2014.873613

Pimenow, S., Pimenowa, O., Prus, P., & Niklas, A. (2025). The Impact of Artificial Intelligence on the Sustainability of Regional Ecosystems: Current Challenges and Future Prospects. *Sustainability (Basel)*, *17*(11), 4795. DOI: 10.3390/su17114795

Possati, L. (2023). Ethics of Quantum Computing: An Outline. *Philosophy & Technology*, *36*(3), 48. Advance online publication. DOI: 10.1007/s13347-023-00651-6

Prastyo, A. B. (2024). *Indonesia's Approach on Cyberattack Attribution through its Foreign Policy*. ResearchGate. https://www.researchgate.net/publication/376656684_Indonesia's_Approach_on_Cyberattack_Attribution_through_its_Foreign_Policy

Pratiwi, A. D., Hennida, C., Susanto, J., Mikhael, T., Totokusumo, R. A., & Viona, A. (2024). COVID-19 infodemic in Southeast Asia: Regionalism approach and responses. *Asian Security*, *20*(3), 158–176. DOI: 10.1080/14799855.2025.2500091

Prilliadi, H. (2025, May). *Harnessing AI for ASEAN's future: Governance, adoption, and sustainability under the DEFA* (Policy Brief No. 2025-1). Economic Research Institute for ASEAN and East Asia (ERIA). https://www.eria.org/uploads/Harnessing-AI-for-ASEAN%E2%80%99s-Future.pdf

Proto, L., Lamoso-González, P., & García, L. B. (2025). The EU's FIMI Turn: How the European Union External Action Service Reframed the Disinformation Fight. *Media and Communication, 13*, 13. DOI: 10.17645/mac.9474

Puaschunder, J. M. (2016). *Global Alliance for Information and Communication Technologies and Development (GAID) as an International Platform for Cross-Sectoral Solution Finding and Policy Dialogue on Information and Communication Technologies for Development* (SSRN Scholarly Paper No. 2726399). Social Science Research Network. https://papers.ssrn.com/abstract=2726399

Puaschunder, J. M. (2019). Artificial diplomacy: A guide for public officials to conduct artificial intelligence. *SSRN, 1*, 39–54. DOI: 10.2139/ssrn.3376302

Pukallus, S., & Brouwers, L. A. C. M. (2023). Peacebuilding and social change through soap opera: The two elements of moral authority of Team Kenya. *Journal of Peacebuilding & Development, 19*(1), 32–47. DOI: 10.1177/15423166231220706

Rachmawati, I., Kuncoro, H. R., Sari, D. L., & Tahalea, S. P. (2024, September). Digital diplomacy in the 21st century: The Transformative role of social media platforms in public engagement. In *2nd International Conference on Advance Research in Social and Economic Science (ICARSE 2023)* (pp. 567-576). Atlantis Press. DOI: 10.2991/978-2-38476-247-7_57

Radanliev, P. (2025). Cyber diplomacy: Defining the opportunities for cybersecurity and risks from Artificial Intelligence, IoT, Blockchains, and Quantum Computing. *Journal of Cyber Security Technology, 9*(1), 28–78. DOI: 10.1080/23742917.2024.2312671

Ragnedda, M. (2017). *The third digital divide a weberian approach to digital inequalities*. Routledge. DOI: 10.4324/9781315606002

Ragnedda, M. (2018). Conceptualizing digital capital. *Telematics and Informatics, 35*(8), 2366–2375. DOI: 10.1016/j.tele.2018.10.006

Ragnedda, M., Ruiu, M. L., & Addeo, F. (2020). Measuring digital capital: An empirical investigation. *New Media & Society, 22*(5), 793–816. DOI: 10.1177/1461444819869604

Rahmat, A., Wahdaniah, W., Bahasoan, A. N., Hayadin, M. R., & Fausiah, F. (2024, August 11). *Digital Giants Duel: How Go-Jek and Grab Are Transforming Indonesia's Economic Landscape.* ProBisnis: Jurnal Manajemen, 15(4), 533–542. Retrieved from https://ejournal.joninstitute.org/index.php/ProBisnis/article/view/529

Rai, V. (2023). *The G20 and India's digital public infrastructure.* Institute of South Asian Studies, National University of Singapore. https://www.isas.nus.edu.sg/papers/the-g20-and-indias-digital-public-infrastructure/

Rajah & Tann Asia. (2025, February 12). *Expanded ASEAN Guide on AI governance and ethics.* AI Toolkit. Retrieved from https://aitoolkit.rajahtannasia.com/2025/02/12/expanded-asean-guide-on-ai-governance-and-ethics/

Rana, V., & Azeez, G. K. (2025, March 19). *Southeast Asia's quest for digital sovereignty.* The Diplomat. Retrieved from https://thediplomat.com/2025/03/southeast-asias-quest-for-digital-sovereignty/

Rashida Farsath, K., Jitha, K., Mohammed Marwan, V. K., Muhammed Ali Jouhar, A., Muhammed Farseen, K. P., & Musrifa, K. A. (2024). AI-Enhanced Unmanned Aerial Vehicles for Search and Rescue Operations. *2024 5th International Conference on Innovative Trends in Information Technology, ICITIIT 2024.* DOI: 10.1109/ICITIIT61487.2024.10580372

Raymer, M., & Monroe, C. (2019). The US National Quantum Initiative. *Quantum Science and Technology, 4*(2), 020504. Advance online publication. DOI: 10.1088/2058-9565/ab0441

Reese, B. (2020). *Yapay zeka çağı dördüncü çağ: Akıllı robotlar, bilinçli bilgisayarlar ve insanlığın geleceği* (M. Doğan, Çev.). Say Yayınları.

Regus, M., Epafras, L. C., & Madung, O. G. (2024). Security governance, non-governmental actors, and the limited statehood legitimacy in the Southeast Asia landscape: A conceptual analysis. *The Journal of Politics, 10*(2). Advance online publication. DOI: 10.7454/jp.v10i2.1235

Reinhardt, R. (2020). Tweets vs. the Officialese: How the Language of Russian Diplomacy Is Changing amid the Global Transition. *Valdai Papers* 114. Retrived May 13, 2025, from http://valdaiclub.com/a/valdai-papers/

Reinhardt, K. (2023). Trust and trustworthiness in AI ethics. *AI and Ethics, 3*(3), 735–744. Advance online publication. DOI: 10.1007/s43681-022-00200-5

RGC. (2022). *Cambodia digital government policy 2022–2035*. Royal Government of Cambodia, Phnom Penh: Ministry of Post and Telecommunications. https://asset.cambodia.gov.kh/mptc/media/Cambodia_Digital_Government_Policy_2022_2035_English.pdf

Riedel, M., Kovács, M., Zoller, P., Mlynek, J., & Calarco, T. (2019). Europe's Quantum Flagship initiative. *Quantum Science and Technology*, *4*(2), 020501. Advance online publication. DOI: 10.1088/2058-9565/ab042d

Roco, M. (2020). Possibilities for global governance of converging technologies. *Journal of Nanoparticle Research*, *10*(1), 11–29. DOI: 10.1007/s11051-007-9269-8

Rodríguez, S., León-Prieto, C., Rodríguez-Jaime, M. F., & Lugo, L. S. (2024). Spielen für den Frieden: Ein Scoping-Review über Sportprogramme als Botschafter des Friedensvermittler. *German Journal of Exercise and Sport Research*. Advance online publication. DOI: 10.1007/s12662-024-00967-1

Rookwood, J. (2021). From sport-for-development to sports mega-events: Conflict, authoritarian modernisation and statecraft in Azerbaijan. *Sport in Society*, *25*(4), 847–865. DOI: 10.1080/17430437.2021.2019710

Rovira-Más, F. (2023). Agricultural Robotics. In *Encyclopedia of Digital Agricultural Technologies* (pp. 34–46). Springer., DOI: 10.1007/978-3-031-24861-0_147

Rühlig, T., & Seaman, J. (2019, June 28). *5G and the US–China tech rivalry – a test for Europe's future in the digital age* [SWP Comment No. 2019/C 29]. Stiftung Wissenschaft und Politik (SWP). DOI: 10.18449/2019C29

Ryan, M. (2020). In AI We Trust: Ethics, Artificial Intelligence, and Reliability. *Science and Engineering Ethics*, *26*(5), 2749–2767. Advance online publication. DOI: 10.1007/s11948-020-00228-y PMID: 32524425

SAFEnet. (n.d.). Southeast Asia Freedom of Expression Network. Retrieved September 26, 2025, from https://safenet.or.id/

Sahmeni, E., & Afifah, N. (2019). Using critical discourse analysis (CDA) in media discourse studies: Unmask the mass media. REiLA. *Journal of Research and Innovation in Language*, *1*(2), 39–45. DOI: 10.31849/reila.v1i2.2764

Sahu, S. K., & Mazumdar, K. (2024). State-of-the-art analysis of quantum cryptography: Applications and future prospects. *Frontiers in Physics (Lausanne)*, *12*, 1456491. Advance online publication. DOI: 10.3389/fphy.2024.1456491

Said, F., & Nabilah, F. (2024, July 4). *Advancing ASEAN's digital economy: Challenges in cybersecurity and IP protection.* Fulcrum. Institute of Strategic and International Studies (ISIS) Malaysia. Retrieved from https://fulcrum.sg/aseanfocus/advancing-aseans-digital-economy-challenges-in-cybersecurity-and-ip-protection/

Saleem, F. (2025, September 23). *Which way for ASEAN's AI governance approach?* The Interpreter, Lowy Institute. https://www.lowyinstitute.org/the-interpreter/which-way-asean-s-ai-governance-approach

Saliu, H. (2022). Rethinking media diplomacy and public diplomacy towards a new concept: Digital media diplomacy. *Online Journal Modelling the New Europe*, *39*, 4–24.

Saliu, H. (2023). Narratives of public diplomacy in the post-truth era: The decline of soft power. *Communicatio Socialis*.

Samal, A., & Misra, L. I. Mohit, Pougajendy, S., Chandel, P. S., Manjunath, T. C., & Selvakumar, P. (2025). Musealization and tourism practices. In S. Oflazoğlu & M. Dora (Eds.), *Preserving Cultural Heritage in Post-Disaster Urban Renewal* (pp. 115-142). IGI Global Scientific Publishing.

Samal, A., & Misra, L. I. Mohit, Pougajendy, S., Chandel, P. S., Manjunath, T. C., & Selvakumar, P. (2025). Musealization and Tourism Practices. In S. Oflazoğlu & M. Dora (Eds.), Preserving Cultural Heritage in Post-Disaster Urban Renewal (pp. 115-142). IGI Global Scientific Publishing.

Samir, I., ... (2023). *Developing a strategy to activate the role of the League of Arab States during the period (2022–2027).* Democratic Arabic Center. https://democraticac.de/?p=91023

Scheufele, D. A., & Tewksbury, D. (2007). Framing, agenda setting, and priming: The evolution of three media effects models. *Journal of Communication*, *57*(1), 9–20. DOI: 10.1111/j.0021-9916.2007.00326.x

Schmalz, S. (2024). Varieties of Digital Capitalism and the US–China Rivalry: The Rise of Competing Technological Spheres. *Critical Sociology*. Advance online publication. DOI: 10.1177/08969205241291645

Schreiner, L., Kastrup, V., & Mayer, J. (2022). Coordination processes in partnerships between German governmental organizations and German sports federations in jointly implemented SDP projects. *Frontiers in Sports and Active Living*, *4*, 989284. Advance online publication. DOI: 10.3389/fspor.2022.989284 PMID: 36406771

Secretariat, A. S. E. A. N. (2007). *The ASEAN Charter*. ASEAN Secretariat. https://asean.org/wp-content/uploads/images/archive/publications/ASEAN-Charter.pdf

Secretariat, A. S. E. A. N. (2018). *ASEAN Framework on Digital Data Governance.* ASEAN Secretariat. https://asean.org/wp-content/uploads/2021/08/ASEAN-Data-Management-Framework.pdf

Secretariat, A. S. E. A. N. (2021a). *ASEAN Digital Masterplan 2025.* ASEAN Secretariat. https://asean.org/book/asean-digital-masterplan-2025/

Secretariat, A. S. E. A. N. (2021b). *ASEAN Cybersecurity Cooperation Strategy 2021-2025.* ASEAN Secretariat. https://asean.org/wp-content/uploads/2022/02/01-ASEAN-Cybersecurity-Cooperation-Paper-2021-2025_final-23-0122.pdf

Secretariat, A. S. E. A. N. (2022). *Digital policy action areas for a connected ASEAN: ASEAN best practice benchmarking and an action plan for regional harmonization.* ITU Publications Asia-Pacific Region. https://asean.org/wp-content/uploads/2024/03/Digital-Policy-Action-Areas-for-a-Connected-ASEAN.pdf

Secretariat, A. S. E. A. N. (2024a). *ASEAN Annual Report 2024.* https://asean.org/wp-content/uploads/2024/12/ASEAN-AR-2024_e-pub_web.pdf

Secretariat, A. S. E. A. N. (2024b). *ASEAN Guide on AI Governance and Ethics.* https://asean.org/book/asean-guide-on-ai-governance-and-ethics/

Secretariat, A. S. E. A. N. (2025a). *Expanded ASEAN Guide on AI Governance and Ethics - Generative AI.* https://asean.org/book/expanded-asean-guide-on-ai-governance-and-ethics-generative-ai/

Secretariat, A. S. E. A. N. (2025b, January 17). *Joint Media Statement of the 5th ASEAN Digital Ministers' Meeting and Related Meetings.* https://asean.org/joint-media-statement-of-the-5th-asean-digital-ministers-meeting-and-related-meetings/

Secretariat, A. S. E. A. N. (2025c, April 23). *ASEAN digital senior officials call for the development of a secure, innovative, and inclusive digital ecosystem to shape ASEAN's digital future.* https://asean.org/asean-digital-senior-officials-call-for-the-development-of-a-secure-innovative-and-inclusive-digital-ecosystem-to-shape-aseans-digital-future/

Secretariat, A. S. E. A. N. (2025d). *ASEAN Community Vision 2045.* https://asean.org/wp-content/uploads/2025/05/ASEAN-2045-Our-Shared-Future.pdf

Sefrina, M. (2024, March). *An inclusive digital economy in the ASEAN region* (ERIA Discussion Paper Series No. 505). Economic Research Institute for ASEAN and East Asia (ERIA). https://www.eria.org/uploads/An-Inclusive-Digital-Economy-in-the-ASEAN-Region.pdf

Şehitoğlu, R.,& Eren, E. (2022). Konferans diplomasisi perspektifinde Antalya diplomasi forumu'nun uluslararası ilişkilerdeki rolü. *İletişim ve Diplomasi, 7*, 185-204. DOI: 10.54722/iletisimvediplomasi.1111491

Selim, M. E. S., ... (1983). *The Arab League: Reality and ambition* (p. 176).

Sevin, E. (2015). Pathways of connection: An analytical approach to the impacts of public diplomacy. *Public Relations Review, 41*(4), 562–568. DOI: 10.1016/j.pubrev.2015.07.003

Sevin, E., & Ingenhoff, D. (2018). Public diplomacy on social media. *International Journal of Communication, 12*, 3663–3685.

Shaaban, A.-S. (1989). Journal of Social Sciences. *Kuwait University, 7*(4), 19–20.

Shahrizal. (2025, May 2). *SEA businesses face 50 million offline cyber threats in 2024: Kaspersky*. Business Today (Malaysia). Retrieved from https://www.businesstoday.com.my/2025/05/02/sea-businesses-face-50-million-offline-cyber-threats-in-2024-kaspersky/

Sharikov, P. (2024). International Regulations of Lethal Autonomous Weapons Systems: Transatlantic Security Dialogue. *World Economy and International Relations*. DOI: 10.20542/0131-2227-2024-68-12-38-48

Sharma, M. (2018). Decrypting China's Quantum Leap. *China Journal (Canberra, A.C.T.), 80*, 24–45. DOI: 10.1086/697232

Sherman, J. (2024, July 29). *Russia's digital tech isolationism: Domestic innovation, digital fragmentation, and the Kremlin's push to replace Western digital technology*. Atlantic Council. Retrieved May 9, 2025, from https://www.atlanticcouncil.org/in-depth-research-reports/issue-brief/russias-digital-tech-isolationism/

Shin, D. (2025). *Debiasing AI: Rethinking the Intersection of Innovation and Sustainability*. Routledge., DOI: 10.1201/9781003530244

Shoaib, M., Wang, Z., Ahvanooey, M. T., & Zhao, J. (2023). Deepfakes, Misinformation, and Disinformation in the Era of Frontier AI, Generative AI, and Large AI Models. *2023 International Conference on Computer and Applications (ICCA)*, 1-7. DOI: 10.1109/ICCA59364.2023.10401723

Singh, S., & Kumar, D. (2024). Enhancing Cyber Security Using Quantum Computing and Artificial Intelligence: A Review. *International Journal of Advanced Research in Science. Tongxin Jishu*, 4–11. Advance online publication. DOI: 10.48175/IJARSCT-18902

Smuha, N. (2019). The EU Approach to Ethics Guidelines for Trustworthy Artificial Intelligence. *Computer Law Review International, 20*(4), 97–106. DOI: 10.9785/cri-2019-200402

Snow, N. (2023, February). A Reliable Friend and Strategic Partner in the Indo-Pacific Region: Japan's Strategic Communications and Public Diplomacy. In William & Mary Global Research Institute/Gates Forum Paper.

Sommer, U., & Fassbender, F. (2024). Environmental Peacebuilding: Moving beyond resolving Violence-Ridden conflicts to sustaining peace. *World Development, 178*, 106555. DOI: 10.1016/j.worlddev.2024.106555

Song, W., & Ai, W. (2023). Role conflict, its compromise, and the European Union's public diplomacy in China. *Journal of Contemporary European Studies, 31*(1), 35–49. DOI: 10.1080/14782804.2022.2056731

Soundariya, A., Behera, N. K., Selvakumar, P., Chandel, P. S., Gupta, S., & Manjunath, T. C. (2025). AI and Environmental Ethics: The Role of AI in Addressing Climate Change Ethical Considerations in AI-Driven Environmental Solutions. In Chakraborty, S. (Ed.), *Human Values, Ethics, and Dignity in the Age of Artificial Intelligence* (pp. 321–346). IGI Global Scientific Publishing. DOI: 10.4018/979-8-3693-9035-1.ch013

Spanaki, K., Karafili, E., & Despoudi, S. (2021). AI applications of data sharing in agriculture 4.0: A framework for role-based data access control. *International Journal of Information Management, 59*, 102350. DOI: 10.1016/j.ijinfomgt.2021.102350

Spaniol, M. J., & Rowland, N. J. (2023). AI-assisted scenario generation for strategic planning. *Futures & Foresight Science, 5*(2), e148. Advance online publication. DOI: 10.1002/ffo2.148

Spry, D., & Lockyer, K. (2022). Large data and small stories: A triangulation approach to evaluating digital diplomacy. *Place Branding and Public Diplomacy, 18*(3), 272–286. DOI: 10.1057/s41254-021-00248-w

Sreekanthaswamy, N., Anitha, S., Singh, A., Jayadeva, S. M., Gupta, S., Manjunath, T. C., & Selvakumar, P. (2025). Digital Tools and Methods. In Çela, E., Paliktzoglou, V., Sengar, S., Eappen, P., & Vajjhala, N. (Eds.), *Enhancing School Counseling with Technology and Case Studies* (pp. 25–48). IGI Global Scientific Publishing. DOI: 10.4018/979-8-3693-8392-6.ch002

Stivachtis, Y. (2018, October 4). *Conflict and diplomacy in the Middle East*. E-International Relations. https://www.e-ir.info/2018/10/04/conflict-and-diplomacy-in-the-middle-east

Su, H., Fang, S., & Young, C. (2011). Relationship transparency for partnership enhancement: An intellectual capital perspective. *Journal of Business and Industrial Marketing, 26*(6), 456–468. DOI: 10.1108/08858621111156449

Su, S., & Xu, M. (2015). Twitplomacy: Social media as a new platform for development of public diplomacy. [IJEP]. *International Journal of E-Politics, 6*(1), 16–29. DOI: 10.4018/IJEP.2015010102

Suskind, D. (2022). Daha az iş olan bir dünya (H. Dölkeleş, Çev.). In Cohen, J., & Chasman, D. (Eds.), *Yapay zekayı yeniden tasarlamak: Otomasyon çağında iş, demokrasi ve adalet* (pp. 31–35). Elif Yayınevi.

Swartz, D. (2013). *Kültür ve iktidar: Pierre Bourdieu'nün sosyolojisi. (Çev. E. Gen).* İletişim Yayınları.

Syvertsen, A., Erevik, E. K., Fodstad, E. C., Girard, L., Kaur, P., Kristensen, J. H., Kolberg, E., Mentzoni, R. A., Morken, A. M., Sagoe, D., & Pallesen, S. (2023). An empirical study on attitudes toward gambling when sportswashing is involved. *Frontiers in Psychology, 14*, 1147332. Advance online publication. DOI: 10.3389/fpsyg.2023.1147332 PMID: 37915529

Tahat, K., Mansoori, A., Tahat, D. N., Habes, M., Salloum, S. A., & Almaleki, S. (2025). Navigating influence: Exploring soft power strategies in the digital journalism landscape. *Innovative and Intelligent Digital Technologies. Towards an Increased Efficiency, 2*, 767–777.

Tamuno Miegbam, A., & Bariledum, K. (2022). Artificial intelligence and diplomacy in the 21st century: The African perspective. *Central Asian Journal of Theoretical and Applied Sciences, 3*(10), 49–65.

Taylor, T. (2012). *Yapay maymun: Teknoloji insan evrimini nasıl değiştirdi* (A. Muhaddisoğlu, Çev.). Alfa Bilim.

Te Velde, D. W., Chandarany, O., Hokkheang, H., Monyoudom, Y., Kelsall, T., Lemma, A., Krishnan, A., Banga, K., Broden, A., Nourrice, M., & Evans, J. (2020, July). *Fostering an inclusive digital transformation in Cambodia*. Supporting Economic Transformation. https://set.odi.org/wp-content/uploads/2020/06/Fostering-an-Inclusive-Digitalisation-Transformation-in-Cambodia-Final.pdf

Tech for Good Institute. (2023). *Towards an ASEAN Digital Community 2045*. https://techforgoodinstitute.org/blog/perspectives/towards-an-asean-digital-community-2045/

The ASEAN Magazine. (2024, February 1). *The ASEAN Digital Economy Framework Agreement.* https://theaseanmagazine.asean.org/article/the-asean-digital-economy-framework-agreement/

Thorhallsson, B. (2019). Small states and the changing global order: What small state theory can offer New Zealand foreign policymaking. In Brady, A.-M. (Ed.), *Small states and the changing global order: New Zealand faces the future* (pp. 379–395). Springer., DOI: 10.1007/978-3-030-18803-0_22

TMT Law Practice (AP Law Solution). (2025, May 27). *Preparing for Enforcement: The Role of Indonesia's Upcoming PDP Body in Shaping Personal Data Protection.* https://www.ap-lawsolution.com/actio/preparing-for-enforcement-the-role-of-indonesias-upcoming-pdp-body-in-shaping-personal-data-protection

Tom, J., Anebo, N., Onyekwelu, B., Wilfred, A., & Eyo, R. (2023). Quantum Computers and Algorithms: A Threat to Classical Cryptographic Systems. *International Journal of Engineering and Advanced Technology*. Advance online publication. DOI: 10.35940/ijeat.E4153.0612523

Tran, E. (2024). Twitter, public diplomacy and social power in soft-balancing China–France relations. *Journal of Contemporary China, 33*(146), 267–294. DOI: 10.1080/10670564.2023.2193150

Tsvetkova, N., Sytnik, A., & Grishanina, T. (2023). Digital international relations: Uncertainty, fragmentation, and political framing. In *The Routledge Handbook of Russian International Relations Studies* (pp. 381–395). Routledge. DOI: 10.4324/9781003257264-29

Tung, R., Zander, I., & Fang, T. (2023). The Tech Cold War, the multipolarization of the world economy, and IB research. *International Business Review*, *32*(6), 102195. Advance online publication. DOI: 10.1016/j.ibusrev.2023.102195

Turan, A. (2024). External Factors Affecting Türkiye-Russia Rivalry in the Second Karabakh War. *European Journal of Transformation Studies*, *12*(2), 172–195.

ul Haq, S. (2025). Russia's Digital Diplomacy and Cyber Governance: Strategic Narratives, Hybrid Tactics, and Global Implications (2000 2025). ASSAJ, 3(02), 1287-1302.

United Nations Economic and Social Commission for Asia and the Pacific. (2022). *Asia-Pacific digital transformation report 2022*. United Nations. https://www.unescap.org/sites/default/d8files/knowledge-products/ESCAP-2022-Flagship-Asia-Pacific-Digital-Transformation-Report.pdf

Ünver, A. (2023). *The role of technology: new methods of information manipulation and disinformation*. ResearchGate.

US-ASEAN Business Council. (2023). *AI governance in Southeast Asia*. US-ASEAN Business Council. https://www.usasean.org/sites/default/files/2023-10/%5BUS-ASEAN%5D%20AI%20Governance%20in%20Southeast%20Asia.pdf

USC Center on Public Diplomacy. (2023, June 8). *AI and the future of public diplomacy*. USC Annenberg Center on Communication Leadership & Policy. https://uscpublicdiplomacy.org/blog/ai-and-future-public-diplomacy

Üste, A. N., & Aydın, U. S. (2022). A New Era in Diplomacy: The Case of the Antalya Diplomacy Forum. *PERCEPTIONS: Journal of International Affairs*, *27*(2), 197–217.

Uunona, G. N., & Goosen, L. (2025). Navigating Ethical Consideration of Artificial Intelligence and the Metaverse in Scientific Research. In Navigating AI and the Metaverse in Scientific Research (pp. 213-236). IGI Global Scientific Publishing. DOI: 10.4018/979-8-3373-0340-6.ch011

Uwizeye, J., Asbaş, C., & Tuzlukaya, Ş. E. (2024). Exploring the Intersection of Cyber Security and Digital Diplomacy: Perspectives and Challenges. Perspectives on Innovation and Technology Transfer in Managing Public Organizations, 38-51.

Vaithilingam, P., Arawjo, I., & Glassman, E. L. (2024). Imagining a Future of Designing with AI: Dynamic Grounding, Constructive Negotiation, and Sustainable Motivation. *Proceedings of the 2024 ACM Designing Interactive Systems Conference, DIS 2024*, 289–300. DOI: 10.1145/3643834.3661525

Valle, S., Wang, Y., & Lian, D. (2025). A vision from China on artificial intelligence: Implications for soft power in global cultural exchange. *Revista UNISCI,* (67).

Vann, B., & Heng, K. (2020). Youth's role in advancing Cambodia's digital diplomacy. *Asia Times*. https://asiatimes.com/2020/08/youths-role-in-advancing

Varela, D. T. (2024). Diplomacy in the Age of AI: Challenges and Opportunities. *Journal of Artificial Intelligence General Science (JAIGS) ISSN:3006-4023, 2*(1), 101–128. DOI: 10.60087/jaigs.v2i1.101

Varela, D. T. (2024). Navigating Cyber diplomacy in the governance of emerging AI technologies: Lessons from transatlantic cooperation. *Journal of Artificial Intelligence General science (JAIGS), 2*(1), 172-180. DOI: 10.60087/jaigs.v2i1.104

Ventura, S. (2025). War and its imagery: The visual narrative of the Ukrainian state's Instagram account Ukraine. Ua as a tool of digital public diplomacy. *International Journal of Strategic Communication, 19*(3), 379–403. DOI: 10.1080/1553118X.2024.2395407

Vichana, S. (2023). *Digital government in Cambodia: Challenges and solutions* [Master Of Public Management, KDI School of Public Policy and Management]. https://www.researchgate.net/publication/376686542

von Eschenbach, W. J. (2021). Transparency and the Black Box Problem: Why We Do Not Trust AI. *Philosophy & Technology, 34*(4), 1607–1622. Advance online publication. DOI: 10.1007/s13347-021-00477-0

Wall, P. J., Saxena, D., & Brown, S. (2021). *Artificial Intelligence in the Global South (AI4D): Potential and risks*. In *Proceedings of the 1st Virtual Conference on Implications of Information and Digital Technologies for Development*. DOI: 10.48550/arXiv.2108.10093

Wang, J., & Dubbins, A. (2024, August 12). *What Artificial Intelligence Means for Public Diplomacy*. USC Center on Public Diplomacy. https://uscpublicdiplomacy.org/blog/what-artificial-intelligence-means-public-diplomacy

Wang, P.-H., Chen, J.-H., Yang, Y.-Y., Lee, C.-S., & Tseng, Y. (2023). Recent Advances in Quantum Computing for Drug Discovery and Development. *IEEE Nanotechnology Magazine, 17*(2), 26–30. DOI: 10.1109/MNANO.2023.3249499

Wang, R., & Xu, W. W. (2023). Hashtag framing and stakeholder targeting: An affordance perspective on China's digital public diplomacy campaign during COVID-19. *Journal of Information Technology & Politics, 20*(3), 250–268. DOI: 10.1080/19331681.2022.2096742

Wang, Y. (2016). Offensive for defensive: The belt and road initiative and China's new grand strategy. *The Pacific Review, 29*(3), 455–463. DOI: 10.1080/09512748.2016.1154690

West, D. M., & Allen, J. R. (2020). *Turning point: Policymaking in the era of artificial intelligence*. Brookings Institution Press.

White, C. L. (2015). Exploring the role of private-sector corporations in public diplomacy. *Public Relations Inquiry, 4*(3), 305–321. DOI: 10.1177/2046147X15614883

Wijermars, M. (2020). The Digitalization of Russian Politics and Political Participation. In *The Palgrave Handbook of Digital Russia Studies* (pp. 15–32). DOI: 10.1007/978-3-030-42855-6_2

Wike, R., Fetterlof, J., & Mordecai, M. (2020, November 15). U.S. image plummets international as most say country has handled coronavirus badly. Pew Research Center.

Williams, S. (2025, May 13). *Bruteforce cyber attacks surge in SEA, over 53 million blocked.* SecurityBrief Asia. Retrieved from https://securitybrief.asia/story/bruteforce-cyber-attacks-surge-in-sea-over-53-million-blocked

Willoughby, K., & Seskir, Z. (2021). Global innovation and competition in quantum technology, viewed through the lens of patents and artificial intelligence. *International Journal of Intellectual Property Management.* DOI: 10.1504/IJIPM.2021.10044326

Wilson, N. (2025, July 17). *The Digital Economy Framework Agreement: ASEAN's anchor in a turbulent digital economy.* TechWonk Blog. Information Technology Industry Council. Retrieved from https://www.itic.org/news-events/techwonk-blog/the-digital-economy-framework-agreement-aseans-anchor-in-a-turbulent-digital-economy

Wise, N., & Ludvigsen, J. A. L. (2023). New notions of soft power: Impact rhetoric in mega-event bid documents. *Local Economy, 38*(4), 306–322. DOI: 10.1177/02690942231213590

Wohlforth, W. C. (2015, April). *The Return of Realpolitik.* Russia in Global Affairs. Retrieved May 4, 2025, from https://eng.globalaffairs.ru/articles/the-return-of-realpolitik/

Woodward, R. (2025). Sport, soft disempowerment and the 1966 FIFA World Cup. *British Politics, 20*(4), 707–724. Advance online publication. DOI: 10.1057/s41293-025-00281-w

World Bank. (2023). *Cambodia economic update: From recovery to reform (Cambodia Economic Update).* World Bank. https://documents1.worldbank.org/curated/en/099112023082512660/pdf/P1773400acb58a0260905e06ed54ad7edf5.pdf

World Bank. (n.d.-a). *Digital.* World Bank. Retrieved June 7, 2025, from https://www.worldbank.org/en/topic/digital

World Bank. (n.d.-c). *Economy profile: Cambodia.* Data360. Retrieved August 25, 2025, from https://data360.worldbank.org/en/economy/KHM

Wu, F., Lu, C., Zhu, M.-L., Chen, H., Zhu, J., Yu, K., Li, L., Li, M., Chen, Q., Li, X., Cao, X., Wang, Z., Zha, Z., Zhuang, Y., & Pan, Y. (2020). Towards a new generation of artificial intelligence in China. *Nature Machine Intelligence, 2*(6), 312–316. DOI: 10.1038/s42256-020-0183-4

Xin, J., & Matheson, D. (2018). One Belt, competing metaphors: The struggle over strategic narrative in English-language news media. *International Journal of Communication, 12*(1), 4248–4268.

Yale Review of International Studies. (2025, July 26). *Data colonialism in the Global South: Who owns Asia's digital future?* https://yris.yira.org/column/data-colonialism-in-the-global-south-who-owns-asias-digital-future/

Yamin, M., Ullah, M., Ullah, H., & Katt, B. (2021). Weaponized AI for cyber attacks. *Journal of Information Security and Applications, 57*, 102722. DOI: 10.1016/j.jisa.2020.102722

Yawar, M. E., Sharify, J. A., & Sadat, S. A. (2025). Artificial Intelligence and International Peace and Security. *Acta Globalis Humanitatis et Linguarum, 2*(2), 49–61. DOI: 10.69760/aghel.02500205

Yesina, M. V., Ostrianska, Y. V., & Gorbenko, I. (2022). *Status report on the third round of the NIST post-quantum cryptography standardization process*. Radiotekhnika., DOI: 10.30837/rt.2022.3.210.05

Yin, J., Cao, Y., Li, Y., Liao, S., Zhang, L., Ren, J.-G., Cai, W.-Q., Liu, W.-Y., Li, B., Dai, H., Li, G.-B., Lu, Q.-M., Gong, Y.-H., Xu, Y., Li, S.-L., Li, F.-Z., Yin, Y.-Y., Jiang, Z.-Q., Li, M., & Pan, J.-W. (2017). Satellite-based entanglement distribution over 1200 kilometers. *Science, 356*(6343), 1140–1144. DOI: 10.1126/science.aan3211 PMID: 28619937

Yin, R. K. (2009). *Case study research: Design and methods* (Vol. 5). SAGE.

Yun, S.-H. (2022). Against the current: Back to public diplomacy as government communication. *International Journal of Communication, 16*, 3047–3064.

Yurdakul, H. (2025). *Tekno-i leti şi m çağinda di ji tal sermaye eşi tsi zli ği ni n gündeli k hayata yansimasi üzeri ne bi r alan araştirmasi* [Unpublished Doctoral Thesis]. Ankara Hacı Bayram Veli Üniversitesi.

Yurdakul, H. (2024). Yapay zekâ, sermaye ve toplum. In Hülür, H., & Yaşin, C. (Eds.), *Yapay zeka, toplum ve kültür* (pp. 326–342). Ütopya Yayınları.

Zaki, A. (2015). *The role of functional theory in analysing the policies of the Arab League 1954–2014* (pp. 1–2).

Zaki, F. (1992). *Diplomacy in a changing world.*

Zamorano, M. M. (2016). Reframing cultural diplomacy: The ınstrumentalization of culture under the soft power theory. *Culture Unbound, 8*(2), 165–186. DOI: 10.3384/cu.2000.1525.1608165

Zaorski-Sikora, Ł., Braniewicz-Zaorska, O. E., & Olaosebikan, O. (2024). Challenges in artificial intelligence management–selected aspects. Zarządzanie Innowacyjne w Gospodarce i Biznesie, (2/39), 13-26.

Zeleznikow, J. (2021). Using Artificial Intelligence to provide Intelligent Dispute Resolution Support. *Group Decision and Negotiation*, *30*(4), 789–812. Advance online publication. DOI: 10.1007/s10726-021-09734-1 PMID: 33867681

Zhang, J. (2013). A strategic issue management (SIM) approach to social media use in public diplomacy. *The American Behavioral Scientist*, *57*(9), 1312–1331. DOI: 10.1177/0002764213487734

Zhong, X., & Lu, J. (2013). Public diplomacy meets social media: A study of the US Embassy's blogs and micro-blogs. *Public Relations Review*, *39*(5), 542–548. DOI: 10.1016/j.pubrev.2013.07.002

Zhou, A., & van der Meer, T. G. (2024). Computational strategic communication in a data-driven world. *Public Relations Review*, *50*(102496), 102496. DOI: 10.1016/j.pubrev.2024.102496

About the Contributors

Ahmet Turan was born in 1991 in Azerbaijan. In 2008, he graduated from the Military High School named after Heydar Aliyev in Nakhchivan. In 2009, he left the Military Academy named after Heydar Aliyev in Baku. In 2017, he graduated from Sakarya University, Faculty of Political Sciences, Department of International Relations. In 2020, he completed his Master's Program in Middle Eastern Studies at Sakarya University Middle East Institute. He took PhD at Sakarya University Institute of Social Sciences. He works as a Head of the International Relations Office at Inonu University and speaks English, Turkish and Russian.

Hasan Ucuzal was born in Malatya, Türkiye, in 1979. He earned dual bachelor's degrees, in Software Engineering from Fırat University and in Business Administration from Anadolu University. He completed his master's degree in Biostatistics and Medical Informatics at İnönü University in 2020, where he is currently pursuing his Ph.D. in the same field. His academic expertise lies in video and image processing, artificial intelligence, and deep learning. He is currently affiliated with İnönü University, where he continues to contribute to interdisciplinary research at the intersection of AI and medical informatics.

***

Munir Ahmad is a seasoned professional in the realm of Spatial Data Infrastructure (SDI), Geo-Information Productions, Information Systems, and Information Governance, boasting over 25 years of dedicated experience in the field. With a PhD in Computer Science, Dr. Ahmad's expertise spans Spatial Data Production, Management, Processing, Analysis, Visualization, and Quality Control. Throughout his career, Dr. Ahmad has been deeply involved in the development and deployment of SDI systems specially in the context of Pakistan, leveraging his proficiency in Spatial Database Design, Web, Mobile & Desktop GIS, and Geo Web

Services Architecture. His contributions to Volunteered Geographic Information (VGI) and Open Source Geoportal & Metadata Portal have significantly enriched the geospatial community. As a trainer and researcher, Dr. Ahmad has authored over 50 publications, advancing the industry's knowledge base and fostering innovation in Geo-Tech, Data Governance, and Information Infrastructure, and Emerging Technologies. His commitment to Research and Development (R&D) is evident in his role as a dedicated educator and mentor in the field.

Md. Shoeab Akhter is a passionate researcher and practicum student with a B.Sc. in the Agriculture Department of the College of Agricultural Sciences at IUBAT—International University of Business Agriculture and Technology, Dhaka 1230, Bangladesh. He is doing an internship at the Bangladesh Atomic Energy Commission. His research title is 'Green Synthesis of Nanoparticles for Agricultural Use.' Loved by nature and with a passion for the environment, his pursuits include areas of interest like agricultural sciences, food security and food science, environmental science, waste management, green energy, AI, IoT-based farming, and agritourism, among others. Along with his objective of creating an impact through writing and research, he combines new, innovative, suitable technologies and nature conservation with real-world issues. He has contributed book chapters (Emerald, CABI, Bentham Science, Springer, Cambridge Scholars) and has participated in various major projects on research. With the hope of bringing about a change in the world, he aspires to contribute to global knowledge and create a lasting impact on sustainability in society.

Anorgul Ashirova is working as an Associate Professor at the Department of General Professional Sciences, Mamun University, Khiva, Uzbekistan

Mallikarjun Badiger is a professional with nine years of experience as a lecturer and system administrator. He holds a Master of Science in Computer Science and a Bachelor of Engineering in Electronics and Communications. His technical skills include programming languages like C and C++, as well as expertise in various operating systems, hardware, and networking. He has experience teaching subjects at the MBA, BCA, and PUC levels.

Ashwini Basavaraju is an Assistant Professor in the Department of Commerce and Management at Dayananda Sagar College of Arts, Science and Commerce, Bengaluru, Karnataka. With over 17 years of teaching experience and one year of industry exposure, she brings a strong blend of academic expertise and practical insight to her role. Her areas of specialization include Accounting and Management. Currently pursuing a Ph.D. in Commerce from Dayananda Sagar University, she has actively contributed to academic research by presenting several papers at both national and international conferences.

Sumanta Bhattacharya from Salkia, Howrah, West Bengal is an Expert commissioner member IUCN Environmental, economics and social policy, Individual Policy Analyst (ADB) . He is among the top 2% world scientist (AD Index), Special civilian member Ministry of Defence, (USI) Member at Ministry of Culture (AS) . Member of Ministry of Defence { [Defence and strategic analysis] IDSA }, Member of World Economic Forum, littérateur at National Economic Research Bureau, Member of Ministry of Personnel, Pension and Public grievance (IIPA) He completed his B.Tech, M.Tech in Textile Technology along with that he has MA in Development studies, M.Sc in Environmental Science, LLB, MA in security and defence law from NALSAR, MA in Economics, MBA, Post Graduate Diploma in Environment and Sustainable Development, DIA&D, DS&DS, MPI(Oxford University) . Being a research scholar he has 290 research papers published in International and Scopus index journal, Wiley, Springer, Hindawi in various sectors like law, economic, Development studies, Textiles, Climate Change, SDGs, Public policy, Nanotechnology, Biotechnology, cancer, environment studies, 100 Book chapters published, Edited 2 books, wrote 4 book, 95 patents International and National, 4 copyrights, attended 150 International and National conference and presented papers and won 29 awards for his excellent in education, policy making and innovation which includes Best Water Management Solution Award 2022, Young Researcher Award 2020, Bravo International Book of Records, Mahatma Gandhi Ratna Award 2020, Sustainable Technology Award 2022, Global Change Maker Award 2020, Best Water Management Solution Award at the Rural & Urban Development Summit & Awards 2022, New Delhi, The Progress Global Awards 2023 for Excellence in Research, GIS -Person of the year – Water Conservation, Green India award, 2023, Global Legend Award 2023 by GSIL Educational Society . He is also a member of various International and National organization which includes IEI, IICHE, Asiatic Society, IIPA, IDSA, YOUNGO, IUCN, USI and many more .

Upoma Chowdhury, Faculty of Food Science and Technology, Chattogram Veterinary and Animal Sciences University, Khulshi-4225, Chattogram, Bangladesh. E-mail: mintuchowdhury1974@gmail.com;

Datla Ganesh is currently working as an Assistant Professor in the Department of Computer Science and Engineering at CVR College of Engineering, located in Hyderabad, Telangana. He holds a strong academic and research interest in the areas of Image Processing, Deep Learning, and Machine Learning. With a passion for emerging technologies and their real-world applications, he is dedicated to imparting knowledge and guiding students in cutting-edge domains within computer science.

Md Rakibul Hasan (mohammadrakib5522@email.com), College of Agricultural Sciences, International University of Business Agriculture & Technology, Dhaka-1230, Bangladesh.

Noprita Herari, M.Ikom, is an academic with a professional background in digital communication. She was awarded Best Graduate of the Master's program in Business and Communication Management at LSPR Institute, where her thesis on digital omnichannel strategies for local culinary MSMEs received high recognition. Her academic credentials include a Diploma in Communication Science from Bogor Agricultural University (IPB), a Bachelor's degree in Communication from Universitas Terbuka (UT), and a Master's degree from LSPR Institute of Communication & Business

Sovanna Huot is a scholar, currently pursuing a Ph.D. in Political Science at the University of Delhi, India, under a prestigious ICCR scholarship (2022). He serves as the Vice Principal of a government-recognized high school in Cambodia, where he actively leads academic innovation and institutional development. Sovanna's academic journey reflects a breadth of interdisciplinary expertise. He completed a two-year teacher training program (2010–2012) and holds bachelor's degrees in English and Educational Administration. His postgraduate achievements include master's degrees in law and TEFL, both earned through competitive scholarship programs, and a Master of Education in School Leadership with a specialization in Upper Secondary School Principalship from the National Institute of Education, Phnom Penh (2021). His research centers on educational reform, digital pedagogy, and the intersection of policy and practice in glonacal (global–national–local) contexts. With a growing portfolio of peer-reviewed publications, he contributes actively to the fields of political science and education. His scholarly work is indexed in Scopus (Author ID: 59316244400).

K. R. Gopalan is an academician and researcher specializing in International Relations (IR), holding postgraduate and doctoral degrees in the field. Expertise spans global diplomacy, peace and conflict resolution, international law, political science, public policy, and education systems

Past Novel Larasaty, MA (Assistant Professor) is a senior lecturer at LSPR Institute of Communication and Business. She is a communication expert specializing in digital public relations, communication governance, and crisis communication. She holds a Master of Arts in Communication Studies from the University of Leeds,

UK, and a Bachelor's degree in Communication Studies from LSPR Jakarta. Her research focuses on government PR, social media, and digital PR.

T.C. Manjunath was born on 6th February 1967. He did his B.E. from RV College of Engg. in 1989 (B'lore Univ), M.E. in Robotics & Automation from Govt.'s LD College of Engg., (Gujarat Univ., Ahmedabad) in 1992 with FCD-First Rank & PhD in Systems & Control Engg. from IIT Bombay in the year 2007, got best research scholar award for the entire IITB. He is currently working as the Dean Research (R & D) and as Professor in Dept. of Computer Science & Engg. with specialization in IoT, Cyber Security, Blockchain Technology in Rajarajeswari College of Engineering, Bengaluru, Karnataka. He has got a teaching (academic), research & administrative experience of more than 35+ years (10 years as Principal & 8 years as HoD, 1 year as Dean Research & rest as faculty) and has published more than 1500+ research papers in various national & international journals & conferences, with 175+ patents, 100+ book-chapters, 25 awards, 100s of Keynote talks and also published 25 text books in various field of science, engineering & technology, completed projects worth Rs. 9 Crores till date & guided 10 PhD scholars in VTU. He is a member of 30 Professional Society Chapters and is a fellow of IE, IETE, AMIEE, Sr. Member of IEEE and a chartered engineer.

P. Selvakumar is currently an Associate Professor in the Department of Science and Humanities at Nehru Institute of Technology, Coimbatore, Tamil Nadu, India. Prior to joining Nehru Institute of Technology, he held positions as an Assistant Professor in the Department of Science and Humanities various engineering colleges in Coimbatore, Tamil Nadu, India, spanning from 2011 to 2023. Dr.P. Selvakumar's academic and research interests lie primarily in the field of phytochemistry. He has made significant contributions to his field, with an impressive record that includes 30 journal publications, 12 patents, and 20 conference papers. Additionally, he has organized 5 seminars and conferences, further demonstrating his commitment to academic and scientific exchange. Throughout his career, Dr. P.Selvakumar has been recognized for his dedication and excellence in teaching, having been honored with several awards, including the Best Teacher Awards. He holds a prominent position in the academic community, contributing actively to research.

Budi Riyanto, S.IP., M.HI (Assistant Professor) is a senior lecturer at LSPR Institute of Communication and Business, specializing in international relations, and public diplomacy. He is pursuing a Ph.D. in International Relations at the University of International Business and Economics (UIBE), Beijing, under the ASEAN-China Young Leaders Scholarship (ACYLS) 2022. His research focuses on global governance, ASEAN regionalism, public diplomacy, and strategic narratives.

S. Pougajendy is a seasoned academician with over 23 years of experience in management education. Currently serving as a Professor in the Department of Management Studies (MBA) at Sri Manakula Vinayagar Engineering College, Puducherry, he specializes in Marketing and Human Resource Management. He holds a Ph.D. in Marketing from Bharathiar University (2015), along with an MBA and M.Phil in Marketing. His expertise spans subject matter proficiency, curriculum development, research, and mentoring. Dr. Pougajendy has an extensive research portfolio, with 45 international and 7 national publications, 4 patent publications (2022-2024), 2 books (2022-2023) and 2 Scopus indexed book chapters(2025). He has successfully supervised 30 M.Phil scholars and is currently guiding 7 Ph.D. candidates. His dedication to academia and research continues to contribute significantly to the field of management studies.

Hemendra Singh is a Lecturer of Law at Jindal Global Law School, situated within O.P. Jindal Global University, Sonipat. He pursued his LL.M. in Intellectual Property Rights from National Law University, Jodhpur, following his graduation with a B.A. LL.B. (Hons.) from Rajiv Gandhi National University of Law, Punjab. With a focus on corporate law, intellectual property law, criminal law, and constitutional law, he has authored numerous research articles and book chapters published in both national and international journals and books.

Arun Thapar Associate member of The Institute of Company Secretaries of India (ICSI), Arun is an educationist and administrator with a passion for learning, innovation, and meaningful storytelling. He is currently serving as an Senior Accounts Officer. Earlier, had contributed to reputed institutions including the Indian Institute of Information Technology (IIIT) Bhopal and the Indian Institute of Science Education and Research (IISER) Bhopal. With over a decade of experience in finance, administration, and institutional development, he has cultivated a deep understanding of how education and creativity can transform lives. Beyond his professional role, Arun finds joy in the little things that make life vibrant. A true ambivert, he balances his love for basketball and coffee-fueled conversations with quiet moments spent reflecting or watching movies. His curiosity about technology and entrepreneurship has also led him to explore the potential of 3D printing cafés as spaces for creativity, skill-building, and business opportunities. What defines Arun most is his belief in resilience, growth, and the power of human connection. Through his writing, he aspires to inspire readers to reflect, dream, and pursue their own journeys with courage and heart.

Geetali Tilak is a distinguished academician currently serving as Professor and Vice-Chancellor of Tilak Maharashtra Vidyapeeth, Pune. With a strong background in higher education and leadership, she has played a pivotal role in shaping the academic and administrative framework of the institution. Under her guidance, the university continues to uphold its commitment to excellence in education, research, and cultural values. Dr. Tilak is known for her dedication to fostering academic growth, innovation, and holistic student development, while also carrying forward the rich legacy and vision of Tilak Maharashtra Vidyapeeth.

Gundepogu Venugopalrao is serving as an Assistant Professor in the Department of Computer Science and Engineering at CVR College of Engineering, located in Hyderabad, Telangana – 501510. He has a keen interest in the fields of Image Processing, Deep Learning, and Machine Learning. His academic focus and research efforts are directed towards advancing these emerging technologies, and he is committed to fostering innovation and excellence in computer science education.

Index

A

B

C

D

E

F

G

H

I

L

M

N

P

Q

S

www.ingramcontent.com/pod-product-compliance
Lightning Source LLC
LaVergne TN
LVHW080906300926
849162LV00003B/582